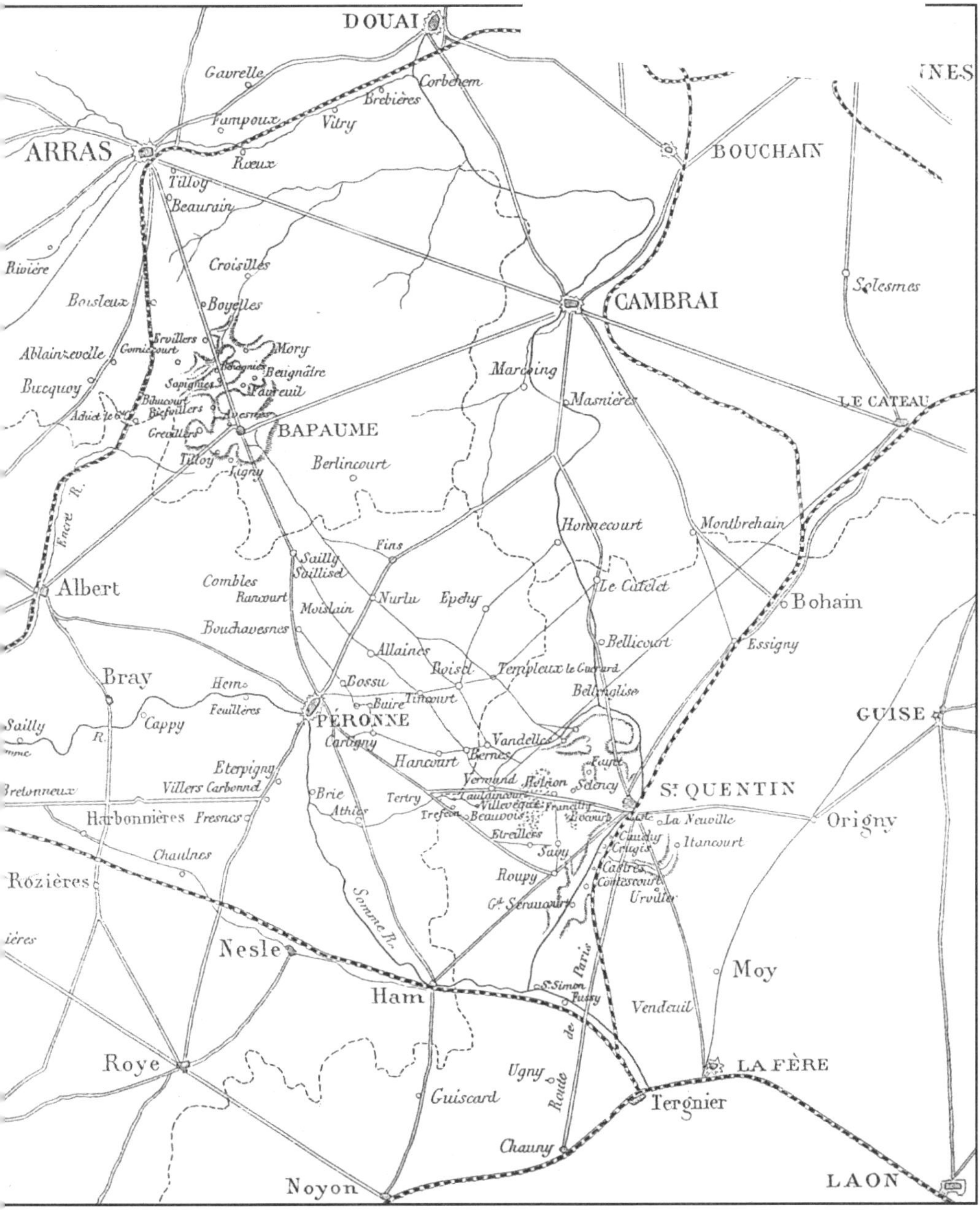
DOUAI
Gavrelle
Corbehem
Brebières
Fampoux
Vitry
ARRAS
Rœux
BOUCHAIN
Tilloy
Beaurain
Rivière
Croisilles
Boisleux
Boyelles
CAMBRAI
Solesmes
Ablainzevelle
Ervillers
Gomiecourt
Mory
Beugnâtre
Sapignies
Favreuil
Bucquoy
Marcoing
Masnières
Biefvillers
Avesnes
LE CATEAU
Grevillers
BAPAUME
Tilloy
Ligny
Berlincourt
Ancre R.
Honnecourt
Montbrehain
Fins
Sailly
Saillisel
Le Catelet
Albert
Combles
Rancourt
Nurlu
Epehy
Bohain
Moislain
Bouchavesnes
Bellicourt
Essigny
Allaines
Roisel
Templeux le Guérard
Bray
Hem
Bossu
Bellenglise
Feuillères
Buire
Tincourt
GUISE
Sailly
Cappy
PÉRONNE
Cartigny
Vandelles
Bernes
Hancourt
Eterpigny
Villers Carbonnel
Vermand
Holnon
Fayet
Selency
S^t. QUENTIN
Brie
Tertry
Caulaincourt
Villevêque
Francilly
Harbonnières
Fresnes
Athies
Trefcon
Beauvois
Dallon
La Neuville
Origny
Etreillers
Gauchy
Itancourt
Chaulnes
Savy
Grugis
Roupy
Castres
Rozières
Contescourt
Urvillers
G^d. Seraucourt
Somme R.
Nesle
Moy
S^t. Simon
Pusy
Route de Paris
Ham
Vendeuil
Roye
Ugny
LA FÈRE
Tergnier
Guiscard
Chauny
Noyon
LAON

THE REALITY OF WAR

Léonce Patry

THE REALITY OF WAR

A Memoir of the Franco-Prussian War
and the Paris Commune (1870-1)
by a French officer

Translated with a foreword and notes by
Douglas Fermer

CASSELL&CO

Cassell & Co
Wellington House, 125 Strand
London WC2R 0BB

First published in Great Britain 2001

Originally published as *'La Guerre telle qu'elle est (Campagne de 1870–1): Metz, Armée du Nord, Commune' par Léonce Patry, Lieutenant-Colonel breveté en retraite,* Paris, 1897.

British Library Cataloguing-in-Publication Data
A catalogue record for this book is available from the British Library

ISBN 0-304-35913-0

Distributed in the USA by
Sterling Publishing Co. Inc.,
387 Park Avenue South
New York, NY 10016-8810

Edited and designed by
DAG Publications Ltd
Edited by Michael Boxall
Typesetting and layout by Roger Chesneau
Printed and bound in Great Britain by
Creative Print and Design (Wales), Ebbw Vale

This translation is dedicated to the memory of

My father, Walter Fermer (1899–1964)
who in 1918, as a young conscript in the 7th Battalion, The Lincolnshire Regiment, marched down the same roads as the Army of the North in 1870–1 to encounter 'the reality of war'

and of

My brother, Robert Fermer B.A. Hons. (Cantab.) (1949–74),
a gifted naturalist and linguist, and devoted student of French life, language and literature.

J'écoute encore tomber la pluie:
Elle n'a plus le même bruit. . .

CONTENTS

MAPS

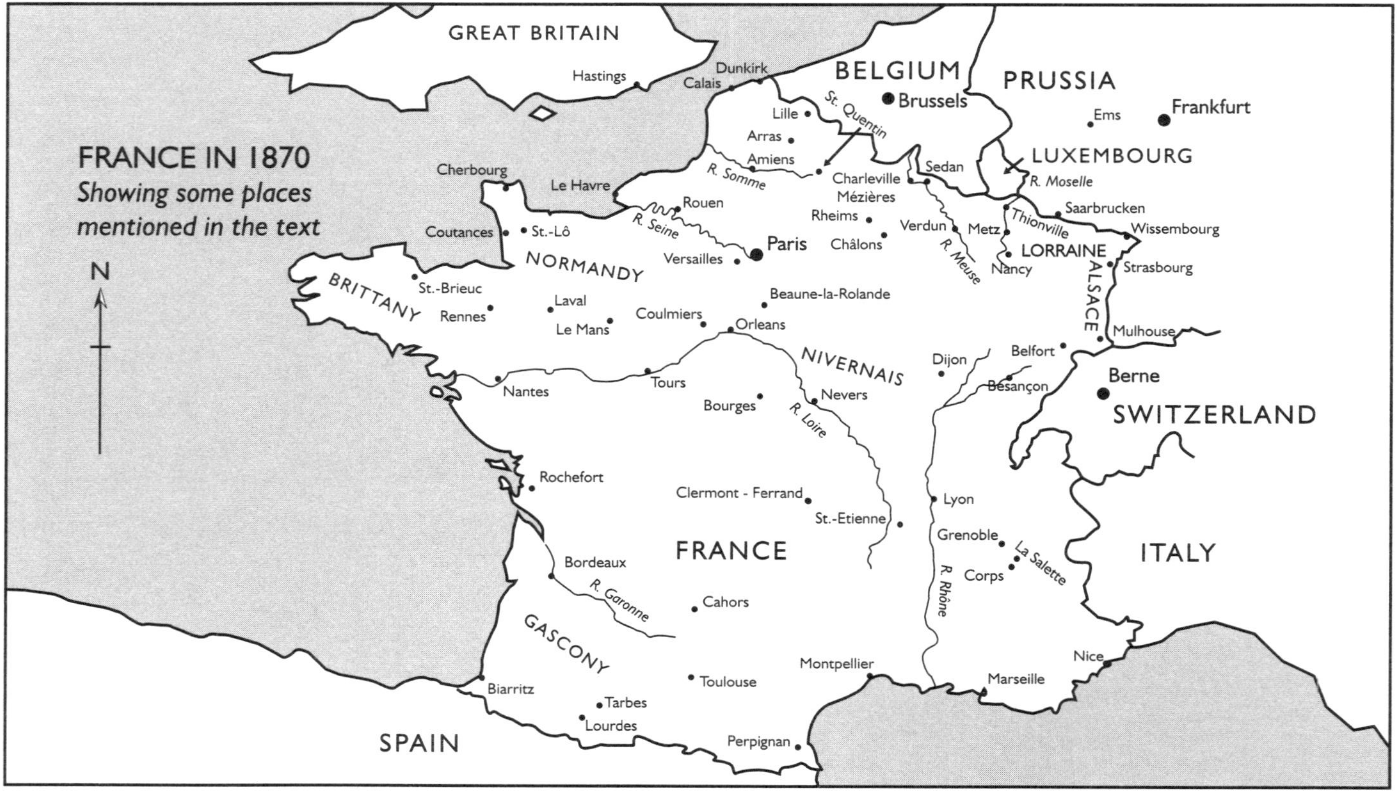

FRANCE IN 1870
Showing some places mentioned in the text

TRANSLATOR'S FOREWORD

1. The Franco-Prussian War and its Legacy

In the long and sombre chronicle of European wars, the Franco-Prussian War of 1870–1 is an episode that now attracts little attention. Nor are the reasons for this comparative neglect of an event that has passed beyond living memory hard to understand.

In its day the war was the greatest armed clash in western Europe since Waterloo, involving the mobilisation of mass armies by telegraph and railway and murderous battles in which hundreds of thousands of men were engaged. It saw the use of breech-loading rifles by both sides and the introduction of an early French machine-gun – the *mitrailleuse*. German breech-loading steel artillery, far surpassing anything used in the Napoleonic wars, was used to terrifying effect both on the battlefield and in the bombardment of French fortified cities. Yet from beyond the watershed of the world wars of the twentieth century, it takes a feat of the imagination to grasp the impact the conflict had on its generation. In any statistical ranking of horrors, its dimensions appear almost modest in comparison with later wars, whether in terms of duration, geographical extent, casualties, or the destructiveness of its weaponry. In the six months of fighting until the armistice in January 1871, Germany lost just over 50,000 soldiers dead (about half killed in battle, the rest by disease) and nearly 90,000 wounded. The impact of these figures is muted when set beside her loss of 2 million in 1914–18 and 4.2 million, plus more than half a million civilians, killed in 1939–45. France, as the defeated and invaded nation, lost more heavily in 1870–1; perhaps 139,000 soldiers dead and 143,000 wounded. Another 384,000 men, including the greater part of her professional army, became prisoners of war, of whom possibly 17,000 died from disease. Yet even these numbers were to pale beside her loss of 1,358,000 killed in 1914–18 and 600,000 in 1939–45.[1]

In terms of comparative destructive power, one example will suffice without labouring the point. At the climactic battle of Sedan on 1 September 1870, at which France's secondary army and her Emperor, Napoleon III, were bombarded into surrender, 606 German guns fired 33,134 shells.[2] Yet half a century later mankind's proficiency in the science of obliteration had advanced so far as to make even this unprecedented hurricane of flying metal and explosive seem almost paltry by comparison. During the first five hours of their spring offensive in March 1918 the Germans employed 6,473 guns of much heavier calibres which fired 1,160,000 shells,[3] and the German army that week was said to have fired off two and a half times more ammunition than was used in the whole of the war of 1870.[4]

However, it is more than the matter of scale that has cast 1870 into the historical shadows. It is not so much that the war has gradually faded from historical consciousness, as that for the sake of its future modern Europe has turned its back on all that it represents. For it left a sinister and dangerous legacy that in a sense blighted the peace of Europe and the world for well over a century. The war is decidedly not 'usable heritage'.

War broke out in July 1870 when France confronted Prussia over the candidacy of a member of the Prussian royal house for the vacant throne of Spain. The conflict was the third in a series fought by Prussia in the space of six years which established her dominance in Germany, and endowed her General Staff with a fateful prestige. War with France was the catalyst which produced the unification of Germany under Prussian leadership, sealed by the acclamation of her king as Emperor Wilhelm I in the Hall of Mirrors at Versailles in January 1871. The creation of the German Empire fostered an era of growing nationalism, militarisation and mutual apprehension of a first strike among the European powers, which led to an armaments race and created the conditions for disaster in 1914. From the Great War came the seeds of a further world war, and from that emerged yet another generation living in fear of war.

Thus in retrospect the war so recklessly begun by both governments in 1870 appeared to have been the opening of a Pandora's box, with appalling consequences flowing down from generation to generation. It came to be viewed as the first in a cycle of three German wars that brought hideous suffering and culminated in the ruin and division of Europe in 1945. Before 1914 the war had been enthusiastically celebrated in the Kaiser's Germany as the glorious founding of the nation. After 1945 nobody had any inclination to dwell upon, let alone to celebrate, a disturbing militarist past that even the nation that had been victorious in 1870 preferred to leave behind.

2. France and the War

For France, 1870 was one of the worst defeats in her history. There is a nightmare quality to the campaign, in which virtually everything went wrong. A recurring nightmare, it might be added with hindsight, for some French children alive in 1870 would live to experience two more German invasions. The sudden diplomatic crisis and mobilisation amid wildly cheering crowds in July, leading to ghastly frontier battles in August, prefigured 1914. Bewilderment, retreat, divisions and suspicions of treason leading to disaster at Sedan foreshadowed the crushing defeat of 1940.

Instead of consolidating the Bonaparte dynasty, reversing the verdict of Waterloo and restoring France as arbiter of Europe, as Napoleon III had hoped, the Franco-Prussian War set the seal on the reduction of French prestige and power. Until that moment the French army had enjoyed the reputation, not without cause, of being the best in Europe. It had taken years of struggle by the united powers of Europe to defeat France in 1814 and 1815. Yet in 1870 Germany alone was able to dispose spectacularly of the main French armies in six weeks, then to besiege Paris and to overcome hastily mustered provincial armies, achieving decisive victory by January 1871. After fatal overconfidence about France's military capability in July 1870, her leadership proved hesitant and inept. Following a clumsy mobilisation, her armies failed to bring their strength to bear to any effect. French movements were leaden, and attempted blows failed to connect against an aggressive, purposefully led enemy who seemed to be everywhere at once; in front, on the flank, in rear, all around. Sedan provoked the toppling of the Second Empire and Napoleon went into captivity, then exile. The improvisations of the succeeding Government of National Defence staved off submission for five months, but could not avert it.

And if invasion and defeat were not enough, civil war followed in their wake. The year 1871 saw horrific bloodshed and destruction in Paris as the newly elected national government headed by Adolphe Thiers used the army to crush the insurrection of the Commune, which had taken control of the city in March in the aftermath of the armistice and the election of a large conservative majority in the National Assembly. The ensuing peace with Germany, signed at Frankfurt in May 1871, subjected France to the loss of two of her eastern provinces – Alsace and the greater part of Lorraine – and to the payment of an indemnity of 5 billion francs. German troops remained on French territory until 1873 when the agreed instalments had been paid.[5] It was Victor Hugo who christened 1870–1 'The Terrible Year', and that stark epithet has deservedly endured.

Had France used her military force effectively, 1870 might indeed have proved her last chance to check German power and assert her own dominance. But her bid for mastery failed decisively, and in the decades following defeat the question changed to whether France would be able to defend herself in the face of growing German superiority in population and industrial and military strength. If active French desire for revenge is now discounted as a direct cause of the Great War, French attitudes to Germany at the political, military and social levels were nevertheless conditioned by her defeat, and 1914 cannot be understood without reference to the earlier catastrophe. If German troops marching into France in 1914 wanted to re-enact the glories of 1870 which their grandfathers had told them about, and which had been sedulously inculcated in the classroom, in the barracks, and through the rituals of commemoration,[6] their French opponents had equally imbibed a determination to redeem the shameful defeat of forty-four years earlier. In this sense pre-1914 French nationalism owed much to the humiliating memory of 1870,[7] but it was a memory which France sought above all to exorcise in 1914, and quite understandably has preferred to lay to rest since.

3. A Missing Perspective

In the decades following its end the Franco-Prussian War was better documented than any previous war, and there appeared a mass of official histories, regimental histories and more or less self-serving memoirs from participants and newspaper correspondents.[8] Unsurprisingly, interest waned markedly after 1914. The spate of strategic and tactical studies concerned with the supposed lessons of 1870, which were of absorbing concern to a generation of military students, suddenly became obsolete.[9] The centenary of the Paris Commune briefly revived some interest, but military events were often sketched merely as a background to the siege of Paris and to political and social events in the capital. Since then there has been some academic debate about whether the war of 1870 was really 'modern' or not, a question which becomes increasingly sterile as warfare enters the missile age. Much manuscript material that might have inspired a more fruitful re-examination of the conflict was lost in the bombing of 1939–45.

English-speaking readers have naturally felt less interest in the Franco-Prussian War than in the larger conflicts in which their own nations took part. Compare, for instance, the outpouring of books about the First and Second World Wars, and particularly about the American Civil War of 1861–65, with the trickle of volumes about 1870 written in recent decades. It must be admitted too that the language barrier and the relative inaccessibility of source material acts to some extent as a restraint on the inquisitiveness of the English-speaking world. It may well be felt too that Michael Howard's magisterial single-volume history, *The Franco-Prussian War: The German Invasion of France, 1870–1871* (London, 1961), says so much so well in clean, classical prose that there is little more to be added. There seems to be a general consensus that from the diplomatic, political, military and strategic viewpoints the war has been exhaustively analysed by competent critics.

Yet, below the level of statesmen and generals, we may be left with the conviction that there is a dimension missing from the history of that war. English-speaking readers have little sense of what the war was like for participants. Only a handful of visitors today find their way to the macabre (to Anglo-Saxon tastes) ossuaries at Bazeilles and Gravelotte, or wander around the grass-covered burial mounds on the slopes below Saint-Privat and Amanvillers, where the peace is now disturbed only by the vibration of traffic on the nearby motorway. Those who ponder what stories the men who fought there could have told do not find the answer readily accessible. We may take our literary impressions of the French view of the war from Zola's epic of Sedan and the Commune, *The Debacle*, and from the short stories of Maupassant. But direct accounts by the vanquished remain rare. The letters of a French officer who served in Normandy and the Loire valley were published in London in 1970, but have long been out of print.[10]

Nor apparently do many photographic images survive from the rapid summer campaign of 1870 to seize the imagination as do those of the American Civil War. Engravings from the period mostly remain buried in the pages of contemporary illustrated journals. In the history of art, the war is now generally noticed only in passing as the event which drove several Impressionist painters to London for a few months – and incidentally killed one of the most promising of their circle.[11] The most striking pictures of the war, the military paintings of Alphonse de Neuville and Édouard Detaille (much more popular than the Impressionists in their day) are little reproduced in works in English. For all their arresting 'realism', we remain aware that de Neuville's canvases present carefully crafted and dramatically posed images of French defeat: affirmations of heroic defiance and nonchalance in the face of overpowering hordes of fierce barbarians. Purporting to illustrate 'the reality of war', they emphasise a vision of defeat without shame or dishonour, helping Frenchmen to come to terms with the bitterly humiliating reality. Widely reproduced as prints, they offered the succeeding generation a nationalist legend which reasserted French prowess.[12]

How can we better understand the experience behind these images? What of the testimony of the men who fought in battles larger and as momentous for the future as Chancellorsville and Gettysburg? Many of the men in the French army in 1870 were semi-literate peasants, and critics noted that many French NCOs and officers were very badly educated. Indeed, there was a strong anti-intellectual streak in the pre-war French officer corps, where many despised study as a dangerous irrelevance.[13] Yet such generalisations should not obscure the fact that there existed in the junior ranks of the French army intelligent, critical and reflective observers capable of setting down invaluable accounts of what they experienced and saw in the trying months of defeat. None more so than Léonce Patry.

4. Patry's Testimony

For his framework of his memoir of the war of 1870–1, written twenty-five years later, Patry used the note book he kept at the time. Readers will have inferred the existence of such a diary even before he quotes from its perfunctory entries in his last chapter. The day-by-day structure of his narrative, with occasional topical digressions, helps to impress a strong sense of the exhausting and monotonous reality of the infantryman's life on campaign: the routines of making and breaking camp, the apparently aimless marching back and forth, the overriding preoccupation with obtaining and cooking food. But Patry's writing is no mere artless chronicle, solely of anecdotal interest. As he makes clear in his discussion of the difficulties of discovering the truth of the events of the battle of 16 August 1870, he has reflected on the writing of history and on the behaviour of men in combat. His experience of battle leaves him deeply sceptical about accepted accounts in the grand narrative tradition: 'I became certain that most of the great feats so preciously reported by history were nearly always invented.' After the armistice, in Dunkirk and Paris, he is astounded to talk with civilians whose fanciful picture of military events bears no relation to the experiences he has just lived through.

As the title of his book suggests, Patry was therefore concerned with describing without pretension the facts behind the 'stories that are always poeticised to inflame hearts'. In doing so, however, he did not aspire to the Olympian detachment of the historian, although he was well aware of the canons of objective and impartial history. A contrast between his approach and that of a close colleague is instructive. His friend and messmate in the battles around Metz, Léonce Rousset, was later to become a lecturer at Saint-Cyr and a very fine military historian. Rousset's histories of the war of 1870–71 remain authoritative and invaluable, based as they are on careful scholarly comparison of the sources available to him in the interests of producing an objective narrative. In Rousset's measured account of the battle of 31 August 1870, there is no hint that he himself was badly wounded, save for the formal inclusion of his name in an appendix listing officers killed, wounded and missing.[14]

Patry was of a different temperament, and chose to make his account of the campaign entirely personal. This is not to imply that his narrative is therefore less than reliable. On the contrary, where his facts can be checked against official records and other sources, they are generally accurate in detail, with only a few very minor slips. But he deliberately keeps to what he saw, did and felt at the time, giving us the junior officer's confined view of the daily unfolding of the war. He recounts rumours that were current among the officers, but never attempts to describe what he does not see. He does not attempt to give an overview of what history records as the Battle of Rezonville; only to describe his participation in a desperate encounter with the enemy at the edge of a smoke-filled ravine: 'I knew that I had fought close by a certain place; but what the general position of our army was I had never known.' He tells his story with great verve but is aware of, and strives to avoid, the natural human tendency to be 'drawn into embellishing everything, even without the least intention of pushing oneself forward'.

His self-confessed limitations thus help to give his memoir focus and vitality, and make him a most valuable eye-witness to the events in which he took part. Not for him the coolly detached euphemisms and evasions of the official histories. Only towards the end of the last chapter of his book does an unaccustomed reticence creep in. He provides illuminating testimony of the events of 18 March 1871 in Paris, the day the insurrection which led to the Commune broke out. But he has very little to say of the culminating events of 'Bloody Week' at the end of May, during which parts of central Paris were burned by the retreating Communards as the army advanced to regain control of the city, and appalling atrocities were committed. As Patry makes clear, he felt revulsion for the civil war and tried to avoid serving in the campaign, which he found mostly tedious, uneventful and ignominious. He is deeply critical of the Versailles government for provoking the conflict, but he is also contemptuous of the 'madmen' of the Commune, of whom 10,000 at the very least were killed during the two months of fighting and the brutal aftermath. It may well be that his post prevented him from seeing much at close hand of the final events that were to become legendary. He tells us that his unit suffered casualties, but gives few particulars of the circumstances. We are left wondering why his gift for frank and well-observed description seems to run dry just when we feel that he could tell more.

For the war itself, however, Patry's memoir must surely count as one of the better personal narratives to come out of that conflict. He makes no pretence of giving us an elevated, insider's view of command decisions and grand strategy. His strictures on the failings of his superiors, particularly on those of Marshal Bazaine whose decisions led to France's principal army being surrounded in Metz and taken prisoner and to Bazaine's post-war trial, are certainly less than objective. But Patry's passionate judgement conveys the anger of one soldier who, like thousands of others, felt betrayed at having risked his life at the command of inadequate leaders who needlessly sacrificed their troops and French territory. He reminds us of the truth that in 1870 the great majority of French regular soldiers fought well enough, but were outgunned and outgeneralled through no fault of their own.

In one sense Patry's book is in a tradition of personal war narratives well established even before 1914–18, dealing with the perennial theme of the loss of innocence and the journey from illusion to disillusion through the horrors of war. He describes ironically his early romantic illusions and thirst for glory which lead him to lie and disobey orders in order to get to the front. But in both Lorraine and Picardy his heroic aspirations end in an undignified headlong run for his life through an irresistible hail of German shells, against an infernal backdrop of burning farms and burnt and smashed bodies. War, as he tells us and shows us, is an abomination which leaves terrible suffering in its wake. Yet his theme is not the futility of war, in the vein of post-1914 literature, so much as the consequences of waging it ineptly.

If Patry is a forthright critic of the shortcomings and follies of the high command in 1870, his book should not be lumped with the spate of bitterly anti-military and pacifist literature which was appearing in France in the 1880s and 1890s even before the Dreyfus Affair heralded an avalanche of attacks on the army and its values.[15] Nor on the other hand are his concerns those of the political right which, as was shown by its reaction to the frank depiction of the disaster of Sedan in Zola's *The Debacle* (1892), regarded any aspersion on the army's competence, even in fiction, as almost treasonable and took it as an article of faith that only numbers had given the Germans victory in 1870.[16] Such ideological posturing is foreign to the independent-minded Patry, a pragmatist and political sceptic. He is first and foremost a patriotic French officer who loves his profession and accepts the warrior's code. While he has little patience with popular hatred of the Germans, whose officers he has come to respect, he has no qualms about the unquestioned duty of killing the invader in combat. Like most Frenchmen, he has little doubt that sooner or later the contest must be renewed, and he cares passionately that the complacency and fatal lack of initiative which proved so disastrous in 1870 should not be repeated. He shows from hard experience that without intelligent will and higher standards of professionalism in commanders at all levels, soldiers' lives and efforts will be needlessly squandered and their cause lost.

If Patry's book were just a military treatise, it might be left to gather dust with dozens of other strategic studies and tomes dealing with the movement of brigades and divisions in ponderous detail. But it lives precisely because Patry was not afraid to put himself into the story and let us see events through his eyes. We may smile at his excessive protestations of indifference to matters of promotion and decoration, which are in fact one of his preoccupations. If at times he is inconsistent and judgemental, with strong likes and dislikes particularly with regard to his superiors, he only makes us appreciate his foibles and his humanity, which shines through in the warmth of his family feelings. He is in many ways the Gallic warrior *par excellence*; spirited, impatient, witty, with a slight taste for the macabre, and deeply concerned with food and good wine even in the bleakest circumstances. Presenting idealised and chivalrous portraits of women – Madame Surmay the doctor's wife, the Protestant widow, and the elderly aristocrat Madame de Becquencourt – he is not without an appreciative eye for the Parisian demi-mondaines. In all, he is a cultivated and congenial narrator, a sharp and often humorous observer of human behaviour, who quickly wins our attention and keeps us absorbed in the story of his war.

Many of the events Patry narrates will be unfamiliar to English-speaking readers, even though the campaigns of the Army of the North described in Part Two were fought only a few miles beyond the English Channel, over terrain and around places that were to become all too familiar to British soldiers of 1914–18: Amiens, Albert, Bapaume, Arras, Saint-Quentin, Villers-Bretonneux, the Somme. The story of France's soldiers in the ordeal of 1870–71 has been unduly neglected, and the voice of the defeated should not be lost. Over one hundred years after its first publication in France, Patry's eloquently told story deserves to be rescued from oblivion, and is here offered in English for the first time.

5. Léonce Patry

Marie Gabriel Léonce Patry was born in Paris on 18 April 1841.[17] His father, Nicolas Édouard Patry (1814–80), was at that time a language teacher whose subsequent assignments as a deputy head and head teacher of state schools took him to various provincial towns, including Tarbes and Cahors in south-western France.[18] It was from Toulouse Academy that Léonce gained his baccalaureate in 1859. The following year Édouard Patry sought a free place and uniform for his son at the officer-training academy at Saint-Cyr, pleading that his modest salary was all he had to support Léonce and his elder sister, a 91-year-old great-grandfather, and his wife, Sophie Florentine (née

Guilleminot)[19] who had been an invalid since Léonce's birth. The town council of Tarbes, the mayor of Cahors and the local prefect supported his application for a bursary, which was approved by the Minister of War. So in November 1860 Léonce, described as having an oval face, large nose and chestnut eyes and hair, voluntarily enlisted in the army.[20]

Graduating from Saint-Cyr in 1862, Léonce joined the 6th Infantry Regiment as a second lieutenant, serving on garrison duty at towns near the north-eastern frontier: Thionville, Bitche, Metz, Lille (where he became a lieutenant in 1867) and then at Mézières near the Belgian border. He was in Charleville, just across the River Meuse from Mézières, when war with Prussia broke out in July 1870, and it is from this point that his vivid narrative of his personal experiences begins: the marching and counter-marching on the frontier in the heat and rain of summer; his baptism of fire in the great battles around Metz and his endurance of the subsequent blockade of the city; his escape to Belgium after the capitulation of Metz, and service in the makeshift Army of the North, which struggled on under General Faidherbe in a series of hard-fought winter battles until its rout at Saint-Quentin preceding the armistice in January 1871.

His commanding officer in the Army of the North, Colonel Fradin de Linières, reported that Patry was a very well brought-up and educated officer; very brave in the face of the enemy, liked and respected by everyone. If he was rather bookish and did not show all the zeal desirable in matters of routine, if his dress was spruce but not strictly regulation, here nevertheless was an officer with excellent principles and a bright future.[21]

That future seemed to be unfolding well in the fifteen years following the war. Although his health was impaired for a while from campaigning in the open during one of the coldest winters of the century, Patry apparently recovered and flourished in duties which challenged his lively and versatile mind. In 1872 the Commission for the Revision of Officers' Ranks, which reduced the ranks of so many officers rapidly promoted in the emergency of war, recognised his worth by confirming his wartime promotion to captain. That summer he married Marie Clémentine Morel, heiress of a Parisian publisher, with whom he would have two children.[22] In 1872–4 he was employed at Versailles on a commission testing firearms, for which he had a strong taste and aptitude. He was sent to Holland in 1874 in connection with tests on the Beaumont rifle. In 1877 he received a ministerial letter of thanks for a general study of the recent war, and from 1880 to 1883 was military attaché at the French embassy in Berne, Switzerland. Reports on him praised his physical and intellectual vigour, his facility in drafting, his memory, sound judgement and capacity for work. His promotion to major in 1879 was seen as overdue, and following his meritorious service in Switzerland he was appointed chief of staff of the 32nd Infantry Division at Perpignan and made a lieutenant-colonel in 1884.[23] A colonelcy seemed within easy reach.

Then the bottom fell out of Patry's career. Although a regular soldier, with all the professional's contempt for ill-disciplined militia, Patry often showed a distinctly cavalier approach to obeying orders which did not suit him. His propensity for clashes with his commanders in wartime, the story of which he skilfully interweaves with the unfolding of military events, evidently did not leave him afterwards. His 1884 report noted that although he got on very well with his peers and that his men were very attached to him, he had differences with his superiors. After returning from staff duties to service in a line infantry regiment – the 125th – Patry's previous luck in getting away with defying authority finally ran out.

By 1886 he was borrowing large sums of money, evidently in connection with some private industrial venture. His failure to repay 800 francs to a Monsieur Auriol, a Perpignan banker, provoked a complaint to his commanding officer. The matter reached his corps commander at Tours, General Carrey de Bellemare, who in October 1870 during the Siege of Paris had shot to popular fame for his spectacular if unfruitful victory at Le Bourget. De Bellemare claimed that he had shown indulgence to Patry, inviting him to disclose the extent of his debts and to offer a proposal for repayment. But Patry gave dilatory and evasive responses, whereupon de Bellemare, fuming at such 'insolence, flippancy and bad faith', ordered an inquiry and then his arrest and strict confinement in January 1887. Patry had already been informed that his nomination for the rank of colonel, for which he was otherwise well qualified, would not go forward.[24]

He confessed to debts of 10,350 francs, approximately double the annual income of a lieutenant-colonel, and he was given three months to begin repayment. Instead, Patry went on sick leave before completing his 30 days' confinement, and subsequently got his leave extended twice, absenting himself from de Bellemare's supervision for five months and adding insult to injury by having his absence authorised by another command and appealing direct to the Minister of War. Although it had been noted that Patry's health seemed to be shaken and that he was preoccupied with private affairs, de Bellemare was not convinced. He wrote two blistering reports to the Minister of War, charging that Patry was not sick at all and was simply defying authority. Having ignored all warnings, indulgence was no longer appropriate: 'To me, Lieutenant-Colonel Patry is a dishonest man, without conscience, without scruples, and absolutely lacking in moral sense. He merits exemplary punishment, and dismissal from active service will be a lesson to him from which he may profit.'[25] Recommendation approved by the Minister of War, 21 June 1887. Approved by the President of the Republic, 28 June. At the age of 46, Léonce Patry was out of the regular army and living in Nice.[26]

Although he did pick up a post in the Reserve in 1888, his career was irreparably blighted, and it seems that we owe his fascinating account of the war to that circumstance. *The Reality of War* (*La guerre telle qu'elle est*) was apparently the product of his enforced leisure, completed in 1896 and published in Paris in 1897. Eventually the army did at least find some further use for his talents. In 1896, being clear of debt, he was assigned to staff duties, becoming chief of staff of the 80th Reserve Division. On successive annual exercises in the Alps he showed that he was still capable and energetic, again receiving excellent reports.[27] He was also employed in the military administration of the Paris garrison. Although he never advanced beyond lieutenant-colonel, he was promoted from Chevalier to Officer in the Legion of Honour in 1909 in recognition of his services in the Reserve. He was still serving on manoeuvres in 1913, aged 72, and was formally retired only in April 1914.[28]

The outbreak of war in August 1914 found him eager to rejoin, though like the French Government itself he prudently moved from Paris to Bordeaux as the Germans advanced on the capital. He wrote to the War Ministry, offering his services and explaining that had remained in the Reserve 'in order to be certain of having a place in case of war'.[29] He was made commandant at Lourdes, far from the front, that autumn. But by now, however willing the spirit, his strength was failing. In 1915 the French Army took a hard second look at the number of superannuated Reserve officers it had employed at the onset of the national emergency. In January 1916 the army doctors concluded that signs of arteriosclerosis and senility made Patry definitely unfit for service, and he was retired for the final time in March.[30] The following year, as Frenchmen of a new generation were being slaughtered in droves by German artillery and machine-guns along the Chemin des Dames in eastern France, the old veteran of 1870 died, ten days after his 76th birthday, on 28 April 1917.[31]

A Note on the Translation

This translation is unabridged and is taken from the original French edition published in the *Librairie Illustrée series* by Montgredien and Company, 8 Rue Saint-Joseph, Paris, in 1897. Some minor misprints have been corrected (Grammont to Gramont, Bistroff to Rustroff, Itterstroff to Ittersdorf, Kirschnahmen to Kirschnaumen, Habouville to Habonville, Lersy to Lessy, Emery to Esmery, Tilloy to Thilloy, Pittie to Pittié, Guévillers to Grévillers). As Patry was (to modern tastes) unduly fond of the semi-colon, punctuation and paragraphing have occasionally been modernised, but only where this could safely be done without altering his meaning. Although for certain passages (particularly battle-narrative) Patry enhanced the immediacy of his account by adopting the present tense, he did not always use this technique consistently or tidily, and to avoid confusion to English language readers the translation renders these passages in the past tense. With the exception of the last two chapters, chapter titles have been supplied by the translator, who also selected the opening quotations in each case.

Acknowledgements

This translation has had a long gestation, and although nobody else is responsible for any errors and shortcomings in it, I would like to acknowledge several debts incurred in its preparation. First to my friend William Bellchambers, who long ago unknowingly introduced me to Patry's memoir. When clearing out some musty old books, knowing my curiosity about such matters, he handed me a little blue-bound volume called *Famous Modern Battles* (London, 1913) by Andrew Hilliard Atteridge, a leading military writer of his day. I had no great expectations of a book of that vintage with such a quaintly antique title, and in my ignorance I had vaguely assumed that the Crimean War was the only event of note in European warfare between Waterloo in 1815 and Mons in 1914. Yet, passing an idle hour in the wet summer of 1969 in reading Hilliard Atteridge's elegantly written account of Rezonville and Gravelotte, the scale, significance and horror of those little remembered but portentous events in Europe a century before began to dawn upon me. I was particularly struck by the inclusion of short quotations from a frank and spirited witness to the chaos of battle – Patry. However, it was nearly three decades before an intermittent intention to 'do something' about Patry's book crystallised into resolution. The stimulus came in September 1997 when I had the good fortune to join a party which visited the battlefields of 1870 with an inspiring guide, Professor Richard Holmes. It was towards the end of our tour, discussing books about the war and the lack of available French accounts with some knowledgeable fellow travellers one warm evening at a café under the arches of the Place Ducale in Charleville, that I was finally stirred to begin the work. For help during my pursuit of it, I would like to thank the staffs of the British Library, the Institute of Historical Research, King's College London, Croydon Public Libraries, Le Musée de L'Armée at Les Invalides, Paris, and the Service Historique de l'Armée de Terre at Vincennes. My thanks too to Colonel Michel Perrodon, Army Attaché at the French Embassy in London, Monsieur François Robichon, President of the Association des Amis d'Edouard Detaille, and Monsieur Frédéric Lacaille and Madame Aleth Depaz of Le Musée de l'Armée, for their courteous responses to my enquiries; and to my colleague Isabelle Carslake for help and advice at various points. It is also a pleasure to record personal debts to Owen Rhys, my good companion and driver at Amanvillers in the sun, Saint-Quentin in the rain, and on many another field; to my mother for her encouragement and faith; and last but not least to my patient wife and children who, but for this book, might have seen a great deal more of both me and the kitchen table over the last two years.

Douglas Fermer
2000

GLOSSARY

abattis Felled trees used as defences against infantry attack. Laid side by side in front of earthworks, with the overlapping branches pointing towards the enemy, they were intended to break the momentum of an assault while the defenders fired into the attacking troops. Abattis were used during the investments of Paris and Metz, where both armies were stationary. (Barbed wire, which was to serve the same purpose even more effectively, was patented in the USA in 1867, came into use there in 1874, and was first put to military use in the Spanish-American War of 1898).

billet A house or other building requisitioned by troops for overnight shelter. In the war of 1870–1 the Germans generally billeted their troops in French villages, while the French kept to their Algerian and Italian campaign habit of pitching tents overnight. The German practice had several advantages in northern European conditions, not least that the men did not have to carry such heavy packs with cooking utensils and shelter tents; they also rested and ate better, and it was usually easier to guard against surprises. Patry's account illustrates all the contrasting rigours of French camp practice in the summer campaign. However, he shows that in the severe cold of the winter campaign in the north, French troops necessarily adapted to using houses, farms and factories for shelter.

chassepot A breech-loading, bolt-action rifle developed in the 1850s by Antoine Alphonse Chassepot (1833–1905) and adopted for army use by a decree of Napoleon III on 30 August 1866 in the wake of Austria's crushing defeat by Prussian troops armed with breech-loaders. The 1866 model chassepot, though not without its faults, was the best army rifle in Europe in 1870, far superior in range (1,200 metres), accuracy, rate of fire (6–7 shots per minute) and reliability to the Prussian Dreyse needle-gun. It fired a relatively small (11mm) conical lead bullet with an integral paper and gauze combustible cartridge. Although not always well trained in the chassepot's use and tending to waste shots, French troops in good positions were able to inflict terrible casualties on attacking German infantry. Impressed with its killing power, French generals became more inclined to a passive and defensive strategy which undermined their tactical advantage. The French had a million chassepots in 1870, but a large proportion of these were captured at Sedan and Metz. In the later stages of the war French forces had to turn more to inferior converted 1857 rifle-muskets or imported weapons. The chassepot was superseded as the standard French infantry weapon in 1874.

Commission for the Revision of Officers' Ranks A commission established by the National Assembly in 1871 to review wartime promotions. Because of the desperate need for more officers during the war, in October 1870 the Government of National Defence suspended the normal regulations governing promotion. At the end of the war (as after the American Civil War) there was thus a large surplus of officers at inflated ranks, and the Commission's task was to determine who should be retained in post and who demoted. Inevitably, this generated much bad feeling and accusations of bias among those who were reverted. The chairman of the Commission was General Changarnier, a monarchist who had been close to Bazaine during the capitulation of Metz and who was suspected of putting the honour of the army above the claims of patriotism. The Commission, which continued its work well into 1872, was particularly hard on officers who had broken their parole to the Germans by escaping to serve the Republic. There was criticism that the conservative Commission used the opportunity to re-establish the dominance of the officer corps of the old imperial army at the expense of those more recently appointed by the republican Gambetta. Patry's promotion to captain in the Army of the Rhine, dating from 12 September 1870, was confirmed by the Commission.

Commune The left-wing Government of Paris proclaimed on 28 March 1871 and bloodily suppressed in the last week of May by the forces of the National Government based at Versailles. The election of the Commune resulted from grievances at the acts of the monarchist-dominated National

Assembly, which in the strongly republican working-class districts of Paris appeared deliberately provocative. In the wake of the privations of the siege, it also represented a patriotic reaction against the peace terms. The word *commune* (community) carried an almost mystical significance as an expression of Parisian aspirations to self-government. It evoked legends of the revolutionary Commune of Paris of 1792–4 which had dominated France during the Terror and the Revolutionary Wars. It embodied a range of radical, socialist and revolutionary ideals and programmes for greater social justice and equality: hence the Commune and its martyrs were to be a source of myth and inspiration to the left for a century to come. To its enemies, at the time and afterwards, the Commune was a conspiracy of criminal anarchists, atheists and foreigners, deliberately inciting the 'dangerous classes'. To the Communards, conversely, those opposing them were ignorant, priest-ridden royalist reactionaries. Patry's undramatic account of his part in the military operation against the capital provides a more plausible insight into the motivation of professional soldiers reluctantly caught up in a civil war.

cuirassiers Cavalry shock troops wearing steel breastplates and backplates (the *cuirass*) as body armour and crested steel helmets for protection in close-quarter combat. Although cuirassiers did fight hand-to-hand at Mars-la-Tour on 16 August 1870, and their belief in traditional tactics remained undimmed, their eventual disappearance from European battlefields had been presaged by the massacre of cuirassier regiments in sacrificial charges into German rifle fire during the frontier battles of 6 August.

depot The permanent administrative base of a regiment, where it was concentrated before setting out for the front. Reservists had to report to their regimental depot on the outbreak of war for the issue of uniforms, equipment and weapons. In line with the policy of not allowing units to stay too long in one town, more than half of all French regiments were garrisoned far from their depots in July 1870. The transportation of these units clogged the railways just as thousands of individual reservists were crowding onto trains to reach their depots. Stories became legendary of men travelling the entire length of the country, or even to North Africa, to join their depot, only to have to travel hundreds of miles back to near their starting-point once their regiment set out. The delays involved in this process, and in forwarding reservists from depots to the front, contributed heavily to French loss of the strategic initiative. Patry's regiment at least had the advantage of being garrisoned at its depot, Mézières.

dragoons Mounted troopers trained to fight either on horseback or on foot, typically wearing a crested brass helmet and armed with a carbine and sabre.

francs-tireurs Military companies formed on the initiative of private individuals or communities with the aim of waging guerrilla warfare against the Germans. Some had their origin in pre-war shooting clubs. The *francs-tireurs* often bore exotic titles and wore fantastic uniforms, and included foreign volunteers; particularly Spaniards and Italians. The Government made some effort to control them by attaching them to the *Garde Mobile*, making them subject to the orders of local military commanders, and providing pay, but with varying success. Some 57,000 men enrolled in these units. Their performance was mixed. Some delivered nothing but braggadocio: others were no better than marauders terrorising French communities. But some performed well enough to cause the Germans to detach large numbers of troops to protect their rail communications and rear areas. A few units under capable leaders performed outstanding feats. However, the Germans refused to recognise the *francs-tireurs* as anything other than murderers. They responded to rear area attacks brutally, with hangings, shootings and burnings, not always very discriminately. A cycle of mutual reprisals greatly embittered the latter phases of the war.

Garde Mobile (*Garde Nationale Mobile*) An auxiliary force created by the Niel Law of 1868. Intended to take France a step nearer to a universal military service obligation, it was widely unpopular for that reason. The *Garde Mobile* was meant to include all men of military age who had not been conscripted (i.e. those who had drawn a 'good number'), or who had bought a substitute to serve for them in peacetime or had been exempted. It was hoped that it would provide an equivalent to the Prussian *Landwehr*. However, such was the hostility to the new force in the Legislature that their training was set at a derisory fifteen days per year, with no overnight camps.

Pre-war attempts to organise training met such a hostile reaction in Paris and other towns that the experiment was not repeated, and after Minister of War Niel's death in 1869 the army did not much concern itself with the *Mobiles*. Thus in July 1870 the force existed only on paper. Its mobilisation, instead of providing garrison troops to relieve the army in rear areas, proved an outright hindrance. The Paris *Garde Mobile* was so undisciplined that it had to be sent back to the capital from the camp at Châlons. Some 280,000 *Mobiles* served in the war, but after it they were disbanded as a failed experiment and replaced with a new territorial force. Nevertheless, some units of '*Moblots*' who served in the provincial armies, braving the contempt and neglect of regular officers, and despite their inferior arms and equipment, showed courage and self-sacrifice on the battlefield.

Guards regiments The Imperial Guard was the élite of Napoleon III's army, created in 1854 in imitation of his uncle's redoubtable force, and expected to be personally loyal to the Emperor. The Guard was formed by taking the best soldiers from the line regiments, for which it was sometimes criticised, and its better pay and conditions created some jealousy among line troops. Nevertheless, it proved itself in the Crimea and Italy. In July 1870 it was a corps numbering more than 20,000 men of all arms, and in an army renowned for its resplendent uniforms the Guards regiments were the most colourful and stylish. They fought at Rezonville on 16 August, but were held out of battle on 18 August by their temperamental commander, Bourbaki. Several generals who held senior commands in the provincial armies were Guards officers who had escaped from Metz, for example Lecointe and du Bessol in the Army of the North. The Guard itself was abolished by decree of the new Republican Government on 21 October 1870.

hussar A light cavalryman, typically wearing a busby and a dolman jacket with a fur-lined short cloak.

kepi (from the German-Swiss *käppi*) A military cap with a close-fitting headband, a smaller flat round or oval top sloping towards the front, and a horizontal peak. As an infantry officer, Patry's kepi would have had a red top and a dark-blue headband. In wide use in the French army from the late 1850s, the kepi was imitated in America as a forage cap and is forever associated with the characteristic image of troops in the American Civil War.

Legion of Honour The highest civil and military honour in France. Napoleon Bonaparte, who believed that 'it is by baubles that men are led', initiated the order when First Consul in 1802. Napoleon III introduced major changes in 1852. The head of state was grand master of the Legion, which was administered by a chancellery presided over by a grand chancellor. The order was normally awarded for a minimum of twenty years' distinguished service in civilian life (as for Patry's father after his years as a head teacher) or for exceptional bravery or distinguished service in war. The Legion had five classes, with 80 grand crosses, 200 grand officers, 1,000 commanders, 4,000 officers, and an unlimited number of chevaliers (knights). The highest aspiration of most junior officers was to retire as a captain with the scarlet ribbon of the chevalier's cross, which carried with it various civil privileges and an extra allowance. During their retreat from the centre of Paris in the last week of May 1871, the Communards burned the Palace of the Legion of Honour, which to them was a symbol of hierarchy.

light infantry (*chasseurs à pied*) Specially trained assault troops able to march and attack at a faster pace than normal infantry. They were equipped with carbines, and their *élan*, mobility and firepower had by 1870 gained them a formidable reputation in combat. In 1870 France had 20 battalions of *chasseurs à pied*, each with a nominal strength of 933 men.

line regiment Most French regular troops served in line regiments, of which there were 100 in July 1870, including four in Algeria and two in Rome. The total strength of these regiments on the outbreak of war was over 190,000 men out of some 367,000 military personnel on duty in France or overseas. Once the reservists were called up, France was able to put about a quarter of a million men of all arms on her eastern frontier by mid-August. The line regiments were distinct from the more prestigious Imperial Guard, the Army of Africa, the artillery and engineers and various other specialised units. The uniform of line infantry included red trousers and kepis, with dark-blue coats and tunics. A line regiment was typically composed half of conscripts, and the other half about equally divided between volunteers, men who had chosen to re-enlist for a second term, and substitutes (men paid to take the place of wealthier conscripts). See also *Regiment* under *French Military Formations in 1870*.

mitrailleuse An early machine-gun with 25 tubes within one barrel, fired consecutively by turning a handle. By inserting blocks of 25 pre-loaded 13mm rounds, it was possible to fire up to 125 shots per minute. Developed in great secrecy by Captain Reffye in 1866–8, under the patronage of Napoleon III, the *mitrailleuse* failed to have the expected impact on the campaign. There were various reasons: officers trained in their use were erroneously assigned to other duties on the outbreak of war; the firing-pin tended to break and the weapon had a limited traverse. Mounted on wheels like a conventional cannon, it was often used as one rather than in close infantry support – but in either case it was vulnerable to German artillery. Despite inexperience in its tactical use by its operators and field commanders, it nevertheless could and did occasionally work to murderous effect.

National Guard A citizen militia originating in the revolution of 1789. Napoleon III had severely reduced the National Guard after his seizure of power in 1851, but it was revived in August 1870 with enthusiastic republican approval. It was greatly expanded by the Government of National Defence, but was rarely of much military value. In the Army of the North, Robin's National Guard Division proved worthless in battle. In Paris, this armed force of 350,000 men proved easier to activate than to control. Having little to do but man the ramparts, the National Guard became highly politicised during the siege. Some 'Red' battalions incited demonstrations at the Hôtel de Ville on 31 October 1870 and 22 January 1871. On the first occasion loyal battalions came to the Government's rescue. On the second, Breton *Gardes Mobiles* fired on and dispersed the dissidents. After the armistice, four-fifths of the strongly republican Paris National Guard battalions were unsympathetic or hostile to the newly elected Government, and formed themselves into a Federation. It was in attempting to disarm this volatile force that the Government precipitated insurrection on 18 March 1871. The operation against the Commune that followed was in effect a civil war fought between the regular army on one side and on the other possibly 50,000 National Guards in April, shrinking to perhaps 20,000 at the end of

May. After the Commune was crushed, the National Guard was formally abolished in August 1871.

Orleanists The members of the House of Orléans – the junior branch of the bitterly divided Bourbon royal family – and their political adherents. The House of Orléans, in the person of King Louis-Philippe, had ruled France from the revolution in 1830 until overthrown by the revolution of 1848. Unlike the Legitimists – adherents of the elder branch of the royal family – the Orleanists acknowledged and accepted the gains of the revolution of 1789. However, while embodying the cause of liberal monarchy in France, they opposed full democracy, preferring a narrowly based parliamentary constitutionalism representing the power of a wealthy élite. In the National Assembly elected in February 1871 the monarchists had an overall majority. The Orleanists, the largest single group, had 214 seats and the Legitimists 186. But despite the willingness of the descendants of Louis-Philippe to reach an accommodation with the elder branch, restoration of the monarchy was effectively ruled out on 5 July 1871 by the reactionary intransigence of the Legitimist pretender, the Comte de Chambord. Initially expected to be only a temporary expedient, the Republic thereafter gradually came to be accepted as the only viable form of government.

pickets (*grand'garde*) Outpost guards which Patry aptly describes as 'squads drawn from companies which, posted at a sufficient distance from the regiment on the enemy's side, give it security while it rests and, by their resistance if attacked, allow it to get under arms and prepare itself for combat before any surprise'.

régiment de marche A temporary regiment constituted for wartime service, and usually commanded by a lieutenant-colonel. In July 1870 it was intended that new *régiments de marche* should be formed by amalgamating the fourth (depot) battalions of existing regiments. With the exigencies of the later phase of the war, however, it became a case of patching together regiments from whatever battalions were available. Thus Patry recounts that in December 1870 two battalions of the 75th Line Regiment, including the one he was serving in, were joined with one from the 65th Line Regiment to form the 67th *Régiment de marche*. These composite regiments were not intended to outlast the war, though to minimise disruption some, like the 67th, were later formally reconstituted as line regiments.

reservists Men eligible to be called up for army service on the outbreak of war. Every year an annual contingent of men was conscripted by lot, divided into the first and second portions. Until 1868 men of the first portion who did not qualify for exemption served seven years in the army. For budgetary reasons, men of the second portion were only required to attend for at most a few months' training – but also remained subject to recall in time of war. The 1868 Niel Law reformed this system. All men of the first portion were henceforth required to serve five years in the army followed by four in the reserve, while training for the second portion was fixed at five months over three years. But the benefits of the new system, which was intended to give France a larger and better trained army, had not worked through by 1870. On the evening of 14 July 1870 a telegram from the Minister of War ordered the recall of the Reserve and second portion men of the 1863–8 contingents: a measure rather optimistically expected to produce 173,500 men ready for combat in fifteen days. In fact, after a chaotic mobilisation, by 1 August nearly two-thirds of these men were still at their regimental depots.

Saint-Cyr (*L'Ecole Impériale Spéciale Militaire*) The French national training academy for infantry and cavalry officers. The institution was founded under the first Napoleon in 1803 and was located at Fontainebleau before moving to Saint-Cyr in 1808. It was dissolved in July 1815 after Waterloo but was reorganised in 1817–18 by Marshal Laurent Gouvion-Saint-Cyr, Minister of War. About 250 second lieutenants per year graduated after a two-year course. Patry entered in 1860 and graduated in 1862, placed 233 in his class of 249. A report by a commission in 1861 found much to criticise in the academic standards, course content and state of morale among students at the academy at that time.

Uhlans German cavalry troops armed with lances and wearing the characteristic *czapska* head-dress. (The French, however, tended to describe all German horsemen as Uhlans). Used in small scouting patrols to screen the German advance, and boldly raiding behind French lines to cut telegraph wires, their effectiveness contrasted with the general lack of enterprise of French cavalry reconnaissance. Rumours of their exploits soon magnified their numbers, and fear of the ubiquitous Uhlans and Prussian spies in 1870 was similar to that inspired by German paratroopers and 'fifth columnists' in 1940.

FRENCH MILITARY FORMATIONS IN 1870

In descending order of size

Corps The largest constituent units of an army, ranging in size between 20,000 and 41,000 men. The larger corps were commanded by marshals, the others by generals of division. The corps system had been revived and refined under the first Napoleon. Each corps was intended to be a self-sufficient entity of all arms for the purposes of manoeuvring and fighting, strong enough to take on a larger enemy force until the army could be re-united. The success of the system caused it to be imitated in other countries. In 1870 France concentrated eight corps (including the Imperial Guard) on her eastern frontier, five of which took part in the campaigning around Metz. Patry served in the Fourth Corps under General Ladmirault, which on 1 August had a combat strength of 27,000 men. Later, in the northern campaign, Patry served in the Twenty-Second Corps under General Lecointe which formed half of the Army of the North. In the Army of Versailles which fought the Commune in 1871 he served in the First Corps, again under General Ladmirault.

Division An army corps was composed of three or four divisions of infantry and one of cavalry. At the beginning of August 1870 the infantry divisions of the Army of the Rhine, each commanded by a general of division, had a nominal establishment of 13,134 but an average strength in the field of about 8,000 men.

Brigade Each division was made up of two infantry brigades, commanded by brigadier-generals or senior colonels. In its turn, each brigade consisted of two regiments. The 1st Brigade in each division included a battalion of light infantry as well.

Regiment The basic unit for recruiting, mobilisation and fighting, commanded by a colonel. While men might be indifferent as to what corps, division or brigade they were in, they identified much more strongly with their regiment. Patry was originally in the 6th Line Regiment, but finished the war in the 67th *Régiment de marche* (see Glossary for the distinction). A regiment had a nominal peacetime establishment of 2,785 (including administrative and support personnel) and was in theory able to put more than 2,400 men in the field on the outbreak of war. In practice, strengths were variable and lower than this. On 12 August 1870, two days before its first battle, the 6th Line Regiment numbered 67 officers and 1,735 men present for duty.

Battalion In peacetime infantry regiments were divided into three battalions of eight companies each. In July 1870 each battalion was ordered to leave two companies at the regimental depot to form a fourth battalion and a garrison. The three field battalions thus campaigned with six companies each. At the beginning of the war France had 374 infantry battalions. Patry was in the 1st Battalion of the 6th Regiment and in the 2nd Battalion of the 67th. A battalion was commanded by a major (*chef de bataillon*).

Company Nominally 112 men commanded by a captain, assisted by a lieutenant and a second lieutenant. Each company had its assigned place on the march and in the firing line. Patry indicates that his company (the 3rd) went into the August battles with 102 men. Because of the shortage of officers after the surrenders of Sedan and Metz, the provincial armies had larger companies. Patry tells us that the company he commanded (the 5th) started out on the northern campaign with a strength of 200 men.

THE
REALITY OF WAR

INTRODUCTION

In publishing these entirely personal recollections, I certainly have no desire to draw attention to my own very modest personality. The utterly unobtrusive part that a lieutenant or captain can play in a war in which hundreds of thousands of men are engaged can cover him in neither glory nor notoriety. My aim in writing these few pages is to show, by the narration of day-to-day events as they were lived, the general state of mind among a group of officers belonging at the outbreak of the war to one of the good regiments of the French army: for it had taken a brilliant part in the campaigns of the Crimea[1] and Italy,[2] and was a front-line regiment, having been on garrison duty on the extreme north-eastern frontier for eight years. I aim to bring out the material and moral campaign conditions imposed on troops subjected to the pernicious influence of deplorably mistaken ideas during ten years of peace and, lastly, to illustrate the part played by a junior officer in a great modern war.

The luck which always favoured me in sparing me even a slight wound or any illness allowed me to be present at the most important stages of the campaign: first, in the operations of the Army of Metz, from July to November, in Cissey's division which suffered the greatest losses (44 per cent of its effectives); secondly, in those of Faidherbe's army, in the division of General Derroja, known as the Achilles of the Army of the North; and thirdly, in the repression of the Commune in the Army of Versailles (Laveaucoupet's Division).[3]

Being constantly in the thick of things during this year of campaigning, I was in a position to witness events at close hand, and can vouch that the account of them which I have set down twenty-five years later is absolutely faithful, and that nothing in it is exaggerated or not strictly true.

The reader may perhaps find some interest in following step by step the experiences during this turbulent period of an officer who, through a combination of the most bizarre circumstances, began by making war for two months without receiving a sou in pay nor a gramme of rations and who, by way of concluding the campaign, found himself twice decorated with the Chevalier's Cross of the Legion of Honour[4] (in orders of 3 June and 24 June 1871).

PATRY

PART ONE

METZ

CHAPTER I

THE OUTBREAK OF WAR

July 1870

'I was in a state of the highest enthusiasm . . .'

Charleville – The declaration of war – State of morale among the officers in 1870 – The regiment prepares for war – My situation – The first, then the second batch of reservists – En route – Thionville – Letters from father and mother – A vow to Our Lady of La Salette

In the month of July 1870 I was a lieutenant in the 6th Infantry Regiment[1] garrisoned at Mézières, a rather ugly little fortified town bristling with bastions and outworks, encircled by two or three ditches, but otherwise absolutely incapable of resisting a few volleys from the cannon in use at that time. Happily for me then, but unfortunately a little later, the company to which I belonged formed part of the regimental depot and occupied a small barracks situated at Charleville, a pleasant, quite unfortified town sitting prettily in green meadows in one of the numerous loops of the Meuse.

We had lived there for three years, dividing our time between the tasks imposed by the career which I liked a great deal and the customary distractions offered by small garrison towns, which were less to my taste – I valued only the relative proximity of Paris – when our quiet was brusquely disturbed by the events of early July. Thenceforward our minds turned to war and, it must be said, we expressed the most ardent wishes for affairs to become more embroiled and for a short and brilliant campaign, like those of 1859 and 1866,[2] to put an end to Prussian bluster. Personally, I was in a state of the highest enthusiasm, and so were the rest of my young comrades who, having left Saint-Cyr[3] after the Italian War of 1859, had not had the chance of a serious campaign in Europe.

We had prayed long and fervently for this war that we so desired! Let our hopes not be dashed again this time! We had really believed that we were going to set off once before, in 1867, at the time of the Luxembourg affair.[4] Our swords were all but jumping out of their scabbards, only to be put back again, and we had resumed the monotonous garrison life.

The desire of we young men to make war was all the greater as our regiment had figured gloriously in the campaigns of the Crimea and Italy; most of our comrades wore on the breasts of their parade uniforms the medal given by the Queen of England[5] with four clasps: Alma, Inkerman, Balaclava, Sebastopol, and the Italian campaign medal. Some comrades, the most favoured by fortune or with the best connections, complemented these medals with Ottoman or Italian decorations, and it was with truly envious stares that we saw all these riches spread on their dress tunics while ours stayed eternally bare and deprived of these most honourable embellishments. We listened, eyes shining with emotion, hearts palpitating with interest, to stories of combat in which everyone had his share of glory; it was with a pious respect that we eyed the colour-bearer's cross-belt with the proudly preserved hole made by the Russian bullet which had killed the officer who wore it at Inkerman.[6] When would our turn come to join in such spectacles? When would we be able to associate ourselves with such memories?

We thought the government too yielding; we wanted to see window smashing straight away. Then we were in despair when the Emperor William[7] announced that his kinsman had renounced the throne of Spain.[8] Fortunately, there remained a tiny red point at the tip of the match, and under the eager puffs of Gramont, Leboeuf,[9] etc., the fire rekindled. They managed to light the fuse and blow up the building.[10]

If our desire to make war was great, our means of doing so assuredly did not reach the same heights, but we took no account of that. We considered ourselves, our officers, NCOs, and troops, very brave, and we did not doubt for a single instant that our spirit would succeed easily in bowling over the Prussians, whose clumsiness would be no match for our dash. Besides, were we not also trained in even the most difficult tasks of our profession? For my part at least I knew perfectly not only my regulations for manoeuvres, for drill by squad, by battalion, for field service, etc., but was equally familiar with the line drill which had been taught me thoroughly by my old captain of grenadiers when our company had been detached for two months to a central prison[11] where we could not leave the premises. During those exercises I had dutifully fulfilled the most important office of adjutant. At every inspection I had put in efforts that had won me praise. I was therefore confident in the belief that I was fit to lead my little troop in the proper manner. The devil take me if I ever suspected that a fortnight later I would not know how to place a picket guard or to push out a reconnaissance. And yet we were all in the same state, even those who had been on earlier campaigns and who, under the influence of mistaken old doctrines, had no idea of the methods to employ to conduct the daily operations of modern war.

Although the declaration of war was not notified to Prussia until 19 July, it was considered certain from the 15th.[12] It was from that day that we started to take the steps necessary to put the regiment on a war footing. The offices of the sergeant-majors were stirred into feverish activity which manifested itself by the arrival of a crowd of additional secretaries to fill out the call-up orders of the men on indefinite or temporary leave. All our time was absorbed in issuing items of every kind to the men present and sorting out their equipment and so forth.

One thing surprised me amid all these preparations which reeked strongly of gunpowder, and that was to see the coolness, the lack of enthusiasm, with which all the old officers (and by old, I mean all those who had campaigned in the Crimea and Italy) had greeted the opening of this new campaign. Most of them, confronted with our outburst of joy, silently shook their heads, as if to say, 'You'll soon draw in your horns.' Their markedly reserved attitude struck me as rather shocking.

A year later, how I understood the good sense of this behaviour! For war, modern war at least – so seductive for young minds full of illusions fostered by reading and by stories that are always poeticised to inflame hearts and make them find the most painful sacrifices glorious – war considered as it really is by those who have seen it at close hand is nothing at bottom but an abomination.

My astonishment was greater still when I saw several of the older captains, the most experienced in war service, scurrying to grab jobs distant from the front. Two of them surreptitiously slipped off into the *Garde Mobile*,[13] another into the job of adjutant, another, as soon as the campaign had begun, into the post of commandant of a little depot of invalids left in Metz while we were fighting on its outskirts. Yet a few months earlier these brave officers had been full of brag that they were ready to slice up every army in Europe, one after the other.

It was at this period of my life that I was assailed by the most terrible and grievous tribulations. Certainly I have had plenty of torments since, plenty of cruel anxieties, but nothing ever approaching the agonies which I suffered during this second half of July. I belonged to one of the six depot companies. Now, as everyone knows, while the three field battalions of the regiment set out for the frontier, the depot troops constituted as one battalion under the orders of a major stay in garrison to receive the men earmarked to fill up the gaps left by enemy fire and illness, equipping them, instructing them, and finally getting them ready to be incorporated in the battalions operating in the field.

A lucky chance meant that a vacancy for lieutenant existed in the 3rd Company of the 1st Battalion: the post-holder was detached in an Arab bureau in southern Algeria and could not possibly return in time to fill his place at the commencement of operations. My first concern was to rush to the colonel and urge him as strongly as possible to give me this place. But, for the five years that Colonel Labarthe[14] had commanded the 6th Line Regiment, I had never been in great favour with him. In fact we had had some serious disagreements which had led to severe punishments for me when (as was most frequently the case) superior authority had overruled my protests; and to some more or less harsh reproaches for him when it had upheld me. Thus there was an extreme tension in our relations. But the war had made me forget everything and I would have embraced him (though he was not good-looking) in order to get permission from him to go with the field battalions. Naturally, he showed me the door, not without an air of mocking satisfaction. I returned to the charge the next day and would have gone on my knees to him, but with no more success, alas!

I was then seized by an intense fretfulness which robbed my days of charm and my nights of sleep. I continually saw my comrades following the victorious flag, triumphantly entering Berlin, returning covered in glory, in promotions, in medals; whilst I, shamefully sheltered in my depot, would be consumed by my chagrin, burying all my dreams of combat and of a brilliant future in gloomy despair. I reached the point of contemplating the most extreme solutions. I would hand in my resignation and depart with my knapsack on my back like any private. But would I be allowed to resign?

And then the formalities take so long, thanks to the channels of hierarchy, that they must drag on painfully before any decision as to who was in the right. So I would desert and enlist under a false name, free to unmask myself when I should have won the Legion of Honour after some brilliant action which I had set my sights upon. Good sense being restored, I abandoned these impracticable projects; but then, not knowing what else to resolve upon and seeing no other way open to me to obtain my goal, I became profoundly disheartened, which made me very wretched.

Then on 20 July I had the immense heartache of seeing the three battalions of the regiment depart for the frontier. Meanwhile, our life was becoming busier and busier; five hundred recalled reservists had just arrived. We had to clothe, equip and arm these men, get them back in military habits and train them at the very least to load their chassepots,[15] although they were familiar only with the old hammer and percussion cap weapon.[16]

While this was going on I received my appointment as lieutenant instructor at the Academy of Saint-Cyr. This official letter, which I would have received with the greatest joy if it had arrived a few weeks earlier, seemed to me the height of mockery. What! While my regiment was speeding to victory after victory on the battlefields of Germany, I should be lurking in a desk job without even the hope of replacing a killed or wounded or sick comrade, or of being included in some company of reinforcements? I wrote immediately to Colonel Hanrion, who commanded the Academy at that time, that my duty was too plain to think of withdrawing into some bolt-hole, and that I emphatically refused to hide myself away at the Academy. He responded, telling me that it was not my place to debate an order which had been formally issued, and that I must report immediately to my new post on pain of exemplary punishment. But during these negotiations events had marched on, and I no longer had to preoccupy myself with this business, which threatened to take a disagreeable turn for me.

On the 25th, two hundred of the newly recalled men were ready to be sent to the field battalions, which were on the frontier near Sierck, on the Moselle. Leadership of this battalion between Charleville and that place was entrusted to a lieutenant or second lieutenant, assisted by three or four non-commissioned officers who were supposed to return to the depot and take up their normal duty once their troop had been delivered to the regiment. On the announcement of this departure, I bounded over to the major and asked him as a favour to give me command of the detachment, pleading among a thousand good reasons that I intended to make every effort to find employment in the company with a vacancy for lieutenant. I met an absolute refusal. I was not the most senior; the officer assigned, more senior than me, had accepted the post which besides he had no plausible reason for refusing. So I had to yield, promising myself nevertheless to put things right later, for from that moment the idea began to germinate in my mind, vague at first but becoming clearer every day, of arranging matters in my own fashion.

The opportunity was not long in coming. On the 29th a fresh convoy of three hundred reservists was to set out for the frontier. The second most senior lieutenant was assigned to conduct it as far as the frontier. This officer was old, having already passed forty, worn out by numerous campaigns and moreover, what was rare at that rank, married and the father of several children. My plan was decided. I went to find him and asked him if he intended to try to stay with the regiment once he reached it. When he replied in the negative, I begged him to yield his place to me. He agreed, but only on the understanding that I got the approval of the major, which I had to make sure of. I left him in order to report to the major, but scarcely had I reached the street when I took a turn in another direction and went into the first café I came to. I stayed there a good half-hour, then returned to my comrade and told him that the major had given his permission for our swap. Without further explanation I returned to quarters and spent the rest of the day preparing for the departure of my detachment, which was to board the train at Charleville station at two o'clock in the morning. Not wanting to give the game away, I made no ostensible arrangements for departure, and on quitting my little bachelor's quarters I left all my effects as if I was going to return a few hours later.

Towards midnight, on reaching the barracks at Mézières where the detachment was due to assemble, I was in terrible apprehension. Supposing that on arrival I should see in the courtyard the silhouette of the major, coming to inspect the troop before its departure! Luckily I had to go and deal with a man who had overslept, whom a visit to his quarters at half past midnight could not arouse at all. With the aid of three non-commissioned officers or corporals who had joined me I put my troop in order, then 'By the right, march!' and we left the barracks. So long as the figure of the commanding officer did not confront me menacingly on the station platform! But there was nobody: the god of stratagems was definitely on my side. I got my three hundred men embarked somehow or other. In eight years as an officer, this was the first time I had ever had to contemplate such an operation, let alone take charge of it. As two o'clock struck, the railwaymen closed the carriage doors and every slam reverberated in my heart. A long blast on the whistle, and my campaign had begun.

Once en route, all alone in my first-class compartment, I started to put a little order into my thoughts, which had been in complete turmoil since the day before. Had I even slight remorse for the unspeakable act which I had just committed? None. My conscience gave me no reproach. I had tricked my comrade, it is true; but that could do him no harm, for it would be easy to exonerate himself with the major by putting all the blame on my back, as was only just, indeed. As for the major, I confess that I thought with a certain pleasure of the crestfallen expression he would wear when he learned that the bird he was charged with keeping caged had taken flight. But soon a cloud, small at first then ever blacker and more menacing, darkened my blue sky. Obviously the major, furious at having been made a fool of, would write to the colonel and tell him of my escapade. Perhaps the letter would travel faster than me, and then how would I be received on my arrival, given the still extreme tension in my relations with the colonel? Bah! Let luck decide! Perhaps on leaving the train a lucky chance would hurl me with my detachment into open battle, and then if with my three hundred reservists I carried off a signal victory they would be forced to keep me.

The day began to dawn when the train was at the station in Sedan; we were subjected to a long wait. Despite the early hour, a good part of the population was about. The station was you might say invaded and the train almost stormed by the inhabitants who, mounted on the running boards, passed all sorts of food and drink through the open doors. I had absolutely forbidden my men to leave the wagons and it was just as well I did so or they would have been lured, with no ill intentions, into the buffet or the taverns near the station and scattered in all directions, and I would never have been able to reassemble them in time when the train was ready to depart.

While I was walking up and down the platform, keeping a watchful eye on the carriage doors, several leading citizens surrounded me, as if I were an important military personage. They asked me a mass of questions, in the midst of which I sensed a certain anxiety breaking through about the size of our army, or at least about its state of preparedness. Now then, what business was that of these civilians? We not ready! Were we not always ready to fight? What? They seemed to doubt our superiority! I assured them that we would be at the Rhine in a fortnight, if not beyond it. Were we not the soldiers of Sebastopol and Magenta?[17] Despite the warmth of my assertions, it seemed to me that I did not succeed in dispelling the cloud of uncertainty which hung over all these people.

As for my men, whether from natural high spirits or from the effect of the cheering feast which had been so generously offered them, they were very boisterous, singing their heads off. They kept it up for the whole journey, which ended on the 29th towards two o'clock in the afternoon after numerous halts caused by the congestion of the Ardennes railway line.

We were at Thionville, a small fortified place on the Moselle frontier which had been designated as the base of operations for our army corps (the Fourth). Before getting the men off the train, on the advice of an old sergeant who was accompanying me I enquired of the stationmaster whether the commandant of the place had left him with any instructions to be handed to me on arrival. But the stationmaster had nothing for me. The officer in charge of the military post office at the station had nothing either. I searched in vain on the platforms and in the area around the station for an officer-in-charge able to give me instructions. Time was pressing. The train had to be evacuated and returned to the rear as soon as possible. I got the men off and mustered them in the confined and deserted market square. Then I set out towards the local headquarters.

Thionville was no longer recognisable. This little town where I had lived for about two years from 1863 to 1865, so dreary, quiet, boring even, had become the centre of extraordinary activity. In every street there was a continual coming and going of soldiers, carriages and horses in the midst of an indescribable hubbub. I had difficulty in making my way through.

Headquarters was full of people seeking every kind of information. A brigadier-general was kicking up a great row because nobody could tell him where his troops were. I eventually managed to accost an officer and present him with my marching orders. 'That's in order,' he said to me, and as I did not turn quickly enough on my heels for his liking he added, 'Well! What are you still waiting for?'

'But captain, I wanted to know where I should lead my detachment, as they can't stay penned up in the market square for ever.'

'Wherever you want, to be sure!'

'I'd like to take them to my regiment, the Sixth of the Line, which must no doubt be somewhere hereabouts, and to do that it is quite necessary for me to know where it is camped.'

The captain, in very bad humour, went into another office and returned a good half-hour later to tell me that the 6th was encamped on the frontier itself, close to Sierck, and that I should pass the night at Thionville and set out the next morning to rejoin it. Of course there was no question of billeting the men with the inhabitants. Where should they sleep then? After much negotiation, finally a barracks empty since the morning was earmarked for my detachment.

After having gone to the commissariat to get the necessary provisions of all kinds for issue to my troop, I returned to the station and by about five o'clock all my lively lads were in the afore-mentioned barracks, at the door of which I set a guard with the strictest orders for the night. The issue once made, and my men provided with four days' biscuit, rice, coffee, etc., plus the regulation camping utensils – small tents, mess-tins, water-bottles, etc. – but not however in sufficient numbers, I thought of finding myself a lodging for the night.

After a hasty dinner at a hotel in the town where the diners, nearly all military men, succeeded each other like figures in a diorama, I went and sat down outside a café and as night was falling – a splendid summer night lit by legions of glowing stars – I little by little withdrew into my own thoughts. Suddenly seized by a sort of weariness mixed with vague sadness, my mind drifted back, far from there, to affections which I was perhaps leaving for ever.

A few days earlier I had received a letter from my father to which I had paid little attention at the time, my mind being completely absorbed in my plan to take part in the campaign. But at this moment when my goal appeared to have been attained and my task for the day completed, I could give it my whole attention. Reading this letter caused me strong emotion, which comes back to me almost as keenly twenty-five years later. I cannot resist the urge to quote it.

Poor dear father! It is sixteen years since death took him from me, though he was in flourishing health and good spirits, as strong in body as in mind, and the grief of this irreparable loss is still as stinging as on the first day.[18] For in him I lost my only friend, and what a friend! Come, let us unfold the old paper, yellowed by time, which for twenty-five years has been sleeping in the pocket of the wallet which I carried with me during the campaign. The neat and clear writing attracts the eye and proclaims an honest hand, a strong character, an upright mind and an enemy of all compromise of principle. The ink has faded, and yet for me this letter is so expressive that it might be burned into the paper with fire.

Grenoble, 20 July 1870[19]

My Dear Boy,

Here you are, exposed to fire for the first time.

It is your duty. I have nothing else to say. But you must understand how much we suffer, your mother and me.

So be careful.

Remember that between the timidity which fears everything and the rashness which fears nothing, there is a nobility which confronts necessary dangers and a caution which knows how to protect itself from unnecessary risks.

So think of your mother, your sister and me. We all say, 'March forward like the brave man you are,' but we add, 'Don't be rash. Don't put our lives at hazard by needlessly risking your own.'

Put yourself in the hands of God who demands from us and you this supreme sacrifice for the defence of the country.

Go, my fine son, face the fire covered with God's protection, our kisses and our blessing.

Your father who dotes on you.
E. PATRY

If I have quoted this precious letter at length, it is certainly not with the intention to offer it to the reader as a model of the epistolary art, nor as a unique fund of paternal and patriotic sentiments. In suchlike circumstances in novels and plays one could easily find grander, more literary and more dramatic expressions of those sentiments: but these were from life. It was to his son, his only son, whom he loved not as a father but as a friend and long-time comrade, and by whom he was adored: to his son who was leaving to undertake a campaign which the great reputation of the enemy promised to make hard and bloody, that this excellent man wrote these few lines marked by such a high degree of despair and noble resignation. Despite his immense sorrow, he sought only to make his son more aware of the path of duty and, although his heart was breaking with anxiety, he nevertheless told him plainly, without reservation, 'March onward! Do your duty!' How many fathers have done as much?

Are there not grounds for drawing a profitable lesson for the future from this admirable letter, to make it a sort of catechism for the future for we who have grown old, and whose sons may perhaps have to reap the great harvest of revenge? Ah! When that terrible moment comes, let us armour our souls in the purest steel and lift up our hearts! *Sursum corda*![20]

Let us utterly reject as a crime any idea of shielding them in any way from the performance of their duty. Let us not try to keep them from combat by seeking to find them jobs away from danger, but also from honour. Let us on the contrary urge them, intellectuals and nobles, to stay in the ranks to set an example of courage and the fine public virtues that a superior education develops, for their place is in the firing line and not in the rear in offices or in the hospitals.[21]

Certainly, reading this letter at the doorway of the café in Thionville did not inspire me with reflections of this kind, but it impressed me strongly. I understood with complete clarity how great was the sacrifice which their country asked of these poor parents. And I who a moment before, doubtless under the influence of fatigue and of the thousand vexations of the day, felt ready to pity my lot, understood that the most to be pitied were not those leaving for the frontier, whom the lively and varied life of the camps bore along, almost carefree, in its continual bustle; but rather those who stayed at home, turned inward on themselves, without even daring to own their fears, kicking their heels in incessant worry.

My mother had sent me two little medals by the same post; one of gold, the other of silver, bearing the image of the Holy Virgin and of Our Lady of La Salette. These two medals were sewn into the corner of the letter she had written me. Under the influence of an intense religious feeling, sustained by an ardent faith, my mother viewed the approach of the harsh trial with that irrational confidence which belief in providential help gives. While waiting, she had taken precautions and had made a vow to Our Lady of La Salette that if I returned from the fray she would lead me to her in her mountain sanctuary.[22]

That journey, however, would be an enterprise not without great difficulties for my mother, for she had been unable to walk properly since my birth. She lived always stretched out on the *chaise-longue*, avoiding even a carriage ride. But to go from Grenoble to La Salette, in 1870 at least, you had to spend a night in a coach which took you down to Corps, I believe, then from there you had to climb to the church perched on a plateau 1,800 metres up. Three hours at least on mule-back were needed to complete the ascent and up there you could find only the very basic facilities of a convent in which to pass the night.

To conclude the tale of this engagement made in writing, I have to say that it was fulfilled to the letter. In August 1871 my father, my mother and I made the pilgrimage. Strange to relate, my mother, sustained no doubt by her faith and her happiness at seeing me safe and sound again after so many wanderings, cheerfully bore the hardships of the journey of four or five days up hill and down dale. As for me, I caught a chill there which brought on a serious illness. That would have been the limit! To have escaped the manifold dangers of battles to die of pneumonia contracted right in the middle of a pilgrimage undertaken to thank heaven for having been preserved during the war!

Be that as it may, my mother and I agreed that in the next campaign she would convey her prayers and promises to a Virgin dwelling in a flat region served by a railway.

CHAPTER II

ON THE FRONTIER

30 July–4 August 1870

'Nobody had the least idea of the situation. . .'

From Thionville to Sierck – A lucky encounter – The divisional chief of staff – Arrival at camp – A letter from the major – A night alert – On the march – A tricky situation – Bivouac – Camp at Bouzonville – Reconnaissance on Sarrelouis – We retrace our steps – Picket guard

For me, 30 July was one of the most tiring days of the whole campaign. I had fixed reveille at four o'clock so that we could set out at five, for there were still some issues of rations to make before departure. At the stroke of four I was at the barracks. Everyone was already up: the night had passed in the greatest turmoil. Having only a little straw available, the men had preferred to stay in the courtyards to take the fresh air. They had thus had no rest. A large number had managed, I know not how, to come by some brandy, and by now many heads were on fire. With my three NCOs I tried in vain to be everywhere, but I could not assemble them or hold them together. Fortunately for me a passing battalion of the 73rd had also been quartered in the barracks that night. Their commander took pity on me. He lent me half-a-dozen NCOs to establish and maintain order, and two quartermaster-sergeants to issue the rations. Without this truly providential help I should never have got out of that mess.

Finally at five o'clock we got on the road, heading for Sierck. The head of the column marched along tolerably but at the tail, despite the presence of my old sergeant, disorder was at its height. After an hour's marching my three hundred men were strung out over nearly four kilometres of road, some stretched out in the ditches and refusing to get up, others lying around in the fields, gathered in small groups wherever there was a little shade: the rest tramping along slowly, swearing about the sun, about their knapsacks, about the whole business.

I felt a real rush of despair. To think that we were almost in the presence of the enemy! What would become of us if a party of cavalry suddenly showed up? How could we resist with these men who had lost all sense of shame and discipline? What was to be done? I went from one man to another, reasoning, imploring, threatening, but nothing succeeded in persuading them. I had scarcely fifty men in hand.

Suddenly I saw on the road, in the direction of Thionville, a great cloud of dust which thickened as it advanced. It could be nothing other than troops on the march. I ran towards it . . . Oh what happiness! It was the battalion of the 73rd which was also headed for the frontier. Their commander immediately deployed two sections in extended order to right and left of the road, and in a few minutes all my gallants, with bayonets pushed in their backs, were pressed back onto the highway. The commander formed them in four ranks and once order was re-established I resumed the march. Ahead of me were three companies of the 73rd which drew us along by their example, and behind us three other companies which, forming a solid rearguard, forced the stragglers to march in spite of themselves. After a meal halt of an hour in the village of Koenigsmacker, the march was resumed in the same order. A few kilometres before arriving at Sierck the 73rd left me, but the men had been put back in their stride and I had very little difficulty in leading them the rest of the way.

Besides, we had for some time already felt ourselves in a military atmosphere. Camps had been seen on the heights in the distance, and tethered horses and wagon parks in the vicinity of the road we were following. These sights, reassuring for me, rid my lads of all inclination to indiscipline.

Here we were at last in Sierck without too much bother. I halted my troop in the village square, which seemed packed with soldiers of all arms. Then I went to the town hall for some instructions on the location of the 6th, but nobody could give me any. Someone pointed out a house where a general was to be found. I reported there and had the good fortune that it just happened to be the headquarters of General de Cissey, commander of our division. I asked to speak to him, but he was absent. The orderly indicated a room where I found, attired in a rather comfortable gown, the colonel who was chief of staff of the division. I explained my position and asked him where I should lead my detachment.

With an attitude full of nonchalant dignity he said to me, 'The Sixth?' then, looking at a little chart which hung on the wall, 'Yes, the Sixth is part of the division. Now then. The Sixth is on the Rustroff plateau, where the whole division is camped.'[1]

'What road should I take to get there?'

'Oh! Anybody will tell you that. Goodbye.'

Dear God. At the time, this way of doing things did not shock me. It was so much the custom of the epoch where 'muddling through' was still in fashion. But later, when, reflecting on the events of this disastrous war, I recalled the haughty casualness of this agent of the high command, I could not help shuddering, and suddenly the cause of all our disasters appeared to me as clearly as if it had been written in the sky in letters of fire. A chief of staff who, after eight days of campaigning, had to refer to a memo to know whether or not the Sixth was one of the *four* regiments which made up the division, was that not the lowest depth? And everything else was of a piece.[2]

I enquired the way of more than a dozen people without being able to get proper directions. I would still be in the village square if chance had not put me in the path of a man of our regiment who had been sent to Sierck on army business and was returning to camp. I followed in his footsteps and, after a stiff climb of several kilometres, I at last had the pleasure, on arriving on top of the plateau, of seeing the promised land stretching before me in the distance. There, laid out as far as the horizon, serrating the blue of the sky with neat triangles, was a camp of ten thousand men. Ah! All was forgotten; fatigue, impotent rage, and the rest. I went straight to find my colonel and turned my detachment over to him, fortunately complete (thanks to the 73rd).

The dear colonel seemed to me to be in good humour! I took advantage of it to repeat my request, and I begged him to allow me to fill the vacancy for lieutenant which existed in the 3rd Company of the 1st Battalion. My conviction shook his resolution, and in the end he told me that if the general of division consented to it, he would keep me. On this promise, I left him and went immediately to take my place.

I found, settled in a small tent made of four squares of canvas, the men who were to become my wartime companions and who at that moment were thinking of taking their evening meal; for it was quite six o'clock by the time I could consider my day as finished. I was received with open arms

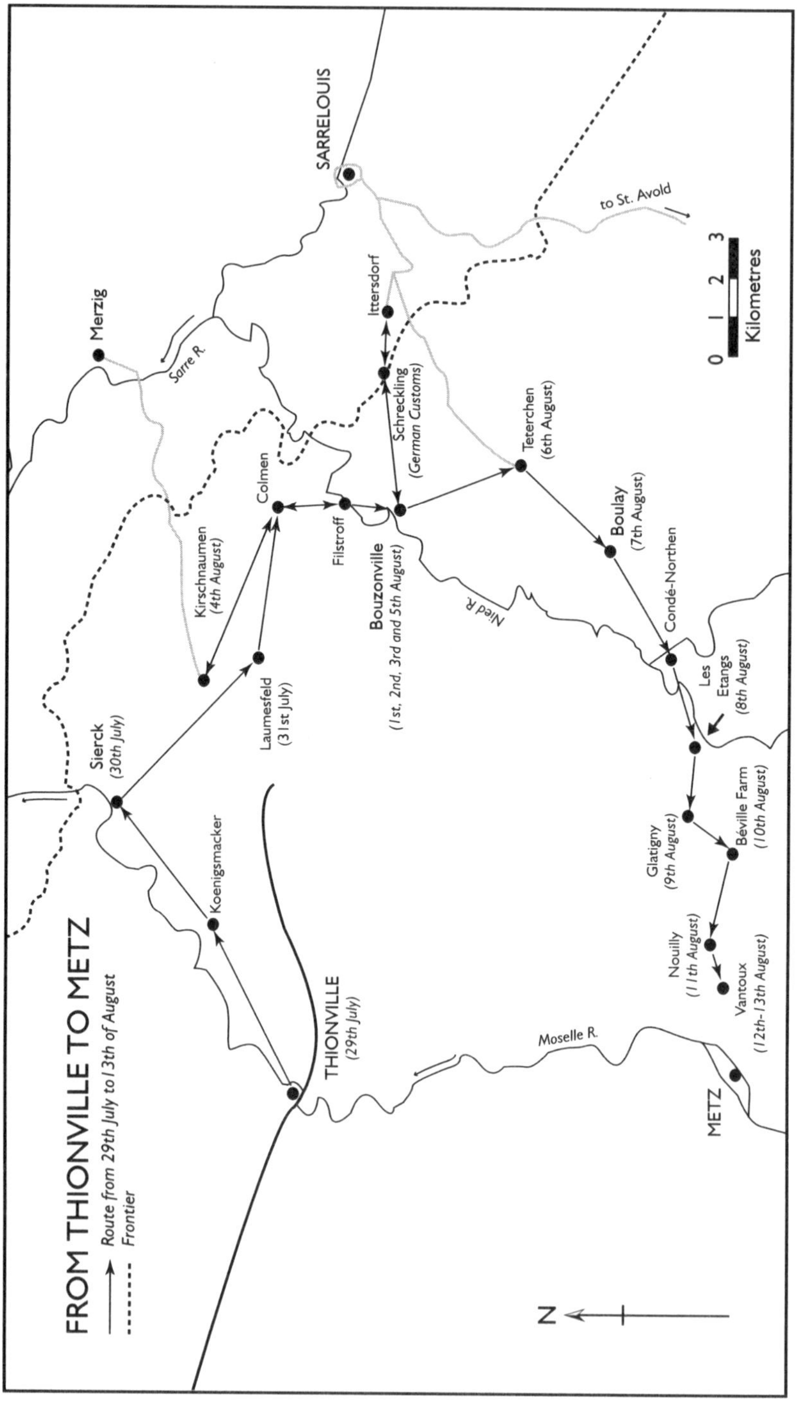
FROM THIONVILLE TO METZ
Route from 29th July to 13th of August
Frontier
SARRELOUIS
Merzig
Sarre R.
to St. Avold
Ittersdorf
Schreckling
(German Customs)
Teterchen
(6th August)
Boulay
(7th August)
Condé-Northen
Les Etangs
(8th August)
Béville Farm
(10th August)
Glatigny
(9th August)
Nouilly
(11th August)
Vantoux
(12th-13th August)
METZ
Moselle R.
Nied R.
Bouzonville
(1st, 2nd, 3rd and 5th August)
Filstroff
Colmen
Kirschnaumen
(4th August)
Laumesfeld
(31st July)
Sierck
(30th July)
Koenigsmacker
THIONVILLE
(29th July)
0 1 2 3
Kilometres
N

by my old comrade Frondeton, who had been a captain for several months, and by young Second Lieutenant Rousset,[3] who had arrived the day before straight from the Academy of Saint-Cyr where he had completed his second year. We quickly made acquaintance, and I promptly ascertained that I would have in him a comrade as agreeable as he was staunch.

Abundance reigned in the field-mess; I enjoyed one of the most delicious meals of my life. Then, night having come and after several good pipes smoked under the stars, we rolled ourselves in our greatcoats and, having crept into the tent, pressed closely one against the other, we were not long in going to sleep.

From dawn on the 31st everybody was astir and in line of battle on the outposts. Why? We never knew a reason, any more on that day than on those following. After a few hours of waiting, ranks were broken and the men were left free in camp.

I took the opportunity to slip down into Sierck to see the general in command of the division. I had the luck to meet him. He listened to me with benevolence and told me that the colonel could address a request to him which he would receive favourably. Ecstatic, I left him and returned smartly to camp. I hurried towards the colonel's tent to announce the good news to him. I was scarcely before him, not yet having opened my mouth, when I was received with a storm of abuse and invective. He was trembling with rage, and was feverishly waving in his hand an opened letter from the major at Charleville which recounted my escapade. 'Leave immediately,' he told me. 'Return to the depot where you will remain under close arrest for a week. If you haven't left camp in five minutes I'll have you seized by the military police.'

I turned on my heels, completely annihilated. Farewell my dreams of glory! They were all going up in smoke. I sat down at the foot of a tree to calm myself after this outburst, which had staggered me. After having reflected well and having weighed the pros and cons in the scales of my conscience, I made up my mind, determined to see things through cost what it may. I went first to my company and told my captain that, having been unable to see the general, I must go back down to Sierck and perhaps stay there all day, for I could not return without seeing him. Then I returned to the village immersed in my thoughts, which were the colour of ink. Lord, how long the day seemed to me! If only the shooting had broken out at that moment! How quickly I should have returned to my post without anyone's permission! I wandered around all day like a soul in torment. At nightfall I returned to camp. I slid into the tent and after a few brief words of explanation fell asleep, absolutely broken down.

I was in the heaviness of early sleep when I felt myself brusquely shaken. I could scarcely open one eye.

'Get up quickly,' said the captain, 'we're breaking camp.'

'But what time is it then?'

'Half past midnight. We're leaving at once. It seems that we intend to surprise the enemy.'

I was quickly awake and on my feet. How fortunate this alert was for me. At night all cats are grey, and if I had the luck that we should fight the enemy the colonel would not dare to send me back to the depot! Come, the gods are with me. Let's march! But we did not march at all. The battalions were in line on the plateau: it was pitch-dark. Only some lanterns of mule drivers finishing their loading up streaked the profound darkness with a few rays of light. All three of us were speaking in whispers, commenting on events and, faced with this long inactivity, beginning to miss our sleep.

Finally we got on the road. Where were we going? Nobody knew. We marched the rest of the night, then the whole morning, but at a funereal pace. Most certainly we were not making three kilometres an hour. No enemies, but dust, heat, then in the long haul fatigue and boredom. Halts were frequent, sudden stops more numerous still. In the end we left the road and settled ourselves in a meadow. It appeared that we were within the bounds of a little village called Laumesfeld, still in French territory. Where were we in relation to Sierck, which we had left the night before? Or to the Moselle or to the frontier? How could we tell? Nobody had maps, not even the senior officers.

Once camp was made, I went to present myself to my major, Monsieur de Saint-Martin, and told him that, the general of division having authorised me to address a request to him on the subject of the vacancy for lieutenant, I was in the company awaiting his final decision. He found all this entirely natural. Besides, it was a matter of very little importance and scarcely one to divert anyone's attention from the great events which we expected to unfold from one moment to another.

In my captain's eyes my position was also very reasonable, and he only awaited receipt of the instruction from the general of division to confirm my transfer. Now everybody well knew that the general had other fish to fry, and to process my request would certainly take many days! As for the colonel, he rarely showed himself: in camp he stayed put in his tent; on the march he rode at the head of the regiment without ever turning round. With a few precautions it was thus easy for me to avoid his sight. Only an unforeseen circumstance could bring us together face to face and lead to a clash, the very idea of which made me shudder. This circumstance did not arise and it was not until 17 August that chance put us in each other's presence.

In saying earlier that camp had been made I committed a slight error; the tents had stayed folded in our packs. The regiment, remaining on the alert, had simply stacked arms and the men, having put down their knapsacks, rested stretched out on the ground, waiting impatiently for the order to cook. The whole day passed thus. When evening came tents were pitched, fires lit, and forthwith feverish activity reigned amongst the men. It was a case in fact of one thing being of the first importance, of being indeed the only thing truly worthy of interest; in a word, it was the matter of cooking a meal. It is sad to say, perhaps, but on campaign, whether it is that life in the open air turns a man back towards nature or as a consequence of the many fatigues of war and one's strength being in constant need of replenishment, it is incontestable that one thinks of absolutely nothing but eating and sleeping. I am of course speaking only of the junior officer who, once he has his men settled in conformance with the orders he has received, has nothing to occupy his mind. And this was all the more natural for us, who in the twenty days of marching around Metz never knew where we were, whether we were advancing or retreating, whether the enemy was far or near or to the right or left. Having nothing better to do, driven into indifference to what we were doing by the complete ignorance in which we were kept, we gave all our care and attention to the smooth running of the field-mess and to fixing ourselves up with somewhere to sleep.

Personally, I have a horror of everything to do with housekeeping and cooking, etc. I would much rather eat badly, even not eat at all, than have a feast if I had to do the work myself. I am aided in that by a most accommodating stomach, for it very rarely grumbles, knows how to wait, contents itself with very little and accepts pretty well anything one offers it. Thus during the whole campaign I never loaded myself with even a piece of chocolate. Besides, at this time I had a stomach disorder as peculiar as it was painful. As long as my stomach was empty I got along splendidly, but as soon as it was full the least movement became painful to me, to the point of forcing me to stop to let the crisis pass. Little wonder then that I was always apprehensive of food, whatever it might be, taken in the course of an existence as full of movement as that which one leads on campaign; and that far from longing for mealtimes, I almost always came reluctantly to the table, except in the evenings when I had the night before me to digest in peace.

On 1 August we were up at dawn. We stayed in ranks for two or three hours, awaiting what? Finally we got on the road. After several hours of a march as slow as it was enervating we came to a pretty valley, crossed the river which we were told was the Nied at a place called Bouzonville, and climbed up onto the table-land on the right bank. The regiment was halted in the middle of a large plain which allowed us a view of a vast horizon. We had stacked arms and the tents were already pitched when we suddenly heard shouts: 'To arms!' echoed from every side. We rushed to our stacked arms, checked our guns, put cartridges within reach. The men seemed to me full of spirit: would it be the real thing this time? Were we at last going to see some of these Germans whom we imagined ourselves to have been running after for several days? We waited one hour, two hours: nothing. Finally the decision was taken to re-stack arms and attend to the cooking.

The whole day passed baking in the sun on this immense plain without shade. I made use of the time to write to my parents. Besides, 1 August is my mother's birthday, and I do not think that I have ever let the date pass without sending her my best wishes. Ah! That is by no means a duty, but truly a pleasure. I know that it pleases her, and as I love her very much I take every opportunity to prove it to her. I would moreover have been delighted to let her know, as a birthday present, that her son had been under fire for the first time and had conducted himself becomingly. I also wrote to my orderly whom I had left at Charleville in my little bachelor's quarters, and whom I had told that I should return in two or three days. I charged him with putting all my things in trunks and carrying them to the home of one of my friends living in the town, and with making up my campaign trunk and sending it to me through the good offices of the regimental depot which was in constant communication with the field battalions.

A few days later I did in fact receive my campaign trunk, but it would have been better if it had never been sent to me, for it fell into the hands of the Germans on 18 August, with our whole camp. My orderly had had the unfortunate idea of packing with it a letter-case containing my papers, which meant that my letters of appointment, my two bachelor's diplomas in literature and science, my certificates for the Nicham's Cross that I had brought back from a little expedition in which I had taken part on the frontiers of Tunisia, and for the Cross of Isabella the Catholic of Spain, went to be scattered in Germany.[4]

On 2 August, early in the morning, the regiment was sent out to make a reconnaissance towards Sarrelouis. The camp was left under the guard of one company. The men were lightly equipped, without knapsacks or camping utensils. They had passed a good night, were well rested and appeared to be in fine fettle and very good spirits. We were off! Matters would be handled briskly if we met the enemy at last! While ruminating on these happy thoughts I was marching alongside my company when all of a sudden there rose up, a few paces ahead of me, the frightful statue of conscience in the form of the colonel. Having halted at the point where the regiment was leaving the ploughed fields and stepping onto the main highway to Sarrelouis, he was watching all the units march past. To turn back towards my troop, take my handkerchief from my pocket and bury my whole face in it was the work of a second, and I passed in front of him, brushing his horse's nostrils with my shoulder-blade. He noticed nothing, being in any case one of those men who, always absorbed in some petty trifle or other, most often some piffle, look without seeing and hear without listening. As for me, so great had been my emotion that I was sweating all over and my legs had turned to jelly.

I do not know whether the column comprised our regiment alone, or the brigade, or the whole division. In any case, for the first time we marched properly, at a good pace with no sudden stops. In two hours of marching we were at the frontier itself and passed beyond it. At last we had set foot in Prussia. It seemed to me that heads were held more proudly, and that legs struck the ground more boldly, as if well and truly to take possession. The march was pressed to just beyond the village of Ittersdorf. But at the junction of our road with another which, coming from France in nearly the same direction, joined it at rather an acute angle, the battalion was halted: then, after several minutes, it was put back on the march in the opposite direction. The commander of the battalion left me at the fork of the roads with my section of about fifty men, telling me that I was the extreme rear-guard, and that I had to keep about 500 metres in rear of the tail of the battalion. There I met a peasant who told me that some days previously the Prussian customs, whose post was at Schreckling on the same road, had been attacked by our customs officers. The post had been occupied by infantry from Sarrelouis. The French customs men had driven them out of ambush, killing their leader, and had suffered serious losses. This story inflamed my ardour and I prayed with all my heart for a similar opportunity where with my section I should be able to inflict a first-class trouncing on the Prussians. While the column turned about and began to move off, I climbed a little hill near the road and contemplated the surrounding terrain. About three or four kilometres ahead of me and barely distinct was the town of Sarrelouis, upon which I could see two main roads converging, thanks to the trees lining them: the one we were following and another to the right, one or two kilometres distant (which I later understood to be the road from Saint-Avold). Between the two roads the terrain was slightly undulating with scattered woods, covered with harvest crops and meadows. In front of the town, on a little plateau sloping slightly in my direction, a group of three Prussian companies was occupied in exercises which seemed to me to be something rather similar to our battalion drill. Moreover, although we were entirely visible, they did not seem to be at all interested in us. I had a foolish longing to deploy my section as skirmishers and to go and disturb their security with a volley of bullets. But it was necessary at the very least that I should be authorised to do so and that I should feel supported.

I turned round to go back down the road and acquaint my commander with what I had seen. Great was my surprise to find myself completely alone with my section, unable to discern the shadow of a soldier as far as my view extended along the road. In the twinkling of an eye I returned to my senses. Of my warrior's ardour of a moment ago nothing more remained than a sudden fear of having compromised the situation of my little troop by lingering thus on my observatory. I immediately got my section on the road and for a long time I could not prevent myself from turning around at every moment to see that we were not being followed by the Prussians who, observing our weakness and isolation, could have had the intention of surprising us. During the day we returned to camp and, alas, were never to set foot in Germany again other than as prisoners.[5]

Dinner that evening was very animated. Everybody was discontented; we no longer understood anything. How could it be? We had entered Prussia, we had marched on a strongpoint which appeared not to be defended, and without even attempting to strike a blow we had turned back! We all felt just a little downcast at this miscarried escapade. Our high spirits of the morning had turned to ill humour in which we could not help but encourage each other. Our captain in particular did not stop fuming, but that was for an entirely different reason. The cook had dropped something or other in the stew, which had spoiled it, and the captain was very upset by this. 'Ah! Stew,' he told us. 'Boys, stew is everything on campaign, and wine of course! Drink, my boys, believe me, drink hard, but always wine.' This captain was a good fellow. As we had been lieutenants together for seven or eight years we were on familiar terms and, as is customary, had preserved our former comradely relations. I never held back from sending him to the devil when he bored me too much with his lamentations or his more or less ridiculous advice; but the same was not true of my young friend Second Lieutenant Rousset, who served as his butt. The poor boy, still completely intimidated by the superiority in rank, didn't know where to put himself when the captain started blackguarding him in his moments of ill humour. I intervened several times in his favour, but not as vigorously as I should have done and wanted to because of the falsity of my position, which I feared all the time would be exposed. That evening at mess was truly diabolical. The shrill voice of the captain, who didn't stop sounding off, split our ears. 'Drink my boys, you must drink wine to keep up your strength'; and, very gravely practising what he preached, he swigged glass after glass, so much so that when dinner ended he was deep in his cups. In spite of ourselves we followed suit, at a distance it is true, but in the end not so far behind that we weren't a little sozzled ourselves. That made us see life in rosier colours, and when we got ourselves back into our tent we were as close friends as three fingers on the same hand.

On 3 August the whole day was passed entirely in camp in lamentable inactivity and idleness. A few roll calls, an inspection of arms and ammunition, a parade under arms in the evening, but without purpose, were not sufficient to shake off the boredom which weighed upon us. Although we had made no movement, we felt fatigued under this burning sun from which there was no escape. For this cursed plateau which stretched as far as the eye could see bore not a single tree. We felt torpid and almost despondent, without reason however, for nobody had the least idea of the situation in which we found ourselves. And what now fills me with astonishment is the profound unconcern in which we wallowed. Yet during this interminable day our leaders had ample time to put us in the picture. It is true that our chiefs no doubt knew no more than us. And then we didn't even know them. I can vouch that I had never seen the face of our brigadier. I knew that of our general of division because I had seen him at Sierck, but I had never encountered him amidst our columns or in our bivouacs. As to the commander of our army corps, we did not even know his name.[6]

Among ourselves, in the endless conversations which helped us to kill the time, it was only very rarely that we discussed anything about the war. I do not recall that one of us ever showed a very marked desire to know how we stood in relation to the enemy or to the other parts of the army, any more than I heard any criticisms uttered of the movements made or any views on what should be done; at least, not at the outset. No! We were almost indifferent to these questions, but if we suddenly heard that a cook had been able to buy a chicken for the pot, oh! Then our spirits rose and our discussions waxed interminable on the subject of what was the best part of this windfall to partake of.

Should we be severely censured? Obviously not, since this state of affairs was but the consequence of our previous military education. Thus for eight years since leaving Saint-Cyr I had belonged to a regiment which, for that whole period, had been on garrison duty on the northern and north-eastern frontier. We should have known something of the area around Thionville, where the 6th Line Regiment had stayed from 1863 to 1865, furnishing detachments to Metz and Bitche! But during those two years, which of our generals or colonels had ever, I don't say encouraged, but even advised those little pleasure trips around the garrison which, undertaken with a well-defined goal and with facts and documents collected and studied in advance, become in reality study and reconnaissance trips? What did we even know about our enemy on the other side of the frontier? Did anyone ever talk to us about the Prussian forces at those tedious regulation lectures which came around every winter, or about the political and military state of Germany, and so on.?

I remember that one day in 1865, at exercises which we were carrying out on the slopes of Fort Bellecroix at Metz where my battalion was detached, the major, who was very intelligent and industrious (it was Monsieur Vilmette who later commanded the Second Corps at Amiens)[7] took advantage of the fact that he was no longer under the regulation eye of the colonel, who had stayed at Thionville with the bulk of the regiment, to give us an idea on the ground of the combat formations in use in certain foreign armies. After some explanations had been given to the group of officers gathered around him, each one returned to his post to teach his troops the formation which had just been demonstrated. By chance a general passed by; it was a rare instance as it was hardly six o'clock in the morning. He stopped in front of the battalion and contemplated these manoeuvres which were unknown to him with a completely dumbfounded look. He summoned the major and ordered him to stop this sort of practical joke immediately, and to stick strictly to the regulations which in his eyes were perfection itself. That was how officers were encouraged to educate themselves five years before the war.

Our camp on the plateau was as uncomfortable as it could be. Naturally there was not a drop of water to be found. To procure this essential element it was necessary to organise long and frequent fatigue duties. The men, laden with every possible and imaginable receptacle, had to travel several kilometres to descend the valley below the plateau where a little stream ran, and to climb back up to camp. It seemed that this way of doing things offered the undeniable advantage of keeping troops in the very position where they would have to fight in case of attack. It was then the fashion to reduce the art of war to the occupation of good defensive positions. We had a very vague idea of this principle, and we listened open-mouthed to one of our number who, having had business at army corps headquarters, had met a comrade there who had told him, with an air at once mysterious and reassuring too, that if the Prussians had the insolent notion of entering France they would be stopped immediately by the French army, which was gathering on the impregnable position of Cadenbronn, where it would be unassailable; after which the Prussians would wear their talons[8] down to the knuckle. The name Cadenbronn made us wonder somewhat. Where was Cadenbronn? But we could rest assured that the position had been studied for several years by all those the army reckoned as most eminent in the arms of engineering and artillery, and success was certain.[9]

That day I received my campaign trunk from the depot. For me this was a diversion and a real godsend, for I could now change for the first time since 29 July. On campaign one reverts to primitive man. I also chose an orderly from the company. He was a nice lad with an alert expression and a decided and resourceful air. He was from the Nivernais and was called Guyonne. This good man attached himself to me completely, and rendered me valuable service throughout the whole campaign. He followed everywhere in my rather restless footsteps, and never once complained of the numerous dangers to which his devotion to me exposed him.

On 4 August, early in the morning, the regiment was under arms ready to receive an enemy attack which never came. Camp was struck and the march in column – slow and without interest – was resumed in overpowering heat and dust. We followed the valley of the Nied, without imagining in the least where it might be leading us. The battalion, following many others, entered a village in its turn. Great was my astonishment on seeing upon the road-sign fixed to the corner of the first house the name Filstroff. I recalled that we had passed through a place of this name in coming to Bouzonville three days earlier. I was doubtful, however, for then we would be returning on our tracks; but a few kilometres further on we went through the village of Colmen. Suddenly I was completely sure. We were indeed going back down the same road we had come up. So we were retreating! That was what I thought, for I had no idea of our compass bearing. I shared my discovery with several of my comrades, and as nobody could give us an explanation of this retrograde movement we were none the wiser, though not without being somewhat intrigued.

The regiment was halted at a place called Kirschnaumen. The company was assigned to outpost duty. This was starting to interest me greatly. The company took a road nearly perpendicular to that followed during the day's march. After having gone about a kilometre and a half, the captain halted it and called Rousset and me to give us his instructions. Although he had campaigned in Italy in 1859, the captain seemed to me a little perplexed. I had myself not the least idea of what picket duty might consist of on the ground, although I knew very well what it was according to the book of field service regulations. After many delays, hesitations and useless words, it was at last decided that if the enemy appeared we should defend the road, cost what it may, to prevent him passing. Thereupon we had arms stacked, left a sentry on the road, and occupied ourselves with finding a suitable place to set up the field-mess.

While the stew was simmering and the captain was gazing tenderly at it, Rousset and I, spurred on by curiosity and vaguely uneasy, and moreover without really taking account of finding ourselves isolated in the expanse beyond the lines, stepped out well ahead to see if we could discover anything suspicious. The countryside was peaceful; the last rays of the setting sun lit it with a pleasing soft tint and absolute silence reigned around us. Before this spectacle of infinite tranquillity, we shared our thoughts like old friends of several years' standing – we who had known each other scarcely five days – about the anxieties that we felt, rather vague admittedly but real nevertheless, about the way the operations in which we were taking part were being conducted. Returning to the headquarters of the picket post, that is to say to the field-mess, we were greeted by a broadside of invective from the captain, who was dying of hunger and who was waiting for us before starting dinner.

The night was calm and fortunately fine, for we passed it under the stars, wrapped in our cloaks. I do not know what the successive sentries in front of the stacked arms could really see on the horizon, apart from the heaps of stones bordering the road; but very luckily for us they were not called upon to verify the approach of the smallest troop of the enemy. For I do not know at all how we should have received them, placed thus haphazardly here and there across the road. That was how picket guard was mounted in the year of grace 1870 in a regiment of the French army which had lived on the frontier for eight years.

During the whole evening, the night and the morning of the next day, we were visited neither by our major, nor by our lieutenant-colonel, our colonel or our brigadier; and yet (although we were completely ignorant of the fact at the time) seven kilometres distant from us on the road which we were pretending to guard, strong detachments of the German First Army were occupying the town of Merzig on the Sarre! *Ab uno disce omnes*![10]

CHAPTER III

RETREAT TO METZ

5–15 August 1870

'We sensed battle close at hand . . .'

Teterchen – Boulay – False news of victory – Night march – Les Étangs, bivouac in water – Severe sickness – On reconnaissance – Around Metz – In town – First battle (14 August)

On 5 August at daybreak the company received the order to rejoin the battalion, which had encamped to the rear. The regiment got back on the march and after a long while we found ourselves back on the Bouzonville plateau which we had left the day before. This, most definitely, had become quite incomprehensible. This tramping about over the same ground began to get on our nerves considerably. What's more, the weather was atrocious. A frightful storm burst upon us. We camped literally in water. The captain groused without let-up. Everybody was grumbling as well. To cap our woe, there was no means to light a single fire. We had to imagine dinner. That contributed no little to the general sullenness. Boredom, mortal boredom arising from inactivity of the body and above all of the mind crept over us. Most certainly, war was no fun; instead of laurels, if we had at least had umbrellas! The night passed for better or worse, but rather worse than better.

On 6 August we took the whole morning to cover six or seven kilometres. There were continual halts, often very long; but as we were never warned in advance of even their approximate duration we held the men in suspense, keeping them from putting their packs on the ground and so achieving the fine result of exhausting them to no advantage whatever. Believing that this was unavoidable, there were no recriminations, but we found this way of proceeding entirely without attractions. Finally, we pitched camp in the neighbourhood of Teterchen. The weather was a little better than the day before and the cooking-fires which glowed along the whole line of tents gave the camp an air of animation and gaiety which lifted morale a little.

During the afternoon we learned of the defeat of Douay's division at Wissembourg, but in very vague terms. The fact spoke for itself none the less, in all its cruel reality.[1] Going back over these recollections of military history which still fill my memory, I am utterly astonished that we allowed ourselves to be beaten on that part of the frontier, defended by a fortress and by an arrangement of fortified lines which covered the gateway to Alsace by the Lauter. How could a system of such strength, occupied by a division, fall in one day of battle? That seemed inexplicable to me. But as it was so nevertheless, I felt myself filled with a slight scepticism regarding defensive positions, even fortified ones, and Cadenbronn no longer seemed so impregnable to me. This setback was the subject of every conversation and gave rise to the most doubtful hypotheses. It was a certainty, in any case, that hostilities had commenced in earnest and that in a short while we should at last see the enemy.

On 7 August at two o'clock in the morning we struck tents, then the regiment was formed in line on the plateau. We awaited daybreak in this manner. This was long drawn-out and tedious, but it seemed that the enemy was in the vicinity and that an encounter was imminent. When dawn came everybody was already wearied with the interminable standing, and on every face could be read a strong desire to sleep rather than to fight. As the enemy did not appear, we bivouacked on the spot, but after an hour or two new orders arrived and we set off. This time we were surely going into battle; at least we were convinced so. In the meantime we took the road for Metz and turned our backs to the frontier.

We passed through Boulay, a pleasing little town which was filled this Sunday with considerable animation. In front of a café I caught sight of many tables occupied by groups of officers of all arms holding forth in the midst of great excitement. I would have given anything to mix with them and to know the subject of their conversations. Alas, the regiment passed on, leaving the town, but it started up the heights and soon, having no doubt arrived at a *good position*, it was halted and camp was made. I had not mastered my desire for information. Thus, when my modest tasks left me free, I asked the major to allow me to go after the news. He gave me permission, and off down the hill I went towards Boulay.

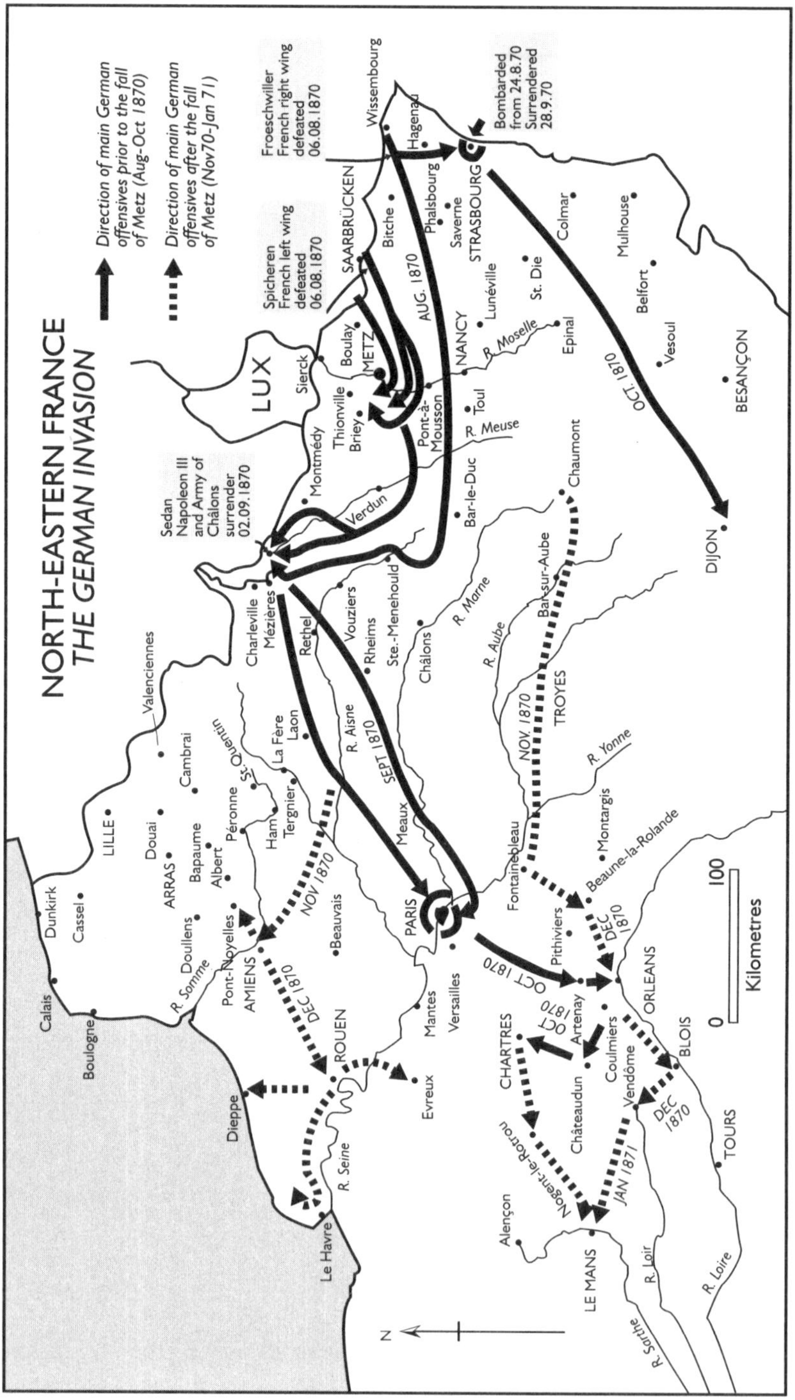

NORTH-EASTERN FRANCE
THE GERMAN INVASION
Direction of main German offensives prior to the fall of Metz (Aug-Oct 1870)
Direction of main German offensives after the fall of Metz (Nov70-Jan 71)
Spicheren French left wing defeated 06.08.1870
Froeschwiller French right wing defeated 06.08.1870
Bombarded from 24.8.70 Surrendered 28.9.70
Sedan Napoleon III and Army of Châlons surrender 02.09.1870
LUX
Wissembourg
Hagenau
SAARBRÜCKEN
Bitche
Phalsbourg
Saverne
STRASBOURG
Colmar
Mulhouse
Belfort
Vesoul
BESANÇON
DIJON
St. Die
Lunéville
NANCY
R. Moselle
Epinal
Toul
Boulay
METZ
Sierck
Thionville
Briey
Pont-à-Mousson
Montmédy
Verdun
R. Meuse
Bar-le-Duc
Chaumont
Bar-sur-Aube
AUG. 1870
OCT. 1870
Charleville
Mézières
Rethel
Vouziers
Rheims
Ste.-Menehould
Châlons
R. Marne
R. Aube
TROYES
NOV. 1870
R. Yonne
Montargis
Valenciennes
LILLE
Douai
Cambrai
ARRAS
Bapaume
Albert
Péronne
St. Quentin
La Fère
Laon
Ham
Tergnier
R. Aisne
SEPT 1870
Meaux
Dunkirk
Cassel
Calais
Boulogne
Doullens
R. Somme
Pont-Noyelles
AMIENS
Beauvais
NOV 1870
DEC 1870
PARIS
Versailles
Fontainebleau
Beaune-la-Rolande
Pithiviers
DEC 1870
OCT 1870
ORLEANS
Artenay
OCT 1870
Coulmiers
Mantes
ROUEN
Evreux
Dieppe
R. Seine
Le Havre
CHARTRES
Châteaudun
Vendôme
BLOIS
DEC 1870
TOURS
Nogent-le-Rotrou
JAN 1871
Alençon
LE MANS
R. Loir
R. Loire
R. Sarthe
0
100
Kilometres
N

Arriving at the main square I approached the first group I came to and learned that MacMahon[2] had avenged Douay and that he had penetrated the Palatinate after giving the Prussians a sound thrashing.[3] Ah! What a good glass of absinthe I drank there! Boredom, fatigue, all was forgotten. So we were going to go to the front, to put ourselves in line beside the victorious troops of MacMahon, to trample enemy soil as masters, to enter towns in triumph, flags floating in the wind. In a week we would be in Mayence. Ah! Prussian gentlemen, you wanted to meddle with us? Well, so much the worse for you.

Moreover, was it not entirely natural that things should stand so? Were we not in fact playing the last act of the great patriotic tragedy that one could call revenge for 1815, the first two acts of which were set in the Crimea and Italy, and which were called Sebastopol and Solferino. The Russians first, the Austrians next, and finally the Prussians. It was their turn. After this campaign we should have reclaimed the rank in Europe which the victories of Napoleon in 1805, 1806 and 1807 gave to us,[4] and France would find herself once again the greatest nation in the world.

When I got back to camp, everyone knew the good news already. I had therefore only to rejoice with my friends after a most lively dinner. Our conversations on this inexhaustible subject carried on rather late into the evening. When we were about to make our dispositions for the night and were preparing ourselves for fine dreams of glory, the order was given to break camp without delay. This was clear confirmation of what we had just learned. We did not want to lose a minute to repel the enemy with our sword-points in his back. After rather a long time we were started on the road. A great part of the night was employed in a march even slower, I believe, than any of those preceding. Our over-excited impatience made us curse against all these unknown obstacles which were constantly halting us and allowing the Prussians to gain distance on us.

Finally, on the 8th at two o'clock in the morning, near Les Etangs,[5] we were led into a meadow all sodden by the rains of recent days and by that which had been falling without cease since the beginning of the night. We made bivouac after a fashion, but in deplorable conditions for health.

I was very thirsty, and a soldier of my company went to find me from somewhere a water-bottle, from which I drank avidly. Where this water came from I do not know, but what is certain is that at daybreak in the morning, when the regiment resumed its march, I was seized by terrible colic. It was a real firework, exploding upwards and downwards; the whole show. I was in despair. I was continually forced to leave the column and recover myself for a few moments away from the road. In vain I tried to spend only the time strictly necessary for these very disagreeable operations. At every halt, and they were terribly frequent, I lost ground to the column, which meant that after an hour I had lost not only my company but my regiment, my brigade, and even my division, for I suddenly found myself quite alone on the road, with nothing more behind me. As I was firmly convinced that we were marching towards the enemy, I had no apprehension; only the fear that my regiment might become engaged without me caused me burning anxiety. Finally, after a last crisis even more acute than the others, I felt my legs give way and refuse me all service; everything whirled around me and I only had time, to avoid falling, to sit down on a little heap of compost, dried leaves and manure which was at hand and there, without my knowing the least thing about it, without my mind even being even able to struggle, I fell into a deep slumber.

When I awoke a reviving sun which had warmed me shone in all its splendour. I was on my feet in an instant, completely restored, but I no longer knew in which direction to go. I recalled, however, that in the midst of my wanderings my tiredness in trying to rejoin the column had been increased by the fact that the road climbed rather steeply. So I resumed the climb through the woods which lined the road on both sides. I had scarcely walked for half an hour when, on reaching the top of the hill, I saw a mass of troops halted and formed on the plateau facing in my direction. I was very puzzled by this sight. How could I, who a few hours before had been behind the troops, now find myself in front of them? I easily found my regiment, and there I learned that instead of marching on the enemy since our departure from Boulay, we were retreating on Metz; that we had lost two battles, on the Saar and in the Vosges, and that the whole army was concentrating before Metz to fight a decisive battle there.

During the day my battalion was assigned to accompany a squadron of hussars which was going on reconnaissance. After an hour of marching we saw the hussars falling back rapidly in disorder. They had met a party of enemy cavalry which had pushed them back vigorously, killing their captain and wounding some troopers. The battalion was halted and put in line of battle, but no enemy troop appeared. We therefore returned to our camp at Glatigny, still innocent of any contact with the Prussians.

On 10 August at one o'clock in the morning we struck tents and got on the road. We tramped for hours and hours. It appeared that we were to make a reconnaissance in the direction of Boulay, but on setting out nobody knew anything about it. It was only on recognising the road followed the day before that we had some suspicion of things. However, for a simple reconnaissance we would not have broken camp and loaded the wagons. Perhaps this was a reconnaissance of the type called offensive; that is to say with a significant body of troops, and which are generally a prelude to a great battle. Let us march to the front and we shall see in due course what it is.

Our battle turned out to be no great matter. We were halted on a plateau from where the view was very extensive, hardly being obstructed by anything; either woods, houses, or hills. In front of us, in the corner of a little spinney formed by a few trees and about a kilometre distant, we suddenly saw a group of four or five enemy horsemen who were trying to get behind the trees, but these were too thinly spaced to form a shelter and hid these imprudent men but very imperfectly. We watched them with eyes burning with curiosity. Think of it! These were the first enemy we had seen in twenty days since the opening of the campaign. We watched them without thinking of anything else. The fortunate but rare possessors of field-glasses were literally assailed by supplicants wanting to see the Prussian horsemen more closely. A squad of hussars lay near us. One of these riders, with or without orders, dismounted from his horse, walked thirty paces forward, then, loading his chassepot carbine,[6] went down on one knee and, setting his sights at eight hundred metres, took aim for a few seconds.

The firing of the shot surprised me, as if we were at the theatre. At once an agitation was observed among the enemy group, of whom one rider was unseated. Then in a few seconds order was re-established and the whole troop galloped off. Why did our hussars not launch themselves immediately in pursuit? Why did we not at least accompany the enemy with a good volley of shots? I still wonder about it. No doubt we were waiting for someone to give the order, and nobody thought of doing so. We were so used then to doing nothing without an order that we would have awaited one to draw our sabres from our scabbards if we had been attacked hand to hand.

After this fine escapade and a sanitary detail for several hours we got back on the road in the reverse direction and returned to Béville farm. The result of the reconnaissance was rather paltry and hardly capable of satisfying ambitions like ours; but I was content nevertheless, for I had seen a specimen of the enemy and had heard a shot fired. Towards evening rain set in and we passed the night literally in water.

On the 11th, after staying under arms for the whole morning, no doubt the better to receive the rain,[7] we were set on the march. As the direction we followed was the opposite to that we had taken the day before to make our famous reconnaissance, we deduced from this that we were drawing closer to Metz. We took nearly the whole afternoon to make two or three leagues[8] and we halted above the village of Nouilly where camp was established. It was still raining, and that was not calculated to cheer up our endless march in retreat and our making camp in the mud.

On the 12th we were made to change our position. We were closer still to Metz. Camp was made among the vineyards which crown the northern crest of the Vallières ravine above Vantoux. The fine weather had returned; we dried out, recovered ourselves, polished our weapons and cleaned our kit. Towards the end of the day the camp and the men had an air of tidiness which cheered the spirits, and their state of morale seemed to me equally good. They were very gay. The view of the camps surrounding us and stretching into the distance made them aware of the strength of the army and gave them confidence in the outcome of the struggle that could not be long in commencing.

For the enemy was near; we sensed his presence by a multitude of unmistakable signs. This produced an effect which we did not fail to remark and which fairly astonished us. Our company, which on departing Mézières counted scarcely seventy rifles, had seen its effectives successively increased by the arrival of reserves and had now reached one hundred and ten men. This was nearly normal wartime strength. This number included a small minority of old soldiers, ten or twelve at most, who had campaigned in the Crimea or Italy. But I noticed that as the organisation of units of all types was completed, so this number diminished. It so happened that most of them had offered themselves immediately when there had been calls for aides-de-camp for generals, stewards, service jobs of various kinds, orderlies, carriage drivers, or employees at the little regimental depot established in Metz. These fine fellows no doubt greatly valued their skins, and I would not blame them for it, but then is it not astonishing that they have been able in perfect safety to collect commemorative medals for the campaign! I was counting on their moral influence in the ranks to set a good example in the moment of danger to young comrades who were on their first campaign; another illusion that can be discarded as moonshine.

The whiff of powder in the air also made impressionable natures more nervous. The captain was very wrought up. He blew up for no reason, like milk boiling over. It was the poor second lieutenant who caught it. At every moment the captain cocked an ear and believed he had heard noises betraying the presence of the enemy. A wagon making a din as it bumped along, the lid of a mess trunk closed too sharply, a puff of wind blowing under a tent making the canvas snap, were cannon! All day long he heard cannon! I suspect indeed that the orderlies, always jokers, amused themselves when his back was turned by purposely knocking over the mess trunks in the baggage wagon to see him jump and hear him say 'It's cannon!'

On the morning of the 13th, at the first glow of dawn, we were under arms, drawn up on our plateau ready to receive the enemy, who did not show himself. We returned to camp and applied ourselves to our usual occupations, that is to say preparing the morning meal and waiting for the time to come when we could think about the evening one.

I was greatly tormented by the desire to go to Metz, from which we were scarcely four kilometres distant. I had not dared to speak about it the day before but today, having dressed as carefully as possible, I could not resist it. I was wondering how to broach the subject with the captain when he came and himself provided the very opportunity I was seeking. 'I have to talk to you,' he said. 'It's now a fortnight since you joined the company and I haven't received any transfer papers concerning you from the captain acting as adjutant. I find that odd. Didn't you tell me that the general of division had promised to keep you here in place of X? It's quite astonishing that in a fortnight that question hasn't been settled at headquarters. What do you think? Do you want me to go and get instructions from the adjutant or the colonel, as it seems to me that this situation needs regularising promptly. You aren't getting pay or rations, and that can't go on much longer.'

While he was talking I must have gone through all the colours of the rainbow. Fortunately he was too short-sighted to be able to tell the end of his nose from his pipe. Recovering myself a little, I gave him to understand that the general of division and his staff, amidst the daily movements we had been making, certainly had not had time to bother themselves with so slight a matter, but that as our proximity to Metz assured us of a semblance of stability for a few days, I would take advantage of it, with his permission, to go to divisional headquarters to regularise my position. He was persuaded by this reasoning and asked me to go immediately, and above all to do everything I possibly could to give him an answer the same day; and I could take the whole day if I needed it. I didn't need him to tell me twice and with a light step, avoiding the tents of the colonel and his administrative staff, I took the road from Saint-Julien which in a short while led me into town.

I had great pleasure in finding myself once more in that fine military city where I had passed such an agreeable time when I was in garrison there during the summer of 1865. It was about eleven o'clock. I went to take lunch in the Rue Serpenoise at the Hôtel du Porte-Enseigne[9] which enjoyed a long-established and well-deserved reputation. I was delighted to eat proper fare, well served on porcelain plates, and to drink from a glass. The tin plates and mugs standing on the lid of a trunk were already just a bad dream to me.

After lunch I went to see once more that beautiful esplanade whose terrace dominates the valley opposite Mont Saint-Quentin with its slopes covered in vines and crowned by a fort of forbidding aspect. I was told that the Emperor's headquarters were at the Hôtel de l'Europe. I went in that direction. The great coming and going of people of every sort gave the street where this hotel was located a most lively air. I went into the hotel, access to which was forbidden to no one; which surprised me very much. It appeared to me that great disorder reigned there, hardly compatible with the presence of such an august personage. I got news from an employee of the Emperor's suite, a groom no doubt, who told me that carriages were ordered for the next day because everyone had to return to Paris. I was absolutely stupefied. What! Was the Emperor going to quit the army before it had won the great victory which must decide the outcome of the campaign? The groom must be mistaken about the facts![10]

I returned quietly to camp at about five or six o'clock. Nothing had come to pass there. I told my captain that I had not been able to see the general of division, who had been absent for the whole day, but that at his headquarters they had promised to hasten the solution of my problem. I had started down the path of lying, and I had to follow it and persevere in it until the end; that is to say until the battle which could not be long in coming.

After dinner, evening having come, I was walking in front of the camp smoking a pipe when my attention was suddenly drawn by raised voices coming from a group which darkness prevented me from making out distinctly, but which I saw dimly outlined on the crest of the plateau. I made my way in that direction and there witnessed the following little scene which seemed to me most suggestive. There were three characters: one little, gesticulating a great deal, seeming very excited and speaking nearly all the time; the other big, strapping, calm, interrupting from time to time with short phrases; the third a simple stooge, a mute. The first man, the little one, said: 'But general, I can't undertake a night reconnaissance in such conditions. You tell me to go there,' and he extended his arm, 'but where does "there" mean? Give me a place name, show it to me on the map you should have, with the road to take me there. I will not assume the responsibility of exposing my battalion to falling into an ambush while leading it against the enemy at haphazard. You don't make a reconnaissance on campaign as if you were going to Mass.' The second character, the big man, he who had been called general, answered in a low voice with a few words which I did not hear, then the group broke up.

The little man headed towards our camp, and I recognised him as Major Payan of the 3rd Battalion. As he passed close to me I approached him and asked him who he had been with just now. 'Can you understand this brigadier who wants to send a battalion out on reconnaissance at this hour?' he asked me. 'As it's my turn to go he summoned me, took me with his aide-de-camp onto the edge of the plateau and, stretching his arm in the supposed direction of the enemy, he tells me to go with my battalion to make a reconnaissance there. Upon my word, I believe they're all mad! My poor friend, we're being led to the devil by people who have no idea of what war on a large scale is, and who are afraid because they don't feel themselves equal to a fight with the Prussians, and because they know very well that they will all be beaten one after the other, all of them, for they are all ignorant cowards.'

I confess to my shame that these words did not make a great impression on me at that moment, but when they came back to me some time later, I understood their entire justness and their full significance. Be that as it may, I fell into a calm and deep sleep, for the day I had spent in Metz had left me befuddled with weariness, and I was exhausted.

At one o'clock on the morning of the 14th, in fine moonlight, we were woken by orderlies who went into each officers' tent in turn and transmitted the order to break camp without noise, for we were to leave straight away. I had great difficulty in waking myself. Once afoot, while going to shake my boys who were snoring like churchwardens, I sought to explain to myself the reason for such a sudden departure, carried out in such mysterious conditions. I came to the conclusion that, the enemy being very close, we were going to try to surprise him. Ranks were formed, wagons loaded, and we waited from one moment to the next to be set in motion. Daylight found us in the same place, numb with cold, weighed down by the desire to sleep, stupefied by waiting and already weary. Nobody around us as far as our view extended seemed to be moving. Besides, we could hear neither cannon nor rifle fire. Why then this alert and this waiting under arms?

It was eight or nine o'clock when we were ordered to cook a meal. Finally, at three o'clock in the afternoon we were ordered to march, but not towards the enemy; quite the contrary, towards Metz. I was quite sure of this since we turned into the road that I had taken myself the day before to go into town. We were going to start down the Saint-Julien road when all of a sudden behind us came the sound of a cannon shot. This time it was no ordinary boom. In the distance a vaporous white cloud rose in the air and swiftly blurred against the blue of the sky. It was followed by another detonation, of less intensity but of an entirely different kind: it was the burst of a shell. But all this was at a good distance from us. Some minutes afterwards the column was halted.

We were at the foot of the slopes of Fort Saint-Julien, which appeared scarcely complete. Taking advantage of this moment's halt, I climbed the slopes bordering the road in order to see. Ah! How I itched with curiosity! This cannon fire had made me look round. I absolutely had to see. The shots succeeded each other rapidly, Soon other shots were heard, closer but with a completely different sound; it was our cannon replying. Then the crackling of rifle fire. But this was all so far away!

I saw the column being faced about and in a few strides I had rejoined my company. We were all very excited, officers and soldiers; we sensed battle close at hand and we accepted it with pleasure. We had awaited it for so many days, had prayed for it even, in the course of our interminable and inexplicable marches and counter-marches or in our bivouacs, soaked by rainstorms or scorched by the relentless sun of the dog-days. The regiment having faced about, that is to say facing the enemy, we marched towards the cannon. Everything was fine now! Who said that our generals understood nothing! And we marched briskly. We left the road and entered the fields. There the regiment was formed in company columns at regular intervals. We were halted in this formation for quite a long time. But the cannonade was growing; it was now in front of us. We saw our artillery going at a gallop up the road which passed in front of the fort. In the midst of a cloud of dust it passed like a whirlwind; the horses pulling flat out at the drag-ropes; the drivers inciting them with their spurs and whipping the unmounted horses with all their strength. The sunbeams darting obliquely on the bronze of the cannon made them sparkle with flashes of gold; the wheels turned so fast that they appeared like solid discs. Sitting on their caissons the crews, shaken like leaves in the wind, clung on like grim death. All this flashed before us in a magic instant. It was truly superb and made us tread with confidence. At that moment war seemed to me a fine thing, and I felt my heart swell with an inexpressible enthusiasm. 'Go on, fine fellows, we are there to support you and you will see how we go about clearing the ground in front of you.'

We marched. In passing into the park of a château, Grimont no doubt, we witnessed preparations which had nothing very cheering about them: medical orderlies assisted by musicians were spreading straw on the lawn and making beds from it for the wounded.

But here came the shells again. They passed over our heads with an infernal noise and went on to burst behind us. Then a few bullets at the limit of their range fell around us, at our feet, embedding themselves in the ground with a muffled sigh, as if regretting not having met some bones to break on their journey. Now we passed many stretchers bearing wounded to the field hospitals; then mule litters, to which the pace of the mules imparted a hard rocking motion which drew cries of pain from the poor devils they carried.

The firing increased in volume. The battalion was deployed in line and we crossed a large open space in perfect order. Because of its number (the third out of six) my company was in the middle of the battalion. Our commanding officer,[11] on his big light bay horse with the white blaze and long nose, marched in front of the centre of the battalion, turning round every moment to keep it well in order. I was thus very close to him. Suddenly I heard a dry crack and the horse, rearing sharply on its hind legs, sent its rider flying ten paces. But the major got up immediately, seized the horse by the nose and, taking advantage of the halt of the battalion, searched for the place where it had been hit. A bullet had struck the horn of the hoof of the left hind foot and split it without cutting into the flesh. The major got back in the saddle and we started off again. The ground descended in a gentle slope. We reached an orchard planted with fruit trees; the battalion was formed in double massed columns and in this order the third (mine) and fourth companies were at the head. We were halted and the major gave us the order to have the men kneel down. We remained in this position for a long while. The bullets were flying thick and fast, nearly shaving our heads. It sounded like the buzzing of bees. In passing through the trees the bullets cut up the leaves and broke the small branches, the debris of which rained down on us. The cannon thundered steadily all around. It was utter pandemonium.

Rousset and I, passing along the front of our sections, reassured our men, who bore themselves very well too, though they appeared a little dazed by this incredible noise. I had never felt so proud and so pleased with myself. I saw myself growing in my own eyes, and finally fulfilling my true role as an officer. I went from one man to another, speaking to each one, making them laugh with some jokes about the ineffectiveness of the enemy's shooting.

Evening had come, but the din was increasing all the time. At last the major ordered us to stand up and deployed the battalion. Then we saw a long line of troops to right and left. After a terrible fire lasting some minutes, this entire mass was sent charging forward towards a wood in front of us from which came thousands of tiny lights sparkling like stars. This was Mey Wood, taken and retaken several times in the course of the battle. We ran across and took possession of it. Night began to envelop friends and enemies with its protective shadow: we went no further.[12]

We had some difficulty in restoring order among the jumble which the battalion had become, with all the companies mixed together, and we remained in position while awaiting new orders. The cannon no longer made its strident voice heard; only a few shots here and there broke the silence which weighed upon the battlefield. The moon soon rose to bathe in its wan light this plain which had so recently been bustling and animated, but was now dismal and silent. I used the opportunity to go and do a little exploring in the woods. The trees were well spaced out; the moon found numerous clearings in which to intrude its beams and thus to form several pools of light. The fighting must have been desperate, for there were many corpses. In an angle, behind a little rise of ground forming an enclosure, six or seven Germans lay intertwined in a pitiful jumble. They must all have been dead, for nothing moved. I was heading in another direction when, in going round a large tree, I found myself face to face with a big devil of a German standing bolt upright with his back against the tree and his left arm in the air. A moonbeam struck full on his ghastly features. I stopped, terrified. Not that for a single instant I had any doubt that the fellow was dead or that he could threaten me in any way. But this sight, in this place at this hour with this lighting, was truly eerie and I felt a shock which one could not describe otherwise than with the banal word fear.

I considered my journey of exploration finished and I hastened to get out of that funereal wood. On the plain starkly lit by the moon lay many cadavers of both armies. Many of our men bore the numeral '64'.[13] Among the Germans, a very young man with blond hair, with immaculate white gloves and sword in hand, attracted our attention. He was a young officer, doubtless fallen at the head of his troops in an effort to retake the wood from us. A typical detail: he was already without boots. No doubt they were already being worn by some sharp fellow on our side who had found a good opportunity to exchange his hobnailed shoes for a fine pair of boots. This was moreover a general practice; each time that the battlefield remained in our possession the enemy dead were stripped of their footwear in the twinkling of an eye, and the operation was carried out with such skill and speed that I was never able to catch anybody in the act.

Night was well advanced when we resumed a regular formation for getting back on the march. It was around midnight when suddenly the air was shaken by three tremendous rounds of cheers given by the German troops established only a few hundred metres from us and no doubt being visited at that moment by some great general of their army. We were astounded by it, for we had little suspected that we were so close to one another.

At last, around one o'clock in the morning of 15 August, we were marched slowly, very slowly, towards the Moselle. During the march we chatted among ourselves about the incidents of the day. Rousset and I had our hearts full of a holy joy at having received our baptism of fire. The captain had complimented us on our attitude and we were delighted with ourselves. Well, I was asked, what effect did this first action, which on the whole was quite hot, have on you? I was much at a loss for a reply, for it had had no effect at all. During the whole time we had been engaged I had been so busy with my men and with my duties that I really had not found a minute to feel my pulse to see whether or not I had a fever of emotion. I had not had to force myself to march. I had not thought for a single moment of the possibility of receiving any wound. Rather, I had felt alert to some degree all the time, but at all events without any exaltation, for the calmness which is fundamental to my character was in no way changed. I have since asked several of my comrades who, like me, were under fire for the first time on 14 August, what kind of sensations they had felt in that memorable circumstance, and all seemed to have felt just as I did. That is the truth, just as it is.

It was full daylight when we crossed the Moselle by a pontoon bridge. But the column was in inextricable disorder. Everybody was hustling to get to the other side, and as there were neither generals nor representatives of the supreme command present in sufficient numbers the jumble of units only increased every minute. Finally we reached the island,[14] and there a little order could be restored in the regiment. At about ten o'clock in the morning we arrived at Longeville, where we were told to make camp. We had taken nine hours to travel just two leagues! In truth, we were tired out! And we were dying of hunger. We had not eaten anything for quite twenty-four hours, we were much spent, and had been on our feet since one o'clock in the morning of the day before. Feeling rather light-headed, I asked the captain to let me drink a drop of a certain green elixir of Grande-Chartreuse that he always carried with him – the flask carefully locked away in a wooden box. He had boasted to us many a time of its remarkable virtues as a stimulant to the point, he used to say, that it would rouse a dead man. He offered me the flask. It was empty. He had drunk it all during the battle without noticing, thinking only to sip a few drops. We both laughed heartily!

We had scarcely settled in when the commissariat,[15] which had hitherto (unsurprisingly, given the disarray of our operations) provided a most irregular service, took advantage of the proximity of the town to give us several issues of rations, one of which was fresh meat. Stew was already in preparation when suddenly the order came to set off again immediately. We were furious. Nevertheless, we had to tip out our cooking-pots in order to be able to fix them to our packs (this was not the first time that this had happened to us) and to resume our funereal pace. After two hours we had reached Woippy. There we were halted and made to pitch camp again. This second camp site was the right one. The fires were quickly lit and the cooking pots filled. It was one o'clock in the afternoon. The men could certainly not eat the stew before four o'clock.

I was dying to go into Metz to know the impression made on the inhabitants by our victory of the previous day. On condition that I bring him back another bottle of elixir, the captain allowed me to decamp.

The town was full of rumours and the streets were packed with people. The numerous groups formed by chance meetings appeared very animated; the conversations among them were at a raised pitch. I mixed with several of them, burning with desire to become involved in order to let the people know that I had taken part in the battle of the day before. 'It's true all the same,' said one man, 'that the army is in full retreat and that before long Metz will be unprotected.' 'In full retreat!' I shouted. 'Now then, where's your spirit? Does any army beat a retreat after a victory like yesterday's? If we have crossed the Moselle, it's because the commanding general wanted to, and because such a movement is part of the working out of his plan. Be assured, with an army made up of soldiers like ours, there's nothing to fear, and we will stop you from being attacked. If only you had seen us yesterday when we trounced those German devils! Go on with you, they aren't worth much, and we've given them a lesson which will make them behave for some time.' Pressed by the bystanders, I told the story of what I had done and seen.

I had occasion then for the first time to take note of a rather strange fact which I have seen repeated many times since; that is how easily one is drawn into embellishing everything, even without the least intention of pushing oneself forward. I was astonished myself at everything that I recounted to them and which I had not even glimpsed in the course of this battle, of which it had been given to me, like so many others, to see only a very tiny corner. Yet I was not born on the banks of the Garonne[16] for all that, being a Parisian by birth and Norman in origin!

Everybody listened to me with an interest that was pictured in their faces, and in the eyes of all these good people I read the pride of national honour satisfied and the desire to hope for new successes which would spare their dear city the shame of being defiled by the enemy.

When I had finished, the man resumed: 'I don't doubt for a single instant, lieutenant, the perfect truth of what you have told us, but it is true none the less that the head of the army is already heading down the road to Verdun and that the Germans have crossed the Moselle at Pont-à-Mousson, that they are there in very large numbers, chasing after you to bar your route. What I am telling you is the exact truth, for I have just come from Pont-à-Mousson.'[17] 'Oh well,' I retorted, 'if they want to block our road, we'll step over their bellies and pitch them into the Moselle.'

At heart I was asking myself: 'What are these civilians poking their noses in for? They understand nothing about it and always want to know more than us.' Thereupon I went to dine with one of my comrades who had not taken part in the battle. I served it up to him all through dinner. Finally, after having clinked glasses again and again to the glory of the French army and to our future victories, we separated. I got back to camp enchanted with the citizens of Metz, with my comrade and with myself into the bargain. Oh well, now I no longer feared meeting the colonel!

CHAPTER IV

DAYS OF BATTLE

16–18 August 1870

'We were soon surrounded by a vast circle of fire and smoke.'

Second battle (16 August) – Unfortunate encounter – At the headquarters of the corps commander – The field post office – Third battle (18 August) – Retreat by night

On the morning of the 16th, at about four or five o'clock, the regiment broke camp and, at the tail of a long column doubtless formed of the whole division, headed up a road which climbed rather steeply through woods. After many sudden halts we emerged at about ten or eleven o'clock on a vast plateau which offered immense horizons to the view. For some time already cannon had been making themselves heard on our left. Once on the plateau we saw in the distance a mass of little puffs of white smoke which were created spontaneously in the air, dissipated, and were immediately replaced by others. These were German shrapnel shells which burst in the air and dropped on our men a veritable hail of iron fragments which tore everything in their path and caused atrocious wounds. We continued our march along surfaced roads leading us westwards. We passed through the hamlet of Habonville and the village of Jouaville. There we veered obliquely towards the south, which brought us closer to the battle; which must have been hot to judge by the cannonade and the rifle fire, which grew steadily in intensity. We passed through the village of Doncourt where we made quite a long halt. Then the march was taken up again directly towards the south.[1]

When we got beyond Bruville and had gained the high ground, we saw the general panorama of the battle. Two almost parallel lines of thick greyish smoke, which formed veritable clouds lit up at every instant by powerful red flashes, were the opposing batteries which kept up a terrific duel between themselves. Approximately mid-way between these lines was a mass of white smoke of persistent opacity which extended along the whole fighting front; sometimes accumulating in the depressions, sometimes following the crests of the hills. This was the fire-fight between the two lines of infantry which in some places were only a few hundred metres apart.

The brigade deployed on the plateau south of the village; but it seemed that matters were pressing, for orders were given to put packs on the ground and the battalions in line were started forward at the double.[2] My battalion, which was marching at the tail of the column, was preparing to go into battle formation too when the major received the order to stay in position to guard the convoy which was following us and which was halted in our rear. This really was bad luck! A fight was so clearly in the offing and was going to take place without us! We surrounded our major and begged him to move ahead, to leave the convoy which had nothing to fear and to follow the other battalions. Quite naturally he remained inflexible. Rousset, luckier than the rest of us, was detailed with his section to conduct a group of wagons towards a farm situated to the west. I saw him leave with regret, for his mission would take him closer to the fighting. The brigade had scarcely been gone half an hour, abandoning us on the plateau, when we heard rifle fire of extraordinary intensity which lasted almost an hour, and which suddenly faded as it moved further away. Orders arrived for us to move up to the line. Packs were quickly put down, with two men from each company left to guard them. Then, moving at the double onto ploughed land, we hurried straight ahead across fields and soon saw our line silhouetted on the crest of a plateau. To join it we crossed a hollow filled with Prussian corpses, all bearing the numeral '16' on their shoulder-straps.[3] Beyond it we rejoined the battalions of the regiment which, from the edge of the plateau, were firing at the enemy occupying the opposite crest. We extended the line to the right and opened fire. The men were completely out of breath, but full of spirit, and they laid down a hellish fire.

All of a sudden, from the bottom of the ravine[4] which separated us from the enemy, a mass of cavalry rushed upon us and passed through us, but without doing us great harm; where I was, at least. It is true that the principal effort of the charge had been made against the centre of our line, and my battalion was on the extreme right wing. This very vigorously led action created some disorder in our ranks. However, several men, seeing the enemy horsemen seeking to regain their lines by going around our rear after having passed through us, turned round and fired several volleys which laid low a number of them. These were blue-clad dragoons whose horses bore on their rumps a numeral above a closed crown. About fifty horses remained in our hands.[5]

Once order had been re-established, firing was resumed against the enemy infantry, who appeared to be not very numerous and rather disorganised. We all wondered why we were not ordered forward. We were there in force, ready and willing; we sensed, privates as well as officers, that there was nobody in front of us. Why not advance? Why not follow up the success already achieved? Instead of that we were ordered to fall back and return to the first position, the one from which the brigade had mowed down the 16th Prussian. We could not understand it at all, and we cursed the generals who did not know how to profit from the advantages which our dash had bought for them.[6]

Soon our attention was drawn towards our right by the strangest din. The earth trembled as if shaken by a volcano, and two or three kilometres distant on the plateau which stretched westward rose a huge column of dust from which came cries, blows and the clash of arms. This was the great cavalry mêlée where more than eighty squadrons came together in a terrific hand-to-hand combat.[7] We saw nothing more of it at that moment, but what we saw distinctly some hours later was the return of solitary individuals, lost on this immense battlefield and searching to rejoin their units. Even during the night still more of them presented themselves at our advance-posts. They were Frenchmen or Germans without distinction, but a fairly common characteristic of both was that they were all on foot and leading their horses by the bridle; at least those that I saw come in.

Night found us in the position we had last been ordered to. Before it was completely dark each battalion in turn was sent to the rear to retrieve its packs. Then the whole regiment went into bivouac where it was, on the edge of the plateau where the struggle had begun.

This battle was straight away the subject of the most animated conversations among the groups of officers who gathered on the field in chance meetings. Each one recounted his exploits. We all believed that we had once more won a great victory. We learned that our brigadier had been killed with his aide-de-camp. This general whom I had never seen was called Brayer.[8] He was, it seems, a very handsome man, very careful of his appearance and

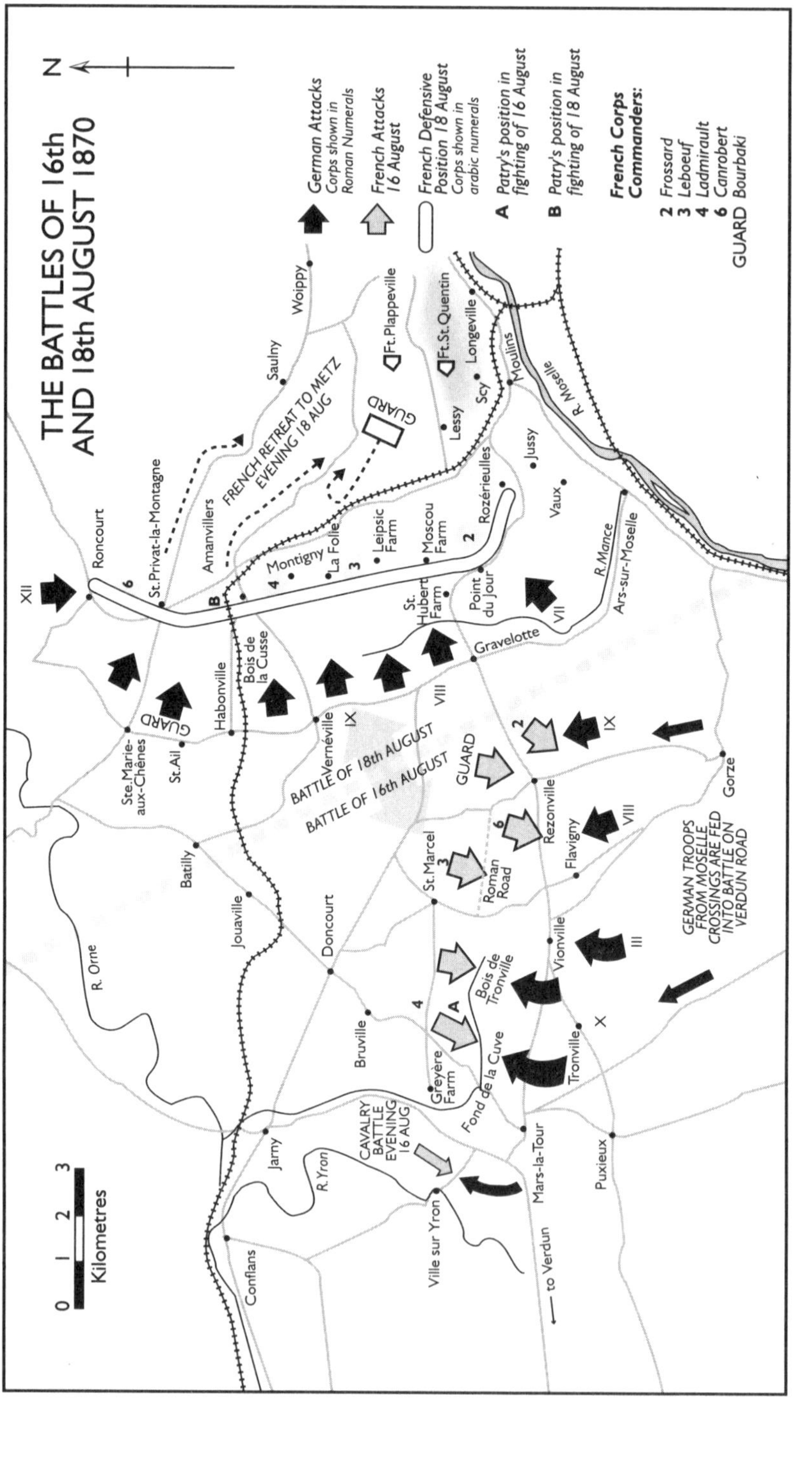
THE BATTLES OF 16th AND 18th AUGUST 1870
N
German Attacks
Corps shown in Roman Numerals
French Attacks 16 August
French Defensive Position 18 August
Corps shown in arabic numerals
A Patry's position in fighting of 16 August
B Patry's position in fighting of 18 August
French Corps Commanders:
2 Frossard
3 Leboeuf
4 Ladmirault
6 Canrobert
GUARD Bourbaki
0 1 2 3
Kilometres
Roncourt
St. Privat-la-Montagne
Amanvillers
FRENCH RETREAT TO METZ EVENING 18 AUG
GUARD
Saulny
Woippy
Ft. Plappeville
Ft. St. Quentin
Lessy
Scy
Longeville
Moulins
R. Moselle
Jussy
Vaux
Rozérieulles
Montigny
La Folie
Leipsic Farm
Moscou Farm
St. Hubert Farm
Point du Jour
R. Mance
Ars-sur-Moselle
Gravelotte
XII
Habonville
Bois de la Cusse
Verneville
Ste. Marie-aux-Chênes
St. Ail
BATTLE OF 18th AUGUST
BATTLE OF 16th AUGUST
Batilly
Jouaville
R. Orne
Doncourt
Bruville
St. Marcel
Roman Road
Rezonville
Flavigny
Gorze
Vionville
Bois de Tronville
Tronville
Greyère Farm
Fond de la Cuve
Mars-la-Tour
Puxieux
GERMAN TROOPS FROM MOSELLE CROSSINGS ARE FED INTO BATTLE ON VERDUN ROAD
CAVALRY BATTLE EVENING 16 AUG
Jarny
R. Yron
Ville sur Yron
Conflans
to Verdun

always occupied, it was said, in waxing his moustaches and dyeing his hair. There was, then, nothing astonishing about his never leaving his tent except on days of battle.

It was on the occasion of this death that I thought of the difficulty there must be in writing history. Indeed, I heard the episode narrated in five or six different ways. According to some he had been killed in seeking to lead his brigade forward at the moment of the encounter with the mass of the enemy at the famous ravine. According to others, seeing the troops hesitate, he had seized the Colour of one of his two regiments and had gone out in front carrying everybody along. It was at this moment that he had received the mortal blow. Some were saying that he had been killed by a horseman at the moment of the charge, others that a shell bursting in the midst of his staff had felled everybody. In the following days I applied the inductive method to reconstruct the facts. This interested me a great deal and I arrived at this result: that not one of those who spoke of it had seen the event any more than those to whom they attributed the story which they told. In the end, I have never been able to find out exactly how our brigadier was killed.[9]

I felt a touch of scepticism enter my mind in regard to the remarkable feats of arms recorded by Dame History, and I came to wonder how a commanding general could lead an army to victory by his example, since in the midst of the hubbub of battle, of the smoke of the cannonade and musketry, this example could hardly be seen by any but the few men around him. The bridge of Arcola might just as well have been taken by a captain of grenadiers: the moral and material effect for the whole army would have been the same, since the greater part of them certainly did not see Bonaparte rush it with a Colour at the head of a company.[10] The men who took the bridge under Austrian fire would just as well have followed the captain as the general, and with equal vigour. Our line of battle on 16 August extended over a front of about ten kilometres. Who would have seen Bazaine drawing his sword and seeking to lead forward his army, which numbered nearly 140,000 men engaged in the struggle? To whom would his dash have been communicated? To whom other than to the officers of his staff?[11] This opinion only developed in me by degrees with the unfolding of the events of the war in which I was subsequently caught up, and I became certain that most of the great feats so preciously reported by history were nearly always invented.

During the night, while walking around among my men, most of whom were exhausted from fatigue and hunger (for we had eaten nothing since the evening of the previous day and had only a small piece of biscuit to put in our mouths, certainly the most repellent of foods), I saw a well-lit building in the rear. I went in that direction, but the lights were much farther away than they had seemed, and I had to walk a long time before reaching them. It was a small farm in which there reigned intense activity. The incessant comings and goings from the courtyard into the building and from the building into the courtyard, the vehicles cluttering the approaches, the loaded mules entering the courtyard led by the tether by soldiers of the baggage train: this was a field hospital. I went timidly into a room on the ground floor. On the floor lay some fifty wounded men whose cries made a confused clamour; continuous, monotonously sad, rent occasionally by a strident scream coming from the middle of the room which was occupied by a large table upon which the poor wounded were being operated on. I was not long in turning on my heels and leaving as if I had the devil behind me. Oh! That cry of pain of the unfortunate man whose limb was being cut off! It rang in my ears for a long time; I could not rid myself of it.[12]

On the 17th, early in the morning, we marched back over the plateau we had traversed the day before, so cheerful and brisk without our packs, to advance against the enemy. Why abandon this battlefield which we had conquered?[13] Mystery and dissatisfaction! From which sprang despondency and intense fatigue, augmented by the protests of empty guts. In the afternoon the regiment halted and camp was made in advance of and parallel to the road from Saint-Privat to Amanvillers, the left very close to the road from Briey to Metz in the vicinity of the milestone which bore by way of an inscription 'Metz 22 kilometres'. Absolutely incomprehensible! We were facing Metz, turning our backs on the direction from which the enemy would come. Incredibly, we placed picket guards that evening in front of our camp, that is to say between us and Metz, and the crowning folly was that these pickets fired shots all night long. At what? [14] Behind us, separated from the camp by the road, all our baggage trains were spaced out in several parallel rows. Once camp was made the men started to cook their dinners with enthusiasm.

I was walking quietly behind the camp near the road and following with interest the arrangement of vehicles of all types which formed our long train, when on turning round I found myself face to face with the colonel.

'What, are you still here?' he said to me, and, his anger rising progressively as he spoke, he unleashed a long litany of extremely disagreeable and offensive remarks at me. I did not flinch under this outpouring, for I had instantly decided on my stance. The philippic ended in a formal order to leave pending a hearing and to rejoin the depot at Charleville. I then said to him with perfect calm: 'Colonel, I have twice led under fire the company which I have adopted, irregularly to be sure, but that is nevertheless a fact. But I am telling you that, whatever you say or do, I will not leave it, and I will not return to the depot where I should appear to have been sent back in disgrace. I am going directly to the general commanding the army corps to ask him to judge my case.' Then, saluting militarily, I walked off without listening to another word.

I had to find the corps commander, General Ladmirault.[15] Where could he be? I set out rather haphazardly in the direction of Metz. After many requests for directions addressed to this man or that I met on the road, I was set on the right track and in the end arrived at my goal, though without taking in its exact location. The general was not at his headquarters, but fortunately his chief of staff, General Osmont,[16] was there. I was shown in to him and with a voice thoroughly shaking with emotion, with indignation even, and I informed him of my situation without hiding the least detail from him. I can vouch that he listened to me with great kindness, smiling from time to time. When I had finished he got up and, tapping me on the shoulder, said to me in a very cordial tone: 'My dear friend, your colonel is a ***** imbecile; tell him that from me. In the position we are in, we can't have too many good men.' I was entirely of his opinion but, as I could not decently and reasonably take such a delicate mission upon myself, I asked him not to let me go empty-handed. So he gave me a paper of entirely official nature which said that, pending a definitive decision regarding him, Lieutenant Patry would be retained in the vacant post of lieutenant of the 3rd Company of the 1st Battalion in consequence of the absence of the placeholder. Good old General Osmont! I could have hugged him. The words to thank him rushed to my lips in such a flood that I stammered them out. In the end, when he held out his hand to me I gave it such a shake that he must have known that he had just made me a happy man.

Armed with my safe conduct, I returned to camp. Was it far? Was it near? I had not the least idea. I judged it prudent nevertheless not to go back until as late as possible, and I allowed myself to saunter pleasantly in this superb weather which amply repaid us for the countless showers we had had at the beginning of the month. I passed on to Amanvillers, a village situated on the plateau and from which there was a very extensive view. The troops occupying it were preparing works which made me think that it was the intention to await the enemy's attack there. I came back into camp, somewhat anxious. During dinner I asked, without seeming to attach much importance to it, if by chance the colonel hadn't been prowling in the vicinity. Upon a negative response, I resolved to wait until the next day to hand in my paper. Is it not best to sleep on things?

All through this night of 17/18 August we heard shots, but fired by our own men; at trees no doubt or dogs wandering in search of scraps from the field-mess. At an early hour in the morning we stood to arms and were held in ranks for rather a long time: then everyone returned to his occupations in camp. I was very hesitant. Should I bear the precious paper to the colonel, or send it to him, or wait for another chance encounter in order to show it to him? I had much difficulty in deciding. Finally I made no decision at all and profited from the repose which had been granted to us to write to my parents and tell them the story of our two victories.

I had barely finished when I heard the voice of the captain calling us for lunch. He was in ecstasy. There had been a meat issue in the morning and a sheep had fallen to the company's share. We were thus going to eat mutton chops. These were the first in nearly a month. Lunch was very jolly, although I was always apprehensive of being ordered in front of the colonel by some orderly. The chops were divine.

After the meal we had an inspection of the men, who had put the morning to use to tidy themselves up and get their arms and all their equipment in order. Indeed they made a good appearance; one would never have said on seeing them so well turned out and polished that they had been marching without respite for three weeks and that they had just gone through two great battles in three days.

I thought to post my letter and was heading towards the paymaster's wagon which was parked among so many others on the other side of the road (on the side towards the enemy) when on passing close to the major's tent I noticed him shaving himself. I hailed him and said, 'How handsome you look, major. Are you planning on going to make some conquest in

Metz?' 'Heavens no,' he replied, 'but since by chance I've been able to lay my hands on my uniform trunk, I've changed completely. This way, if I'm killed today I shall go into the other world properly dressed.' 'Do you think anything will happen today? It seems to me that things are dead quiet.' 'Does one ever know?' I left him, and while walking towards the post wagon I could not help thinking that this idea of death expressed by the major, and his preparations made in that expectation, were bizarre. I know very well that these presentiments are quite involuntary and that, unsummoned, they come to haunt the mind. But it seems to me that if I were assailed by them I would do everything possible to chase them away. However, never having had them, I cannot tell whether one can shake off these obsessions.

In front of the post wagon I found the divisional paymaster finishing lunch with his two aides. These gentlemen impressed me as very agreeable men of the world. I joined in conversation with them and we discoursed for a long time about the confusion which had prevailed in our marches, particularly in these last few days. They were seated like lords, with a table, camp-stools, and a complete dinner service. Indeed they had! They had ample means of transport, while for the rest of us poor devils of fighting men the space was measured at just about a cubic centimetre in one of our scarce wagons. I was about to leave them and post my letter in the box next to the wagon – it was about midday – when a terrific noise resounded very close to us. It was a shell which had burst in the middle of the wagons of the train. It was soon followed by a second, then by a third. The ball had opened once more.[17]

To describe the pandemonium which broke out among this mass of wagons packed almost one against the other, among the tethered horses which, breaking their ropes, were galloping furiously in every direction, or the cries of their drivers trying to recapture them, or the terror of the civilian crews who thought of nothing but flight, would I think be impossible. I ran to rejoin my troops. The men, leaving the tents standing and the whole camp just as it was, had picked up their rifles after having emptied into their pockets all the cartridges kept in their packs. We had our backs to the shelling; we were about-faced to the rear and the regiment, with its three battalions deployed, was led forward, that is to say towards the enemy. We marched straight ahead, having the village of Amanvillers well to our left. In this formation we climbed a rather steep slope which led us to the top of a hill from where the view was very extensive. In front of us the ground sloped down towards some woods, the boundary of which could well have been between one and two kilometres away. Beyond the woods was a crest thick with artillery which was cannonading us heavily. On our right some way off was a village on an isolated hillock. On our left was Amanvillers; about a kilometre behind us was the camp we had just left. Our divisional artillery was not long in arriving and going into battery on the height.

There being no enemy infantry in front of us, we were withdrawn a few hundred metres to the rear, leaving matters to the guns. The regiment, still deployed, was halted among the furrows half-way up the slope and the men lay down on the ground awaiting developments. In a short time the contest between the opposing artillery became terrific. The greater part of the Prussian projectiles passed over us and went on to burst in our camp. The big drum of our band took a shot which tore its parchment.[18] But soon the shooting became more regular and we started being well and truly peppered. I grumbled resolutely, for I find nothing more idiotic than being shot at without being able to reply.

After having talked to my men for a long while to distract them and to distract myself as well, I decided to lie down in my place likewise. I had my coat rolled up around my body. I took it off, put it on the ground and used it to rest my head on. It was very hot and I had passed an almost sleepless night. Little by little, in this state of forced inaction, I felt myself overcome by an irresistible torpor, and I fell asleep. I was brusquely awoken by a shell splinter which, falling in the circle formed by my rolled coat, had thrown up a whole packet of earth and had completely covered me in dust. This dust was so well encrusted in my hair, even though it was very short, that it was still with me many days afterwards. (Admittedly, shampooing did not flourish in our bivouacs). I was on my feet straight away.

The situation had taken a rather grave turn. Our artillery was now responding only feebly to that of the enemy, and our infantry was engaged; but my battalion, being in the second line, maintained its original position. The shells fell thick and fast. Several of my men were badly wounded, particularly one who had taken a burst in the back. He writhed and yelled, and at the same time his coat caught fire. He was carried a little further away by two men next to him, whose return I took care to supervise.

I was startled to see our major's big light bay horse walking on only three legs. In looking more closely I saw that the fourth limb was cut off at the height of its white stocking. The hoof and half the hock of the left hind leg had been carried away by a shell burst. The animal was going laboriously on three legs without appearing to suffer a great deal, but for all that it was not missing a mouthful and was browsing the dry and sparse grass with a good appetite. That sight filled me with anxiety about the fate of the major, whom indeed I could not see. But I learned that he had come to no harm. Behind us a great mass of cavalry, principally dragoons, were receiving random shells. In vain they changed their position at nearly every moment, but just the same they caught shots which, though not intended for them, struck them no less cruelly.

The battalion was moved forward. We followed a railway under construction,[19] in a cutting at first, then emerging on level ground into a plain swept by well-sustained rifle fire. We extended our line on each side, with the railway at about the mid-point, and we commenced firing at the wood in front of us. The men fired kneeling. Passing continually behind the ranks, we officers put all our efforts into making them aim, making them get the required range, and stopping them from wasting cartridges. But we had great difficulty in getting even the shadow of a result. The men, excited by the danger, affected by the gaps torn in their ranks by this murderous fusillade, fired – fired without listening to anything, apparently wishing to escape the enemy's sight by surrounding themselves with an impenetrable cloud of smoke. Their position indeed was not the most enviable, particularly that of the soldiers whose neighbour or neighbours were killed or wounded, and who were obliged all the same to stay in their place with these most discouraging pictures before their eyes. The longer the fighting went on, the less our artillery behind us made itself heard. A *mitrailleuse*[20] battery which had just taken position on the hill to the right of the railway did not stay there for a quarter of an hour, for certain. The coffee-grinders, as the men called the *mitrailleuses*, didn't have time to grind many beans.

At this moment the battle was at its height. Along the whole line as far the eye could see there was nothing but smoke and detonations. My battalion had to change positions and bear right for a few hundred paces. In effecting this movement we met a caisson of infantry ammunition near the unfinished railway line. Several men per company went over to it and carried back in the flaps of their coats a great many packets of cartridges which were shared out among all those present. At the moment when the first three companies reached the height – the only ones to push that far, the other three having been left on the railway line – they were greeted by a most intense artillery fire. We immediately had the men lie flat on their stomachs and, pressed to the ground, they began a lively fusillade against the troops coming at us from the Habonville road.

The captain, Rousset and I were stretched out in a furrow behind the centre of the company and were sharing our impressions, which were entirely lacking in jollity, when a frightful noise was heard to the rear and very close to us, at the same time that the earth was violently shaken. It was a caisson blowing up. A mass of debris of every sort was thrown in the air and fell back down in a grotesque hail all around us. The captain was lying at full length on his stomach, his nose against a clod of earth. Rousset and I saw him indulge in a violent pantomime which seemed intended to testify to a profound disgust, and with his right eye, always adorned with his eternal and irremovable monocle, he examined with extreme repugnance an object which had just fallen from the sky right beside his face. We went to see what it was: with the end of his baton Rousset turned over and over something which had the appearance of a piece of sausage. It was the thumb of an artilleryman which the explosion of the caisson had removed from its owner, and which had rolled onto the august nose of our captain. He was so indignant that, had he dared, he would have got up and would have had this impudent artillerist, or at least the largest lump of the unfortunate man that could have been found, thrown into a cell for a week. Despite the gravity of the situation, we curled up with laughter at this episode. At this point our artillery disappeared and we saw it no more, at least on this part of the battlefield.

It began to grow late. The Germans, encouraged no doubt by the silence of our cannon, determined to deliver a heavy attack against our positions. Large masses left the woods and advanced resolutely. They did not head directly for our height, but towards our left, towards Amanvillers; we therefore took them somewhat at an angle. Firing at will was opened immediately by our three companies, who in a short time sowed murder and disarray in their ranks. As the reception reserved for them in their front was quite as courteous, they were not long in disbanding and regaining their woods.[21] This affair, coming after the incident of the artillerist's thumb, restored my self-possession and gave me a little nerve, which I had been completely lacking until then. I was feeling completely apathetic and this battle appeared in a very gloomy light to me. Was this lassitude due to having been too frequently in danger in such a little time, for this was our third big battle in five days? Was it bad morale? Yet I was in very good health and had no reason to feel depressed in spirit in any way. But in spite of myself, when we were lying in the furrow, inactive and impotent under that hellish fire which tried us without our being able to return blow for blow, I was overtaken by a strong desire to be elsewhere; not, however, at the regimental depot.

How long did we stay in this position, exchanging pot-shots with the enemy without great results and receiving his shells passively? I could not say. But, despite my passing excitement, the time seemed long to me and I found night very slow in coming to cover us in its protective mantle. From time to time we chatted among ourselves in rear of our soldiers. The commander of the 2nd Company was a lieutenant named Ravel, a colleague of mine from Saint-Cyr, to whom I was very attached. He was a charming boy, ordinarily very cheerful with a joke for every occasion. He looked a very steady Flemish type, almost without hair and always smiling. But on this 18 August he sang another song altogether. 'None of us will get out of here alive,' he told me. 'As for me, I'm quite sure that I won't make it.' I tried in vain to buck him up, although I did not feel very enthusiastic myself. Not that I had the slightest apprehension concerning my own fate, but because it seemed very clear to me that we were engaged in a bad business, and ineptly engaged at that. Thus we could not forbear from criticism that the mass of cavalry standing around behind us, uselessly losing many men, had not been thrown upon the German infantry at the point when, disorganised by our fire, it had been forced to retreat. And then the artillery! Could one conceive of such a thing? Batteries which cannot sustain the contest for more than a few minutes and which are obliged to bring up their limbers straight away! It was always we, the infantry, who bore the brunt, and for the whole duration of the combat at that. We were being sacrificed wantonly. And then we never had regular issues of rations. We always had to fight on empty stomachs, and so on.

Our conversation was interrupted by one of the most unfavourable developments in our situation for some time, the effects of which were to prove almost overwhelming.

The village which we could see on a hill to our right, Saint-Privat, had been evacuated by Canrobert's corps[22] and subsequently occupied by the enemy who was hastening to establish a line of batteries there, the fire from which enfiladed our positions. Fire from the front, fire from the right flank; that was the last straw. In a few minutes our losses were considerable. Our major, rattled by this new danger that threatened to destroy all his troops, strode about, exceedingly anxious. Our unsupported position on this hillock gave us a sensation of complete isolation. Finally, taking an energetic course, he resolved to advance on the batteries facing us as far as the point where we would be within range, and once there to let them have it with our chassepots until the turn which the battle was to take on our side might indicate what we should do. To stay on this height and allow ourselves to be decimated uselessly there any longer was folly. If we were going to take losses, it was better to suffer them while inflicting them on the enemy.

The major, having communicated his intentions to the leaders of his three companies, put himself at the head of the troops and started them forward. Here we were descending the slope in good order to conquer about a hundred cannon which had been raking us for many hours. Everybody advanced resolutely; we had understood our leader's idea and were determined to see it through to the end. We had gone two or three hundred metres when the major, who was marching in front, received a bullet in the head. He fell, and immediately, as if the mainspring of the machine had just broken, the companies halted. The men knelt and fired straight ahead.

Our little group, isolated in this plain without the slightest cover, was then struck by the converging fire of all the enemy batteries, which it served for a target. We were soon surrounded by a vast circle of fire and smoke. To our left Amanvillers was ablaze and from it immense columns of flame and sparks leapt skywards; in front of us and to our right were the muzzles of the German guns from which every second came red flashes, sinister points of light which made the falling dusk even more terrifying. The shells beat down like hail around us, and their murderous splinters made grievous gaps in our ranks. Vaillot,[23] captain of the 1st Company, fell never to rise again, his face burned and blackened by powder. His second lieutenant was severely wounded and, knocked to the ground, thrashed about in a pitiful nervous spasm. Ravel,[24] commander of the 2nd Company, had his head half carried away by a shell; he dropped on the body of the major.

Many soldiers were struck and lay on the ground filling the air with piercing screams.

The adjutant of the battalion, Laguire, a southerner, took command of our little troop. He drew his sword and, stalking along to right and left, made a speech of sorts in which he exhorted us not to be cowed, to keep our cohesion and to resume the forward movement. I saw him coming and going, taking great strides and making grand gestures with his sabre, and despite myself – for the moment seemed solemn – his words pronounced with a strong accent of the Midi made me want to laugh. Suddenly the captain, who was stretched out on the ground, was lifted violently into the air by a shell which buried itself in the ground and exploded beneath him. I thought he must be in pieces, when I saw him get up smartly, completely unharmed, and with feverish haste set about finding four objects he had lost in the tumble which were indispensable to his existence: his glasses, his pipe, his cane and his kepi. He did not recover any of them.

Adjutant Laguire ordered: 'On your feet!' and 'Forward!' We did indeed get up; but as soon as we were on our feet, without any signal having been given, without the enemy threatening us more directly, everyone took off at a run, and certain it was that before five minutes had passed we found ourselves more than a kilometre in the rear, north of Amanvillers and out of reach of the projectiles of the enemy, who could no longer see us. There is no denying that we were all there, soldiers and officers and Laguire as well. How could that have happened? After twenty-five years I still cannot explain it, and God knows that I have often thought about that quite unanimous aberration of the spirit which drew us in just the opposite direction to that in which we had meant to go. I have scrutinised and analysed the feelings which could have motivated me at that moment; I can still see myself repeating Adjutant Laguire's 'Forward!', firmly resolved to carry it out myself and to ensure that my men executed the movement ordered. But, as for finding the transition between that state of mind and that which made me turn my back and run away as fast as my legs would carry me, I have never discovered it. There is a gap in my moral existence at that point that I have never been able to fill. It certainly was not example which drew me along. It was not the tide of fleeing men which carried me with it. It was I alone who acted spontaneously in those circumstances. And, if there is anything more astonishing it is that two hundred other men did as much at the same moment.

Later, once minds were cool, I talked about this transformation to several of those who had experienced it like me. Whether their memories failed them, as they nearly all affirmed, or whether they felt embarrassment slightly tinged by shame at awakening this memory which did us such little honour, nearly all told me that they remembered nothing.[25]

We halted on reaching a little rise situated between Amanvillers and the location of our camp, where the tents were still pitched just as we had left them at midday, though some of them were burning. We tried to put a little order back into the companies, but we found the rest of the regiment there, quite decimated, and our men were mixed up with the thinned units of the other battalions. I pulled myself together fairly quickly after this scandalous scene; then I was seized by a kind of savage rage against myself. I very nearly blew my brains out. Tears of anger and shame burned my eyes without bringing any relief to my exasperation. There it was! For ten years of your life you are raised in an atmosphere of ideas of honour and self-sacrifice; for ten years you aspire only to the moment of putting these fine ideas into practice, and all that goes up in smoke in one second, and why? You don't know. You think you are sure of yourself, sure of being a man of duty, and the next moment you find yourself running like a coward!

When one is young, if emotions are vivid they are fortunately transient. My attention was drawn to a group in which great excitement seemed to reign. I approached it and saw several officers of the regiment surrounding the colonel, who was blubbering like a calf. In normal times he most certainly was not handsome, but at this moment he was repugnant. He believed the Colour was either lost or taken, for it was impossible to find it. The Colour-bearer must have been killed and the Colour, fallen with him, must have remained on the battlefield which we had just left so smartly. This fact hardly lessened my remorse, which I felt more burning than ever. But in the gathering dusk a joyful sound burst out and Pincherelle appeared to our delighted eyes, grasping our dear Colour with both hands, safe and sound.[26] The colonel almost fell into a faint. He took the Colour-bearer in his arms and, seized with a sudden tenderness, kissed him on both cheeks. Alas, the emotion of the battle had not kept the colonel from his strong habit of taking snuff, and during the hug of congratulation Pincherelle received a most grotesque black smudge on his cheek. That was enough to cheer us up. The appearance of my captain who, deprived of his glasses, was as blind as a bat at two paces and who was constantly blinking his grey eyes, which gave his ruddy face a truly comic expression, contributed no little to restoring my equilibrium and to driving away the black thoughts which had been agitating me a few minutes beforehand. Moreover, no longer having his kepi, he claimed to have a cold head and to protect himself had wrapped his red flannel sash around it, which gave him the air of a pantomime Turk. He bemoaned the loss of his pipe, which had just reached the very peak of its perfection, and which would have been an inexhaustible source of future delights to him.

The three officers of our company were safe and sound. But how many men were left on the field of carnage? It was quite impossible to reckon our losses because of the considerable disorder which had mixed up all the companies of the regiment, and even with those of other units, and because of the darkness which was growing minute by minute.

A fresh body of artillery had just positioned itself beside us and was scarcely in battery when it opened a violent fire against Saint-Privat, from which the Prussian columns were emerging. They were brought up short. At last, around nine o'clock, everybody took the road which descended through woods in the direction of Metz. Rousset and I, having been unable to find a single man of the company, followed the movement. Like everyone else, no doubt, we were ravenously hungry. At the start of the descent we met a headquarters wagon full of fresh bread. Men who had climbed on the heap held out loaves to the lucky men who passed close to them. Rousset caught one and we had a delicious supper. The whole night was spent tramping along that road, but when daylight came we were not yet close to Metz. It was not until ten o'clock that we arrived at Le Sansonnet where we were halted.[27]

CHAPTER V

TWO SORTIES FAIL

19 August–1 September 1870

'If we go on at this rate, none of us will get out of this.'

Philosophic reflections – Re-organisation– Advance on the Plappeville plateau – Abortive attack of 26 August – A night in a railway carriage – Camp at Longeville – Battle of 31 August at Servigny – To horse – Cannonade of 1 September – Return to camp

The morning of 19 August was employed in restoring a little order to the units; but we could not tally our losses, for at every moment men were returning singly. We were completely destitute since we had left our camp in the enemy's hands. Fortunately Metz was well provisioned with materials of every sort; in the afternoon fatigue parties were sent to the military stores and from there brought back tents, blankets and cooking utensils, and it was possible to set up a more or less habitable camp. We also had to reconstitute our field-mess. Rousset, being the most junior, was charged with this task. He acquitted himself very well and in a few days we were provided with very agreeable fare for the table. During the four days that we occupied this same site, very close to the suburb of Metz called Devant-les-Ponts,[1] our spirits revived almost completely. After this rest, rendered so necessary by the fatigues of every kind that we had had to endure in recent days, we were materially, and it must be said morally too, all ready to resume the campaign.

The officers found themselves in a much worse state of destitution than the soldiers. The latter in fact, when the state of supplies permitted, received a complete issue of kit identical to what they were missing, and better indeed because it was new. The same was not true for the officers; there were no stores on which they could draw, even by paying. We were therefore obliged for the most part to apply to the tailors of the town who, not having been able to foresee so many orders, did not possess raw material in sufficient quantity and found it impossible to supply us. Fortunately the amount of kit in store for the troops exceeded requirements, and a coat and trousers could be issued to each officer. Each made what arrangements he could to have braid indicating rank fixed to his sleeves. This article was entirely lacking. I myself found a large piece of gold braid of unknown provenance at a merchant's in the town and I had some black piping sown over it which divided it along its length. But as a result of an error by the tailor, when I picked up my coat from him two sets of piping instead of one had been sown onto the large gold braid, so giving me the insignia of a captain. This did not inconvenience me much, for I had saved my regulation greatcoat from the fray and I never put on this soldier's coat, which I did not like at all. In my opinion, in order for an officer to retain all the prestige among his soldiers which he needs to lead them to war, it is necessary for him to be dressed differently from them; a single glance should enable him to be quite clearly distinguished, and he should appear to his men as essentially different from them from every point of view.

Looking at this soldier's coat and trousers of coarse cloth, how I missed my full dress uniform, now in the hands of some German who was perhaps decked out in it as if for a masquerade, parodying the former owner whose name was written in full in the papers in my writing case! My beautiful brand new epaulettes, my gilt belt, I imagined hung on some trophy! I who would have made such a great display of wearing them on the day of our entry into Berlin! Oh yes! We were well on the road that leads to triumphal entries![2] To start with, we should not have begun by giving way in fright on the 18th, even abandoning the regimental Colour!

I could not come to terms with this affair of the 18th. Great Heavens, I know well enough that we cannot always be the victors. We had been so on the 14th and 16th, at least that was my private conviction, and that was all very fine, but that was one reason the more for us to retire with dignity and steadily like brave men before an enemy much more numerous than us. After all, there are such things as honourable retreats! But to fly like pigeons! No, that was beyond my comprehension, and all the time, while analysing all the sensations I had felt in that terrible moment and which were still vivid in my memory, I sought to explain to myself how it had all come about, in my own case at least. Like an old philosopher, always philosophising, I clutched at all the theories that my memory summoned successively, but without discovering a satisfying solution. After all, it had been necessary for my will to intervene to make me take a direction quite opposite to that which I had decided to follow a few seconds before. But to intervene it was indispensable that the will should have been activated by a sensation perceived through my senses, or by a feeling perceived by my conscience. But this was not so at all; and yet in skedaddling my legs had indeed obeyed someone or something which could be nothing else but my will. As I had the most absolute certainty that my will had not made itself felt, I was none the wiser about the causes. After racking my brain, I concluded that perhaps this flight must be attributed to a reflex movement. Just as, if I see a sharp knife suddenly coming towards my hand, I withdraw the hand very smartly in the opposite direction from the threat without the intervention of my will, because the sensation of imminent danger is not even transmitted to my brain, so also no doubt the sensitive nerves of my legs, strongly impressed by the constant and growing peril, would have communicated the sensation to the motor nerves without going through the intermediary of the brain, and the motor nerves instantaneously made my legs move in the direction that distanced them from the fight.

I was sufficiently satisfied with my reasoning, and I was beginning to excuse myself just a little when a ray of common sense brought me back to the truth. In good conscience, there could be no point of comparison between these two cases, any more than between a well-defined material object and something of a moral order such as the apprehension of a danger, the imminence of which cannot be judged except with the aid of reasoning. To admit the possibility of reflex movements in phenomena of a moral order is to destroy free will. Who will assure me that tomorrow my arm, by a reflex movement in which my will consequently will play no part at all, is not going to slip my hand into my neighbour's pocket and take whatever it finds there! Who will dare to find me guilty, since my conscience will have played no part in this misdeed, not having been able to perceive the dishonest intention since this intention did not exist! Seeing in the end that I would never find an acceptable explanation of a fact which I still believe to be inexplicable, I gave up all fresh inquiry and made every effort to think no more about it.

Little by little the men of the company had returned. Several, completely lost, had spent one or two days in another regiment. By the 22nd we were able to give an exact account of the losses we had suffered. In the three days of battle, 14, 16 and 18 August, we had lost 37 men killed or wounded. In the first two battles most were only wounded, but it was on the 18th that the greatest number were left dead on the field. Our effectives were therefore reduced to 65 or 66 men who did not appear in any way demoralised by the lamentable result of the battle of the 18th; they would prove that well enough a few days later.[3]

In the regiments we did not know exactly what our situation was. So far as the ranks knew we had lost an important battle, following which we had been obliged to fall back on Metz in order to rest and resupply ourselves after the losses in the field. But no one thought of a possible investment, and once the troops had been reassembled we quite thought to resume a vigorous offensive, the favourable outcome of which, with our entrenched camp as our base of operations, could not be doubted by anybody. As for the generals, possibly they saw no further than us; at all events they said nothing and gave nothing away when they chanced to show themselves.

The regiment received the order to make recommendations for promotions to fill up the gaps which German shells and bullets had made in our ranks in the course of these three engagements, the last of which had been particularly murderous. I can certainly say in all sincerity that up till then, amid the tribulations of every kind that we had undergone since the end of July, my thoughts had scarcely extended to the subject of promotion, which is of such interest in the normal circumstances of military life. My sole aim had been to seek to maintain myself in my adopted company and, at that, to avoid any unfortunate encounter with the colonel and his immediate entourage. Nevertheless, as I found myself there and having been present at the three battles just as others had, I did not see why I should not profit like them from the promotions which were in the offing. I was sixth amongst the lieutenants in order of seniority. There were seven captains to be replaced, either killed, severely wounded or posted to jobs which put them out of the running. I therefore thought myself assured of nomination. But I had counted without the rancour, sufficiently justified too, of the colonel. As on campaign vacancies are filled alternately and in equal numbers by seniority and by choice, the colonel in making his nominations found the means of cutting off the list just before my name; I was therefore left as number one in seniority. I was not particularly concerned, for I was quite certain that the era of serious fighting was far from being closed.

Numerous nominations were also made for the Legion of Honour and for medals. But it was mostly only the wounded who benefited from this, which at that time seemed to me only just. Finally there appeared in regimental orders a list of several officers and a few soldiers cited particularly for their good conduct during those three days.[4] That caused me great astonishment, for I can affirm boldly that I had seen no one around me do any more than their duty; on the other hand I had seen a few do much less. There were also citations in divisional orders in which I noticed chiefly the names of officers of the general staff and of a few higher officers. This was crowned with a list of citations in army orders in which the names of generals figured almost exclusively.

The various appointments were published under the date of 24 August. Our major, killed on 18 August, was replaced by a captain of the 73rd Regiment of our division, Monsieur Cotte, who had recently been appointed to battalion command. Pending his arrival, Adjutant Laguire retained command of the 1st Battalion.

On 22 August the regiment had to furnish several hundred men to work at raising breastworks for batteries and shelter trenches for the infantry. The line officers had only to supervise the performance of the labour, the direction of the works being the responsibility of the engineer officers. We dug the earth in double time, as if it were feared that we would be attacked in the position; to my great surprise, I might add, for all these entrenchments were made on level ground and in close proximity to the heights which dominated and enfiladed them. Perhaps after all it was only to avoid leaving the men inactive that they were made to work in this way.

On 23 August before daybreak camp was broken and the regiment put on the march. After a stiff enough climb, we arrived at dawn on a plateau bounded by a deep ravine, the opposite side of which was covered with fairly thick woods. We were on the Plappeville plateau; behind us and to our right was silhouetted a newly constructed fort which appeared very imposing. The woods of Lorry were facing us, and the road which ran at the bottom of the ravine was that from Saint-Privat to Woippy, the same which we had marched up so gaily on the morning of the 16th to reach the battlefield of Rezonville, and which we had come back down so sorrowfully during the night of the 18th/19th after the tremendous battering we had received on the 18th near Amanvillers. Thanks to the proximity of Metz, where several of us were authorised to go to renew the outfits completely lost on the 18th, we were better informed of the situation. We had been able to procure some maps of the environs of the town and at last had the satisfaction of knowing where we were. Camp was made on the plateau, where we remained until the morning of the 26th.

The nights of 24th/25th and 25th/26th, for my battalion at least, were rather tiring because for several hours we had to guard the trenches constructed on the edge of the plateau, opposite the Lorry woods. On the first of these nights fairly lively firing broke out in front of our lines, which we forbade our men to join in – with much difficulty too. At sunrise we sought to discover the origin and cause of this firing, but without success. Some patrols were sent into the woods, but found no trace of a recent struggle. This fact, which at first seemed very strange to us, occurred so often during the period of the siege that we came to consider shooting at night on the outposts as part and parcel of guard duty, and thenceforward we no longer attached the slightest importance to it. We kept our eyes open a little wider, and that was all.

On the 26th in the morning we abandoned the hospitable camp at Plappeville. I say hospitable because on the plateau the engineers had pitched a number of large conical tents adequate to house a regiment, and under their cover we had found comfort unknown in the little shelter tents in which you could not move around except on your knees and stomach.

We went down into the valley. Then began an uninterrupted series of marches, halts and tramping about which irritated us no end. Added to this was a torrential rain which prevented us from seeing two paces ahead. Where were we going? Nobody had the slightest idea. Towards midday we suddenly found ourselves on the banks of the Moselle. Great astonishment! There we stood waiting for at least an hour; then we were marched over a pontoon bridge, and there we were on the right bank. The road climbed, turned to the north, crossed a ravine with rather steep banks. But this was the road from Saint-Julien! And this was the Vallières ravine! This was our route of 14 August after the battle. And indeed, through the patchy and intermittent mist of vapour from the storm we saw looming on our left, massive and dominating, the heavy flank of Fort Saint-Julien. We entered its perimeters and were halted at almost the same place from where we had set out on the evening of the 14th to attack Mey Wood. But what were we going to do? Were we going to give battle? It was very dismal weather and it was quite late, three o'clock already! If such was the intention of the commanding general the cannonade would have been heard for a long while, yet all was silent around us.

We stayed in position, massed in battalions, under the downpour which raged at intervals. An hour passed thus, then two, then three; twilight came, and we were marched back on the road by which we had come. No one understood anything about this movement. What had been intended? A demonstration? But it was too ineffectual. A diversion? But in that case there would have been fighting elsewhere and we would have heard the sound of cannon, and we would ourselves have been engaged in order to hold the enemy facing us in place. A practical joke then! That was more than probable. But we found it an awfully bad one, particularly in these boggy conditions![5]

The march over this ground turned slippery and sodden by the rain was one of our hardest, and what's more we made no headway, scarcely moving forward 100 metres an hour. I do not know how but great congestion developed in our column and led to lamentable confusion. With the best will in the world not to lose my company or my battalion, or indeed my regiment, I was separated from the regiment by the influx of troops of other units and arms, little by little at first, then completely. Carried along by this throng which milled about on the Saint-Julien road, scarcely advancing at all in the dead of this night which the gathering clouds had rendered totally dark, I did not know where I should end up.

Suddenly, at the turn of the road which overhangs the valley, I caught sight of the shimmering reflection in water of great red smoky flames. I could not understand what this could be, but the very slowly descending human flood led me to the river bank, and there I witnessed a truly fantastic spectacle.

At the entrance to a pontoon bridge, so loaded with men that towards the middle the decking was submerged in the water, several engineer troops were holding aloft big resin torches which flared without much brilliance, casting on their immediate surroundings a reddish glimmer which was reflected brightly in the ripples on the surface of the water, ruffled by the swaying of the bridge, but which scarcely penetrated the black and teeming mass of the crowd in dark and wet clothing. A regiment of dragoons crossed the bridge. The horsemen, wrapped in their great grey cloaks, wearing metal helmets which here and there threw out a tawny gleam, and perched on their big horses which in traversing the submerged part of the bridge seemed to walk on the water, appeared to me truly like phantoms marching. It would have taken the brush of a Raffet[6] to do full justice to the sight of this night march and its infernal quality.

Towards one o'clock in the morning I found myself, after having crossed the Moselle, up against a black wall which after exploration I recognised as a long line of railway carriages halted on the rails, and which alas would not be moving for a long time. This seemed a godsend to me. I gropingly seized the handle of a carriage door. It was a second-class compartment. A few minutes later, comfortably stretched out on the seat, the padding of which seemed to me softer than a feather bed, I fell sound asleep. He who sleeps dines, and even takes breakfast; and that was true now if ever it was.

It was full daylight when I awoke on the 27th with a terrific appetite. Having got out of my carriage, I set out to reach the Plappeville plateau which we had left the day before and where I counted on finding my regiment and my field-mess. On the way, passing close to a little house under construction, no doubt intended to become in time a fine rustic retreat for some well-to-do citizen of Metz, I heard someone call me: 'Lieutenant!' I went in and found there my sergeant major, a brave and excellent man, an old soldier with three long-service stripes who, beneath a rather rough appearance, hid real worth and a heart in the right place. He had spent the night in the little house and, using a few faggots found there, had just lit a good fire and prepared reviving coffee. He invited me to lunch without ceremony. Seeing that there was ample for two, I accepted gladly.

The meal over, the two of us set off towards the heights. Arriving at midday at the place occupied the day before by the 6th Line Regiment, we saw not a single tent pitched. No sign whatever of any bivouac or encampment; only a few jumbled groups of men of the regiment not knowing what to do. After a few moments of waiting, along came an officer of the regiment sent by the colonel, charged with telling all those who might have returned to the old camp that the regiment was now established in front of the village of Longeville, in the valley. We formed a little column with the men we had at hand and in one hour we were at the new encampment where we found the greater part of the regiment. I say the greater part, for men were returning singly or in little groups until nightfall. For all my optimism, I could not help thinking and saying that it was a rather badly chosen moment to change camp sites.

The camp at Longeville which the regiment occupied, so to speak, until the end of the campaign, was quite agreeable to live in. Situated in the plain astride the main road from Verdun, rising towards the right onto the outer spurs of Saint-Quentin, with its back to the village of Longeville-lès-Metz which offered some provisions, it had many conveniences; firstly its proximity to town, from which we drew the items necessary to our daily lives, then its closeness to the outpost line which avoided too long marches when going to take up guard duty.

On the 29th the regiment furnished a detachment to the village of Scy, situated in a most pleasing position on the strong flanks of Saint-Quentin, amid vines which produced a renowned wine.

On the 30th we were back again at Longeville camp. Hardly had the company arrived when we were put on guard duty. Towards eleven o'clock in the morning, in superb weather, we arrived at our place on the outpost line. Where was this exactly? I no longer recall, but it was a charming location. We were on the slope of one of the vine-covered hills which form the west bank of the valley of the Moselle. From there the view stretched far over this pleasing yet imposing valley, confined by the distant hills of the right bank opposite us. To the left we saw outlined against the blue backdrop of a beautiful summer sky the delicate tracery of the spires of Metz rising from a bouquet of foliage. To the right, upstream, the valley opened out, verdant, rich and fertile, ending in a corridor hung with the most varied tapestries; at our feet lay the plain, all dotted with parks, châteaux and smiling villages, brilliant white under the sun, the plain traversed by the turbid Moselle, lingering in many meanders as if to delay the moment of leaving this enchanted land. This beautiful landscape was a real joy to our enraptured gaze. And to think that we would possess these splendours, these riches, scarcely two months longer![7]

Guard duty was very pleasant. Not the shadow of an enemy; no doubt they were basking in the fine sunshine! Rousset, who the day before had bought a pair of brown canvas waterproof gaiters, never stopped spouting about his purchase and already saw himself renewing the feats of the grenadiers of the First Empire before he had worn out his famous gaiters, which would prove impervious . . . to water, yes perhaps! But to bullets, alas, decidedly not! The captain, put in good humour by the fine weather, teased Rousset no end about his gaiters, which he maintained were utterly worthless, driving the poor boy to despair. Dinner at the field-mess was one of our liveliest. The local wine, bought from the owner of a little summer house in the vicinity, took its effect, and the myopic eyes of the captain flickered shut. He claimed that the rays of the setting sun, to which he had his back turned, were to blame. The setting sun! He had evidently swallowed a wonderful quantity of sunbeams!

After doing the round of the advanced sentinels, we wrapped ourselves in our coats and stretched ourselves out on the grass under an apple tree, and between its leaves, little by little, we saw the stars shine.

On the 31st we were on our feet at daybreak. Nothing new on the outpost line. We sought a shelter so that we could make coffee without the smoke revealing our presence. We lulled ourselves in the sweet hope of passing a most agreeable morning in delicious idleness and sleepy contemplation of the splendid picture unfolding before us in the first glow of a sun rising full of shimmering promise, when the order reached us to leave our post and rejoin the regiment. In scarcely half an hour the sentries were called in, the outposts withdrawn and, the company being reassembled, we again took the road to Longeville. On reaching camp we found the regiment in marching order on the road, facing Metz. We took our place, mightily puzzled. 'It seems that we're making a break-out,' some comrades told me. At all events, as the camp was staying as it was we could not be going very far. We set off at a tortoise pace. How many hours did we use up to travel the few kilometres separating Longeville from the Moselle! How long did we await at order arms, packs on our backs (for we might set off again at any moment), our turn to cross the river on the pontoon bridge which had already served us on the 26th! The fact is that it was nearly three o'clock when we found ourselves in line in the same position as on the 26th, a few hundred metres from Fort Saint-Julien, the left flank of the regiment resting on the Bouzonville road.

During one of the numerous involuntary halts which we made before crossing the bridges, Monsieur Cotte, our new major, appointed in place of Monsieur de Saint-Martin who was killed on 18 August at Saint-Privat, had arrived to take command of the battalion. He struck me very agreeably:

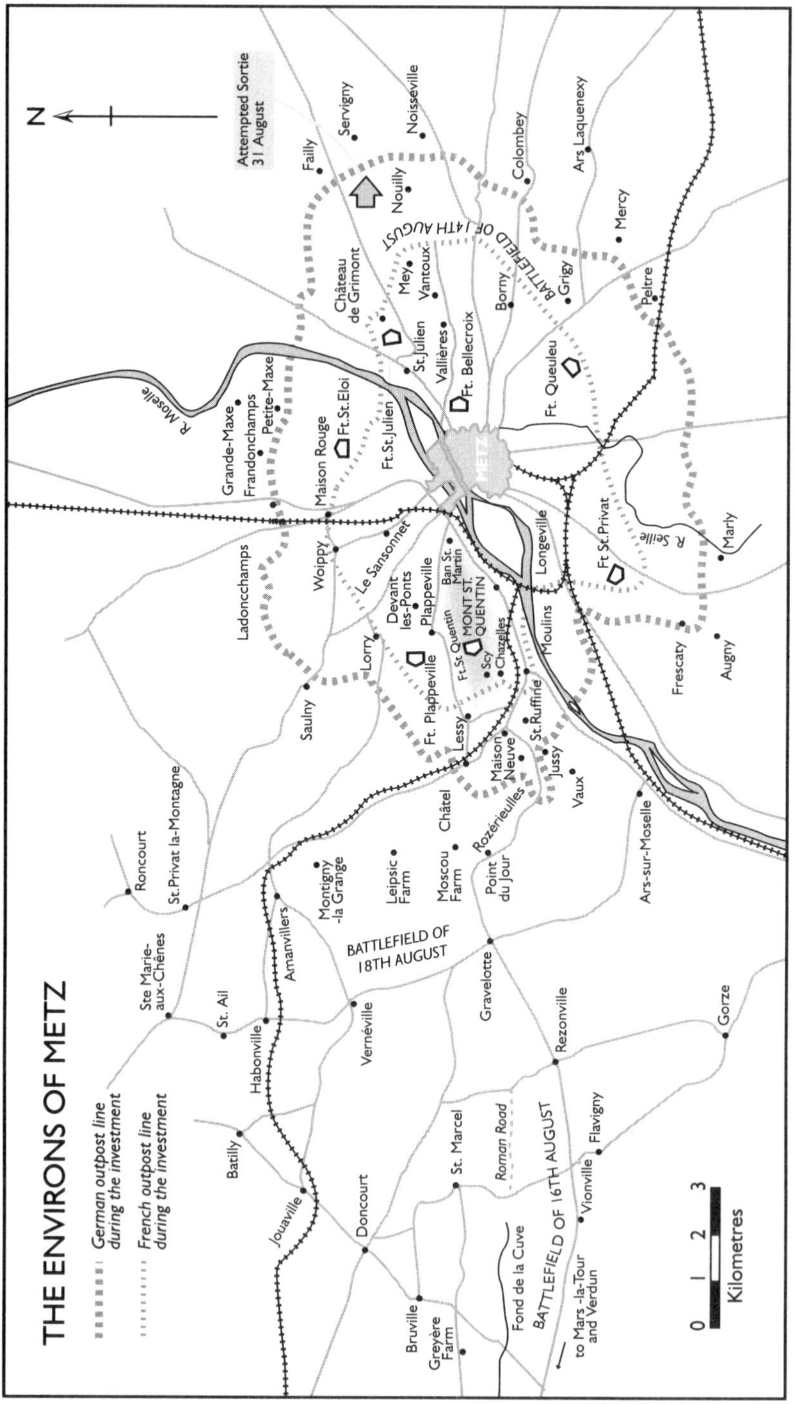
THE ENVIRONS OF METZ
German outpost line during the investment
French outpost line during the investment
N
Attempted Sortie 31 August
R. Moselle
R. Seille
METZ
BATTLEFIELD OF 14TH AUGUST
BATTLEFIELD OF 18TH AUGUST
BATTLEFIELD OF 16TH AUGUST
MONT ST. QUENTIN
Roman Road
Fond de la Cuve
to Mars -la-Tour and Verdun
Failly
Servigny
Noisseville
Nouilly
Colombey
Ars Laquenexy
Mercy
Château de Grimont
Mey
Vantoux
Borny
Grigy
Peltre
St. Julien
Vallières
Ft. Bellecroix
Ft. Queuleu
Grande-Maxe
Frandonchamps
Petite-Maxe
Maison Rouge
Ft. St. Eloi
Ft. St. Julien
Ladonchamps
Woippy
Le Sansonnet
Devant les-Ponts
Plappeville
Ban St. Martin
Longeville
Ft St. Privat
Marly
Lorry
Ft. St Quentin
Scy
Chazelles
Moulins
Frescaty
Augny
Saulny
Ft. Plappeville
Lessy
St. Ruffine
Maison Neuve
Jussy
Vaux
Roncourt
St. Privat la-Montagne
Châtel
Montigny -la Grange
Leipsic Farm
Moscou Farm
Rozérieulles
Point du Jour
Ars-sur-Moselle
Ste Marie-aux-Chênes
Amanvillers
St. Ail
Habonville
Vernéville
Gravelotte
Rezonville
Gorze
Batilly
St. Marcel
Flavigny
Jouaville
Doncourt
Vionville
Bruville
Greyère Farm
0 1 2 3
Kilometres

open and kind features, a decisive air and an elegant figure, albeit in a uniform which did not flatter him as it was in very poor condition. From our first meeting I was well disposed to him, and I believe that this was reciprocal. He introduced himself to each of the officers of the battalion in turn, and this style of making the acquaintance of his personnel, informal yet very courteous, inclined us all in his favour.

The regiment was formed in a single line, with its three battalions deployed; mine, the first, on the left, the third in the centre and the second on the right. It was set in motion in this order and advanced into the plain which stretched before us to beyond Mey, which remained on our right hand. It was halted there in the same order and, as the shells began to fall again, the men lay down on the grass, awaiting events. The officers gathered behind the ranks and exchanged their impressions. By now we were no longer indifferent, as in the first days; besides, such a peculiar and in a way exceptional situation, of an army of close to 200,000 men huddled together around a fortified town, was made to fascinate us and excite our curiosity. What was the intention? To break out in a big battle, doubtless? By all appearances, at least.[8] The terrain on our side seemed favourable; a little open, perhaps, but with our old-fashioned formations such conditions were preferable. The positions occupied by the enemy could be seen indistinctly in the distance and did not appear very formidable to us.

Suddenly there was a great commotion! A large body of riders coming from the right rode across our front towards the Bouzonville road. 'It's Marshal Bazaine!' said some officers. I had never seen him, and I took the opportunity to stare at him as much as the still great distance permitted. He seemed to me very ugly and undistinguished; his face was rather that of a bulldog, his round back and dumpy figure gave him the air of a bumpkin, sitting badly in the saddle and perched on a very poor horse withal. He was followed by a very large staff, among whom officers of all ages and ranks cut capers, seemingly extremely proud of their place and employment. I watched them pass without envy or admiration. I considered myself well above all these hangers-on giving themselves airs; I who had commanded fighting men in three big battles. Certainly, if at that moment I had been offered one of the best staff positions of any kind, even with promotion, I would have refused it, for I considered my role as a leader of men on the battlefield a hundred times superior to that which might fall to a staff officer who has nothing to do but follow a general and pass on his orders. Such was my opinion then, and such is still my opinion when I think of that crowd of officers, mostly young, who aspired to leave their field commands to hide themselves away in some staff bureau, and to pass their time copying more or less interesting documents or grooming the general's horses for Madame or Mademoiselle to mount. But such is not my view when I think of the superior role which should be reserved to the staff if, instead of being what it still is, even now twenty-five years after our disasters, it were to be what it ought to be, that is to say a real command team.[9]

Our attention was suddenly roused by a nearby stir taking place on the Bouzonville road, a few dozen metres from an isolated house situated where that road crossed the road from Mey which passed across our front. A kind of breastwork was being constructed there, behind which several 24-pounder heavy guns taken from Fort Saint-Julien were brought up by the efforts of extra horse teams, and which once in battery began to make their basso-profundo voices heard in the concert where the 4s were the tenors and the 12s the baritones.[10]

Meanwhile we did not budge; neither to right nor left did anyone seem to be moving.[11] Yet we felt that things were about to warm up decidedly. A few enemy shells were coming at us, and nearly all passed over us. During this period of waiting I believe that not a single man of the regiment was wounded.

While strolling behind my battalion I had come upon the neighbouring battalion, the third. I mixed with a group of officers there who were chatting while awaiting orders. Amongst them was a captain who had newly joined the regiment, oldish looking and seemingly completely bewildered. His eyes were a little wild, his voice low and halting. At nearly every puff of his cigarette he said: 'Perhaps this is the last! This time I won't get out of it. All the same it's annoying to have your head blown off when you have an income of 10,000 francs!' This poor devil, who had spent his whole career in recruiting officers, had by bad luck been promoted captain through seniority and forced, in his new rank, to rejoin the regiment a few months before the declaration of war.

Since the commencement of operations, together with another captain of the same battalion (but one who was a braggart, ready to gobble up all the Prussians at one go), he had shown a certain perspicacity. So long as the enemy had not shown himself in our vicinity he had marched at the head of his company, not very happily perhaps, but fittingly at least. But around 11 or 12 August, as soon as contact was made and one could feel that battle was imminent, he gave the nod to his comrade: and the two of them together got themselves admitted to some hospital, no doubt for intestinal disorders. Thus they could rub their hands and offer mutual congratulations at their smart trick while listening to the cannon of Borny, Rezonville and Saint-Privat! As they had heard nothing further to disquiet them since 18 August, and believing no doubt that the army was resigned to the role of garrison of a besieged town – a role in which the chances of danger would be far less frequent than in operations in open country – they left their little retreat on the 30th, only to find themselves on the march on the 31st. What a stroke of bad luck!

To finish the story of these two wretches: in the assault on the enemy positions the first, the man with the last cigarette, was killed, but while marching at the head of his company which he was trying to lead with cries of 'Forward!' which he uttered only with great difficulty with a lump in his throat. As for the other, more artful, fellow, he took advantage of his lieutenant's having just then been wounded and placed on one of the two seats of a mule litter to make himself the counterweight on the other, and thus to accompany him to the field hospital from where the doctor chased him away in shame. Not knowing where to go, he no doubt took cover behind some obstacle during the fighting; then, night having come, gave himself up as a prisoner to the enemy outposts.

It was about six o'clock when the regiment received the order to move forward. We got the men up immediately, places in the ranks were resumed and we set out towards glory! The three battalions of the regiment advanced deployed in one line, as I have described above. For my battalion at least, for I no longer had time to pay attention further afield, our alignment on the march seemed excellent to me. As we closed with the enemy the artillery fire became more and more violent. Shells burst above our heads with a deafening noise and showered us with their splinters, which otherwise did not have much effect against our very thin formation. During a momentary halt, the cause of which I could not tell, the major gave the order to all the officers to place themselves in front of their troops; to all the non-commissioned officers to form a solid third rank behind the battalion to prevent the men from staying in the rear; and to the drums and bugles to group themselves behind the centre of the battalion ready to beat the charge at his signal. The order was promptly executed, and I found myself in front of my company, having Adjutant Laguire to my right and Second Lieutenant Rousset to my left; the captain's place was to the left of the latter. The major, in the centre of the battalion a little further beyond the adjutant, ordered the advance to be resumed. We entered the zone swept by bullets and we began to suffer some losses.

As the firing became increasingly murderous the major, with the greatest coolness, split the companies, placing one section from each in rear in a way to create gaps, veritable corridors for projectiles. This movement was executed in very good order; it was in a voice vibrant with emotion that I manoeuvred my section with regulation commands: 'Mark time. Oblique to the right. Advance!' In this new order we gained a few hundred metres over the absolutely flat terrain swept, or rather shaven, by the projectiles of every kind which the Germans, hidden behind their entrenchments, were throwing at us with desperate abandon.

Not a shot was fired from our side. Besides, with the officers in front of the ranks, firing was of course impossible. A halt was called to our advance for a time and when it was resumed we obliqued slightly to the left. Daylight was fading; we had to make an end to the business. Determined to push right in upon the enemy, the major brought the sections placed in rear back into line and then, with the battalion well re-formed, he ordered bayonets fixed and the attack was carried forward with determination and dash.

It must have made a wonderful spectacle. The men, arms at the shoulder, marched resolutely, following their officers who led them on with oft-repeated shouts, and urged on by the rank of non-commissioned officers who incited them with reiterated calls at the same time as the drummers beat the charge with all their strength and the buglers sounded it at the top of their lungs. Ah! The brave fellows! How proud I was of them! I felt such a shiver that it seemed to me that a glorious breeze passed through my hair and made it stand on end, lifting my kepi above my head. Behind me I heard the heavy breathing of my men, who were panting, roused by the emotion of this victorious charge; I thought I was being followed by a herd of cattle. The major, whose profile I saw about six paces away, seemed enraptured. Captain Laguire, sword in hand, was shouting 'Forward!' fit to make one tremble. I felt very calm, but filled with proud satisfaction. I had not drawn my sword which, not having been sharpened, was merely a heavy and useless weapon, but I had a good stick which I clutched in my hand. From time to time I exchanged a few words with Rousset. It was literally raining bullets; gaps were appearing behind us, but without halting our momentum. Suddenly I saw Laguire roll on his back with his legs in the air; he tried to get up but could not manage it; then, waving his sword about harder and harder, he shouted, 'Avenge me, men!' He was quickly passed and left in the rear.

At the moment when we were about to cross the Bouzonville road, for the battalion had borne a long way to the left, Rousset said to me very calmly, 'If we go on at this rate, none of us will get out of this.' Scarcely had he finished when a bullet caught him in the left leg and laid him on the grass. It was only a few days later, on going to see my dear comrade in the hospital where he was so tenderly cared for (at Monsieur de Bouteiller's) that I learned that the bullet had passed through the ankle of the left foot, holing through and through his superb brown gaiter, brand-new the day before.

We approached the entrenchments occupied by the Germans. A last volley at almost point-blank range greeted us, passing over our heads. The battalion surged forward, clearing the ditches, striding over the banks, and after a hand-to-hand fight of only a few minutes we were masters of the place. Our adversaries were big strapping fellows belonging to the 2nd Regiment of East Prussian Grenadiers, as I learned afterwards. While our men jabbed with the bayonet, they used their rifles as clubs and sought to brain their assailants. In doing so they uncovered themselves and received bayonets full in the body.

But night was coming on apace. We were pursuing the retreating enemy after a fashion until the regiment moving off, followed by the sounding of the assembly, brought us to a stop. We had penetrated a kind of camp formed by huts made of boughs, where we found only a few abandoned weapons. The bugle calls caused us to halt our men, and the captain and I undertook the terribly difficult task of reassembling the company, or at least what remained of it. After having gathered about twenty men together around us we headed rearward, in the direction of the bugle calls. We crossed the trenches that we had taken and halted there at the order of the major, whom we had just met. In the last gleams of dusk, I set to examining the

German works. We were on a road which went down the side of the hill and which was blocked by a broken barricade of barrels filled with earth and rubbish. In the breach lay two corpses, one French, the other German, full-length on their backs, toe-to-toe. They must have come face to face and slain each other. A little further on the right were breastworks for several batteries, though the cannon had disappeared. I could not sufficiently satisfy my curiosity. I went from right to left, examining, scrutinising. This little patch of ground was strewn with many corpses.

Beside one of them I saw small white objects glowing in the darkness. I bent down to pick them up. They were visiting cards, no doubt belonging to the officer stretched out there, who in falling had lost his wallet from which they had spilled, unless some scavenger had already performed his lugubrious task on this unfortunate man. Whatever had happened, this card, which I still have, is inscribed in italic lettering:

Julius Forstreuter
Second Lieutenant, 1st East Prussian Grenadiers
(Crown Prince) Regiment.

I searched for a long time for the wallet, but in vain. It would have given me great satisfaction, once peace was made, to have been able to send it to the family of this comrade, fallen bravely on the field of battle, perhaps killed by one of my own men.[12]

At the moment when, having rejoined my men, I was occupied with the captain in reporting our losses, the colonel arrived accompanied by our major. He threw himself round the captain's neck and hugged him, then it was my turn. As it was dark, I asked him if he had not mistaken me, and I identified myself; but he told me that it did not matter, and that he embraced me gladly. Then he told us the enormous losses which the regiment had suffered, above all the two other battalions. Many officers had been killed, and many had been wounded also.[13] The 2nd Battalion had entered Servigny while we were carrying out an enveloping movement on the enemy's right. He told us a rallying place for the whole regiment; but after wandering about for some time in the dark without having found the prescribed place, the captain decided to halt the company where we were, and to pass the night there in the absence of fresh orders.

What a night that was, that night of 31 August/1 September! What a horrible night! What an endless night! The cold was terrible, penetrating our inadequate clothing, biting the skin, and making all our limbs shiver. There was nothing to make a fire with, but in any case it would have been too dangerous because of the proximity of the enemy. There was nothing to eat and, most of all, nothing to drink! And what a thirst we had after that assault which had literally dried us up! Moreover, we found ourselves on the very scene of the struggle, in the midst of the dead and wounded. The former were hardly bothersome, as we couldn't see a thing, but the latter, the poor wounded who were beginning to feel the effects of fever augmented by the cold, filled the air with their groans and cries. They were asking, either in French or in German, above all for something to drink. That cut me to the quick and chilled my heart. Yet if I had had a full water-bottle, I truly believe that I would have served myself before thinking of them. It is so agonising to feel your gullet cracking with dryness. It brings on such a sapping, burning feeling which invades the inside of your body and prevents you from keeping still. If to this suffering you add that produced by a wound, the agony is complete and it is hardly surprising that after several hours, the fever increasing with the pain, delirium seizes the poor devils who, with a bullet in the chest or a limb broken, are compelled to pass a freezing night under the stars without a drop of water.

Meanwhile I saw some points of light flickering in the shadows, which puzzled me greatly. As I had nothing to do, and as it offered the chance to move about a little, I headed towards one of them as cautiously as possible, for it was as black as pitch. Then I realised that it was stretcher-bearers searching for the wounded and, after giving them a drink from their flask, loading them on to stretchers. Some of these poor people were rescued in this fashion, but many were obliged to await daylight!

In the course of my nocturnal walk, I noticed a sort of red glow; quite voluminous but not very bright at all. I walked towards it and was not a little surprised to come upon a circle of eight or ten men all muffled up in their greatcoats and hoods, squatting like apes around a bivouac fire, the reflection of which illuminated the ends of their noses or moustaches. There was a little gap between two of these Sybarites. I slipped into it, saying to my neighbour on the right, 'You'll permit me a little warmth from the fire, as I'm literally frozen?' I got no answer, scarcely a grunt – of approval no doubt. These men seemed half-asleep. From time to time, however, one of them spoke a few words whose meaning I did not catch properly; yet I kept my ears open, for I had no desire to sleep, my blood still being all astir from the battle. I noticed nevertheless that from time to time they seemed to address the man on my right as 'General'. I was embarrassed, as I have never cared much to rub shoulders with the brass hats, seeing that it is very rare that any good comes of it. But my legs were beginning to warm up and I was in hope that someone would produce something to drink from beneath his coat: and I took the view that, after all, at this moment a good drop of liquid, even coming from a superior, would be very acceptable. A poke of the fire having revived the flames, I recognised that I was sitting next to the general of my own division, General de Cissey. As I was still under the influence of the fierce pride which I had felt during the fight, in which I had led my men in the way I had always dreamed of, I began the conversation: 'You must be pleased with us, general, for we advanced really well! If you had seen how enthusiastic the boys were! They used their bayonets very heartily! That was a fine revenge for the 18th!'

'Yes, yes,' he replied. 'It didn't go too badly. If we had been allowed to do that every time, we would have had a very different result.' 'But General, I imagine that those enemy positions which we conquered and were ordered to leave are now occupied by fresh troops who will have relieved us? The response was evasive, and when I pressed the matter and showed a desire to know where we were, the subject of the conversation was changed to questions about the regiment's losses, and so on.

I had warmed up. Seeing definitely that nobody was about to get out a flask, I resumed the course of my peregrinations, but dissatisfied, despite myself, with my conversation with the general! I wondered how the commander of a division which had seized the enemy positions could be ignorant of whether those positions were or were not still under his control. Certainly my reflections did not have all the clarity which I give them now; but I felt them none the less and gave myself over to depression which, however, was not long in dissipating. I rejoined – I hardly know how – the little core of my company, the men trembling with cold and not knowing what to do to keep warm. I was racking my brains to find some means or other to relieve them when suddenly to our right and almost in our rear an infernal fusillade burst out; at the same moment volleys of bullets passed over us with the familiar whistling sound. We felt warmer immediately. Arms were readied, cartridges put within reach, and we waited with a certain amount of anxiety. The noise lasted about half an hour, but without either receding or drawing nearer. We concluded that it was a counter-attack that had degenerated into a static fight.

I then felt a great weariness and an irresistible need to sleep. I wrapped myself as well as I could in my coat, lay down on the ground, and fell into a deep sleep. So ended this day, the recollection of which will always live in my memory, for it was the only one of the whole campaign on which I saw the ideal, chivalrous battle, such as is dreamed about by those who incite enthusiasm for war.

The first day of September. The freezing night was succeeded by a morning enveloped in such a thick fog that you could literally see nothing a metre from you but dense grey, and ever more grey. Our limbs were so stiff with cold, made worse still by the penetrating damp, that it seemed impossible to make any movement. Little by little and gropingly, however, the scattered elements of the regiment reassembled and we went to take up a waiting position on the plain; but where? Nobody had any idea. Gradually the fog became lighter and more transparent. Then suddenly a very heavy fusillade burst upon several points around us. Soon cannon mixed their deeper voice in this morning concert; yet all this hubbub seemed quite far away from us. When a cheering summer sun had dispelled the white fleece which had enwrapped us so disagreeably, we saw that the regiment was almost on the same spot as the day before at the moment when we had set off for the charge; that is to say to the north of Mey. The brunt of the action, in which we had taken no part, had occurred around Servigny and Noisseville. Shells came at us frequently, but for the most part they passed over and burst behind us. We had the men lie down and they took great satisfaction in basking in the sun, which was becoming hotter and hotter.

A great change had been made in my situation. The major, who hardly knew anybody but me among the officers of his battalion, doubtless because I had been constantly under his eye during the battle the day before on account of my company's position at the centre of the battalion, put me forward to replace the adjutant who had been very seriously wounded. He had been shot through both thighs, one high up and the other low, and his recovery would certainly take a great deal of time. I accepted with enthusiasm, firstly because at heart I considered this as a reward, and also because I would inherit the horse which the state then gave to all adjutants going on campaign. After having warmly thanked Major Cotte, I went straight in search of the horse. I finally discovered it amidst the baggage trains at the rear. The captain's orderly, who had accompanied his officer to the field hospital, had entrusted it to a musician who did not know what to do with it, and who was delighted to rid himself of it by giving it to me. It was fully saddled, but the equipment belonged to the captain, and I promised to come to an understanding with him at the first opportunity about the transfer of this saddlery.

No sooner had I taken possession than I was mounted. I got astride the nag, adjusted the stirrups, and off I went, prouder and happier than I had ever been. The horse seemed excellent to me, endowed with every quality, trotting well, galloping likewise, and so forth. Returning to the battalion, I presented myself to my superior, then went to take up my battle station behind the half-battalion on the right. But my pleasure was promptly spoiled. Indeed the cannonade came closer and the shells fell around us in great abundance; my animal seemed oblivious to it, but not so its rider. Certainly, during the four days of battle in which I had taken part, I had never at any moment been what one would call afraid. Had I had time for it? For an officer fighting with his troops there is so much to be occupied with and so much to be absorbed in! To supervise the firing, encourage the men by talking to them at almost every moment, to have the wounded removed when the line is stationary, to provide for replenishment of ammunition, to be on the lookout for all the enemy's movements on your front, etc. When would one find a minute to be afraid, that is to say to pity your lot and imagine the possibility of a wound, or think of death, and such like? But when I found myself all alone on my hobby-horse, with no other occupation but to stare at its ears, little by little I felt myself unnerved by all the shells falling around me. It seemed to me that, perched thus in the air, I was more exposed than the others who were simply sitting on the grass, and I began to be afraid.

For a moment I had a mad desire to tug the bridle and set my horse hurtling at a gallop in completely the opposite direction to the enemy. I had to make a great effort to stop myself from yielding to it. No longer having to set an example to anyone, I felt myself useless and thought it stupid to be exposed to being killed to no purpose. I was strongly tempted to give up the horse and the job. How would it all end? I did not know; chance in the form of a shell-burst happened to present me with a most honourable solution. One of these projectiles fell very close to me and in bursting sent a fragment of iron into the stomach of my steed, which gave a terrible jump. I thought I was being sent to the devil and was greatly astonished to find myself still in the saddle. I quickly dismounted; then I saw a hole as large as a hand in the lower stomach of the animal, which had returned to a state of perfect calm. The intestines had not been penetrated; it was nothing but a large flesh wound – but what a flesh wound! You could have put your hand through it. The drift of my ideas was suddenly altered, and I thought of bandaging my animal. An old bugler of my battalion who had seen the impact came to my assistance. He was one of those old soldiers who know a little about everything. With his knife he cut a good handful of grass, very neatly chopped it into small pieces and inserted a large plug of this green mixture into the bottomless pocket opened in the animal's side. I left the horse in the hands of my faithful Guyonne, who led him away. Once back to earth I rejoined my company where I regained, along with my job as a leader of men, my aplomb and my spirits.

Towards midday we were set on the road to Metz, and we followed the same route as the day before to return to our camp at Longeville. Everything had returned to the most complete quiet on the right bank of the Moselle.

We were very puzzled. What had been intended? Why had we not taken advantage of our success the evening before? For it is evident that if the positions taken had been strongly occupied during the night by fresh troops, the enemy would not have been able to retake them as he did at Servigny by a single surprise attack; and on the following morning they would have served as bases for continuing the forward movement. No light was ever thrown on the mystery.[14] As for me, I retained a most favourable memory of this day because I had at last taken part in a battle such as I had always imagined, and because the shame of the 18th had been gloriously effaced.

CHAPTER VI

SHUT UP IN METZ

September–October 1870

'There are no heroes. . .'

Into permanent camp at Longeville – Clothing – Food – State of morale and discipline – Interment of a comrade – Proclamation of the Republic – My appointment as captain – Recompense – Adventures on picket duty – Communication by balloons

With the battle of 31 August, terminated at midday on 1 September, the era of active operations of the Army of Metz[1] and of great battles was closed. Not that we were persuaded that it wouldn't reopen, but certainly we had the conviction that this would not be straight away. And so in every regiment each man made the best preparations he could to pass, in as favourable conditions as possible, however long a time we would have to stay under the walls of Metz. What were we awaiting there? Nobody could guess. The daily routine sufficed for the moment to occupy body and mind.

The regiment stayed camped before Longeville, astride the road from Moulins, until 12 September. On that date camp was removed to the southern slopes of Saint-Quentin, the summit of which was crowned by a modern fort constructed in the last few years.[2] Then on the 27th the regiment encamped in the village of Scy, where it stayed until 8 October when it returned to its emplacement at Longeville; never to leave it, alas, but for prison in Germany. In these various semi-permanent camps we were able to make the men as comfortable as was compatible with the very defective equipment we possessed. Nevertheless, the little shelter tents, when you had first dug out the soil inside to a depth of one or two feet and when they were solidly fixed and surrounded by drainage ditches judiciously laid out to prevent rain getting in, made a relatively adequate dwelling. We often wondered why we were not ordered to build shacks or small huts which unquestionably would have been more comfortable and would have allowed the men to live in much better conditions of hygiene. Routine, no doubt, always routine! Personally I was not too badly lodged. Thanks to the exceptional abundance of camping gear accumulated in the Metz stores over a long period, we were allowed to draw from them whatever we needed. With five shelter-tent canvasses a man of my company made me up a very decent tent which I could enter without dragging myself on my stomach. One side of it could be lifted up and, by making it rest on two poles driven into the ground, one got a very passable covered veranda. This opening, turned towards the south, allowed the sun's rays to penetrate the interior of the tent and to air and warm it. A bundle of straw enclosed in a piece of canvas sown in the shape of a sack constituted a mattress, which had no spring, admittedly, but which seemed soft to me beside the clods of dried earth or damp grass on which I had slept for a month. A bolster of the same kind, two woollen blankets, a camp stool purchased in Metz and a sort of small wooden chest containing the scanty effects which I had gathered as I needed them, made up all my furniture.

The men's clothing, worn out by this life in the open air, was repaired or replaced thanks to the supplies of the Metz stores and, towards the middle of September, everybody was just about equipped with essential items in good condition. Munitions were abundant and the wartime quota of cartridges was maintained after a fashion from day to day. Sanitary conditions were excellent and only began to become less good in the course of October, after an exceptional period of rains. During September the weather remained almost constantly fine and warm, but in October a damp cold made itself felt continually, occasioning some diarrhoea which was made worse by deficient nutrition.[3] Rations were issued almost regularly up until about 10 October; bread, horse-meat, rice, etc. Salt was rare. We tried to replace it by making stew with water from a salty spring where the men went daily to draw what they needed. But the result sought was not achieved, for with this water, which doubtless contained other salts than sodium chloride in solution, the horse-meat broth was detestable and the men preferred to eat the meal without salt, but cooked in ordinary water.

Lacking above all were fresh vegetables. At first companies took advantage of the 24-hour spells of outpost duty they put in from time to time in the well-cultivated outskirts of the town to provision themselves with this kind of edible, and above all potatoes which were very abundant that year. But the supply was quickly exhausted and they had to be content with ever thinner horse-meat stew without vegetables or salt. Nevertheless, despite this disagreeable regime, the state of health remained satisfactory. In the last fortnight of October bread was almost completely lacking and was substituted by an increase in the meat ration and larger portions of rice, hash and dried vegetables to the extent that the men stayed sufficiently well nourished to avoid the terrible privations of real famine. Certainly they were not very fat nor their complexions very pink, but, speaking of course for the men I commanded and saw around me, nobody suffered from hunger.

The officers were scarcely better treated: as with the men, their bread and biscuit rations ceased around mid-October. In my field-mess we had had the luck to be able to buy a lot of packets of tapioca; a large batch in fact, for we still had some of it left at the capitulation. Our cook made us stews with horse-meat in which our spoons stood upright. Ah! The orderly who served us could allow the mess-tin which served as a tureen to fall over without fear that the stew would spill on the ground; the stew and its container together made nothing but a large pie in its crust. What I felt most was the total absence of salt in our food for two or three days. We all set out to find some of the precious condiment. I discovered a pound at a miller's in Devant-les-Ponts and paid him 25 francs for it. We found that this was normal. At any rate, famine or not, I have never in my life been so fat as I was at the end of October 1870. It is true to say that I slept very well and led a most regular existence.

Right up to the last the wine ration was issued to the troops; not daily perhaps, but at least fairly frequently. We officers, who had more money than we knew what to do with, always had an excellent bottle on what served us as a table. The environs of Metz, particularly the hills on the left bank, were covered in vines which yielded a little wine of very good reputation. The cellars of the houses of Scy, Lessy and Chazelles were filled with it, and we emptied nearly all of them, paying a good price for old bottles of this wine, the pronounced native tang of which was not without charm. The vine growers of the region made their fortune, for they sold it to us dearly. It's an ill wind that blows nobody any good. Admittedly, these poor vines were so trampled, spoiled and stripped of their leaves by horses and mules that they must have remained unproductive for several years after the war.

I had left Charleville dressed in a brand-new uniform: a tunic with two rows of buttons, opening on a waistcoat, trousers of red cloth, etc. Towards the middle of September this clothing was certainly not worn out, but I was finding it uncomfortable in the extreme and not warm enough. I had a jacket made in Metz of thick dark-blue cloth which I had lined with fur and fitted with an astrakhan collar large enough to cover my ears when turned up, and cuffs of the same kind which could fold down over my hands. Likewise I had a pair of boots made in the leather which is called Russian, coming up to my knees, in which I could tuck my trousers tightly around my legs. Underneath I wore thick woollen drawers, a hunting jacket with sleeves with my uniform waistcoat over it, and a flannel waistband. Covered up thus I could defy winds and floods. In this outfit, which indeed did not lack a certain elegance, I passed many a night outside with impunity in the bitter cold and I never caught even a common cold, let alone the slightest trace of rheumatism! My uniform coat had become almost useless to me and thenceforward I used it only as a blanket or a ground-sheet when I had to sleep under the stars. As for the military greatcoat which had been distributed to every officer at the beginning of August, to tell the truth I never put it on, not feeling at ease in it, morally I mean, as I believe I explained earlier.

When we were not on duty the day seemed long. Happily Metz was very near and, to me at least, permission to go and pass a few hours there was readily given. I therefore went there often. After visiting my wounded friends who were being tended either in hospitals or private homes, it gave me great pleasure to go to a large café on the main square, where the statue of Fabert[4] is, at about five o'clock, for at that time this café was always full of officers from every unit and I was sure to meet some comrade there. Moreover, staff officers of the town garrison or the general staff frequented it a great deal, and through them one could always learn some interesting piece of news which I was happy to take back to camp. There too you could read the town's newspapers, printed on sheets of paper of every colour because there was no more white paper. They contained, particularly towards the end, some very sharp criticisms of the manner in which the affairs of the town and of the army had been conducted by those in authority, and most of the time I thought they were in the right. The question of provisions became bitterly debated by the end of September, and the issue gave rise to such lively polemics that the governor, General de Coffinières,[5] suspended these papers for several days, I believe. But others, more violent, appeared in their place. A collection of them would make interesting reading now.[6]

I often went to have lunch with one companion or another at the Hôtel de l'Europe; it made a change for us from the fare of the field-mess while at the same time the affluence of the diners at the great *table d'hôte* was a real source of diversion for us. At first the prices, while going up, nevertheless stayed within fairly reasonable limits: little by little they increased and ended up at grotesquely exaggerated levels. The last time I took lunch there with one of my friends, consisting of an omelette made with eggs that were not fresh, a horse-meat steak and a scrap of cheese, we had to pay 65 francs for this less than Sardanapalian feast.[7] This hotel made hundreds of thousands of francs from the French army in August and September 1870 and continued to do so happily from the German army in November, December, and henceforward. The bad luck of some is the fortune of others. Sancho's saying is still true.

During the whole of the first fortnight of September, as there were no more oats or hay in the stores, three kilos of corn per day were issued to every horse. Of that I am very sure, as I retained my horse in my capacity as temporary adjutant until 16 September, and during all that time I drew the corn ration for him in that quantity. As we later had to eat the horses it would have been better to have started with them straight away and to save until later the corn which we could have eaten ourselves. But at the time this measure did not seem unreasonable to us, for we were a hundred miles from thinking that everything would end so wretchedly. We supposed that, after several days of rest employed in reconstituting the various elements of the units rather severely shaken up by the events of August, we should recommence the campaign as outside events demanded. Was it not entirely natural to keep the horses in good condition? How could our artillery follow us if the cannon had only emaciated horses to draw them? And in fact, up until the middle of September, the horses remained in excellent condition and sufficiently well nourished given the small amount of work that they had to do.

The morale of the men was very good, in our regiment at least, and no doubt everywhere else if I recall what was said by comrades in other units whom I saw fairly often. Discipline was very adequately observed. Besides, one demands so little of the men on campaign. The details of garrison life which are enforced so severely no longer serve a purpose. Those who have said or written that discipline disappeared in the Army of Metz have deceived themselves or been deceived. Likewise, without parading as heroes, the men did their duty in a very becoming manner on the battlefields where they had to give an account of themselves: and when Bazaine, a man of suspicious and disingenuous mind, had the nerve to say that he could not obtain the best results with such soldiers, he knowingly dissembled the truth, for he could have borne witness himself that the attitude of his soldiers had been entirely proper.[8] Of course there were some shortcomings. Who can say he is without them? Besides, the public deludes itself with the most erroneous ideas about the true nature of military valour. There are no heroes, at least in the sense that the word is commonly used. I have never seen any. What I have seen is men doing their duty worthily and conscientiously, that is to say aiming and firing, taking cover just enough to have some shelter but not enough to hinder them from shooting, standing up when ordered and advancing without allowing themselves to stop because of the enemy's fire, even at its most intense. I have seen many of these men, but I have also seen a fair number who, once lying down or kneeling, had no other concern than to try to escape the enemy projectiles and who sacrificed the efficacy of their fire to do so; and who got up to advance only with the greatest reluctance, despite the exhortations and scolding of their leaders. Finally, I have seen a certain number, a tiny minority certainly but still too many, who sought by every means to avoid their duty as combatants, and who took advantage of every opportunity to stay in the rear, flattening themselves in furrows or ditches, or to abandon their posts during fighting. That is what I have actually seen. Perhaps that upsets accepted ideas, but that is how it is.

Once back in camp, I recovered my appetite for my duties as adjutant, the more so as they seemed full of interest to me. When one company of the battalion had to go on guard duty I went ahead to reconnoitre the place it would occupy, then I led the men there. Quite often I went to visit them next morning in order to be able to report the very latest news from the outposts to the major. As I performed this duty on horseback, for my horse's wound by no means prevented me from mounting it, my pleasure was double. One day indeed I had to ride along the whole outpost line from Lessy as far as the plain; I put in almost the whole afternoon doing this round. I retained these very agreeable duties up until 16 September, at which time I was appointed captain and took command of a company.

Apart from the performance of our daily duties, our work had little variety, but thanks to my being mounted, I got around a good deal and life did not seem too monotonous to me.

The 9th was a very sad day for me. In the afternoon I went to Metz to attend the funeral of my friend Jacques, a young lieutenant of my regiment wounded in the arm on the 18th. The wound had at first seemed slight, passing through a muscle; but in this agglomeration of wounded men the air was infected and carried him off at the moment when he believed himself almost cured.[9] I was grief-stricken, for we had been very close for a long time and I had a genuine affection for him. The day was thoroughly miserable, with rain falling in squalls, and this moroseness of the weather only increased that of my spirit. Yet this was not the first beloved comrade carried away thus in the fullness of youth by the insatiable Moloch who presides over these great slaughters which we call battles. After each fight, when we reckoned up the balance sheet of what it had cost, we saw many gaps in the ranks of our brothers-in-arms. But at the time, in the midst of the action, I had not felt the full magnitude of these successive losses; whether because my thoughts were absorbed by entirely personal preoccupations which were extremely vivid in those moments of acute crisis, or because once the fact of inevitable sacrifice was accepted the consequence appeared natural, so to speak.

On that day, however, my mind, which had had time to recover during the week of relative calm and almost normal life which had succeeded the mental turbulence of the period of great battles, saw in all its horror and cruelty the death of this brave and gentle boy, scarcely 25 years old, whom several years of close familiarity had taught me to admire and love.

Dinner on my return was rather sad: we broke up early, my day having made me very tired. The funeral service had shattered me. It was about eight o'clock and I was getting ready to go to bed when all of a sudden a frightful cannonade burst out. Amidst the growing darkness of the night, the black horizon was torn by great reddish flashes which accompanied the firing of each shot. Shells fell thick and fast in the plain where our camp was spread, but fortunately the ground was soaked by rain and nearly all buried themselves in it without bursting. It was the German batteries on the Point du Jour plateau that were firing at us from cover in this way. But to what end? There was great alarm; we thought there was going to be an attack to break our lines and to bring on a general action, for the cannonade widened and surrounded Metz and its entrenched camp in a veritable circle of fire, as far at least as our view extended. In an instant the men were on their feet with their weapons in their hands. The regiment was assembled in the front line and we awaited orders. I saw the general of our division going down the road, and he had us advance a few hundred metres. The performance did not last long. Little by little the cannonade became less intense, slackened, and finally died out after about half an hour of infernal racket: for Fort Saint-Quentin, with its huge short-barrelled 24s, the heavy shells of which literally made us tremble in passing over our heads, weighed in and replied with vigour. The result of this exchange of insults caused us no harm at all, for in our regiment at least not a man was so much as scratched; but we stayed on the alert for the whole of the night.

It was only long afterwards that we learned the cause of this harmless demonstration. A large convoy of prisoners from Sedan[10] was passing close to Metz, and the German high command took an interest in making them believe that Metz was being bombarded, in order that from Germany they would write back to France about it, and that, in the face of a situation already so far advanced around the last base of operations still held by the French army, peace would be more promptly accepted by our government. Fortunately, the government did not allow itself to be taken in by this little deception in rather doubtful taste, and continued to organise forces in the provinces which were able to hold out against the invader for five more months, and to save at least the honour of the country.

On the 13th a proclamation to the inhabitants of the town made known the disastrous affair of Sedan and the political consequences of the Emperor's captivity, that is to say the advent of a republican government.[11] This news left us rather incredulous at first, then, when the evidence was undeniable, the fact was accepted for the most part with rather marked indifference. It should be said, not doubtless to humanity's credit but because it is the exact truth, that on campaign everything that does not affect the individual directly, particularly his physical well-being, is only of very slight interest to him. Empire! Republic! At bottom it was all the same thing to us, in the sense that we were no less under an immediate obligation to risk having our heads blown off from one moment to the next, to sleep on the ground, to eat horse, and so on. What astonished me most in the course of a visit I made to one of my friends who belonged to a Guards regiment, was to find a very pronounced enthusiasm for the new form of government among the officers of this very select body.[12] It is true that at that time I still knew nothing about politics! I personally attached little importance to this change. I had never shouted 'Long live the Emperor!' even when passing in front of him at reviews, because I thought all that was stupid, and I was no more inclined to shout 'Long live the Republic!' All the same I foresaw no good for the interests of the army from the coming to power of the men of the opposition, for I remembered that in 1863, I believe, at the time of the legislative elections, Monsieur Pelletan[13] had covered the walls of Vincennes, where I was garrisoned, with placards promising the suppression of standing armies.[14] It is true that between words and deeds, in politics as in business, there is an abyss; I have realised that well enough since.

It was not until the 17th that official news was given to the troops of the new state of affairs by way of an order.[15] What it said, in sum, was that we should serve the new government with the same devotion as the old, since our duties to the country remained the same. The reading of this order produced little effect on the troops, who would have much preferred, I believe, to have been told that the war was over and that they were going to go home. Yet some non-commissioned officers showed that they were very pleased to find themselves in a republic at last, and manifested their pleasure rather noisily on several subsequent occasions.

The 15th was a most agreeable day for me because on that day appeared the appointments signed by the Marshal[16] on the 12th to fill up the gaps remaining from the 18th and those newly made on the 31st; and I had the pleasure of learning that I had been promoted to captain. The vacancy that had fallen to me was in the 3rd Battalion. So, not without some regret, I parted from my old comrade Frondeton who, despite his oddities, had received me hospitably into his company and had kept me there for nearly two months despite the irregularity of my position. I imagine that he had not been without his suspicions about that, at the very least, feeding me almost entirely from his rations and Rousset's, and having me share his tent when there was time to pitch it. I also parted with regret from the brave and beloved Major Cotte who had given me such an enjoyable fortnight by choosing me to fill the post of adjutant. Finally I separated reluctantly from the good old horse, on which I had ridden about for duty and for pleasure since 1 September. I would have very much liked to stay in my post of adjutant with my new gold braid, but the colonel preferred, and rightly, to give this job to a lieutenant who had likewise been promoted captain but whom he had kept close to him since the start of the campaign, first as secretary and then, after he took command of the brigade, as an aide-de-camp.

My new battalion commander, Major Payan, the same whose strange conversation with the brigadier-general I had overheard on the evening of 13 August, was a very likeable man and an experienced and energetic leader. He had been in all the campaigns of the Second Empire, and he inspired absolute confidence among all his men. Chance willed that it was our company field-mess that he shared, which in the course of daily contact led to great intimacy between us. The lieutenant of the company, gravely wounded on the 31st, was in hospital for a long time. The second lieutenant was a young quartermaster-sergeant newly made an officer, a well-bred boy but no more, with whom nevertheless I had nothing but excellent official relations. But in the other company which messed with mine was a young second lieutenant, also recently promoted, towards whom I felt almost instantly drawn by a deep fellow-feeling and who from that moment entered completely into my life, for we were not obliged to part until ten years later, and have maintained a sincere and cordial friendship to this day. His name was Fernandez.[17] Shrewd and resourceful by nature, with a mind that was already refined but which he was desirous to expand, curious about new ideas, with a heart filled with delicacy and modesty, absolutely discreet; such was how he appeared to me after a few days' acquaintance, and such have I always known him to be.

Besides the great pleasure which I took in having a third braid put on the sleeves of my excellent jacket and on my kepi, my promotion to captain gained me another satisfaction which was not to be despised. For the two months I had been waging war, as my position had never been regularised I had not received a sou in pay, let alone any wartime supplement,[18] nor any indemnity for replacing my things after the loss of our camp on 18 August, nor any provisions or rations of any sort besides. On 15 September, therefore, I had my lieutenant's pay restored to me, back-dated to 1 July, and I was granted a captain's wartime allowance and everything else. Thus about 1,200 francs suddenly fell into my pocket. I was delighted at this, for my funds were awfully low. I had left Charleville on 29 July with a note for 500 francs which my father's notary had sent me, and I had been living on it ever since. The heavy expenditure I had incurred to rig myself out comfortably and to protect myself against the chill of a season which had already turned cold had almost drained me dry. But this was a major replenishment, and although we had but few opportunities to spend money I was happy to feel myself in funds. The future was amply to justify my gratification.

I was thus a captain at the age of 29, after three years and three months at the rank of lieutenant, and exactly eight years after leaving Saint-Cyr. This, obviously, was not phenomenal, but by this promotion I at least felt myself well rewarded for my tenacity in wanting to follow the regiment. This appointment certainly caused me to gain two years in my career, and that was ample for me. Colonel Labarthe, who did not hail from the banks of the Garonne for nothing, said to me in handing me my commission: 'My dear fellow, if I hadn't kept you with the field battalions, you wouldn't now be a captain, eh?' This gasconade caught me unprepared. It seemed so outrageous that I kept quiet, and could find nothing to say in reply; I who was ordinarily so quick to answer him back. When I think that on the eve of the investment, on 17 August, he was still threatening to have me seized by the military police if I did not leave immediately for the depot!

What I thought remarkable in this whole episode, and perhaps unique in this campaign in which a million men were engaged, was to have waged war for two months at my own expense without receiving a sou in pay or a gramme in rations. As an unorthodox venture, it had turned out rather successfully.

There were numerous promotions among the different ranks. Numerous too were the medals awarded, but to the wounded for the most part, which I could not help thinking was highly irrational. I acknowledge that the wounded are worthy of concern, and that it is charitable to pour the moral balm of reward on their wounds. But in the end those who are not wounded, and who in consequence continue to fight the war and to lead the troops in combat, are just as deserving and indispensable to the forward progress of operations; and it would be at the very least equitable to consider them in the share-out of medals. Decorate all the wounded if you wish, but once this principle is allowed, let a certain number of medals be awarded to those who, having borne themselves well and proved trustworthy at their post, remain at the head of their troops. I have seen only staff officers decorated in any great numbers without having a wound to their credit.

The list of citations for distinguished feats was as long as that for the month of August. One must, however, understand what a distinguished action is. To me this is a worthless term, since it does not correspond at all to facts. Among the officers of the regiment who were cited, several were in my vicinity during the battle. What did they do more than me or others, I ask myself? These citations should be abolished. They are useless and signify absolutely nothing, for there are no distinguished actions, properly speaking. A captain of cavalry receives the order to take, with his squadron, an isolated enemy battery which is causing great annoyance and which appears to be poorly guarded. The captain starts his men at a charge and comes back with the battery. A distinguished action? Indeed not. This captain has quite simply done his job intelligently. He has understood how to put to good use the studies which he has pursued for maybe twenty years in peacetime so that he can act without hesitation on the day of battle. He scarcely has need of a eulogy. By that reckoning, all the officers of my battalion who so boldly led their troops to the assault on enemy positions should have been cited for the action of 31 August, and so should all the men who courageously followed them, and all the non-commissioned officers who so skilfully kept them in ranks, and the drummers who beat their drums so spiritedly and the buglers who wore out their lungs blowing their instruments.

I had a man of my company decorated for the following feat. On 16 August, just as we were taking our place in the line, a German regiment of blue-clad dragoons charged us and caused some disorder in our ranks.[19] Delalain, the man in question, was vigorously set upon by a dragoon who belaboured him with sabre blows which luckily he was able to parry with his rifle. Like a man who does not lose his head, he jumped smartly to the left side of the horseman, and knew how to keep himself there by very nimbly executed bounds and leaps, despite the pirouettes which the rider made his horse perform to catch him again on the right. This singular combat made a most striking picture. In the end the dragoon, uncovered, able to attack only with difficulty and to parry with even more difficulty, was run through with the bayonet and rolled to the ground. Well, in all conscience, where is the distinguished action in that? This brave Delalain quite simply defended his skin, which the enemy dragoon was seeking to slash with an insistence which he found in doubtful taste. He knew how to apply skilfully the principles of the bayonet exercises that had been inculcated in him in barracks and triumphed over his enemy. That is all. It is a good soldier who knows how to keep calm in perilous circumstances, but it is a very far cry from that to making a hero of him, and to cite as such a man who quite simply defended his life when it was threatened. It is said that this kind of reward excites emulation and can set good examples to follow. To that I would answer: no, because nobody has any doubts about the worth of these citations or about the reasons that motivate their award.

Once put in charge of my new company, which numbered hardly more than 50 rifles, I once again began to mount the guard when it was my turn. As everyone knows, picket guards are squads drawn from companies which, posted at a sufficient distance from the regiment on the enemy's side, give it security while it rests and, by their resistance if attacked, allow it to get under arms and prepare itself for combat. After 1 September these picket guards were the only occasions when we found ourselves in contact with the enemy: quite frequent occasions, for our turn came around at least twice a week. The outpost line of the division extended from Lessy to the Moselle, passing through Maison-Neuve and Sainte-Ruffine. Several companies mounted guard for twenty-four hour periods on this advanced line, while at the same time several others, distributed along a second line at Scy, Moulins and elsewhere, served as reinforcements or as a reserve. In the course of these days and nights spent on the outposts in this way, I witnessed some often very singular scenes. I have retained the memory of some which struck me most particularly.

The company had taken up guard duty at Sainte-Ruffine, a village situated on a considerable hill which dominated to northward the Verdun road and to the south the valley of the Moselle, towards which it descended in rather steep vine-covered slopes. At daybreak, from the top of an earthwork from which the view extended far over the plain, I was waiting for the morning fog to clear away so that I could make the usual observations of the positions occupied by the enemy. Soon a light northerly wind blowing down the valley chased away the mist, which receded upstream. I then saw a strange spectacle on the plain which extended to the foot of the hill where I was posted. In front of our trenches, which linked the Ars road with the river, three French soldiers were digging the earth in search of potatoes. The quite sudden disappearance of the fog left them completely exposed and they found themselves without suspecting it very close to a small enemy post. Four armed Germans immediately came out from their ambush and rushed upon the three unwary men to take them prisoner. Unable to run away for fear of being struck by bullets at almost point-blank range, my three lads prepared to resist. One was armed with his rifle, another with a pick for gathering the potatoes, and the third with only a canvas sack in which he was stowing the harvest. The Germans made vain efforts to seize them. The man who had the rifle turned it into a kind of windmill to keep his opponents at a distance; the man with the pick hit out to right and left with his implement; while the third man, grabbing the top of his sack, struck at random and the part containing the potatoes, serving as a pile driver, sent spiked helmets flying and appeared to do the best job. Taking advantage of the astonishment into which their adversaries had been plunged by their aggressive resistance, the three marauders took to their heels and jumped the parapet of the trench before the Germans could load their weapons and send a volley after them. From the top of my earthwork, although they were well beyond the range of my voice, I could not help shouting 'Bravo! Bravo!'

On another occasion, in front of Chazelles, I was doing my morning round in the vineyards occupied by my line of sentinels when suddenly a great devil of a man dressed in a red tunic and black trousers rose up in front of me. Indeed, completely unaware that there could be a soldier in the French army dressed in this fashion, if I had had on me the revolver which never left my trunk I would immediately have used it against this apparition which frightened me at first. But I was soon restored to better intentions on seeing the giant stand still and respectfully await my questions. I then learned that he was a bandsman of the Cuirassiers of the Guard[20] who had come to do his little private harvesting in a place where there were still some grapes left thanks to the proximity of the enemy. I let him carry off his store, telling him to be more careful another time. But this little encounter put me in mind of the numerous mistakes that had occurred in the course of the campaign: light infantrymen[21] taken for Germans and fired upon; Germans on whom we had not fired, believing them to be light infantry; the poor Lancers of the Guard[22] whose blue and white uniform nobody recognised, so that both French and German vied with one another in setting about them during the great cavalry fight of 16 August,[23] and so on. I understand very well that it is necessary to differentiate the arms of the service, because it is unacceptable to impose on an artillerist or a soldier of the army service corps the humiliation of being taken for a common infantryman. But what I do not understand is that among the uniforms of the same army there are no points in common, the sight of which would remove any doubt as to the nationality of the troops of that army. For example, every soldier belonging to the French army should wear red trousers and red head-dress. With these two points of identification, any mistake would be impossible.[24]

When we formed part of the second line we needed to be active only in the event of a serious enemy attack on the picket guards, in order to support and reinforce them. The night usually passed in the most complete inactivity, for we were so used to firing by the outposts, who most of the time were practising on some terrified rabbit fleeing through the vine leaves, that we no longer paid attention to it. We *captains* had acquired the habit of leaving one officer with the troops and meeting at Mother Weber's inn, a place renowned in good times for its fried dishes and its cellar. We passed the night among comrades of different regiments in chatter and draining dry the stocks of the establishment. One day, or to be more exact one night, to shake off the sleep that was gaining on us one of our number put forward the ingenious idea of cutting the cards for a little game of pontoon.

The motion was carried, and cards reigned supreme every night at the hospitable inn. I once found myself there with five or six other officers, and the pontoon was humming along in fine style when longer and heavier firing than usual made us prick up our ears. The hand was dealt and I was about to pick up a four when a very worried messenger from the reserve appeared. We all left our hands with the cards turned up on the table. Everyone went to his post to see what it was all about, then, without any need of prompting, returned to the table when it had been established that there was nothing more than usual to be afraid of. The banker generously conferred a handsome five on me, which allowed me to pocket a few *louis*,[25] of which indeed I had no need, but which gave me pleasure all the same because one always likes to win, even when playing for trouser buttons; and at that period certainly *louis* had no more value than that for us. It seems that higher authority was annoyed by these little gatherings, which, however, had the advantage of keeping us awake while keeping us amused, and had the inn closed. Fortunately there was not a full bottle left in the cellar; our work was done.

Once they have got into campaigning habits, soldiers become really very cunning. I had a most singular proof of this in the following circumstances. My company was on picket duty in the plain. A party of sentinels was concealed behind a rather thinly growing osier-bed where there was an open space of several metres between each willow trunk. As it was very dangerous to relieve these sentinels during the day in view of the proximity of the enemy, each one was posted behind a tree trunk before daylight and was left there until night. I imagine that it must have been the same for the Germans, for you never saw them make a movement the whole day long. As soon as one of our men uncovered himself even a little – bang!, bang! without fail. So the men had dug a hole behind each tree. Thus they could sit down and watch from cover and without fatigue the enemy scarcely a few hundred metres away. Without considering it, I had the unfortunate idea one morning of going on a tour of this line of sentinels. I reached the first without difficulty, but in going from this one to the next I was greeted by two or three bullets which almost grazed my hide. That made me very pensive, for to regain the main road and its protective line of trees I had to pass behind half a dozen tree trunks. And would I have the luck to escape as I had at the first gap? The man beside whom I found myself sharing the shelter of the same tree trunk said to me, 'Captain, leave it to me. When you hear the sound of a rifle shot coming from the enemy, run quickly to the other tree.' And so saying he put his kepi on the end of his rifle and exposed it well outside the shelter and in sight of the enemy who, believing that a man was leaving his hiding place, quickly fired a shot. I took the opportunity to cross the space which separated me from the next tree in a few bounds. I repeated this movement three or four times more and found myself on the road, where no further stratagems were necessary to regain my post.

The post at Maison-Neuve, situated on the Verdun road where we often mounted guard, was very exposed. Opposite to it, in the belfry of the village of Rozérieulles, the Germans had placed a few marksmen who, as soon as they saw someone on the road, did not fail to take at least one shot at him, which never passed very wide of its mark. Thus we had got into the habit of crossing the road in two or three strides, which caused the bullets from the belfry to strike too late. One day I saw an officer of the *Garde Mobile* arrive with permission to visit the outposts. Coming to the road, which we had to cross because the company was positioned on both sides of it, I put him in the picture and set the example by greatly quickening my step. But he, disdainful of the danger, crossed the road at a normal pace. He had not reached the middle before I saw him roll in the dust. He had taken a bullet in the stomach. I was furious, because I had to expose several men, and myself, to go and pick him up. And God knew if the post in the belfry would put paid to us in a shower of lead slugs! Fortunately nobody was hit. I had the foolhardy man carried to the rear, then evacuated to one of the hospitals in town. He was, it seems, a young gentleman of Metz who wanted to be able to recount some tales of his prowess and who, fine butterfly, had just fluttered his wings a little too close to the candle.

We passed an entire night on our feet on account of a troop of young heroes, dressed in grey and green if I remember rightly, who had begged the honour of picket duty in the Moulins cemetery. In the middle of the night, after frightful shooting which had awakened our whole camp, located well to the rear, one of them – a sergeant – came up, thoroughly scared, to tell us that they were being attacked by a force of at least 20,000 men. Everybody was quickly on their feet. We sent some competent people to scout in front of the cemetery. They encountered not a living soul, and did not receive even a single shot from the German advanced posts. The experiment had been tried, and we never saw the over-excitable *francs-tireurs*[26] again, in our vicinity at least.

The first time that I had to lead my company to the outposts, I was given instructions to stop off first of all to see the officer in charge of the divisional front, in order to get complete directions for the post which I had to occupy. This officer was lodged in one of the last houses in Moulins. I went up there, and at its entrance found three or four captains, like me in charge of picket guards, awaiting the arrival of the officer in question. After a good half hour of standing around, we finally saw him appear in all his majesty. He was wearing a fine uniform with much gold braid, but not one belonging to any unit of our army. He made us a speech about the role we had to fulfil, our duties, our responsibilities and a mass of things which we had known for a long time, but which he doubtless found quite novel because he had only just learned them himself. As for particular details about each of our posts, he had nothing at all to contribute. In sum, he struck me as a humbug and a poseur, and I came away wondering why our own much more experienced commanders had been passed over for a mission which by rights should have been theirs, and which they certainly would have performed better. I learned later that his name was Arnous-Rivière, and that he was commander of a battalion of *Mobiles*. Be that as it may, the explanation he had given me of the location of the troops that I was to relieve was so unclear that, following the Gravelotte road to reach Maison-Neuve, I passed beyond the company whose place I was coming to take, so well were their sentinels hidden, and was only brought to a halt on the road by a volley of bullets fired on my troops by the Prussian post stationed at Rozérieulles. In the blinking of an eye the men, none of whom fortunately had been hit, were in the ditches beside the road. So we withdrew, using this shelter so opportunely offered to us, and once out of sight I got things back in order. My first move, in my deep displeasure, was to ball out the advanced sentinels who, without warning us, had allowed us to push our heads into the wolf's mouth; but these men said reasonably enough that on seeing us march out they had thought we were going to carry out an operation in front of our lines. In any case, I made up my mind that next time we were on picket duty I would not call first on Arnous-Rivière, and nor did I, which avoided the loss of time and the boredom of listening to the pontificating of this man, who did not impress me at all.

In the course of one guard duty which I commanded in front of Moulins, on the Ars road which was used in communications with the enemy, I found out for the first time that German officers were very courteous and that the sense of the brotherhood of arms, which animates the officers of all civilised nations in their dealings with one another, was cultivated by them as carefully as anywhere else. Towards the middle of the afternoon the bugle of a bearer of a flag of truce sounded. I went out to meet him on the road, beyond the line of my sentinels, and made contact with him. He was a staff captain who spoke very good French. He handed me a letter, to which he had to await a reply. According to instructions received, I despatched the letter to divisional headquarters and while waiting for the response the two of us stayed in the road chatting about this and that, but mostly of the boredom, from the purely technical point of view, imposed on us by this siege warfare which was so lacking in interest, as much for the attacker as for the defender. 'What causes me most anxiety at the moment', I told him, 'is that my poor parents have not received news from me for six weeks. Perhaps they are weeping for me, although I am perfectly well, and that thought is most painful to me.' 'That need not go on,' he replied. 'If you would like to confide an open letter to me, in which you will speak only of your health or of wholly personal and private matters, I promise you I will get it to them. If I can't use our field post, because of the suspicions which might be aroused by correspondence between a German soldier and someone living inside French territory, I will send your letter to my parents who will undertake to forward it to yours.' At this I sent a man at the gallop to find me a sheet of paper and an envelope. I wrote about a page in pencil to my dear parents and handed my letter in an unsealed envelope to the captain, who tucked it carefully into his wallet. When the reply which he was awaiting arrived, it was with the warmest gratitude that I thanked him and shook his hand. We separated very good friends and both delighted; he at having done a good deed, and I at the certainty that my parents would have my news before a week was out.

The German officer kept his word scrupulously for, towards the end of September, my father living in Grenoble received a letter from Breslau – from whom? From his son shut up in Metz.

From that moment I prayed sincerely that this kind and courteous brother-in-arms would come out of this long and murderous war safe and sound. I hope my prayers were answered and that he now occupies a high military post in his country. If by chance he should read these few lines which I am happy to publish, I should be glad for him to know that the man he obliged is no ingrate, and that the memory of his generous and considerate deed is still fresh in my heart.

Throughout the entire siege I never heard it said that we had received any communications from outside, except those that came from the enemy. There was a rumour current, however, that a lieutenant, named Archambaud

I believe, had managed to cross the German lines and get into the French camps by following an underground aqueduct which carried water from Gorze, but we never had confirmation of this. As for the army's contacts with the outside world, there were none, I believe, in so far as messengers were concerned. But necessity is the mother of invention, and a balloon service was organised which operated from the middle of September. On little sheets of paper, rather similar to cigarette papers in thickness and dimensions, you wrote a few lines on one side, the address on the other, and everything was stowed in the nacelle of a balloon which was launched from the Esplanade. Several times I saw them pass above our camps, and sent my most fervent prayers after them. Two of my little bulletins out of more than a dozen reached their destination; one addressed to my father at Grenoble, the other to my sister at Laval – but I have never found out where the balloons which carried them landed.[27] Naturally we were ordered to say nothing whatever about our military situation, in order not to afford any information to the enemy in case the balloon fell into their hands.

In the section of the line of defence which was assigned to the Fourth Corps, clashes between the opposing forces occurred only very rarely. From the height of our camps on Mont Saint-Quentin, we witnessed at a distance raids carried out by troops on the right bank. It was thus that on the 27th we saw rising in the air the columns of flame and smoke produced by the burning of the Château de Mercy, and on the 28th by the burning of Maison-Rouge.[28]

On the Point du Jour plateau, opposite the front occupied by our army corps, the Germans had raised numerous breastworks for batteries and redoubts, the outlines of which we saw standing out clearly against the sky in broken array. It was a formidable position, defended in front by a natural ditch formed by the very steep-banked ravine of Châtel-Saint-Germain. The heavily wooded western slopes of the ravine had been strengthened by abattis,[29] the impregnable lines of which stretched for several kilometres from Rozérieulles up to Châtel. The heights which dominate the road to their south from Gravelotte, a little further on from Rozérieulles, were likewise covered in earthworks for artillery and infantry. The villages of Rozérieulles and Jussy, opposite Sainte-Ruffine, were strongly occupied. The plain, right down to the Moselle, was defended by barricades, trenches, abattis and fortified posts. If it had been necessary to mount an offensive on this part of the lines of investment it would have been a hard task and success very uncertain. An attack over the plain, on the left bank at least, would lead us into a defile in front of Ars formed by the wooded hills of Vaux, leaving us throughout the movement under the dominating fire of the heights on the right bank and exposed completely without cover to the batteries on the left bank. On the other hand, a direct attack on the plateau was condemned to failure in advance; not so much because of the very strength of the enemy position and the accumulation of defensive works with which the approaches bristled, as by the difficulty that would be presented to the deployment of our forces by clearing the camp at Châtel, which would have had the immediate result of breaking our impetus.

While mounting guard in front of Lessy I had been able to ascertain for myself the importance of the obstacle formed by this Châtel ravine, the mouth of which I had observed when stationed at the advance post of Maison-Neuve. I was therefore filled with great anxiety when one day I heard from a staff officer from army corps headquarters, who had come to assess the configuration of the terrain on the slopes of Lessy where I was on picket duty, that it was the Marshal's intention to make a sortie in this area. This was in the first days of October. I confided to the staff colonel the apprehensions I had on account of the difficulties of every sort which awaited us from the first step, and which my knowledge of the terrain allowed me to describe to him in detail. He went away convinced, and perhaps it was due to this chance conversation that a certain repulse was avoided.

However, as there was a desire at Fourth Corps headquarters to do something, it was decided that a regiment of the 3rd Division (Lorencez),[30] which had been much less engaged than the other two in the August battles, would attack a German advance post installed in a little cottage (called the Biaudel cottage)[31] north of Lessy, from which came continual rifle fire that was most troublesome to our advance posts. It was the 33rd, I believe, which was charged with the operation. The cottage was swiftly taken, but the regiment left a hundred men in the little patch of ground inside the network of wire, abattis and ditches which surrounded the position. That day, 1 October, my company was on picket duty in the area north of Lessy, and at intervals throughout the action we received a veritable hail of bullets which fortunately passed over our heads.

The Germans had from the outset built up their defences on the western side particularly, but with a purely defensive objective; for naturally it was from that direction that a junction could have been effected between the Army of Metz and an army coming from the interior. During the entire duration of the investment they made no attempt at an offensive from that side, any more than on the other sectors of their lines. From time to time, without apparent motive, to us at least, and without following them up with even a demonstration, lively cannonades were fired from their batteries on the plateau and sent a rain of shells crashing down on the villages which sheltered our troops or on our advance posts. So it was that, after the great display on the night of 7 September,[32] the regiment was many times compelled to suffer the effects of their artillery fire, which fortunately were none too lethal but extremely disagreeable all the same. Our outpost line from Lessy to Chazelles was bombarded on 23, 26 and 29 September. On 2 October it was Sainte-Ruffine, where I was on guard duty, which served them for a target. The bombardment even caused some fires in the village that we had great difficulty in extinguishing. On 3 October it was the village of Scy, where the regiment was billeted in reserve, which copped it. On the 6th there was a redoubling of relentless fury on the same point. It even seemed to us that it was going to be followed by an attack on Lessy; but it was only a show which did not become a reality. On the 14th Chazelles and Maison-Neuve where I was on guard duty were utterly ploughed up by shells coming obliquely from the Genivaux batteries. On the 16th there was a bombardment of Sainte-Ruffine, but less severe than the first one. On the 18th the cannon thundered on our outpost line for the last time, in our sector at least.

These cannonades were freely accompanied by very lively rifle fire from the enemy pickets, to which ours replied abundantly, so that after a guard duty of twenty-four hours it was nearly always necessary to issue the men with a complete re-supply of ammunition. The heavy guns of Fort Saint-Quentin kept up their fire at familiar ranges upon the German works on the plateau. It was always quite astonishing to me that it was unable to knock them out completely. In any case, all these demonstrations were quite harmless, for it was only very rarely that a few men were wounded. I had only three in the course of a good dozen picket guards that I mounted on the advance line. The fact is that everybody knew the terrain down to its smallest details.

CHAPTER VII

CAPITULATION

October–November 1870

'I felt myself overcome by a flood of tears.'

Review by the general commanding the division – Alarming rumours – Bad news from the interior – Communications from the commander-in-chief – Break-out committee – 26 October, official announcement of the capitulation – The 6th's regimental Colour – The colonel's farewell – Surrender of the troops – Bitter reflections – Ideas of escape – Cordiality and courtesy of German officers

Meanwhile, time was passing. As the season advanced the weather became worse and worse, the number of horses diminished day by day and provisions were near the end. We had nothing to do but contemplate our inaction. We were not kept in touch with outside events, save in a very summary way through official channels. But on the other hand, when one of us went into town he always brought back ever more grave news about our situation and that of the rest of France.

On 23 September General de Cissey, who commanded our division, reviewed our regiment on the slopes of Saint-Quentin where we had our camp. He had a square formed by the three massed battalions whose total effectives certainly did not reach 1,000 men, and made us a rather involved speech which neither confirmed nor quashed the unfavourable rumours which were current about the future of the Army of Metz. Would we be resuming active operations? Would we remain in position for some time? Would we give up any attempt at a sortie and await events without using our weapons?[1] There were so many points of supreme interest to us that were not even touched upon. This review left us with a very pronounced sense of melancholy, because we all came away from it convinced that the general was aware of ill tidings, but that he had not wanted to communicate them to us for fear of lowering the morale of the troops.

On 7 October, however, we thought that a great battle was going to begin. From morning our cannon sounded to the north; the noise grew louder by the hour and continued uninterrupted till evening. This must be the vanguard of the army opening a passage, and we held ourselves ready from one moment to the next to follow or support it. But in the evening everything reverted to the usual silence and the next day we learned that it had been a simple foraging expedition in the plain in front of the town, and that the farms of Ladonchamps, Frandonchamps and Grande- and Petite-Maxe had been stripped. The result seemed meagre to us for such a large deployment of our forces.[2]

It was not until 14 October that alarming rumours began to circulate in our ranks. The army had no more foodstuffs, no more horses to draw the batteries and baggage trains. If it were not rescued from outside, which there were scarcely grounds to hope for, it would reach the point where it would be obliged to conclude a military convention with the enemy! Alas! We understood what such a euphemism hid in the way of agony and despair! But were we at the point where we were unable to attempt one supreme effort to break out, or if not, to yield after laying low thousands of the enemy? Nearly all of us – I am speaking of those of us who lived on the perimeters, far from the places where news was received, where idle gossip originated and whence it spread all around, magnified and distorted after passing through so many intermediaries – nearly all of us, I say, had great confidence in Marshal Bazaine. 'He's a wily fox,' said the experienced officers, 'a smart fellow who will draw the Germans into a trap in which they will open themselves to being cut off. He is having these rumours spread so that they will come to their ears, and thus they will act according to his plans. You'll see, you'll see; one of these days things will hot up and it will be the Germans who get burned.'

I wanted nothing more than to allow myself to be convinced, but I was none the less deeply demoralised because, without being able to explain it to myself very clearly, I could not help finding our situation extremely perilous, seeing that we were no longer receiving any bread at all, most of our horses had gone into our cooking-pots, and the few that remained were in an unspeakably broken-down condition, having nothing more to sustain such strength as they still had than the bark of trees, telegraph poles, or the tails and manes of their comrades. How could we recommence the struggle with some chance of success in such deplorable conditions? Nothing in the men's stomachs, and no artillery to support us! On top of that the weather was terrible and had a dolorous effect on our spirits, disposing us to look on the black side of everything!

Meanwhile, daily life went on just as it always did; as yet nothing much seemed to have changed. On the 19th we were told that General Boyer, the Marshal's aide-de-camp, had been sent to the interior of France to assess the situation, which the Germans had painted in the darkest hues. There was revolution everywhere; in Paris, in Lyons. Several towns in the Midi had demanded German garrisons to protect them, and so forth.[3] The General would turn to the Empress,[4] who would assume the regency and with the help of the Army of Metz – still intact and, in the eyes of the French people, covered in the prestige which attaches to troops who have not been defeated – would re-establish order in the country and treat for peace with the conquerors.[5] We were enjoined to rise to the accomplishment of this patriotic duty.

Fundamentally, we were being given a hint of civil war after the war between nations. This communication was not gladly received, and in spite of ourselves we had the feeling that all this was totally impracticable, and that we had no other recourse than capitulation pure and simple.

In Metz unrest was at its peak. The struggle between the municipal council and the military authorities had entered a bitter phase and had come to insults and hard truths. But we knew only vague details of this.[6] What interested me most was a sort of oath sworn among the officers resulting in an appeal to willing men to form an escape group which, rather than suffer the shame of a capitulation, would hurl themselves heads down upon the enemy lines during the night and seek to cross them. At least honour would be saved! I confess that at first I was full of admiration for those who had put forward such a heroic idea, and I came to Metz one evening to understand for myself the importance and worth of this very French movement. I was led into a huge room (in the town hall, I believe) which I found thronged with officers. A captain of cuirassiers, if I remember rightly, was indulging in speeches burning with patriotism, but which, too often for my liking, veered towards politics. He was followed by a captain of engineers (perhaps Rossel)[7] who accentuated that note. This displeased me considerably. I was quite ready to give my life for the honour of my flag, but I confess that no political party whatsoever seemed to me worthy of such a sacrifice. Then those present occupied themselves in signing a register which was to become the golden book of the army. I do not know why but I smelt a great practical joke, and I left the meeting in no way disposed to have my skin holed for the subsequent glory of the members of the self-styled 'initiating and directing committee', who would know how to reap all the advantage that might be desired from this escapade. Besides, on the evening of the 27th, the eve of the capitulation, I went out of curiosity to the rendezvous which had been fixed, at the foot of the railway embankment close to the bridge over the Moselle, and there I saw not so much as a cat's tail.[8]

On the 25th I mounted my last picket guard at the barricade on the Ars road. But what a sad duty! The Germans did not fire any more and neither did our men. If we had let them they would have left the trenches and fraternised on that plain whose soil would be French for only a few hours more. How I pined for the day when I had dashed between the willow trees by grace of my sentinel's kepi placed on the end of a rifle and held out beyond the shelter of a tree to invite a shot from the watching Germans. And yet the firing as I carried out my little stratagem had been no laughing matter.

On the 26th an official bulletin told us that, the Empress having refused to accept the regency,[9] and the Count of Paris[10] not wishing to burden himself with the heavy task of governing the country at this time, the army – its strength and provisions exhausted – had no other recourse than to accept the conditions of the victor, namely capitulation. The strangest rumours then began to circulate, evidently launched by those who had every interest in not upsetting the enemy. At first it was put about that only the officers and non-commissioned officers would be sent to Germany as prisoners, but that the soldiers, once disarmed, would be sent back to their homes. This was intended to forestall a military revolt, which the schemings of the famous committee of the wild sortie might cause Bazaine to fear. Then it was said that our arms and all our military stores would be returned to France after the peace. It would therefore be in our best interests not to damage anything and to hand over the weapons in good condition. Finally, the Colours should be deposited at the arsenal where they would be destroyed under the proper supervision of the artillery.[11]

What basis was there for all of this idle gossip? None at all, evidently, as subsequent events amply proved. But at the time we clutched at every straw and did our utmost to find the situation almost tolerable. For my part, I had our arms kept in good condition so far as possible, for it did not seem inconceivable to me that, in order to bring matters to a finish more quickly without risking a last encounter with the Army of Metz that could prove very bloody, the Germans might offer it more generous conditions than usual.[12]

The soldiers took the announcement of the capitulation cheerfully enough. For them it was the end, and that was what they wished for, for they felt that the inactivity in which we had been sunk for weeks could lead us only to final catastrophe; it mattered little whether it came sooner or later! I do not believe that they put great faith in the story running through our camps, according to which they would be returned to their hearths and not led away to Germany as prisoners. The fact remains that they appeared not to understand the gravity of our situation from the point of view of the slur cast on our military honour. In the evening of the day before the surrender of the troops, the 28th, singing and riotous shouts echoed in our camps. At the same time many weapons were broken and thrown in heaps on the roads. But nowhere around me did I see any demonstration whatever of resistance to carrying out the capitulation. That is sad, perhaps, but absolutely true.

During the final days the regiment did not move from Longeville and, the end of everything being near, regulations had gone to some extent by the board and officers had been allowed to lodge in the houses of the village. I therefore moved my modest baggage into a room in a cottage situated on the road which formed the main street of the village. Our field-mess was likewise installed in a house. By this means our existence was made more comfortable, it is true; but at that time what was comfort to us?

On the 27th we were at lunch when from the window we saw the Regimental Colour pass by, being carried to the arsenal. Poor Colour, which had made such a fine display in the Crimea, in Italy, and latterly on the battlefields of Metz: it truly did not deserve to end this way! Such in sum was the drift of our reflections inspired by the last sight of this emblem, around which so many brave men had fallen never to rise again. But the idea occurred to none of us – and I can vouch that this was so among all the officers of the regiment – that our honour was in any way involved in saving the Colour from the fate which awaited it: destruction or surrender to the enemy, which at bottom was all one. And yet the officer corps of the 6th Line Regiment was one of the best. Besides having conducted itself brilliantly in the August battles, of which it had missed not a single one, the desire to take revenge, to continue the struggle and defend the country right to the end was so powerful among the majority of its members that 22 officers of this regiment escaped and returned to France where they served with the utmost self-sacrifice in the various provincial armies, particularly in the Army of the North. One therefore cannot say that such officers had a wavering notion of the obligations imposed by the cult of military honour. And yet everybody thought it quite natural, at the moment when the regiment yielded to the enemy, that the Colour should be given up at the same time, and nobody thought to destroy it. For, truth to tell, in everyone's eyes it no longer existed since there was no longer a 6th Infantry Regiment, only a band of wretched prisoners.[13]

Great was my surprise when, several years after the war, I saw those who had destroyed their unit's Colour, or caused it to disappear instead of handing it over to the enemy, glorified in a most extraordinary way. They were almost made heroes, and their action seemed so meritorious that it was immortalised on canvas so that it could be admired by as many people as possible.[14] I recall the last days at Metz and, finding the sentiments which animated me then still strong and sincere, I hold to the view that, despite the infatuation of the public in regard to those who acted differently to ourselves, we should not incur any reproach either from our own consciences or from the opinions of anyone else.

For a regiment, its Colour is the representation of the idea of the country; it is the bond which ties it to that country. It is what reminds the soldier of his duty towards that country. The sight of the Colour sustains him in the accomplishment of his duty, however hard it may be, because on seeing it he immediately feels that his sacrifice and sufferings are serving the greatness or the salvation of his country. The Colour therefore has no other purpose than to symbolise the country for the group of men around it. But from the moment when that group of men, the regiment, is dissolved and lost to the defence of the land, the Colour by that very fact no longer exists because it no longer represents anything. In a word, the two ideas of a symbol representing the nation and of a union of men around that symbol to defend it are indissoluble; for this symbol has no significance in isolation.

Thus, from the moment when the regiments of the Army of Metz were surrendered to the enemy, from being so many men constituting a fighting unit they became simply the same number of prisoners. The bond which bound them to the defence of the country having been broken, the existence of a symbol, a Colour, intended to hold these men together around it with the goal of fighting for its preservation, has become purely and simply useless; and from the fact of the regiment having ceased to exist, the Colour has become nothing more than a piece of cloth without value. Therefore why seek to deny it to the enemy any more than any other object?

Only 58 Colours were yielded to the enemy in accordance with the terms of the capitulation. Yet there were at least a hundred regiments at Metz.[15] The Germans therefore had the right to claim as many Colours as there were regiments and, if we were unable to present them with an equal number, to have as many made as were lacking; and those made up Colours would have possessed the same authenticity as the actual Colours that were destroyed, whatever might be said on the subject. For in the end it cannot be disputed: did the regiment or did it not surrender on 28 October 1870? The enemy therefore had the absolute right to inscribe its number on the list of his captures, and to include among his trophies the object which symbolises the regiment, that is, the regimental Colour bearing its number and battle honours. That cannot be denied.

There is only one eventuality in which the Colour, though not surrounded by a group of defenders, nevertheless preserves intact its character as an emblem of the honour of the regiment and as a patriotic symbol. That is when the whole regiment is killed to the last man around it and it floats proudly, planted on a glorious plinth of corpses. Only in that case, which I believe has never arisen, would the Colour, despite having fallen into the enemy's hands, not be his trophy of war, for it remains forever the soul of the annihilated regiment and always belongs to the country as the spirit of the great men whose mortal remains have long since disappeared. To conclude this matter I should mention that, once the Colour had been taken away, no one in the regiment concerned himself with what had become of it.[16]

On the morning of the 28th the colonel assembled the officers and made known the exact terms of the capitulation. In consideration of the courage which our troops had shown in the fighting, the enemy allowed officers to keep their swords. This was very courteous, perhaps, but slightly puerile. The value of a sword consists in the fact that it signifies command. From the moment when one has no more troops to command, there is little point in encumbering oneself with wearing such a bauble. I should therefore confess that this provision did not move us greatly, and that it was given only slight attention. After reading out the pact, which we could not listen to without blushing, the colonel added some advice on the absolute obedience to the conditions of the convention that we should require from our men. He ended by saying to us: 'From today I cease to be your commander, but I shall always be your friend.' I felt very moved by these words, and above all by the tone of deep sadness in which they were spoken by this old man, whose utterly drawn features sufficiently revealed that poignant distress was wringing his heart. And I, who certainly had no love for him and who had been disposed at all times to see him as merely ludicrous, now felt completely the opposite, and it was with all my heart that I shook his hand in token of farewell. The announcement was made to companies by their captains. I told my men that, since misfortune had overcome us, they should not aggravate matters by risking making their future position more difficult; that the best thing was to show themselves as brave in the midst of this dreadful disaster as they had been, arms in hand, in the face of the enemy, and to bear stoically this trial which fate had imposed on us. I do not know whether they paid much heed to my words, but in general they seemed to be resigned; perhaps even a little too much so.

On the 29th, at about nine or ten o'clock, the regiment was assembled, without arms naturally, and led onto the Plappeville plateau, where the surrender of troops to the enemy was to take place. What a Calvary to climb! The road, all broken up and covered in mud, climbed steeply in endless zigzags. Above our heads, like the point of a sword which sank into our flesh every time we looked at it, the black and white of the German flag waved from the flagstaff of Fort Saint-Quentin. I came to the point of not daring to raise my eyes any more! Once on the plateau we entered the fields which the continual rains of recent days had transformed into veritable cesspools. The weather was gloomy. A fine rain lashed our faces. Great black clouds seemed like nature's mourning colours laid on for the burial of the honour of our poor army. Melancholy was everywhere. The Germans, at order arms, formed a kind of large square, as it seemed to me. After a rather long wait a *Feldwebel* (sergeant-major) armed with some paper or other came to count my men and took possession of them. Thus we had to part. And these men, who the day before had seemed to accept their lot almost indifferently, did not want to leave me. They wept as they shook my hand and spoke kind words to me: that I had been a good leader, that they liked me well, that they would never forget me, that for my part too I should remember that they had always been brave soldiers. They begged me as well not to leave them, to stay with them a little longer. Some of the more excited ones even regretted having given up their weapons, for at that moment they were ready to use them to recover their liberty. I did my best to calm and settle them, but I had difficulty in speaking. My throat was choked, my tongue all dry, and a kind of shiver shook my whole body, halting my words on my lips. Finally the sacrifice was made and, having one last time shaken a cluster of twenty hands, I made a sharp about-turn and walked away, literally without knowing where I was going. The cup was drained to the dregs and its bitterness had numbed my heart.[17]

After having wandered I know not where nor for how long, without thinking very clearly of anything, I found myself back on the plain quite a distance from Longeville. I was exhausted. I sat down on a fallen tree and stayed there for quite a long time. In short, when I returned to my room it seemed to me that the day was a real low point. I slumped down on the little trunk which contained the few things I possessed, and there I felt myself overcome by a flood of tears. I think that I have never cried and sobbed so much in my life. This outburst calmed me down a great deal, at the same time bringing on a moral numbness which prevented me from seeing the situation in all its ugliness. I was still under the singularly moving but bittersweet impression of the parting, and of the pity which I felt overwhelming me for those poor men whose daily trials in war had made my brothers, my friends, who had always conducted themselves as brave men, and whom I was leaving to an unknown fate, perhaps pregnant with trouble and suffering for them.[18]

Night was approaching. I did not have the heart to dine nor to subject myself to the obligations which contact with other men always imposes. I stretched out on my bed and slept so deep a sleep that I had the very greatest difficulty in rousing myself in full daylight the next morning upon the repeated calls of my orderly, my dear Guyonne (for the Germans had allowed officers to retain their orderlies and horses). Once dressed, having no desire to go out, I sat down on my trunk and began to ruminate on events, seeking to make sense of how they could have led me to the sad epilogue of the previous day. A void which I could not fill lay like a great bar of shadow across the reasoning I was trying to construct, so separating two facts which stood out clearly. Most certainly, for me it was incontrovertible that our army was a match for the Germans: it had amply proved that on the battlefields of August. And it was no less incontrovertible that this army, despite its martial qualities, had just been shamefully yielded to the enemy without having fought for two months. Why? I racked my brains in vain, and was unable to discover any reason whatever. For in the end a commanding general who has under his control an army capable of winning, if he wishes to assure his own honour, does not trifle at allowing it to be uselessly squandered. That would be a piece of insanity which Marshal Bazaine, who was said to be very intelligent and wily, was incapable of. Then why?

Then little by little my mind began to dwell more heavily on the various phases by which the preliminaries of the capitulation had come about. The political aspect, which had to some extent passed me by, suddenly appeared to me in all its sordid reality. Why seek to enter into an arrangement with the Empress, who no longer counted for anything in the country since it had chosen another government, or with the Count of Paris, whose family had been exiled? Was there no government in France? And a real and very active government, seeing that it had been able to continue the war for two months since the imperial armies had disappeared! Marshal Bazaine therefore had no right to offer his army to any other government than the existing one; with that government alone should he have sought to establish contact. Besides, had he not told us himself at the beginning of September that our duty remained the same to the new government as to the old. Why in that case change and tell us a month later that we were going to impose on France a government it no longer wanted, since it had adopted, or accepted, another! To be sure, Bazaine wanted to use us for a restoration from which he would reap all the benefits.

Then I had a flash of illumination, leaving no detail in shadow, revealing the motive which had driven Bazaine not to take advantage of the first-class fighting qualities of his army, nor of the successes which it had gained on 14, 16 and 31 August, and to shut himself up in Metz where his defences could not be breached. He quite simply wanted to wait on events while conserving his forces in order to be able, at his chosen time, to intervene as master with the strength of his reliable army behind him. And it was to gratify such a shabby personal interest that this monster trampled underfoot his dignity as a Marshal of France and the honour of 200,000 brave men! He pushed his knavery to the extent of assuming the appearance of having been forced to shut himself up in Metz by the enemy. And thus it was that victories such as Borny, Gravelotte and Servigny bore no fruit, and why instead of resuming active operations in September we remained sunk in inactivity around Metz! But he had reckoned without the energy and resilience of France which, instead of delivering itself bound hand and foot after Sedan, proudly held up its head and, although almost disarmed, continued the struggle for honour with the stump of a sword in her hand. The peace which he hoped to see concluded in mid-September having failed to come to his rescue, all his shady calculations had ended in the catastrophe which had plunged us all into a cesspit of degradation. Wretch! Thus our glorious struggles on the Rezonville plateau and our brilliant assaults on the entrenchments of Failly and Servigny were merely a sham! A sham which had cost 45,000 men left dead or wounded on the battlefields! Clearly the entire responsibility fell on Bazaine, who held supreme command! But at his side were men who nevertheless had every interest in not allowing a whole tradition of glory and honour to be besmirched in this way. There were Canrobert, Bourbaki,[19] Ladmirault, etc. Why did not one of these men, in the name of all, go to find Bazaine as soon as we started eating our horses and say to him: 'Where are you leading us? When all the horses have disappeared, how will we be able to harness our batteries to give battle? Answer us. We demand it in the name of our honour and that of the brave troops who have confidence in us.'[20] And if, after several days, an honourable position had not been taken, how could one of these men, all of whom we considered as the most perfect examples of military honour, how could one of these generals not have gone back to Bazaine with a revolver in his pocket and eliminated this repellent bulldog of a man in order to give the command to one more worthy?[21]

And then, with the effort of raking up all this filth, I was seized with a great moral lassitude and profound disgust. I felt thoroughly helpless, sunk in utter misery by the collapse of everything which I had loved and respected until that day.

Suddenly the door was opened brusquely and three or four German soldiers came into my room, doubtless with the intention of installing themselves there. I raised my head and stared very fixedly, without speaking, at the man who had entered first and who was a non-commissioned officer. He stared back attentively, then, having seen from my kepi that I was an officer, he halted his men, had them leave and, without taking his eyes off me, stood to attention, gave me an extended salute and disappeared.

These men were evidently obeying an order enjoining them to respect the places occupied by French officers. That is what I thought at first, but this salute completely changed my ideas. So we had not fallen so low, seeing that our enemies observed such courtesies towards us, the conquered, who were entirely at their mercy. Did these marks of respect not proclaim an esteem which one does not accord to those who have not acted as brave adversaries? I felt I could hold up my head again, and no longer regretted the dangers risked, even uselessly, since they were the proofs of my honour. I even found a certain pleasure in contemplating my sabre, which lay in a corner, and I appreciated at its full value the courtesy and deference which the Germans had shown us in not demanding that we should give them up like the weapons of private soldiers.

Much comforted by these reflections, I went out to get lunch. It was the first time that I had found myself back with my companions since we had been separated from our troops, and I feared that a certain embarrassment would exist between us, as between people who have a secret agreement to do, or allow, some evil deed. It was not so. Moreover, the new moral landscape had already been explored the night before by my comrades, who had dined together while I slept for at least twelve hours, worn out by fatigue and emotion. However that might be, the meal was not a cheerful one; we had been too badly shaken the day before! Nevertheless, we did speak of the fate which awaited us. It seemed that we must remain where we were until the moment came to take us away by railway; the time of which would be notified later by posters put up in our camps.

I was finishing lunch when I received a visit from one of my good friends, a captain in the 2nd Battalion, who a little mysteriously gave me a sign that he had something to say to me alone. I left with him.

'What do you plan to do?' he asked me point-blank.

'What? What do I plan to do?'

'Yes. Do you want to go to Germany?'

'How can we do otherwise?'

'Nothing is easier than to give the Germans the slip. This morning I saw someone from Longeville who assured me that by his agency two officers have already escaped, in the course of yesterday evening. He procured them civilian clothing and a reliable guide, and they should have reached the Luxembourg frontier by crossing enemy lines without problems. Do you want us two to do the same? I shall look after all the preparations. When the moment has come I shall give you a sign, and we shall slip away.[22] Above all, not a word or hint about our attempt.'

I think it unnecessary to describe my feelings in accepting this proposition. My spirits were entirely revived and, absorbed in the attempt to escape and in making plans beyond that, I forgot all the vileness which had oppressed me in the course of the last few days.

The house where I had a room was occupied by several German officers. When chance brought us face to face, these gentlemen were inclined always to salute me first with much politeness. But I, slightly shamefaced, like a man who feels himself badly dressed in the midst of elegant society, returned the salute without stopping, so avoiding all conversation. One evening, however, on coming in I was stopped by the proprietor of the house who insistently begged me to spend a few minutes with him. I followed him into a kind of parlour where I found three German officers, the eldest of whom rose on my entering and greeted me, hand outstretched, with great affability. He was a major-general whose name I never knew. I sat down with them and the conversation turned to the campaign which had just ended so sadly for us. Very adroitly avoiding speaking of this outcome, the general, who expressed himself very well in French, praised our resistance on 18 August highly; resistance which, had it not been so absolutely passive, would have caused them grave anxiety for their right wing, very precariously anchored on the Moselle. I confess that had he spoken to me in Hebrew I would have understood no more of what he said. As a matter of fact, I had no idea of the overall dispositions adopted by our army in these great battles. I knew that I had fought close by a certain place; but what the general position of our army was I had never known. I was therefore content to acquiesce without even appearing to dispute anything whatever. He also told me that our infantry attack on 31 August had been admirable; that they would never have believed troops whom such an unfavourable start to the campaign must have somewhat demoralised capable of such an effort, and that they were not very sure of being able to get as much from their troops. I thanked him very warmly for this comforting charity for the heart of a conquered man, and after about an hour of conversation I withdrew. I remained under the spell of these consoling words, which left a deep and lasting impression and helped no little in the convalescence of my poor soldier's self-esteem which had been so grievously wounded.

Another day, finding myself on the Metz road, I saw coming towards me a horseman who stopped level with me and, putting his hand to the peak of his helmet, asked my leave to talk for a little while. He must have been a senior commander of note, for through the gap of his unbuttoned coat I observed numerous decorations on his chest and, hanging from his neck, several Commander's Crosses, among which I clearly recognised that of the Legion of Honour. He told me in an accent that seemed to me thoroughly English, but in very good French, that he was delighted to meet one of his comrades from France in order to be able to express all the admiration inspired in him by the valiant conduct of our troops in the various encounters in which we had opposed each other; that he wished me to know that in his capacity as a brother-in-arms he greatly felt the misfortune which had overcome brave men like us who had fully deserved a different outcome – and finally that he would be very glad to take a good dinner in Metz, where he was headed, and would I be so kind as to recommend a good place, if perchance I knew of one. I could not help smiling at this peroration. I hastened to thank him for the generous sentiments that he had just expressed with such courtesy, and I recommended the Porte-Enseigne restaurant in the Rue Serpenoise as having the reputation for possessing the best cellar in town. 'That's just what I appreciate the most,' he told me. Then, after exchanging a handshake, he set off at a trot and disappeared in the direction of the town.

If I dwell in this manner on the cordiality of these few contacts with German officers which chance afforded me, it is because I have often heard it said since by people animated by an obvious partisanship and having no familiarity with the ways of war, that their officers behaved like savages, with no feeling of the solidarity which should unite all those who exercise the noble profession of arms, whatever nation they belong to. During the whole of this war in which I faced them continually, just indeed as in peacetime, on the few occasions when I have had dealings with them I have found a courtesy and respect in German officers which I have not always encountered in ours.

Meanwhile we had arrived at 3 November. Already the officers of several army corps had been entrained for Germany. There was talk of escapes made by some of our men in somewhat unnerving circumstances which caused me to reflect, without however weakening my resolution in the least. The son of a general had supposedly been stopped and shot on the spot. Others had been able to escape only after the most severe trials, and so on. All these tidings, which it was impossible to verify, came at an exceptionally favourable time for them to gain currency. In our idleness we swallowed them without reserve and our anxiety magnified them in our conversations.

On the morning of the 3rd my comrade burst into my room and told me, not without some embarrassment, that after weighing up everything he was giving up his plan of escape. He would willingly risk death on the battlefield, but to take a dozen bullets in some corner of a wood was stupid. And that was what we were letting ourselves in for by trying to escape. Besides, he added, he had sufficiently proved himself in the Crimea, in Italy and most recently around Metz; he was married and the father of two children and it was folly to expose himself in that way. And then, had we the right to act so? Had not our word been pledged with that of the commanding general? And, notwithstanding any personal pledge that had been made, were we not bound by an oath which honour required us to respect? I was greatly unsettled by all that he said; for at bottom I recognised that he was right. However, I had become so accustomed to this most seductive idea of returning to France and of taking up arms again there to efface the stain of Metz that I asked him for the name and address of the man who was to arrange our attempt. He took me there and I asked him to retain for me the guide whom he had in view, for one day soon.

When I found myself alone I reflected that, after all, my friend's withdrawal might perhaps be a blessing in disguise. These kinds of enterprise need no hesitation, no indecision, in their execution and offer much greater chances of success to a man alone than to a group, however small it may be and however perfect the understanding among the members of that group.

However, as the critical moment was approaching – for notices had been posted in our camps that the officers of the Fourth Corps (the last) would entrain on the evening of the 4th, and that everyone must be at the Serpenoise station at 10 o'clock – I thought I should share my decision with young Second Lieutenant Fernandez, for whom I had a liking fully warranted by his many qualities. He begged me to take him as my companion, which I did there and then, knowing that I would find in him a resolute and co-operative associate. We decided to warn our two orderlies, who would want at all costs to share our fate. But as a group of four (five with the guide) might have given the alarm, we procured another guide for them who would lead them into Luxembourg by a different route from ours, and we invited them to lose no time in providing themselves with peasant clothing.

During the 3rd and 4th we went over and over our plan from every angle, particularly from the point of view of the opportunities its success would offer. On the morning of the 4th, after having thought it over for much of the night, I told myself that after all we were fools to expose ourselves to failure, since we had only to sign an undertaking never to bear arms against Germany again to be free to return to France without running any risk whatever. As for the undertaking, we simply would not keep it, that was all! In war any measures are justified to deceive the enemy. What did we want? To offer our country the slight support of our willingness and devotion. It mattered little whether the means to our end were proper or not! Did a noble goal not justify them? This rather Machiavellian reasoning had taken such root in my brain that I dragged Fernandez to the commandant's headquarters in the Place d'Armes in Metz. We asked an officer there to give us a copy of the declaration in question. The wording of the document was just what we had been told. We had only to fill in our names and sign. But at the supreme moment I felt my face flushing, and I gave back the paper without having dared to write the first of the five letters of my name. Fernandez, who wore a rather woeful expression and who had been no less decided to commit this small infamy, commended my resolution, and we left, delighted to have avoided striking this rock on which we had almost wrecked our reputation as gentlemen.

We were unable to decide every detail of our enterprise as we did not know either on the 3rd or 4th how it would commence. We simply decided, and more expressly so after our visit to the commandant's office, not to try to avoid the journey to Germany until we had fulfilled all the obligations imposed on us by the terms of the capitulation. The only preparatory dispositions which we took were to confide our swords, which might have encumbered us, to the officer who had helped us, with the request that he keep them until the time when we could reclaim them after the war. This excellent man willingly accepted this charge and through his good offices they were returned to us some time after the Commune. We also warned him that our departure would definitely take place the following morning, and asked him to be so kind as to inform the guide he had chosen for us of this, and that we should like everything to be ready at six o'clock in the morning.

CHAPTER VIII

ESCAPE

4–10 November 1870

'How sweet is the air of liberty!'

At Metz station – An eventful evening – An improvised bedroom – At the old-clothes dealer's – Escape – On the highway – A rather dear omelette – At the buffet of Audun-le-Roman station – Our driver makes good his escape – A bad night is soon passed – On the Luxembourg frontier – In the disinfecting hut – Esch-sur-Alzette – Brussels – Return to France

So on the 4th at 8 o'clock in the evening we left Longeville in uniform, after telling our orderlies to be ready to leave first thing the next morning. We stopped for a while in a café on the Esplanade where we met a crowd of comrades who were awaiting the hour appointed for our departure. Finally, at 10 o'clock, we arrived at the Serpenoise station.

A veritable throng of French officers filled the halls and platforms. For an hour we mingled in groups, asking for information about entrainment, the places of internment, and so forth. Some German policemen, easily recognisable by their big brass gorgets gleaming under the gaslights, were strolling along the platforms without seeming to pay the least attention to the prisoners.

Eleven o'clock passed; there was still no question of embarkation nor of a roll call, and the crowd was growing all the time. Seeing that no steps had been taken to secure us, believing that we had fulfilled our duty to the letter and were absolved from any obligation to guard ourselves, since we had put ourselves in the hands of the Germans at the place and hour prescribed, we decided to escape then and there. To this end we followed the platform on the town side right to its end; we passed beyond the last groups of our comrades and went onto the track. Having passed the last gas lamps, we leapt over the flimsy fence, went down the slope of the embankment and came to a street which brought us back to the front of the station. Then, without concealing ourselves, we took the main road and went back into town, which was still very lively despite the lateness of the hour. We ran no risk of being stopped, for there were still a great many French officers in town, authorised to remain there for different reasons.[1]

Now we had to find a resting-place for the night; we could not get back to our camp because the town gates were firmly shut. Our first idea was to go and ask for a room at the Hôtel de l'Europe where I was known to the manager, because several times during the siege I had gone there with some friends for meals at prices as inflated as our usual helpings of horse-meat soup were small.

The hotel was crowded with German officers. On our arrival in the main dining-room the waiters appeared not to understand what we were asking them, even though there were two or three small tables free. I went and spoke to the manager, who with great embarrassment told me that they were all reserved and that he had no place to offer us. The best thing was to look elsewhere, and that is what we did. Thus we looked at five or six other hotels in town; but everywhere our arrival produced a disastrous effect and had the knack of striking dumb the hoteliers who, once they had recovered, sent us on our way with a categorical refusal. In the meantime midnight had long since struck. What was to be done? Chance, in the form of a German patrol, forced us to make a decision rapidly. Although we were followed by this patrol we were able to give it the slip thanks to my knowledge of the town, where I had been garrisoned five years previously. A goods wagon of the Eastern Railway was in front of us, detached and perhaps forgotten in the street. We crept into it smartly. It was filled with packing hay: a ready-made bed. A quarter of an hour later we were sleeping like logs in this improvised dwelling. Our only fear on going to sleep was that we might involuntarily attract the attention of some ferreting patrol by untimely snores.

Fortunately nothing happened; daybreak and cold awoke us. After shaking ourselves and brushing ourselves down, for our hair and beards were full of hay stalks, we left our hotel on wheels and, with many precautions, headed for the Place Saint-Louis where there were several second-hand clothes shops. We entered the first one that we saw open. There for the sum of ten francs each we bought a set of old clothes: frayed trousers, smocks of faded blue linen, and a greasy and battered hat and peaked cap, which made us unrecognisable even to each other. We each made a little bundle of our military clothes and, hiding it under our smocks, took the road for the North Gate. We passed by the sentry, then by the men at the guard post who were getting on with their morning task of polishing their gear. No one so much as honoured us with a glance. We crossed the last drawbridge and found ourselves in open country, as happy as finches escaped from their cage. In half an hour we were back at our camp where we found our orderlies, flabbergasted at seeing us kitted out in this way, but delighted to see us again.

Like astute men, they had already made an arrangement with a local man who was going to Luxembourg that day with his cart to buy foodstuff. They would take with them the two little boxes containing our uniforms; and so we separated. Our rendezvous was arranged for midday the next day in Esch-sur-Alzette, the first village in Luxembourg on the road that they were going to follow. The first to arrive would await the others until midday of the day following, after which each party would be free to reach Lille by its own means.

It was about seven o'clock when we set out with our guide on the Verdun road. Oh! How sweet is the air of liberty! And how easily we breathed as we distanced ourselves from that cesspit of shame in which we had wallowed for two long months! The weather was superb and we hardly noticed the passing of the kilometres.

At Gravelotte we took the northern road, which leads to Verdun via Etain. We crossed the uplands soaked in French blood on 16 and 18 August. Here and there were mounds which perhaps covered some already forgotten comrade! We passed on to Doncourt and arrived at Jarny towards eleven o'clock. As hunger was beginning to dog us, we decided to take lunch in this village. Until now we had met only small numbers of German troops: only a guard post at Gravelotte. But Jarny was full of them. The inn, perhaps the only one in the region, was crammed with them, on the ground floor at least. The guide, who knew the innkeeper, spoke to him privately and we went up to a room on the first floor where three places were laid. The menu consisted of a fatty omelette with ham, salad and cheese; price, thirty-five francs! We protested. The serving girl could do nothing. We summoned the innkeeper, who said to us: 'Take it or leave it. I can guess who you are; you know who is downstairs. You would do best to pay and get out.' This speech

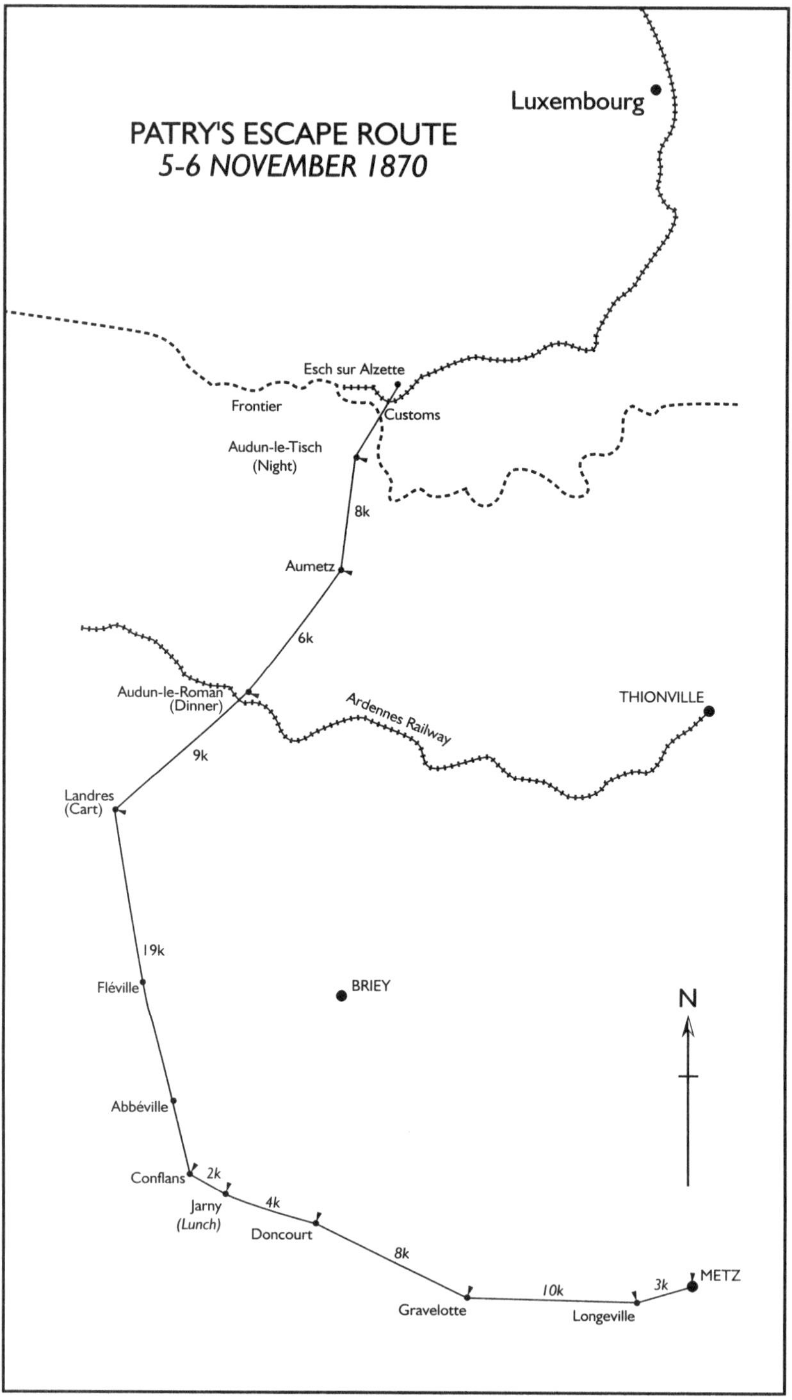
PATRY'S ESCAPE ROUTE
5-6 NOVEMBER 1870
Luxembourg
Esch sur Alzette
Frontier
Customs
Audun-le-Tisch
(Night)
8k
Aumetz
6k
Audun-le-Roman
(Dinner)
Ardennes Railway
THIONVILLE
9k
Landres
(Cart)
19k
Fléville
BRIEY
N
Abbéville
Conflans
2k
Jarny
(Lunch)
4k
Doncourt
8k
Gravelotte
10k
Longeville
3k
METZ

was cynical but explicit. We handed over the thirty-five francs and hastened to get away promptly without even kissing the maid, who treated us like lords because we had tipped her a hundred sous.

Once away, the omelette seemed heavy to us, and to aid our digestion we gave free vent to our indignation. One thing that surprised us was that our guide maintained a prudent reserve and avoided passing judgement on the rather unsavoury conduct of his fellow countryman. But the sun was good, we had well-filled stomachs after all, and the disagreeable impression was quickly dissipated.

At Conflans we left the main road, full of troops marching westwards, and headed to the right, northwards through Abbéville and Fléville, reaching Landres towards half-past four. We were beginning to feel tired. We had covered 42 kilometres since Metz and we still had 26 to go before reaching Luxembourg. For men out of the habit of marching, it was a hard day's walk. As we certainly had no wish to pass the night in a region thick with enemy troops, we decided to hire a light cart. Our guide easily found what we needed in Landres, and the price was fixed at forty francs as far as the frontier. We parted from our guide, to whom we paid the price agreed, that is to say twenty francs. He asked us for forty. We refused, he insisted, but without employing the same method as the innkeeper at Jarny. He appealed to our charity, and to get rid of him we paid up the two *louis*.

There we were rolling gaily along the road to Luxembourg, where we hoped to arrive at about eight o'clock. We had scarcely left Landres when we saw the road black with troops. It was a munitions column composed of thirty vehicles of every kind; caissons, supply wagons, travelling forges, etc. The commander signalled us to halt with an authority that brooked no discussion. We stopped at the side of the road, on its furthest edge, with one wheel almost in the ditch. The column filed past rather slowly. Suddenly there was a great hubbub, shouts, oaths, cracking of whips, and the column halted.

A caisson had tumbled into the ditch and the dismounted drivers were making vain efforts to right it. The commander came up at the gallop to take stock of the accident, then he pointed at us and, in eccentric French rendered comprehensible only by gestures, directed us to get down from our cart and to go and give his men a hand. We hastened to put our shoulders to the wheel. At last we turned the caisson the right way up, then we got it back on the road where it took its place in the column, which resumed its advance without delay. Once alone, we were seized with such uncontrollable laughter that we did not notice the disappearance of our cart. Left to his own devices the horse, taking advantage of our absence, was trotting about on the plain in the distance. We retrieved him and everything was back in order; in an hour we were at Audun-le-Roman. Night had fallen, we were a little tired; we halted in front of the station buffet which looked fairly snug to us, and there we ordered dinner. Towards eight o'clock we were about to get back on the road when several very well-dressed people came and sat down beside us. The conversation turned to events at Metz, and our listeners were not slow to perceive that we were officers who had escaped captivity. We offered them a glass of champagne, then two. By the third we had already told our whole history.

Eleven o'clock was striking when we got back into our cart. A fine moonlight allowed us to see the road and its edges well, which was very necessary, for if we two were rather merry, our driver was completely drunk. We passed through the large village of Aumetz and continued towards Audun-le-Tisch, the last French village. We were about to enter it when, at a bend in the gleaming white road, we saw advancing towards us two German horsemen casting immense shadows before them and followed by two heavily laden wagons. Two more horsemen brought up the rear. Ah! The last effects of the champagne were very quickly dissipated, and for the first time since our departure we were a little afraid. Yet the little convoy passed us and went on its way without paying any attention to our presence on the road.

This encounter woke us up. We thought that the village must be occupied and we judged it more prudent to send off our cart and its driver and to enter it on foot, but not by the main road where there might be a guard post. We offered the driver the two *louis* agreed, but this rogue, made bold no doubt by the power over us which the encounter a little earlier might have given him, was not content and demanded five. We protested; he began to shout. The road was completely deserted. My comrade and I exchanged one of those looks which in one second decide the life of a man. Certainly it would have been easy for us, two strong young men, to strangle this fine fellow whose hair was already half grey. But it was wiser in our situation to avoid a scandal which the proximity of the village, perhaps occupied by the enemy, would have made very dangerous for us. I therefore thrust five *louis* into his hand at the same time that I pushed him towards his cart, which he hastened to remount, but not so fast that my foot, shod in my strong army boot, did not have time to strike the seat of his breeches. He had had enough and made off at speed, and soon the sound of his cart faded in the distance.

And now, what should we do? To enter the village was to risk finding ourselves face to face with the Germans, who perhaps were preparing to depart. We left the road and started across country to go around the village and find the road again on its far side. Our operation was carried out without too much difficulty and in spite of the darkness which made things very awkward for us in the woods. We came in sight of the road again, and about five hundred metres along it we could make out the little customs post with a sentry in front of it. Was he German or a Luxemburger? Not daring to approach, we went back into the woods to try to cross the frontier out of sight of the customs post. Suddenly a frightful uproar broke out near the customs post: shouts, barking, calls. We rushed for cover and put distance between ourselves and this spot, which did not seem at all the place for people in our situation. On our way we came to an unoccupied sawmill. We stopped there to await daylight. A plank made an acceptable bed, and off we went into the land of dreams.

After several hours we were awoken by an intense cold which pinched us cruelly through the worn linen of our smocks. Moreover, day came in with a thick autumn mist. Curiosity drew us back to the edge of the wood bordering the main road. Seeing that all was very quiet around the customs post, and recognising the green uniform of the Luxemburgers, we took to the road and quite boldly walked up to the frontier.

The customs guard whom we were about to pass immediately came towards me, grabbed me by the arm and without saying a word pushed me into a little cabin and locked the door on me. I thought that our Odyssey was finished at a stroke. These customs men no doubt had orders to arrest all suspect persons and to hand them over to the Germans. I gave myself over to these sad reflections in my prison of four square metres at the very most when I was suddenly seized with a terrific stinging in the eyes, throat and nose, and I began to sneeze, cough and cry as if I were shut in a snuffbox. Fortunately my torture did not last long. The customs man reopened the door, ushered me out of the cabin and put in my comrade, who was laughing at my discomfited expression. Then I learned that, as cattle plague had been raging in the region of France adjoining the Luxembourg frontier, orders had been given to the Customs to disinfect every dirty object. Dirty we were, and certainly in all respects we merited fumigation. We also learned from the customs guard, who had become very friendly with us – no doubt because we were clean – that the tumult during the night which had made us so wary was caused by a scuffle between smugglers and customs men, and that the area had not been occupied by the Germans, but that they sometimes came there to make requisitions.

Even the best of friends have to part; so we entered the hospitable territory of Luxembourg and, after a quarter of an hour's walking came to Esch-sur-Alzette, the end of our escape route. While we were having lunch our orderlies arrived with our things. We at once put on our uniforms and left for the station. I asked the ticket clerk for two first-class and two second-class tickets for Brussels, at the same time putting the money in front of the little opening. The employee gave me the tickets and, to my great amazement, gave me back the money. 'When one is travelling for such a noble purpose', he told me, 'one does not need to pay for one's seat'; and, despite my insistence, he would not accept anything. This generous act, in such striking contrast to the coarse greed which we had encountered on the other side of the frontier, moved us profoundly, and with all our hearts we gave this noble man our warmest thanks.

On the evening of the 7th we were in Brussels, where we found paradise. Think of it! For unfortunates who for three months had lived like veritable savages, to sleep in a bed, a good bed, to have a bath every day, to put on clean clothes, to sit at a well-provided table and eat well-cooked food! Can you ask for anything more, above all when you are conscious of having done your duty properly? Brussels was full of life and gaiety. The winter season was in full swing. All the theatres were open, and we took advantage of this with inexpressible pleasure. This fine town had also become the refuge of a crowd of Parisians who had emigrated before the investment. Amongst this lot were a rather large element of *demi-mondaines* from the Quartier de l'Europe. They were our fellow countrywomen and it was difficult for us to disown them, not to say pleasurable not to do so. In short, here were the delights of Capua,[2] but enjoyed for a such a brief time! [3]

On the 10th we thought of leaving the Belgian capital and returning to our dear but unhappy country. To tell the truth, and not to pass ourselves off as paragons of patriotism, we had not a sou left. So we took a morning train, which in a few hours brought us to Lille where we had learned that an army was being formed to operate in the north of France.

Such was our escape, which as has been seen was free of serious misadventures but which in the course of its execution had seemed to me at moments to present terrible dangers. In any case, from the pride that I felt in having undertaken it and the flattering reception which I received in Lille from my new commanders and comrades, I well understood that I had not been mistaken and that I had been right to consider it as a proper action. Later on, however, not everybody took this view and, if many of those who had to judge praised me, others blamed me for it. A Minister of War to whom one of my boyhood friends, an influential deputy, recommended me in order to hasten my nomination to lead a battalion, even made this rather typical response; 'If it were not for respect for you, instead of giving your protégé promotion I would inflict exemplary punishment on him for having, at Metz at least, defied all the rules of discipline, against the orders of his commanding general.' My good friend, who had thought to advance my interests strongly in making the merit of my escape known in high places, kept very quiet. When he did confide this ministerial point of view to me I was at first somewhat troubled by it. But, after reflection, I continued to consider my action as meritorious, for my conscience told me clearly that I had deceived no one; and that the fact of having procured a willing and experienced captain for a company in a provincial army largely compensated for the so-called disobedience of which I was guilty towards a leader called Bazaine. So I thought then, so I still think now, twenty-six years after these events, and so shall I think always.[4]

PART TWO

THE ARMY OF THE NORTH

CHAPTER I

TO THE SOMME AND BACK

10 November–4 December 1870

'This was the beginning of my second campaign.'

Lille – My new company in the 75th Line Regiment – Generous commissariat! – Examples of new officers – Major Tramond – 26 November, starting on campaign – Bray-sur-Somme – Retreat: Bapaume – Cambrai – Douai

It was with real pleasure that I found myself back in the agreeable town of Lille where I had been garrisoned three years previously. It was full of unwonted bustle occasioned by the extraordinary agglomeration of troops and service units intended to form the future Army of the North, by the movement of officials and travellers of every sort which its standing as capital of the northern region and virtual seat of an independent government drew to it, and by the boost given to its population by the numerous refugees from Paris.[1] The life of this mass of humanity spilled out into the streets, and the cafés were always full of people discussing the situation, bearing news, commenting on it, and passing from great confidence to black despair. Despite the approach of the enemy, one of whose armies was heading from Metz towards the north, a very carefree attitude reigned among the inhabitants, who seemed to me just as inclined to enjoy themselves as in the past. Thus it was that, under the pretext of raising funds for the wounded, very well-attended concerts were given in the theatres, where the ladies of Lille once more found a way of vying to out-dress one another. After several days I found myself in the same state of mind as if my sojourn in 1867 had been extended until this moment. The war did not seem to preoccupy unduly the people I mixed with, and I myself had reached the point of not thinking about it any more, giving myself over to the pleasure of living in this pleasant town in which I had resumed all, quite all indeed, of my habits of 1867.

My first concern on arrival had been to present myself at the garrison offices, whence I had been referred to those of the staff of General Bourbaki, who was the commanding general.[2] There I found a colonel of the general staff, a friend of my brother-in-law, who offered to give me any post I would like. But what did I want? I was already well content with having been promoted captain at Metz. I therefore took the command of a company, the 5th, in a battalion formed by the depot of the 75th Line Regiment. I had no trouble in having my friend Fernandez appointed as a second lieutenant of this same company. Then, rather at random, I picked my cadre of NCOs from among a crowd of those available, young for the most part and nearly all of them having escaped from Metz or Sedan. In this way I formed an exceptional cadre of men, very well motivated and already having experience of war. A lieutenant was assigned to me who had qualified as an officer a short while previously and had jumped the rank of second lieutenant within a few days. He was an old soldier type whom I did not like much from the very first, but before reaching a firm judgement, and rising above my dislike, I waited to see him at work. Alas, this bad initial impression would only increase progressively as I lost my illusions about the excessive deficiencies of this wretched officer.

I had arrived at Lille on 10 November; on the 13th I was given an appointment; on the 14th I received notice to present myself at the commissariat, as did Fernandez also. We both arrived there with no idea at all of the reason for our summons. Imagine our surprise, our delight, when we were each given an order for 750 francs; yes, 750 francs, to be drawn on the treasury. For people who no longer had a sou and who suddenly found themselves thrown into a rather expensive existence, it was a fortune! It is unnecessary to add that these 1,500 francs were not spent by the two of us all by ourselves. However, we were obliged to make a few essential purchases: a sword first of all. As there were no more regulation swords available from army contractors, we treated ourselves to English swords with forged steel hilts of very elegant shape. The high command having given orders that all officers must be armed with a revolver, we each bought the smallest model Lefaucheux.[3] I put mine in my waistcoat pocket where it stayed in the warm for the whole duration of the campaign.

Lille was at that time the gathering place for a crowd of officers in search of positions. Some, and these were the majority, were escapees from Metz or Sedan. The others, nearly all newly promoted, came from the depots of the region. The continual formation of battalions and batteries destined to compose the Army of the North had necessitated very many appointments, followed immediately by hasty promotions. Thus many young second lieutenants scarcely a year or two out of Saint-Cyr already found themselves captains, just as long-serving NCOs retained at their depots during the first phase of the war became lieutenants and even captains. I therefore entered on a scene where ambition reigned as absolute mistress, inflamed and encouraged every day by new promotions. I, who was amply satisfied to have received my third braid at Metz, began to regard it as no longer having the same value when I saw it distributed with such ease to officers who had not been put to the test like me. Yet it seemed to me that I was a real captain whereas all these young men were merely make-believe captains. Especially conspicuous among these were those who, having been employed as NCOs in a variety of secondary services little regarded by combat soldiers – recruiting sergeants, prison sergeants, etc. – had never in their lives dared even think of getting their epaulettes and who, seeing themselves adorned with two or three braids, took it as perfectly normal and flaunted them with language fit to make you blush.

A very young captain whom I met often at the Café Jean, our main meeting-place after the day's work, held forth in a particularly bumptious manner, claiming that he had been the victim of an injustice. Having left Saint-Cyr in 1869 and been made captain in 1870, he was demanding something else again; I don't remember exactly what. The best of it was that, having been taken prisoner at Sedan as a second lieutenant and having signed an undertaking not to bear arms against Germany for the duration of the war, he had argued like the very devil on his return to Lille against accepting a post in a combat unit, pleading as a pretext the oath which kept him on the shelf. But, as he was anxious above all to profit from the current rush of promotions, he got himself a job in the garrison offices where the rank of lieutenant, then captain, had come to him in the space of two months. He retained this post during the whole campaign, combining with remarkable craftiness respect for his undertaking to the Germans with looking after his own interests. Such was the state of disorder in command that such enormities could be carried off in broad daylight without anyone thinking of bringing these self-glorifying rascals down to earth.

Another captain, also very young and fresh from Saint-Cyr, seeing that he had not been decorated, profited from some absence which he took – I don't know in exactly what circumstances nor for what reason – to return with a red ribbon in his buttonhole; just the ribbon, for Crosses could no longer be found on the market. If someone had thought to establish a few cartridge factories, they had completely forgotten to set up a factory for Crosses, which, however, would have been no superfluity in view of the infinite number of these much coveted trinkets that were given out at this epoch. 'Hello, so such and such has been decorated?' someone would say. 'Yes,' replies another with the greatest indifference. 'Apparently it was by the governor of such and such a fortified town where he has just served for a while.' Thus the matter ended; no one spoke of it further, and it was accepted by everybody that the fellow in question had actually been decorated. But it came about that after the Commune, when everything returned to normal, no official confirmation arrived from the chancellery for our captain at the due time. Two, three terms passed without bringing anything for him. The colonel, puzzled but unable even to guess at such a bold pretence, called on him to produce his title; and as naturally he had none, the fine Cross which swung so elegantly on his tunic was put back in its case and that was the end of the matter. Meanwhile, his high rank relative to his age, combined with the prestige of the Cross, had procured him what he believed was a very advantageous marriage. But although the term 'immanent justice' had not been invented at that time, once the marriage was concluded it turned out that the young lady did not have a sou. In fact this was almost at the same time that the young bridegroom was reverted to lieutenant by the Commission for Revision of Ranks,[4] and obliged to make away with his honorary ornament. So the two newly weds had nothing with which to reproach each other.

It was not until 16 November that I took command of the men who were to make up my company. For the most part they were conscripts from the class of 1870, belonging to the departments of the extreme north; pale young men of placid and resigned appearance, rather tall and quite well built, but of sluggish disposition. To this element, which seemed to me unlikely to show much steadiness, was added a small group of ten or twelve already mature men, some even middle-aged, with a determined air and very well motivated. These were volunteers who had signed up for the duration of the war. These men formed a solid core in my company which was an enormous help to me. Their absolute devotion and their strength in every trial were a most salutary example to all the young men around them. One of them was forty-five years old and the father of a family. He had left everything behind – his job as a coach-driver, his wife and children – to march against the enemy. His conduct throughout the whole campaign was nothing but a long series of acts of courage and selflessness. I managed with great difficulty to get him decorated with the military medal, for the Army of the North was very stingy with decorations. Plenty of promotions were given because it was necessary to replace the dead, but nothing more. Besides, it was of small importance, seeing that the big chiefs, Faidherbe, Farre[5] and others, came out of it as generals of division and Grand Officers of the Legion of Honour. This brave man was delighted to return to his hearth with this proof of his outstanding conduct. He was very grateful to me for it, but less so for this than for having authorised him almost from the beginning to get rid of his knapsack, which irked him horribly.

Thanks to the activity of my NCOs, the company was quickly on a proper footing; the men clothed, armed and equipped, the weapons in good condition. By the following evening we could already put them at carry arms and were teaching them the first principles of handling a gun: mainly loading. Every day, morning and evening, we went to do several hours drill around the citadel. At about five o'clock in the evening the officers, having finished their task, gathered in the cafés or restaurants in the centre of town. The evenings passed as if we were still in times of peace, whether in gaming or in café singing. Lille scarcely had the appearance of suspecting that the enemy was fast approaching from the Somme; though it was true that they still had some distance to go to reach the city.[6]

On about the 20th we learned that the German advance-guard had entered Tergnier and had taken Ham. The enemy's objective appeared to be Amiens. All the battalions formed in the depots of the various garrisons of the north were concentrated around the town and directed to the Somme, towards Amiens and Corbie. A battalion which, like mine but before it, had been formed by the depot of the 75th Line Regiment and which included two of my comrades of the 6th who had escaped from Metz, left Lille at this time to take part in the defence of Amiens. We were amazed that we too were not designated for this same objective. As always happens in troubled times, a thousand different rumours were flying concerning our destination. Some said that we would be setting out before long, but in another direction; others asserted that we would be following the first battalion the next day; and then there were those who claimed that we would make up part of the garrison of Lille which, as the most important town of the north, would without fail be besieged by the enemy. This last hypothesis could not but cause me bitter reflections. Of sieges I had had quite enough; I had just got out of one. Merely the thought of seeing myself once more caught in a trap, as at Metz, made me shudder. Had I been certain that this would be the case I would have left immediately for the Army of the Loire, the existence of which was known to us through its success at Coulmiers.[7] Nothing would have been easier for me in these times of turmoil and disorder than to conceal my having joined the 75th and to announce myself as having arrived directly from Metz. However, before attempting such a stroke I thought it best to await events.

Meanwhile we were living our rather pleasant garrison life quite peacefully when we were profoundly shaken from our tranquillity by the arrival of a veritable hurricane in the person of our major. His name was Tramond.[8] He was a big, handsome man of military posture, almost theatrical, with a fine bearing and expressive features, sharply spoken and abrupt; he looked as if he had a quick temper. Nevertheless, he knew his job admirably and let us know it straight away. He had been an adjutant at Metz, from which he too had escaped. What astonished me most in him was his very sincere hatred of the enemy; a hatred which indeed he showed at every turn and which caused his face to go purple. My goodness! Had I been able by some means to have annihilated several hundred thousand Germans I would have done it with the greatest satisfaction, and would have felt no remorse for it; but for me there was a great gulf between that and hating them. On the contrary, as a soldier I had if anything fellow feeling for them because I had always found them to be plucky and upright opponents. Be that as it may, he urged on with the utmost fervour the instruction of the men as to their role on the battlefield, skirmishing drill and duties on campaign. He demanded with might and main, though without success, that we should begin target shooting. He often called us together and spoke to us about our duties as leaders of troops and so on. When I knew him a little better I saw that beneath his somewhat brusque exterior he was the finest man you could have met; a good leader, a trusty friend, scrupulous, obliging to a degree. Very brave in action, although very prudent and sparing of his troops, he was amazingly vigilant and far-sighted in all the incidents of life on campaign. Always the first to be up, he never thought to rest until he had assured himself that his troops were provided with everything necessary to them: food, ammunition, and a place to lay their heads. With such a leader mishaps were not to be feared, and we never knew them. Moreover, as he had a great deal of tact he was quickly on the best of terms with the big chiefs, which allowed us always to be in the know about the wherefores of operations, the execution of which thus interested us doubly.

On the 26th we went to bed rather late as usual when, towards one o'clock in the morning, I was awoken with a start by a violent hammering on my door. It was my quartermaster-sergeant who had come to inform me that the battalion had to entrain at the station at 3 o'clock that very night, destination unknown. I was ready in a few minutes. My packing did not take long, seeing that I had almost nothing to take. My orderly, however, put a few things in a little trunk which was placed in the battalion's baggage wagon. Everything was complete confusion at the barracks. The company had already gone down into the courtyard of the citadel and, through the good offices of the sergeant-major, the issue of campaign rations and cartridges had begun. These operations were carried out with some difficulty by the light of a few candle ends carried by the men. Finally, at two o'clock, everything being ready, the battalion was put in motion for the station. A train was there, all ready to receive us. We piled the men into it as best we could, for at that period entrainment did not form part of the exercises normally carried out by the troops, as they do now, and at 3 o'clock exactly the locomotive's whistle announced our departure for the unknown. This was the beginning of my second campaign.

The officers of the battalion, spread out in the compartments of a first-class carriage, were much puzzled by this sudden departure. They had a lively debate about it and commented on this way of doing things in terms very critical of the high command. As I had no information about the reasons for our departure, but which I could not help thinking must be weighty, all these speeches were idle words in my view and, instead of wasting my time paying attention to what did not concern me, I settled myself to resume my interrupted sleep as best I could.

It was 6 o'clock in the morning when our train stopped at the termination of its journey. Dawn was breaking and we were at Albert, a station on the line from Arras to Amiens. The men, numbed by the journey, dulled by lack of sleep, slumped down from the train with a great clanking noise produced by their weapons and camping utensils not strapped tightly enough onto their packs. We got them out of the station and after several minutes the battalion was formed in a body, the companies in line one behind the other at six paces. The battalion, like all those composing the Army of the North, consisted of only five companies. Each company, with a strength of 200 rifles, was commanded by a team comprising a captain, a lieutenant and a second lieutenant as officers and a sergeant-major, a quartermaster, four sergeants and eight corporals as NCOs. The staff of the battalion was formed by the major, a doctor and the paymaster. It had been found unnecessary to attach an adjutant to the major, and rightly, for that job serves no purpose at all on campaign. At Metz where I had filled the post, I could vouch that, just as I saw in the north, the absence of this rather superfluous cog did no harm to the good management of the battalion. At the reorganisation of the army it was judged opportune – and I am still seeking the motive without being able to find it – to re-establish this post, and it was a great mistake. Its sole reason for existence was for instructing the battalion officers. As this instruction was remitted to the care of company commanders in 1875, the justification no longer holds. It would therefore have been much better, after the experiment in the battalions of the Army of the North, to have suppressed them completely. At the present time, in 1897, the saving to the infantry would be about 600 officers and the same number of horses (the equivalent of a regiment of cavalry on a war footing).[9]

An inspection of the men's kit and clothing was carried out by the officers and, once everything was snugly strapped up, the battalion was put on the road. We were followed by another battalion, but of the *Garde Mobile*,[10] assigned to operate conjointly with ours under the command, quite naturally, of Tramond, who was in ecstasy at thus finding himself at the head of 2,000 men. Major Mathis, an excellent man but one who, fresh from his factory, had not the least idea of how a battalion of 1,000 men might be led in war, was delighted to find in his regular army colleague not only a counsellor, but, above all, someone to tell him what to do. Tramond, mounted on a big brown bay horse, was not far from believing himself a little commanding general.

We passed through the suburbs of the little town of Albert. The routes out of town and the railway bridges were guarded by National Guardsmen,[11] who in fact had no uniform except a kepi, belt and gun; but what a gun! Old percussion weapons, not all of which had even been rifled! The men whom I could observe closely, however, appeared convinced of the importance of their role, which they took very seriously. I should have liked to see their reaction if a salvo of shells had suddenly fallen around their post!

After about two hours of a rather slow march we arrived at Bray, a pretty village on the right bank of the Somme. There the two battalions were billeted. While we were busy settling the men in with the inhabitants, the major made a reconnaissance of the place. It was then that the officers' field-mess was constituted for the first time. The first four companies were grouped in twos. My company, the 5th, finding itself alone, the major, the doctor and the paymaster joined me, and so we formed a mess of six table companions. To say that this combination pleased me very much at the outset would be completely untrue. I little relished the prospect of continually rubbing shoulders with my immediate superior, but I could not do otherwise and I resigned myself to it philosophically. I was far from imagining that during the myriad occasions of daily contact I would find the beginning of two precious friendships which have never diminished since. I have spoken about the character of Major Tramond. Medical Officer Michel,[12] who had also come from Metz where he had served in a Guards Regiment, beneath the guise of a rather quarrelsome fellow was a charming man, full of spirit, the most agreeable of companions when he liked you. From the beginning our very different natures meshed and after that we felt drawn towards each other. He was very resourceful. Thus the field-mess was quickly set up and always operated just as one would wish under his masterful eye. As for the third additional messmate, the paymaster, he was a decent boy but a complete nonentity and almost totally lacking in education. That aside, he was a good and obliging fellow.

During the afternoon information reached the major which made him fear a threat coming from up the valley of the Somme. He ordered a reconnaissance which advanced as far as the village of Cappy, also on the river, but which could report only the most complete quiet. In the evening we returned to Bray where we dined joyfully, like people delighted to lead this good life in the open air which kept up our gay and jovial mood.

The morning of the 27th passed very peacefully, but in the afternoon we heard a muffled and distant cannonade coming from the south. It was the battle of Amiens, one of the major episodes of which took place at Villers-Bretonneux,[13] about fifteen kilometres from Bray as the crow flies. Tramond was seething at not being able to march towards the cannon, but he had strict orders to guard the passage of the Somme between Corbie and Péronne very closely with his two battalions. Joining him on the high ground, we listened without seeing anything, straining every fibre of our being towards this sound which seemed stationary.[14] But we could not make even a light reconnaissance to inform ourselves about the fighting on the far bank because the bridge over the Somme had been destroyed several days ago.

A rather weak party of enemy cavalry having come up close to the opposite bank of the river, Tramond, able to stand it no longer, forded the Somme at the head of a company, the men of which were soaked to the armpits, and gave chase. A sword and a carbine were all they brought back from this extremely soggy expedition, and without doubt a few bad colds besides.

Next day, the 28th, a dispatch arrived during the course of the morning recalling our column to the fortified towns of the north with all possible speed. The two battalions were assembled without delay and directed by the road leading most directly northward. The battalion of *Mobiles* marched at the head, then came ours. My company formed the rearguard. On the major's orders I had been obliged, rather against my will, to leave 50 men in Bray under the orders of Fernandez – I no longer recall for what reason. After several kilometres my company found itself far in the rear, slowed in its march by too frequent encounters with a crowd of stragglers from the *Mobiles* who refused to go further despite my threats and scoldings. That caused me no anxiety, for the country was very open and there was no sign of the presence of the enemy as far as the eye could see. Besides, in delaying I might the sooner have the chance to pick up my section left at Bray. Seeing nothing coming, I continued on my way entirely out of sight of the column, very anxious about my detachment and about Fernandez, leaving behind me many groups of *Mobiles* who had settled themselves in the roadside ditches. Two or three kilometres from our destination for the day, I was very much perplexed by the appearance on my left of a large black column of infantry which at a very rapid pace was following a road converging towards the same point as ours. I thought at first that these were enemy troops seeking to cut off our retreat, and as the distance between us progressively diminished I expected at every moment to see some of them halt and open fire on us.

I was very worried, and the prospect of sustaining such an unequal struggle with my green troops who had never fired a shot hardly cheered me. I tried to put the best face on it I could, but I could see well enough all the anxious faces automatically turning to the left, all eyes fixed on the great black serpent moving over there at about 1,000 or 1,200 metres. Finally, when the distance between us had come down to a few hundred metres, we were able to see that they were a battalion of our light infantry.[15] There was a general sigh of satisfaction and relief. The light infantry had not had the same apprehension as us, for they had very quickly been able to distinguish our red trousers and kepis.

Towards four o'clock in the afternoon we arrived at our resting-place. We had done about twenty kilometres and we were in the little town of Bapaume, to which the old, half-demolished fortifications gave a mildly reassuring air of strength. About an hour later I saw Fernandez arrive with all his men. He had had a brush with a few German cavalry who had approached through Cappy and had delayed his march from its outset.

Here we learned about the failure of our army in front of Amiens. Our first battalion, or at least the battalion formed before ours by the regimental depot of the 75th, had been seriously engaged at Villers-Bretonneux. Without the strict orders which had been given to Major Tramond to remain at Bray, we would certainly have marched towards the sound of the nearest cannon the day before, and we would have arrived just at the moment of the battle when our men, pressed by superior force, were obliged to retreat. Chance would thus have allowed our battalion to rescue its twin, and perhaps to have re-established matters by its intervention on the enemy's extreme flank.

On the 29th we left Bapaume and moved to Cambrai, where we remained for two days. The weather was very mild and our young troops were in very good shape both physically and in morale. The hurried retreat and the bad example set by the *Mobiles* had left no mark on their spirits, and we soon built up their confidence in themselves, which we had been trying above all to inspire in them. The army had been brought back behind the line of fortified towns, there to be reorganised, for the defeat had degenerated into a rout. Fortunately the enemy, though well provided with cavalry, had not pursued on the right bank of the Somme. He had entered Amiens and halted there.

On 2 December we were ordered to fall back on Lille. The reason for this retreat was unknown to us. It was said, however, that in view of the unsteadiness of the troops in open country, the idea of active operations in the field had been abandoned, and that we were going to form an army corps at Lille with the intention of defending the approaches to the capital of Flanders. It was also said that now that General Bourbaki had yielded command to a newcomer, General Faidherbe,[16] the latter wanted to reunite all his troops to constitute a real army corps, composed of several divisions, with which he would resume the campaign as soon as his organisation was fully complete. I preferred to believe the second version to the first, given my obvious dislike of fortifications, particularly since the possibility of my getting away elsewhere was no longer open to me. We arrived at Douai in the afternoon, but there everything was changed. News had been received that a great victory had been won outside the walls of Paris by its army, which had broken the blockade and inflicted a serious defeat on the enemy. Now finally we were halted at Douai, where we remained throughout the 3rd and 4th. But it appeared that the great victory of the Parisians had shrunk to quite simply a repulse,[17] and the dispositions of our commanding general were accordingly modified.

CHAPTER II

THE CAPTURE AND DEFENCE OF HAM

5–18 December 1870

'We were very proud of our success. . .'

5 December – Forward! – First picket guard – Capture of Ham, evening of 9 December – At Doctor Surmay's – Ambush on the Tergnier road – A German column attempts to retake Ham, 12 December – En route for Amiens – Billancourt – Vauvillers – Reconnaissance of Villers-Bretonneux – Corbie

On the 5th we started out early in biting cold which had set in two or three days previously. After a very tiring march of 30 kilometres on roads hardened by the frost, we halted at Marcoing, south of Cambrai. There I learned from the major that a column of several battalions with artillery would be concentrated at Fins the next day in order to launch an offensive on the flank of the enemy advancing on Rouen.[1]

Consequently on the 6th we marched for the whole day in the snow and at nightfall we arrived at Nurlu, having made only twenty kilometres, but on side roads and with numerous halts. On the 7th we continued southwards and in the evening found ourselves at Roupy, midway between Saint-Quentin and Ham, which we knew to be occupied by the enemy.

We had completed a very difficult march of about 27 kilometres on bad roads covered in snow. These three days of hard marching, accomplished in rather punishing conditions, had been very cheerfully borne by our young soldiers, encouraged indeed by the example of their NCOs and of some volunteers interspersed in their ranks. At Roupy, the proximity of the enemy (Ham is ten kilometres away) necessitated the employment of a picket guard. My company was designated for this duty. It was almost night when I established my posts. Fortunately the sky was clear and the ground was all white with snow, which greatly eased my task. I placed my main post about 1,500 metres from Roupy on the road from Ham, and a cordon of double sentries roughly 500 metres further out, the two wings anchored on the two roads from Séraucourt-le-Grand and Péronne. The cold that night was intense. Despite the wear and tear of these three days, my soldier boys bore themselves very well in their new duties, the importance of which I had magnified to them. I stayed on my feet all night, on the prowl along my line of sentries to keep them wide awake. The view was very extensive, and I asked each man for a report of what he could see in the distance. In this way I received some rather original replies. Many were those who were convinced of having seen the enemy, who was sleeping quite peacefully in the citadel of Ham eight kilometres away unaware that we were so close.

On the 8th we left Roupy at about 8 o'clock in the morning, heading for Saint-Quentin. As soon as my sentinels and guard posts were pulled back and my company reassembled, I congratulated my men on the manner in which they had fulfilled their mission, and assured them that it was thanks to their vigilance and steadfastness that the battalion billeted at Roupy had been able to sleep peacefully. Saint-Quentin was said to be occupied by the enemy, and I took advantage of the men's good spirits to tell them that in a short time we might perhaps encounter the Germans, but that this caused me little anxiety, being very certain after having seen them at work for a week that they would conduct themselves like brave men. This prospect did not seem to disturb them unduly, and they set off down the road at a very resolute pace.

We reached Saint-Quentin towards 10 o'clock after having put in a short march of nine kilometres. Instead of Germans, we were greeted by hundreds of workers who hailed us as liberators. The whole battalion was billeted in a spacious factory at the lower end of town. My men, once they had eaten their meal and savoured its effects a little, stretched out on the floor, laying their heads on their knapsacks by way of a pillow, and were not long in finding wholesome amends for the weariness of four days of marching and a night spent in the snow under the stars.

It was at Saint-Quentin that I learned the composition of the column of which we formed a part, and which was, as it were, the advance-guard of Twenty-second Army Corps. It comprised three line battalions furnished by the 65th, 75th, and the 91st, plus the 17th Battalion of Light Infantry in addition to a battery of six 4-pounder guns. It was to proceed to the east to threaten the communications of the German army which was marching on

Rouen. Among these battalions I found several of my comrades of the 6th who like me had escaped from Metz: Oudard, Vinciguerra,[2] Martin, and others, whom it gave me great pleasure to see again. This column was commanded by Colonel de Gislain,[3] who had the reputation of being a very energetic officer who really knew his business. We were all full of confidence and desirous of redeeming our failings at Metz by a great show of vigour and willing spirits. We passed the day at Saint-Quentin in pleasantly renewing acquaintances and in gossip in which the hope of forthcoming success was the major topic.

On the next day, the 9th, we were all gathered at the same table eating lunch at a hotel next to the main square, when a man entered the dining-room briskly and asked to speak to the officer in command of the troops, which was Major Tramond. He told him in a perfectly confident tone that the town of Ham, eighteen kilometres from Saint-Quentin, was occupied by two weak German companies and that nobody suspected that we were in the vicinity. He had left Ham the same morning in his carriage, and he vouched that the Germans, having no misgivings, were virtually unguarded.[4] He offered the major many references in Saint-Quentin; he was a commercial traveller known in the best houses in town. Tramond, who was very enterprising by nature, received this news with enthusiasm and immediately took the travelling salesman to the colonel.[5]

At about midday the battalion was set on the road. The snow was thick; our feet sank in it up to the ankle. The men had no suspicion of what we were going to demand of them in a few hours. Believing that it was a change of billets, they marched along in a carefree way. The good rest that they had enjoyed for twenty-four hours at Saint-Quentin had put them in fine humour; they would be easy to lead forward when the moment came. The march was slow. Once night had fallen, the battalion was halted in an open field and silence was ordered. Then we headed towards the town. Suddenly, to our right, the quiet of the night was broken by a sharp volley of rifle fire, followed by a muffled din. It was the toll house, situated at the entrance to town and guarded by German troops, which had just been taken. We immediately made our way into the streets, which fortunately were lit by gas. My company, marching on the left wing, passed along a boulevard, searching the adjacent streets as we went. A few shots were fired by isolated men, but the main work was done in the houses, where we picked up several prisoners.

In an alley running perpendicular to the boulevard I heard an infernal hullabaloo. I entered a small house and found two of my soldiers in a state of unaccountable fury, getting ready to bayonet a hapless German who had taken refuge under a bed. The people living in the house were yelling at the top of their voices to prevent this abominable slaughter; the soldiers were shouting louder still. The German was saying nothing. With great difficulty I was able to stop these frenzied fellows, who did not even deign to listen to me. Finally, after having made them put their (happily unbloodied) bayonets back in their scabbards, I laboriously summoned the four or five words of German that remained to me after having had lessons for five years at college. Despite having won prizes every year, all I could manage after long efforts was to articulate the following phrase in a deplorable accent: '*Auf! Kein Schade wird ihnen gemacht werden* (Stand up! No harm will come to you).' Without needing further entreaty, a big man with a blond beard, distress written all over his face, emerged from under the bed with effort and, once on his feet, stood to attention. His clothes were all torn in shreds by the bayonet points which, by good luck, had not touched the skin. In truth, to penetrate the vital organs they would have had to pass through a thick protective layer of lard. I gave orders for him to be led to the town hall and my two men, with that characteristic French ability to pass almost instantly from one extreme to the other, laid a friendly hold on him, one on each side. Then, arm in arm like old comrades, they led him off . . . to a bar, where they bought him a drink.

About one hundred prisoners had been taken in the town. The remainder of the garrison, about 150 men, had taken refuge in the château, an old fortress with round towers of considerable thickness and surrounded by broad and deep moats which it was impossible to seize by a surprise attack.[6] From the battlements and loopholes the defenders were shooting for all they were worth into the streets, which could be raked by their fire and which were marked out for them by the gas lamps which were still alight.

Once the action was over, I reassembled my company in one of these streets where we were severely troubled by the firing from the château, which might have become extremely dangerous due to an unfortunately placed gas lamp burning a few feet in front of us. One of my men, as agile as a monkey, quickly climbed up to the lamp, which had had all its glass panes smashed by bullets. But the key had been bent and despite his efforts he could not manage to turn it off. After having served as a target for enemy riflemen for several seconds, he came down more quickly than he had climbed up and came to report his misadventure to me. Straight away another man, swiftly putting his pack on the ground, mounted the lamp-post on the run, hoisted himself up to the lamp and, instead of renewing his predecessor's attempts, put out the light like a common candle using his kepi as a snuffer.

Meanwhile the major had sent an order to billet the troops where we were. Amid the shadows I made out a large villa separated from the road by a rather wide flower bed and bordered by railings, with the gate wide open. I entered and rang at the door of the house. A servant came to open it and eyed me with a mistrustful stare. I asked to speak to the master of the house. He was absent. He was Doctor Surmay, the doctor in charge of the hospital, where he was at that moment in order to care for the wounded. I was rather embarrassed when, drawn by this conference, there appeared in the hall a dark young woman with a comely face and a decided air, in elegant indoor attire. She asked what I wanted.

'A resting-place, madame.'

'The house is at your disposal.'

'But there are many of us.'

'I have several guest rooms. If they are not sufficient, we will double up the beds. It will be a case of making do in wartime.'

'But there are about two hundred of us.'

'Two hundred! Where do you expect me to lodge such a troop?' Then, after a moment's reflection: 'Come in all the same. We shall see. Now then, you must first give me a strong NCO and ten men for a working-party. These people will need to obey me in everything. I am going to make ready the ground floor of the house. The billiard room and my husband's office will be emptied; each room will easily hold 50 men. The rest will find room in the coach house, from which the carriages will be removed. Bring your men into the garden. Make sure that they spare my lawns and that no one enters the house before everything is ready. You and your officers will find your rooms on the first floor.'

After scarcely an hour everybody was settled in, and in the carefully rinsed-out wash-tub simmered a fine onion stew which the men ate piping hot before going to lie down with a roof over their heads on a bed of straw thickly strewn over the floor.

'Above all, no one must smoke in the house.'

This was the last order of our generalissimo in petticoats. I immediately ordered the NCOs to take care that it was observed. And during the four days that we invaded her house in this way this valiant lady, this fine Frenchwoman, never for a single instant lost her good humour, her prudence or her patience, and was always full of delicate attentions to improve the comfort of the soldiers, but checked the slightest transgression promptly and with a firm hand.

After everyone was settled in I went to the town hall to learn the news. I was a little anxious, not knowing the reason for some cannon shots we had heard during the evening. Most of the leaders of the expedition were gathered there. I learned there that the Germans in the château had refused to come to any agreement when called upon to surrender. They had been given to understand under flag of truce that they were surrounded by the powerful Army of the North, and as proof several cannon-balls were fired into the door of the fort. Matters proceeded no further while we awaited daylight and events.

The baggage of captured German officers was searched in the hope of finding information about the enemy position in the region. The harvest yielded little, but what was found in the cases was a heap of unusual odds and ends. That of the commanding officer, named Otto, contained ill-matched pieces of material, bits of lace, babies' garments, a child's silver-gilt goblet, a pair of candle-holders from a piano in poor-quality gilded bronze, embroidered handkerchiefs of various French makes, two ladies' trimmed and embroidered chemises, etc.

During the night the garrison surrendered after being summoned anew by my comrade Oudard of the 91st. No doubt by mistake, the bugler was killed while bearing the flag of truce. A protocol of capitulation was drawn up with strict formality and was signed by the two parties concerned. At six o'clock in the morning the château was handed over to us. In total we captured nine officers, 221 men,[7] several wagons, 20 horses and an abundance of provisions, including among other things heaps of sausage made with peas. It was very bad. In the rooms they had occupied the German soldiers had left a distinctive smell that could not be dispelled for several days: an odour of rancid tallow and damp leather mingled with a vague aroma of bad pomade.

We were very proud of our success, even though it had been achieved by a column of four battalions, of which indeed we were completely unaware, for up until the evening I had for my part believed that my battalion had operated alone. This success was not without results.[8]

On the 10th we learned that an enemy detachment coming from La Fère and ignorant of the events of the evening before was due to arrive at Ham during the morning. Tramond left early in the morning with three companies to oppose the enemy. Mid-way between Ham and Tergnier the road passed through a quite considerable wood. The undergrowth was dense; the snow heaped on the branches increased the opacity of the curtain formed by the edge of the wood. The place was made for an ambush. On each side of the road, in the wood and several metres from its boundary, the men lay down amid the dead leaves. Their weapons were not loaded, but bayonets were fixed. At the agreed signal, when the enemy had entered this living corridor without challenge, the two human walls would rush together all of a sudden and crush the life out of him.

After about an hour of anxious waiting a little horse-drawn omnibus for interchanges on the Northern Railway approached at a funereal pace. Four officers were lolling in it peacefully, smoking their cigars as if they were taking a stroll in the Tiergarten.[9] The omnibus was followed by a company of about a hundred men, marching without much order. The soldiers, bowed under their knapsacks, moved at a heavy, straggling pace; nearly all wore their little round caps,[10] with their helmets hung from their equipment by the chin-strap, their rifles slung, big china-clay pipes in their mouths. Well to the rear came four 4-wheeled wagons, each drawn by two horses. Upon a shot being fired as a signal, before anyone could even take any kind of defensive position, the German column was surrounded, apprehended, jostled a little and placed in a situation where the slightest resistance was impossible. Tramond had leapt at the door of the carriage and forced the officers to hand over their swords. Thoroughly sheepish and dumbfounded, they opened their mouths as wide as ovens without being able to utter a single word. They were made to get out of the carriage. The men were disarmed, their weapons loaded onto wagons, and off we went to Ham!

In our little haul we had gathered four officers, 127 privates and four wagonloads of provisions and equipment, and this without firing a shot and without even a scratch.[11] To console the unfortunate officers for their misadventure, on arrival at Ham we invited them to lunch, after having given them back their swords. The next day all the prisoners were sent to the strongholds of the north under good escort.

Put on his mettle by this escapade which had succeeded beyond his expectations, Tramond, on rather vague information given him by a local person, set out on the morning of the 12th with four companies in some direction or other – I have forgotten where. He left me at Ham with my company which would temporarily form the entire garrison of the place. At about 10 o'clock my two officers and I were about to sit down to lunch at a hotel in town when from the dining-room windows we saw a very agitated crowd. Women were shouting, men were gesticulating, all arms were pointing in the same direction. I was about to go outside to find out the cause of this stir when several men entered the room and, all out of breath, told me: 'Captain, the Prussians are here. They are arriving in great numbers by the road from Nesle. Peasants who were working in the fields have seen them sure enough. They are going to enter the suburbs in a few minutes.'

How could the Prussians be so close to Ham, since the whole surrounding area was at that moment being patrolled by our columns? I besought my second lieutenant at all costs to go and find his section and to bring it up as quickly as possible on the Nesle road. My lieutenant would take up a reserve position among the houses at the edge of town to support the movement of the first section. I also sent a warning to the officer in charge of the château to have the drawbridge raised if the enemy appeared. Then I headed towards the threatened point, escorted by the men who had seen the Prussians and who told me that there were troops on foot and horseback, with cannon. The crowd followed, thinning out progressively as we approached the point where the road led out of town, to such good effect that after having passed beyond the last houses I found myself all alone.

Before me the road, bordered with trees and piles of stones, climbed with quite a perceptible slope straight ahead towards the summit of the hill which barred the horizon about half a kilometre away. On the slope of the hill running down towards the town were orchards planted with fruit trees. To the left of the road was a factory with its chimney under repair, surrounded by scaffolding. To the right, about two or three hundred kilometres away, was a line of trees marking the course of the canal; otherwise not a Prussian on the horizon. At this moment I was joined by my quartermaster-sergeant, fully armed, who announced that trustworthy people had sighted the enemy on the Ercheu road. I resolved at once to find out the situation for myself. To this end, marching along in the middle of the road accompanied by my sergeant, I headed towards the top of the hill from where there would be a view of what lay on the other side. We had reached a point about 150 metres from the top when all of a sudden the crest of the road was lined with a row of rounded helmets and a discharge of about twenty shots came right in our faces. I entertained no further doubts, at least as to part of what I wanted to know. With a bound we were on the shoulder of the road. Then, running from tree to tree, I made my retreat smartly under the protection of the sergeant who halted now and then and fired at the heads showing themselves above the sky-line.

On entering the suburbs I found my second lieutenant with his section; a hundred rifles. I apprised him of the enemy's position. He deployed his men in extended order on both sides of the road in the orchards, his right resting on the canal. The firing began, but the enemy showed no sign of advancing. I installed my second section in a large, easily defended house in such a manner as to be able to recall the skirmishers in the event that they should become too closely pressed.

Still bent on the idea of discovering the strength of the enemy, I thought of the scaffolding erected around the factory chimney; the ladders were right there. From up there I could see over the summit of the hill which sloped towards us. A body of infantry that I estimated at five or six hundred men was massed in the plain, covered by a fairly heavy line of skirmishers who lined the crest of the hill, of which my men held the lower slope. A fair number of horsemen were patrolling and appeared to want to move around our left. Finally, a cluster of artillery, a battery no doubt, was halted in march formation, probably on the Ercheu road. This discovery did not fail to cause me very acute anxiety. If the whole of this force were to launch a vigorous attack, what would become of us? Descending from my observation post, I requested a willing townsman to go and explain the situation at the town hall, so that express messengers could be sent out immediately on horseback or by carriage to find our columns operating in the vicinity. Then I urged my second lieutenant to increase the firing to mislead the enemy, and at the same time I sent my sergeant with ten men to my left to prevent the horsemen from seeing our situation, which we had every interest in concealing for as long as possible.

After an hour and a half or two hours I saw a battalion of marines[12] coming out of the town. I was saved. A naval captain was in command. I explained to him what was happening and entreated him to support me. He unfolded his map, oriented himself and began to draw up battle plans. He would send troops to port to outflank the enemy on his starboard, etc. While awaiting the execution of these grandiose plans, I begged him to reinforce my desperately weak line. Our conversation was fortunately interrupted by the arrival of Tramond at the head of the battalion. An understanding with the sailor was reached in short order. It was Tramond who did all the talking: 'Start by deploying two companies here, send one of them that way, post the rest over there, and everybody forward!' The enemy, disconcerted by this resolute forward movement, began to retreat and we pursued him for about seven kilometres as far as the village of Esmery (I believe).

In the evening we returned to Ham, delighted to have thwarted the enemy's intentions so handily. My little second lieutenant, who had behaved very intelligently, was recommended for lieutenant. He was promoted to that rank three weeks later. I nominated my sergeant, a very spirited young Parisian, for the military medal, which he got at the close of the campaign. From that day too dates the first submission of my name for the rank of major, a submission which was renewed after Bapaume, after Saint-Quentin, during the Commune itself, and which succeeded . . . in September 1879.

The consequences of these three little feats of arms were considerable for our morale. The officers could take note that the supposed infallibility of German officers in military skill was not after all as absolute as was made out. We had just surprised them twice in rapid succession while they were completely off their guard. We could vouch besides that their famous boldness in the attack was a little overrated, since with a thousand men of all arms they had allowed themselves to be held up for two hours by a small company of infantry. Lastly, their spirit of resistance was rather second-rate, seeing that the garrison of the château, though provided with food and ammunition and sheltered behind ramparts which were unassailable, at least with the feeble means at our disposal, had capitulated without putting up so much as a semblance of defence. Our confidence in ourselves, who for the most part had come from Metz or Sedan,[13] increased in proportion as our opponents in our eyes lost the superiority which we had accorded them. To the soldiers, these little fights in which the losses were insignificant gave a taste of warfare and a certain enthusiasm which veteran troops do not often have.

In concluding this tale I would like to cite a passage from the work of Colonel Wartensleben[14] relating to the day of 12 December:

> The events at Ham were known at Amiens on 10 December. The general commanding,[15] who was at once warned at Rouen by telegraph, immediately ordered General Groeben to march on Ham directly. It was possible furthermore that the detachment was still holding out in the château. Thus General Groeben had a battalion, a squadron of cavalry and four pieces of artillery under the orders of Captain von Lukowitz set off on the evening of the 10th. But on the 12th these troops, which were marching on Ham through Ercheu and Esmery, were sharply attacked in front and flank at Eppeville (about four kilometres west of Ham), while strong enemy detachments threatened to surround them. Captain Lukowitz then retreated on Roye under the protection of his rearguard and returned to Amiens on the 13th.

Dear comrade Lukowitz, I hope that you had the good luck to escape the dangers of the campaign of 1870 and are still of this world. It is my fervent desire that perhaps you even occupy a high military post in your country. If chance should bring this narrative under your eye, I guarantee you that it is completely genuine (besides, you know that better than anyone for the day of the 12th, when for two hours the two of us were commanding generals) and you could take stock of the fact that on the afternoon of 12 December, in the vicinity of Eppeville, you utterly lacked boldness and even the most elementary flair. For even if you had not attacked – though that was the goal of your mission – but had sought to discover your opponent's strength, you would have entered Ham straight away. With your numerical superiority you might have ventured cutting off the retreat of my company and at the same time you could have retaken the citadel before the arrival of the reinforcements which allowed us to inflict such an agreeable 'Grenoble escort'[16] on you.

On 14 December the battalion remained at Ham. We even thought for a moment that it would be detailed as the garrison of the little place, for in the morning we were ordered to quit our billets and we installed ourselves in the rooms of the citadel. Fortunately, the next day we left those horrible quarters and found ourselves once more on the highway in the fresh air and in open country. The weather had become much milder, and what a pleasure it was to breathe in the good air of the fields without having our view confined by the monotonous and oppressive outline of some rampart. We passed through Nesle and headed towards Roye where there was apparently a concentration of enemy troops. We were halted at Billancourt. My company and the staff of the battalion – my field-mess, in a word – were lodged in a very pretty château belonging to Madame de Becquencourt. This lady, though now advanced in years, had not fled before the German invasion like so many others. She received us with much kindness, putting her whole château at our disposal: the cellar, the kitchen, the store-room, etc. 'I should be delighted to invite you to dinner,' she told us, 'but I can offer you nothing to eat. I haven't seen a scrap of meat on my table for a fortnight. The area has been cleaned out by the requisitions of the Germans and yourselves alike, and not a single head of cattle is left for several leagues around.' We invited her to share our dinner, in which meat was not lacking. She ordered her cook to prepare our rations, and we had her eat an excellent dinner, for which she had furnished the wines, the utensils and the plates, and we the wherewithal to fill them. One makes do in wartime!

Not feeling entirely secure, I had placed two guard posts at the corners of the park facing Roye and I passed part of the night watching with them. But my precautions were needless, for nothing out of the ordinary happened either during the night or in the morning.

On the 15th we got on the road at about eight o'clock. We retraced our steps, passed through Chaulnes and arrived at Vauvillers towards two o'clock. While going through Chaulnes my attention was attracted by a statue representing a churchman. I went closer to see to what benefactor of humanity this monument had been erected. And what did I see inscribed on the plinth? Lhomond, yes Lhomond[17] the grammarian – *rosa*, the rose. I could not believe my eyes. What! This fellow whose indigestible old books had brutalised my youth, who had caused me so many torments, clouts to the head and punishments at school. This good man had his statue! Bronze and stone must cost nothing in this country! I wished heartily that fortune might bring a small act of war to this place, with just a little violence, and that the same fortune, taking advantage of the occasion, would send a good shell through the fellow's head and scatter the grammatical treasures it contained to the four winds.

We had been settled in Vauvillers for about an hour when a great tumult was heard towards the southern end of the village. The men came out of their billets with their rifles in their hands. We could see nothing in the street where we were; all seemed quiet. I headed in the direction of the noise, and there I learned that some enemy horsemen, surprised by our arrival in the village itself, had hidden themselves in an outhouse which had not been searched by our men. The Germans had lain low for some time, then, calculating that everyone must be out of the way or that the village had been evacuated, as they could no longer hear any stir, they had emerged from their hideaway and dashed towards the nearest exit from town at a gallop. A few shots were fired at them, but without hitting anyone. This was unfortunate indeed, for it meant that our game was given away. Had there been complicity by the locals? I do not believe so because, seeing that we were in strength, they would not have feared compromising themselves. However, with peasants, particularly those from Picardy, you can never tell.

During the war and afterwards I often heard the peasants of the invaded regions reproached in the most severe terms for having given the enemy a better welcome than they gave our troops: of having hidden their foodstuffs when our men arrived and of having got them out eagerly when the Germans appeared in our place. There is evidently much exaggeration on this subject. Certainly there could have been cases where this sort of thing happened, but this was very much the exception. For myself, who for two months moved about in countryside occupied successively by us and by the enemy, I can vouch that we were never badly received. Nevertheless, one must be forbearing towards these poor people, whose lot was most pitiable. In a war of invasion the inhabitants can choose between two extreme courses: either to arm themselves with anything that comes to hand and resist the invader, which leads inevitably to the destruction of all the centres of habitation, or to confront him with absolute passivity, and so to allow themselves to be pillaged of everything, which is not long in bringing famine and the worst miseries. Quite naturally it continually happens that neither of these courses is adopted because they are extreme, and human nature tends always and in everything towards accommodation. The result is that, alongside some spasmodic acts of resistance, which give rise to equally spasmodic reprisals, the majority of inhabitants try as best they can to carry on with their lives in the presence of the enemy. Should one judge them so very harshly? And should we expect that, after having given their sons to the army to defend the soil of the country step by step, they should expose themselves and their kin – women, old men, children – to having no roof for shelter and to dying of hunger? Then it would be well to admit that their best course is to act as they acted in 1870, as their forbears acted in 1814 and 1815,[18] and as all civilised peoples have acted in like circumstances.

Without doubt in the north at least, to speak only of what I saw, certain irregular troops like the National Guards and the *francs-tireurs*, badly commanded for the most part and unrestrained by any tie of discipline or military dignity, sometimes left the most disagreeable memories in the places they passed through, and those who came after them found everything completely stripped. The indignation of the inhabitants in the face of this conduct worthy of Bashi-bazouks,[19] and not of fellow countrymen, no doubt led them to complain in such terms as might make it seem that they preferred the presence among them of strongly disciplined German troops who took from them only what they strictly needed and who paid for it most of the time. But there is a wide difference between that and saying that the population of the North generally preferred to give lodging to the Germans than to the French, and I can bear witness in good conscience that such was not the way of thinking of all those that I encountered in my travels and whom I had cause only to praise.

To speak quite frankly, it has to be confessed that our soldiers have a temperament which is essentially, if not thieving, at least wasteful. And to prove it here is a deed that I witnessed. In the last days of the campaign I was on picket guard in the vicinity of Bapaume. I had established my principal post in an isolated farm abandoned by its owners. As it was very cold, my men had settled themselves in the main room on the ground floor. In the courtyard in several well-stocked piles was the winter's supply of firewood for the needs of the farm. I allowed my men to take the few logs and faggots necessary to keep the fire going in the fire-place during the coldest hours of the night.

The proximity of the enemy obliged me to pass the whole night out of doors with my guard posts and sentinels. When I returned to the farm in the morning I was dumbfounded. In order not to give themselves the trouble of walking ten paces into the courtyard and going to fetch the wood from the pile, my scamps had found it much more convenient to burn the wooden staircase which led up to the first floor and which was already destroyed up to a man's height. This act of vandalism sent me into a terrible rage. If I had had the authority to do so I would have called a court-martial and I would have shot one or two of these marauders. I was forced to content myself with giving them a tongue-lashing, for on campaign punishment does not exist since it is without sanction. And yet my soldiers, for the two months I had them in hand, were well disciplined. They were brave men who were waging war *pro aris et focis*,[20] since they were fighting for their native land. But there it was; instinct, abetted by laziness, was stronger than duty and the farmer's staircase fell victim to it. After such an example it is best to gloss over with a little indulgence the misdeeds of the National Guardsmen and the *francs-tireurs* who obeyed no rule and recognised no authority, since a far too naïve government had allowed them to elect their own leaders.

It must also be said in defence of the inhabitants that, in the face of the invading flood which threatened to engulf them, they were abandoned to their own moral resources for most of the time. The rich landowners, the lords of the manor, had almost all emigrated, either to Belgium or to those parts of France which were not threatened, leaving some caretaker with the trouble of disputing their property of every kind with the enemy. This was a great error, for the prestige of their nobility, of their fortune, of their position of influence in the region would have benefited all the people of the neighbourhood with the German commanders, who were naturally very respectful of these special titles. And, thanks to the intervention of the lords of the manor with the German military authorities, many vexations could have been spared the local communities, many disputes settled, many difficulties smoothed over: whereas the commanders, settling themselves in the empty châteaux, met no counterweight to the natural inclination of conquerors to abuses. The great landlords who abandoned their residences at the approach of the enemy were thus much to blame. They should have remembered that if wealth has its privileges it also has its obligations, which in certain circumstances become duties. Madame de Becquencourt, although very old and having nobody around her for support but a young girl and her governess, did not hesitate to remain on her estates. She told us that she had considered it as a sacred duty and that she had not had cause to repent it because, thanks to her daily relations with the German commanders lodged in her château, she had obtained many alleviations of the lot of the inhabitants of the community and saved some of them from the reprisals which an unfortunate act of impulse or of resistance to the demands of the enemy would have brought upon them.

On the 16th we left Vauvillers early in the morning. My company was at the very head of the advance-guard. I marched with twenty men, three or four hundred metres ahead of the main body of the company, with nothing in front of me. Having arrived at the crossroads with the road from Péronne to Amiens, I turned to the left and, after having passed through a little village – the name of which I have forgotten – I found myself in the middle of a wide plateau with a view stretching away without interruption. Behind me I heard the trot of several horses. I turned around and was immediately joined by an officer with a still youthful face and a heavily braided kepi, and he told me that he had come to observe our march for a little because there was every reason to believe that the village of Villers-Bretonneux, which we must pass through four or five kilometres ahead, was strongly occupied by the enemy. He put his horse at a walking pace and marched alongside me while watching very attentively to the front and flanks. I took advantage of the proximity of an officer of his entourage to ask who this person was. He replied that it was General Derroja,[21] who had escaped from Metz, where he had been colonel of the 15th Infantry, and that he was in command of the column. Then it was no longer de Gislain in charge? It seemed indeed that in between these two there had been General Lecointe.[22] So many changes in so little time!

When we came to within about a kilometre of Villers-Bretonneux, which we saw amid a mass of trees, the general, introducing a manoeuvre which would become regulation a few years later, had me disperse my company in many groups of a few men. In this order, with a reserve of fifty men who followed along the road at a distance of about 200 metres, I advanced towards the village, my two wings spreading out as we gained ground in such a way that when we were within about 600 metres of our objective the groups of men forming my line stretched round a wide arc of 1,500 metres, the concave face to the village. I confess that from this moment emotion began to get a strong hold on me. Would a hail of rifle shots suddenly come from the thickets which bordered the village? At moments I wished for it, to escape from the uncertainty which oppressed me. I halted my line about 500 metres from the village. The general urged me to deploy the groups in skirmish order to avoid presenting too good a target to the enemy's fire, as they were no doubt waiting for us to come within easy range before opening the ball. We remained thus for several minutes without any change occurring in the situation. In the end, not being able to control my impatience and nerves any longer, I pushed my skirmishers forward. We had scarcely gone a hundred paces when we saw emerge from a footpath leading from the village a group of three or four men who were going to the fields. They told us that there was not a single German in Villers-Bretonneux, and that only a few horsemen came there very occasionally. I reassembled my men and we entered the village. All the same, I had learned a good lesson which I was eager to profit from later when the opportunity presented itself.

At midday we crossed the Somme at Fouilloy and entered Corbie. I was lodged in a room of the château which seemed to me to have a most artistic character. On the 17th we returned to Villers-Bretonneux, then came back to Fouilloy where we were billeted that day and the next, the 18th.

CHAPTER III

PONT-NOYELLES

19–29 December 1870

'Severe cases of frostbite appeared by the dozen. . .'

On the Hallue – Contay, the château and the parish priest – Organisation of the Army of the North – Tempting offers – 23–24 December, Battle of Pont-Noyelles – A Protestant view – An unfortunate mistake – In retreat – Heroic duel with a chicken – Behind the Scarpe

On 19 December, after a short march of twelve kilometres, we arrived at Contay on the Upper Hallue.[1] My company was lodged in a château belonging to Madame de Ranchey, the care of which in the absence of the owners had been entrusted to the village priest, who discharged his obligation better than a squad of gendarmes would have done. Be that as it may, we established our field-mess in the kitchen of the château and ate in the dining-room. The priest consented to hand over wine from the manorial cellar at 1fr. 50 a bottle. That might seem dear in Montpellier, but in Picardy it's a very good bargain, particularly when the wine is old and from a good area, like that which we were sold. The priest was very annoyed because, with Fernandez, we made a complete and detailed inspection of all the rooms in the château. However, we might at any moment be called upon to defend this château. It was very necessary that we should familiarise ourselves thoroughly with its outlooks and interior layout. He was choked with anger because we even entered the room which served as the wardrobe of the mistress of the house, and he thought it in very bad taste that our gaze should fall even for a single instant on the very elegant ball-gowns which looked terribly bored on the nail which held them suspended in the air. Indeed we exchanged some rather sharp words on this subject, and it took nothing less than lunch taken together at our field-mess, and well washed down with a few bottles at 1fr. 50, to seal our reconciliation. But I believe that, in order that harmony should be more securely established, he pulled out the best. For he did the office of purveyor himself and we discovered, on this occasion even more than others, that good wine was not dear in Picardy.

It was at Contay that, following the new and definitive organisation of the Army of the North, my battalion was allocated to a new regiment, which was numbered 67 (67th *de marche*[2] be it noted). For commander of the unit we got Lieutenant-Colonel Fradin de Linières,[3] who from the very first made a most favourable impression on us. As we got to know him better this impression was confirmed more and more. He was in fact a charming man, likeable, courteous and with excellent manners. An indulgent commander, experienced, giving generously of himself, he knew how to imbue this regiment, formed of three battalions which were absolute strangers to one another, with intelligent leadership which soon gave it unity and cohesion. Major Tramond soon collared him and introduced him to our field-mess, which he adopted permanently. Consequently I, who until that point in my career had shunned all too intimate contact with my direct superiors, found myself obliged much against my will to rub shoulders daily with my battalion major and my colonel in all the most intimate of life's routines. Contrary to my expectation, I was never embarrassed by this and I fell into the easiest and most cordial relations with these two men whose close proximity I had dreaded. Only one point still troubled me. I was afraid that my comrades might think that I had taken the initiative from motives of ambition in putting together this group which chance alone had formed. It is a fact that the spirit of comradeship prevailed so little in this officer corps composed any old how, in which no one knew anyone else! As for my old comrades of the 6th who were part of it, they knew me well enough to understand that I could have had no hand in the matter.

From this time our regiment, the 67th *de marche*, composed of one battalion formed by the 65th and two battalions formed by the 75th, belonged to the 1st Brigade of the 1st Division of the Twenty-second Corps of the Army of the North. The brigade, besides the 67th *de marche*, comprised the 2nd Battalion of light infantry and the Pas-de-Calais Regiment of *Mobiles*. It was commanded by Colonel Aynès. The 2nd Brigade was led by Colonel Pittié. These two brigades formed the 1st Division commanded by General Derroja. Finally, the Twenty-second Corps was led by General Lecointe, former colonel of a Guards Regiment at Metz. The division possessed three batteries, two of 4-pounder guns and one of 8-pounders, and one company of engineers. The Army of the North included one other army corps, the Twenty-third commanded by General Paulze d'Ivoy; but this corps really possessed only one sound division. The second consisted only of regiments of mobilised National Guards commanded by the all too well-known General Robin![4] That was all I knew at the time of the composition of this little army, which in truth was everything essential.

On 19 December my company was on picket duty. On the morning of the 20th I made a reconnaissance far to the south-west, but without discovering the slightest trace of the enemy. Yet that day a German column, leaving Amiens, came to attack our outposts at Querrieu, which resisted valiantly and forced it to retreat.[5] It is true that Querrieu is at least eight kilometres from Contay.

On the 21st and 22nd nothing disturbed our stay at Contay. One morning during lunch, however, we saw a disreputable cabriolet with its hood lowered pull up in front of the château, and from this boneshaker descended a tall gentleman dressed in a blue smock, wearing a fur cap, his nose adorned by a pair of spectacles with very thick lenses. He asked to speak to the colonel. He was shown in, and it was none other than our commanding general, General Faidherbe, who after a reconnaissance which he had pressed for some distance had come to ask us for lunch. He shared his plans and intentions with us. I was all eyes and ears. But I could not stop wondering why, instead of going to do his reconnaissance quite peacefully on horseback with a good escort, he had adopted this disguise which, despite myself, I found absurd because it was unnecessary.[6]

The night of 21/22 December was a sleepless one for me, and yet I passed it very comfortably in a bed in the château. But in the evening after dinner Major Tramond, who during the course of the day had had a long interview with General Derroja, general of our division, took me to one side and told me: 'The general called me in a little while ago and offered me the post of divisional chief of staff. After reflection I have declined this offer, believing that I would render far more service to the army and to myself by remaining at the head of my battalion. Besides, commanding troops suits my temperament better than staff duties. The general then asked me to suggest someone capable of filling those functions. I straight away gave him your name, so he has charged me with putting the proposition to you. You know that would mean assurance of your fourth braid immediately. Think about it and let me know tomorrow morning. I strongly urge you to accept.'

The moment was opportune! The offer was tempting! Twenty times I would have accepted, twenty times I told myself that it was folly. What! Take on a job for which I did not even know the requirements! Did I even know what a division was? And was I about to expose myself blithely, for the gratification of becoming a major straight away, to the exercise of command over ten thousand men for an uncertain period if the general should be killed or seriously wounded: I who was not yet all that sure of being able to command well a company of 200 rifles! No! I would have been wrong to throw myself into such an adventure and I declined it; but only in the morning, and I had nothing to regret but my sleepless night.

Besides, during the first days of my sojourn at Lille, on 10 or 12 November, my brother-in-law's friend who held a high position on General Bourbaki's staff had proposed that I should take command of a group of seven battalions of National Guards, a large number of whom had been assembled at Marchienne. I went to have a good look at them. They were a rabble, not soldiers. No uniforms, old percussion rifles and an awkward appearance! I hastened to refuse these gifts of Artaxerxes,[7] preferring my two hundred lads in red trousers, armed with good chassepots and soundly officered by NCOs who asked only to go to the front, to these thousands of poor fellows who were utterly incapable of taking part in active operations.

And it was lucky for me that I remained in my little sphere where I moved comfortably. For it is probable, as it subsequently proved, that in these more elevated jobs I should have found only what others have done who have gone blundering into them: disappointments and troubles of every sort.

On the 23rd, early in the morning, cannon boomed heavily on our left. It was the beginning of the Battle of Pont-Noyelles.[8] We took up our arms and, instead of taking position on ground to the west and south-west of Contay that we had become familiar with for three days past, we were marched across to the left bank of the Hallue where we took position halfway up the hills. As the enemy had not yet appeared in front of us we kept our men in ranks, well in hand. Major Tramond strongly criticised this way of doing things. According to him, instead of submitting to the enemy's moves and awaiting him passively, we should have gone forward and advanced squarely to meet him. Besides raising the morale of our young troops, by doing so we would have had the advantage of taking the enemy by his left flank while he was making a frontal attack on the line of the Hallue at Pont-Noyelles. I thought he was perfectly right, for since Metz I had had enough of defensive battles.

Only in the afternoon did the enemy appear on the heights of the right bank of the Hallue. A battery was established straight away and opened fire. Our divisional artillery was not slow in answering, and the cannonade became general. The shells fell around us and burst on the hard frozen ground, throwing up showers of earth like great fountains. The companies of the battalion were separated from one another by fairly wide intervals. I held mine under fire for some time. Fernandez and I walked up and down our company front reassuring the men, telling them that all this was causing more noise than harm and joking with them when a projectile passing too close to us made everyone duck their heads. It was all I could manage not to do likewise; I do not know why as I was well accustomed to this saraband. Seeing that the firing was becoming more accurate, I ordered a change of position and sheltered my company behind a screen of large trees which bordered a field. I sent a few squads under the command of Fernandez to the bottom of the valley to fend off an infantry attack which I judged was imminent but which did not materialise. The men deployed as skirmishers had to deal only with groups of cavalry who retired at once under the fire of our chassepots.

Major Tramond went from one company to another and appeared satisfied with the manner in which his young soldiers were behaving. The artillery duel went on for several hours in this way. Seeing no serious attack developing, Tramond, who well understood that we must have only an insignificant force in front of us, became indignant that we were not led forward. As General Derroja came passing by, he made his appreciation of the situation known to him, pressing to be allowed to advance against the enemy with his battalion. The two of them moved away, talking with great animation. Doubtless the advice seemed sound, because before nightfall we crossed back over the Hallue and retook possession of Contay. But when we arrived on the plateau on the right bank there was no longer any trace of the enemy in front of us. If this offensive movement had taken place two hours sooner the Germans who had got a foothold in the villages of the valley would have been obliged to evacuate them and to fall back before the threat of an attack on their left flank by the whole division. Instead of an indecisive affair we should have had a real success to record. However, during the afternoon the commanding general had come to see what was happening on his right wing. General Derroja had explained the situation to him. Why had we not acted, particularly as we were risking nothing? Faidherbe had passed his whole military life far from the command of troops. An engineering officer and doubtless very intelligent, he was most interested in the study of colonial questions. His republicanism alone had got him appointed to the high post which he occupied. On that day he should have realised, if indeed he was a man able to estimate his own actions impartially, that one cannot improvise a commanding general. For he held in his hand a unique opportunity to inflict a first-class lesson on the enemy, but he either did not know how or did not dare to take advantage of it.

Night put an end to the fighting. The regiment was billeted in Contay, protecting itself with a strong line of outposts. My company held a post on the hillside on the right bank near the village of Bavelincourt. I had established it as best I could, but with much difficulty given that the night was very dark. At last my sentries had open terrain before them with a view extending for some distance. That was the main post. I posted the bulk of my company a little higher up, only one hundred paces to the rear, and I ordered everyone to keep their eyes open and to have their arms ready. I also made, and caused to be made, frequent visits to keep the sentries awake and to maintain the state of alert. This part of the task was accomplished without great difficulty, helped as we were by the terrible cold, perhaps the sharpest of the whole winter. In certain units severe cases of frostbite appeared by the dozen. Fortunately, in my company I had none to report. But what numbness of the fingers!

While going from one man to another, as much to warm myself as to supervise them, I thought of the events of that day and congratulated myself that circumstances had given my men a post of such little danger for their first battle. In this way they were becoming inured to warfare effortlessly. They had maintained their position very well under a fire to which they could not respond, which nearly always gives rise to great nervous tension followed by profound demoralisation. Their morale was very good, and I was optimistic after this first trial. Personally, although I do not find battle the most pleasant affair, I was delighted to have received this second baptism which washed me clean of all the ignominy of that dreadful capitulation of Metz.

During one of my numerous nocturnal walks I noticed a window lit up. I approached and made out a little house with a low roof and a rather wretched appearance. I knocked on the door and entered. Inside, in front of a feeble fire, a peasant woman sitting on a stool seemed to be absorbed in melancholy thoughts. She was still a young woman, whose features expressed great strength. She got up and asked me what I wanted. 'Nothing,' I replied, 'or at least, if you will allow me, I should like to get warm a little at the fire, for it is a freezing cold night.' She offered me a place at the hearth and, after having revived the fire which was dying out in the fire-place, she began a conversation. I was surprised to hear almost correct speech and, above all, unusually elevated feelings from a woman of her station. I asked her if she had not been exceedingly frightened by the cannonade that afternoon. 'Afraid, no,' she told me, 'for in these times of calamity there is no use in being afraid. I had sheltered my little daughter as best I could,' and in saying this she turned towards the bed which held a sleeping child. 'Several times Prussian or French bullets have skimmed my roof. Certainly it would be a great misfortune for me to see this cottage, which is everything I have, destroyed. But what do you expect? I was resigned in advance. Must we not pay for our faults, our crimes? Was it not a great crime on our part to have declared war without reason? We have been much to blame, and God punishes us for it justly. We must therefore resign ourselves and be ready to bear with courage all the evils that come to us. In any case, what are these tribulations which we suffer through our own immoderate ambition beside what Christ suffered for us? Who sows the wind must reap the whirlwind. However, now that the Prussians, in continuing the war for no reason, reveal in their turn ambitious plans of conquest, the righteous cause is with you who defend the soil of our country. My good wishes and prayers go with you, for you are fighting for the right.' Seeing that I was astonished to find so much resignation in a woman still so young, she quoted me several evangelical texts appropriate to the circumstances. I had no difficulty in guessing that she was a Protestant, for a Catholic in her situation would have served me up only jeremiads accompanied by a lot of monotonous prayers in Latin or French, but without any meaning or relation to the present circumstances. I withdrew, entirely under her spell and wishing every possible happiness to this young widow who was bearing her solitude so bravely, and who accepted the misfortunes of her country and her own privations with a resignation so full of dignity.

I awaited daylight with impatience to see where I was and how I was situated with respect to an enemy threat. In consequence I modified the line of my outposts. A fairly extensive wood five or six hundred metres in front of my line worried me particularly. I took twenty men and we searched it up to its far edge without encountering anything suspicious.

Towards eight o'clock very lively fighting broke out again on our left in the direction of Pont-Noyelles.[9] Being certain that the woods in our front held no enemy troops, I had no anxiety about that quarter, for the moment at least, when suddenly I saw emerging from them at the double dark-uniformed troops who were advancing on us resolutely. I immediately gave the order to open fire. But from the shouts of these pseudo-attackers, then, when they were close up, by their uniforms, I recognised them as *Gardes Mobiles*.[10] I had much difficulty in stopping the firing. Some of them lay on the ground, struck by our bullets. So why were they running like that without any reason? For nobody was pursuing them; the wood was not occupied by the Germans until at least an hour later. After a few shots exchanged with the enemy posted in the woods I pulled back my men on the major's order and rejoined the battalion. We went to take position in front of Contay, on a plateau which a body of enemy infantry was making as if to occupy. After the exchange of a few thousand bullets the enemy abandoned his attempted attack. The major, judging the moment opportune, wanted to pursue them, but General Derroja sent the order to return to the positions on the left bank which we had occupied the day before. So we abandoned both Contay and the right bank, never to return, having perhaps once again let slip the opportunity, by turning the enemy's left flank, to relieve our centre which had given way at Pont-Noyelles and to inflict a serious setback on the Germans.[11]

We stayed in our positions for part of the afternoon, once again to suffer the German artillery fire which, however, did us almost no harm. Then towards three o'clock we were ordered to retreat by stages. This movement,

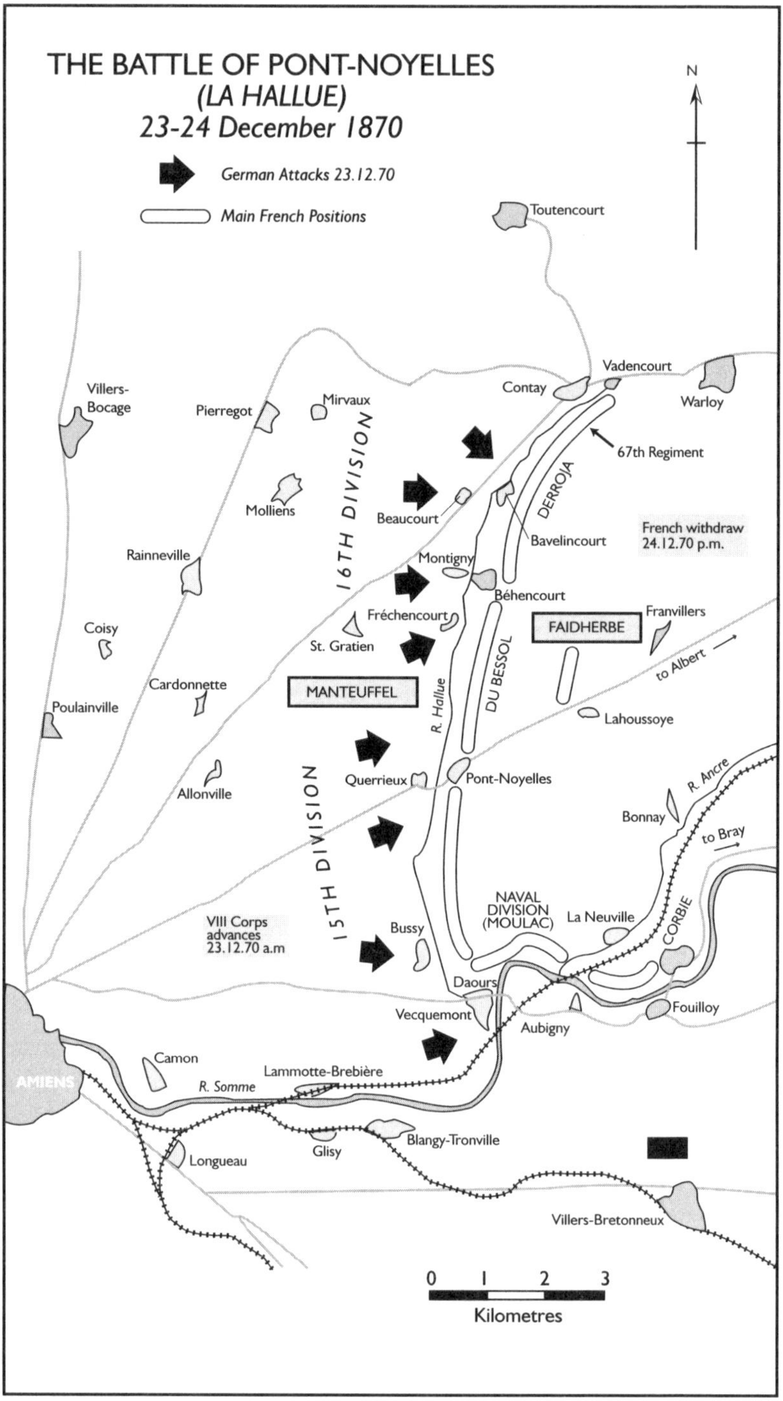
THE BATTLE OF PONT-NOYELLES
(LA HALLUE)
23-24 December 1870
German Attacks 23.12.70
Main French Positions
N
Toutencourt
Vadencourt
Contay
Warloy
Villers-Bocage
Pierregot
Mirvaux
16TH DIVISION
67th Regiment
DERROJA
Molliens
Beaucourt
Bavelincourt
French withdraw 24.12.70 p.m.
Rainneville
Montigny
Béhencourt
Fréchencourt
Franvillers
Coisy
St. Gratien
FAIDHERBE
DU BESSOL
to Albert
Cardonnette
MANTEUFFEL
R. Hallue
Poulainville
Lahoussoye
Querrieux
Pont-Noyelles
Allonville
R. Ancre
Bonnay
15TH DIVISION
to Bray
NAVAL DIVISION (MOULAC)
La Neuville
CORBIE
VIII Corps advances 23.12.70 a.m
Bussy
Daours
Vecquemont
Fouilloy
Aubigny
Camon
AMIENS
R. Somme
Lammotte-Brebière
Blangy-Tronville
Glisy
Longueau
Villers-Bretonneux
0 1 2 3
Kilometres

harassed only by enemy shells, was executed with remarkable order and precision. Once out of sight of the enemy the regiment was reassembled. Then I realised to my great shame that I had forgotten to pass on the order to retreat to a detached squad at a river crossing in the valley. I was in mortal anxiety. I sent Fernandez to find it; luckily we had not yet gone very far. Scarcely half an hour later he led it back at full strength. The blunder which I had just committed gave me food for thought and made me understand how difficult the art of war is, even in its little details; how much foresight is necessary, and how the mind must always be kept alert and held to the accomplishment of professional duty.

After having marched six or seven kilometres we arrived in a little village called Senlis-le-Sec where the battalion was billeted. For our billet my company got a big farm in the village. I hoped to find provisions for all my people there, but the farm had been evacuated several days before and there was nothing at all left. Fortunately the same was not true elsewhere, and my men were able to prepare a good hot meal before going to sleep. They had great need of it, for since midday of the 23rd they had eaten how they could, whether the few rations they carried in their packs or some food bought in Contay while passing through. These two days and the intervening night had been hard, and fatigue, coming on top of their excitement, had somewhat affected them.

The field-mess had not been operating for me either, for at least the same period, and I had been able only to take a bite now and then as opportunity presented. So I took delight in dining properly. The colonel and the major, having gone off with some senior commander, I believe, were not with us and there remained the four of us, the doctor and the three company officers. Michel straight away went searching in the village, but there were so many of us that there was not enough for everybody. Finally he returned with a pan of milk and a packet of potatoes which his orderly was carrying. He was holding a chicken by its legs. When he came back in I was alone in the main room of the farm, in the process of blowing on the fire, which did not want to take, with a large metal tube which I was puffing into. The lieutenants were seeing to settling the troops. Michel put the creature in my hands and said, 'Well, kill the chicken while I go to find some bread. You know that it's most important to bleed it.' And he left, leaving the victim and the executioner face to face.

Kill the chicken. Easy to say, but how to do it without using one's hands? I was very perplexed, and I found it repugnant to kill this beast; at bottom I did not dare. Certainly, if it had concerned myself alone I could well have foregone eating the chicken, particularly at this price. But I did not want to appear a booby in my comrades' eyes, and in these circumstances I recognised the stark reality of the sad fate awaiting me and the chicken. I drew my knife bravely; my intention was quite simply to cut its head off at one blow. But when the moment came to act I did not have the strength. The chicken took advantage of my hesitation to escape and to run around the room in fright, clucking all the more. For two pins I would have begged it to be quiet. It seemed to me that it was calling for help, that it was crying Assassin!. Yet the job had to be finished, for Michel was about to come back and my warrior's pride was pledged to the accomplishment of the chicken's murder. Then, believing that I would have more courage for killing it at a distance, I drew my big sword and tried to run it through, but feebly. Moreover I could not trap it, for it ran around like a lost soul, fluttering this way and that and shrieking! Weary of this pursuit, which I well knew I was not in earnest about, I threw my sword at it sideways on, hoping that it would be more or less knocked senseless by it; but I succeeded only in increasing its agitation. I then took extreme measures. I went out and asked a man to send the bugler to me. When he presented himself I had resumed my place and my occupation of bellows man. Turning towards him quite calmly I said: 'My friend, be good enough to take this chicken and kill and pluck it. Go and perform the task in the courtyard or somewhere else.' It did not take long! Ten minutes later the chicken was brought to me all ready to be put on the spit or in the pot. At this moment Michel returned. 'Have you at least prepared the chicken, for it is late and it will be a long time yet before we can eat.' By way of reply, I pointed with dignity to the corpse of the victim lying on the table. He examined it, turned it over, and gave his approval.

All these operations had taken us very late into the evening. The stew was not ready until midnight. But then it would be midnight supper,[12] and this idea filled us with joy! It evoked old memories; joyful Christmas Eves in stylish restaurants with elegant company! It was three o'clock when the last bone of the famous chicken was picked clean. Our menu had nothing regal about it: milk soup, potatoes, chicken. Happily it was washed down by a few good bottles of wine, which did much to sustain our good cheer. In the North the wine is always good. The prices are very high, so it is better to pay for good-quality wine than for thin stuff.

On the 25th, Christmas Day, we took the Arras road. At Bucquoy we turned left and went to spend the night at Bailleulval, near the road from Doullens. The whole day was consumed in doing this long stage of about thirty kilometres. In the evening the major told us a good story. General Derroja, in returning on horseback to Contay on the evening of the 23rd, got entangled in the stacked arms of the sentry post at the entrance to the village, no doubt placed too far in the middle of the road. Man, horse, the orderly who was following, and rifles were all reduced to a jumble which the men of the post, who came out on hearing the commotion, had the utmost difficulty in untangling. The general was set on his feet again, all bumps and bruises. The next morning he could not move at all. However, he was bent on marching into combat with his division. Mounting a horse was out of the question. The coach-house of the château contained several carriages. He had a victoria brought out and had one of his horses hitched to it, and off he went to the battle. But he had counted without the parish priest, who was not having this and refused to allow the Countess de Ranchey's carriage to leave. Finally, after much negotiation, he demanded a formal written receipt from the general and, although much against his wishes, he tolerated what he could not prevent and what he considered almost as kidnapping. The victoria did duty for the whole campaign and even had the honour of enabling the wounded Fernandez to get away from the disaster of Saint-Quentin.

From the 26th to the 31st the regiment did not leave the eastern outskirts of Arras. General Faidherbe had pulled back his army, a little disorganised by the two days of fighting on the Hallue, behind the fortified towns and had put it on the defensive on the line of the Scarpe, its two wings resting on Arras and Douai. In our billet at Athies we had a very pleasant existence thanks to the jovial character and good humour of our colonel. Yet signs of anxiety were not lacking in him. At Béthune, his last garrison, he had left his wife with seven children, the youngest of whom was scarcely three or four years old. His eldest son, aged seventeen, had enlisted for the war in a regiment which had suffered a great deal at Pont-Noyelles; indeed he had been taken prisoner and for several days news of him was anxiously awaited. In spite of everything the colonel was always affable and joined in with our merry chatter like a good comrade. In the evenings after dinner Major Tramond, who assiduously called on the high commanders (as much to not let himself be forgotten as to keep informed about plans), left us to pay his visits. My lieutenant and the paymaster got on well together and fled our society. The four of us, the colonel, Michel, Fernandez and I, therefore passed our evenings together talking over a variety of subjects, most often far removed from the war; literature, music, philosophy, anything. One day at our modest camp table we had the good fortune to receive Madame de Linières, who had come to bring her husband the good news that their son had succeeded in escaping from German hands and that he would rejoin his father in a few days.

The return of the major was the opportunity for us to ask a mass of questions, to which he gave very interesting replies. Thus we learned from him that General Derroja had not yet been able to console himself for the inaction which had been imposed on him on the days of battle of 23–24 December; that the commander of the army corps, General Lecointe, was furious that Faidherbe had thus held back his first division which had no enemies to speak of in front of it, while his second division under General du Bessol[13] was almost crushed. Assuredly the co-operation of the first would have relieved the second and would have led to the certain defeat of the enemy. Much criticised also was the mania of the commanding general for taking cover in defensive positions and remaining there passively.

The enemy had not pursued us; only his cavalry had accompanied our retreat. Now it came up to the opposite side of the Scarpe to find out what we were doing. A few parties were even prowling far in our rear and had tried to cut the line from Arras to Lens. As for us, sheltered behind the almost impassable line of the Scarpe, we did not move, and we awaited events while providing ourselves with as much comfort as possible.

CHAPTER IV

BAPAUME

30 December 1870–15 January 1871

'The Germans put up a desperate resistance. . .'

Offensive towards Péronne, 30 December – Conquer or die – Ambush, 1 January 1871– The New Year's gift that got away – Battle of Bapaume, 3 January – Inexplicable retreat – Rest at Croisilles – Surprise attack at Sapignies – Bapaume – Albert

On the 30th our regiment made a reconnaissance in force south of Arras, through Beaurains, Mercatel, Wailly, Dainville and back through Saint-Nicolas. On the 31st we left our billets at Athies. The line of the Scarpe was finally abandoned and we launched ourselves into a very determined offensive movement. The commanding general had shared his intentions with us beforehand in an order of the day which said that the moment had come for the Army of the North to conquer or die.

Already, on about 10 December, on taking possession of his command, the general had opened communication with his troops through an order of the day as naïve as it was peculiar, in which he enjoined us in a strict and threatening way that we should arm ourselves with the three essential virtues of the true man of war: discipline, moral austerity and contempt for death.[1] Discipline went without saying: but moral austerity! How could the morals of these poor devils not be austere, seeing that they spent all their days floundering in snow or mud and their nights either keeping watch in these endless plains of the north where the horizon is always out of sight, or snatching a miserable nap in a barn or hovel? In short, grant that this moral austerity was very easy to practise at that time; but contempt for death! To be sure, Faidherbe was a very intelligent man, but in truth this was a lame philosophy. Death, danger, privation and the strength of the enemy are subjects which one should take care never to broach with soldiers if you want to keep them in a good state of morale.

When I had to lead my men virtually every day in small operations which the lack of cavalry obliged us to carry out ourselves, I always avoided these grand words. The boldest spirit might suspect that they would come back to haunt him. If the men asked where we were going:

'To such and such a village.'

'Do we know if it is occupied by the enemy?'

'How could the enemy be there? He cannot be everywhere at once, and all his forces are in front of Paris.'

When we were fired at:

'Oh, they are there and in strength,' said the men. 'How the bullets whistle!'

'You didn't think they'd be firing blanks? But their bullets do no harm. They always pass over your head.'

'Not always, for at Pont-Noyelles and Bapaume they laid many men low.'

'Those were big battles. One can't make an omelette without breaking eggs. But most of the men were only wounded, and those are the lucky devils who are pampering themselves in hospital while we are slogging hard at it. Well, let's advance a little and you'll see how they clear off.'

If on the other hand I encountered resistance which I was in no position to overcome, I said to my lads: 'You see, they dare not come out; but by withdrawing a little we shall compel them to follow us and uncover themselves.'

Thus we set out for victory or the banks of the Acheron.[2] We marched all morning and part of the afternoon and arrived at Beaumetz-lès-Loges, a fairly large village situated on the Doullens road. As my company had been designated for picket duty, I led it to the appointed ground and disposed my guards. It was very cold, but a dry cold, easy to bear, for the north wind was not blowing.

In passing through the village which was entrusted to my company to guard that night, I had learned that every morning for several days past a party of enemy cavalry of about twenty men had come there to reconnoitre, and indeed that a requisition had been ordered for the next day. I immediately conceived the idea of setting a trap for the enemy, who did not know of our presence in this area. Several good horses, which we were almost entirely lacking, would fall into my hands as a result.

The night passed in the most absolute quiet. I could not prevent myself from becoming very restless, ruminating over my idea, considering every angle, adopting one plan, then another. Finally daylight came: a greyish glow at first, scarcely allowing objects to be distinguished by its feeble light, then the cheering, totally red face of the sun which the wintry mist allowed us to stare at without being dazzled. It seemed to say to me: 'The attempt is sound. You will succeed.'

Before me stretched a great undulating plain which rose towards the horizon. Nothing broke the monotony of these rich farmlands, save a few isolated spinneys all adorned with hoarfrost and the double row of tall trees lining the road leading directly south towards the line of the horizon. A light mist lifting from the earth little by little hung in fleecy wreaths in the highest branches of the trees, then gathered in little clouds which the rising sun strove to dissipate.

My line of sentinels was posted on the edge of a little wood which stretched at right angles on each side of the road that the enemy must follow to reach the village. Along almost its whole length it was bordered by a fairly low quickthorn hedge. The wood was about a hundred metres deep on each side of the road. The enemy was naturally obliged to pass through it to get to the village.

I placed a group of fifty men without rifles or packs on each side of the road and hid them as best I could behind the thickets and hedges. I gave them strict orders to allow the enemy horsemen to enter into the natural trap formed by the woods, then, at the given signal, to rush at the horses' heads, forcibly seize the bridles and bring the riders down by heaving them over by their legs. I left them their sword-bayonets, which would be quite sufficient to assure their personal defence in a hand-to-hand fight and to overcome resistance from any riders who proved excessively recalcitrant. Above all they should do no harm to the horses! Twenty armed men had the mission of blocking the road beyond the wood, towards the village, in order to prevent any of the enemy escaping that way. In case of need they would add their bayonets to the attack.

I had in addition placed, one hundred metres in front of the wood, a small post of eight men whom I had planted behind a heap of beetroots in a ditch covered with branches which hid them from view completely. They had instructions that as soon as the enemy party had entered the wood they were to take position on the road with their rifles levelled to cut off its retreat.

These men had been chosen from among the best; to them fell by far the heaviest task. They alone had retained their cartridges, which they were to use only against riders who succeeded in escaping. I had placed them under the command of an old soldier of about forty in whom I had every confidence, for I had seen him show great resourcefulness and firmness on many occasions. He had experience of war, having been in the campaigns of the Crimea, Italy and Mexico,[3] of which he proudly wore the commemorative medals.

I had positioned myself in the wood to the right of the road in the angle formed by the hedge, which was very thick at this spot, and awaited the appearance of the enemy with impatience. It must have been about eight o'clock when the NCO who stood at my side with his gun loaded, ready to fire in order to give the signal at the chosen moment, leaned towards me and in a very low voice whispered in my ear: 'Captain, here they are!' I felt myself turn pale. I immediately fixed my gaze on the point on the horizon where the road crested the rise and I saw halted there two silhouettes of horsemen standing out strongly in black against the blue-grey of the sky. These men were easily a kilometre away from us. We could have sung the *Marseillaise* and they would hardly have heard us. Yet it was in an almost smothered voice that I said to the sergeant : 'Let's lie flat on our stomachs so that they don't see us. Above all, don't fire until I tell you.'

There we were lying flat on our bellies in a mixture of dead leaves and old snow. I observed the movements of the enemy through a gap in the branches. The two horsemen separated, one to the right, the other to the left of the road, advancing from the crest in such a way that their outline could scarcely be distinguished against the terrain, rather than showing clear and sharp against the sky. They explored the plateau for a few hundred metres at right angles to the road, on which two other horsemen soon appeared who likewise halted in front of the crest, abreast of the two scouts. This little riding display lasted for about half an hour, during which I was kicking my heels with impatience and indescribable anguish.

Then the two horsemen on the flanks regained the road at an angle and there joined their two comrades who had been proceeding along it at the very slowest pace. The four riders, reunited about 600 metres away from me, appeared to hold a little confabulation. It was at this moment that I noticed that they were armed with lances, at which I rejoiced greatly for, encumbered on their right-hand side by that most inconvenient weapon for defence in combat at close quarters, and on their left by the sabre which they would be able to draw only with great difficulty, these fine Uhlans[4] were at the mercy of my chaps. The enemy group was then 200 metres at most from my most advanced post hidden in the ditch behind the beetroots.

After a few minutes of conversation two horsemen turned back and soon disappeared beyond the horizon at a rapid trot while the two others stayed in the road. Hardly had a quarter of an hour passed when I saw a substantial body of horsemen appear, breaking into the trot at first, then slackening their pace and proceeding slowly towards us. When they got to within 100 or 150 metres of the two men who had remained in the road, those two resumed their advance and the whole group moved forward slowly along the road: the two horsemen riding almost side by side at its head, the leader of the detachment 150 metres further back, then the squad of Uhlans riding three abreast, seven ranks deep – twenty-three riders in all, for the last rank consisted of only two men.

Motionless, breathing hard, I watched this prey coming towards me, considering it as good as devoured. My heart was thumping fit to burst my chest. Never had I experienced such an agonising feeling. Yet it was not the apprehension of danger, for I was not running any risk, nor was it thirst for vengeance, for I very much hoped that everything would pass off virtually without bloodshed. No, the feeling which prevailed in me and grew in my mind with an almost painful sharpness was very complex: the satisfaction of the huntsman who, after ingenious calculations, sees the game fall into the snare he has set; a glimpse of the rapture of triumph when I would re-enter the village at the head of my company with these twenty-three captured horses followed by the same number of prisoners; and finally the excitement produced by this interminable waiting following a night of agitation and sleeplessness.

The enemy troop was still advancing, but so calmly and so slowly that it seemed to me to be marking time. The two horsemen in the lead had already passed my post dug in behind the pile of beetroots, and they were about to pass between the two lines of hedges bordering the road. One of them was only a few paces from me and the impact of his horse's hooves on the ground hardened by frost echoed in my brain like hammer blows. I glanced at my sergeant to warn him to be ready to fire. He looked completely green. With the moment for action approaching, I felt my whole body relax, and calm gradually return to my mind. The leader of the squad, a good-looking boy with a blond beard, proudly sitting astride a superb chestnut horse which I already accounted mine and whose attributes I was appraising thoroughly, was just level with the heap of beetroots. I did not take my eyes off him. Suddenly, one of the men of my advance post emerged from the branches covering him, jumped onto the heap of beetroots, and with his weapon raised I heard him call out in a stentorian voice: 'Who goes there!' backing up his shout with a simultaneous shot from his rifle.

In less time than it takes to tell it the squad had turned about, regained the crest at the gallop and disappeared over the horizon. The eight men of the advance post had emerged and had begun firing a useless volley which hit nobody. As for the two most advanced horsemen, I did not even see what became of them. Taking the hedge at a stride – after a fashion, as it was rather high – I immediately rushed over to my advance post and found, standing on the heap of beetroots as if in a daze, his rifle still smoking, who? The old fellow in whom I had so much confidence.

I climbed up beside him and, grabbing him by the strap that fastened his knapsack at the back, I began to shake him like a plum tree. 'Scoundrel! You gave us away, but now you're for it! I'll have you court-martialled! If I had my way I'd run you through with my sword!" This was a rather idle threat, for I had taken care to deposit that encumbering and useless instrument at the main guard post. I gave emphasis to my words with a flurry of kicks vigorously applied to the area below his cartridge pouch. If this summary punishment calmed my anger it unfortunately did not bring back the Uhlans, and I returned to my post thoroughly crestfallen, and doubtless to be on foot for a long time to come.

My major, the gallant Tramond who never slept, had hurried to the sound of gunfire at daybreak. I recounted my misadventure to him, and poured out my chagrin to him as my commander and friend. He did his best to console me and told me that, after all, it was no great misfortune and that I would make up for it another time.

As for my old fellow, I did not have him arrested because on reflection I persuaded myself that he had been suffering under the irresistible influence of an hallucination. He disappeared and I saw him no more in my company. I fancy that he must have blown his brains out in some corner.

We departed at about ten o'clock on the morning of 2 January 1871 and continued our forward march. It seemed that we were going to the relief of Péronne, which was tightly invested on both sides of the Somme and close to the end of its resistance.[5] The possession of this stronghold was of the utmost importance for us because it was the only crossing point of that river which remained to us and which would allow us to take the offensive. After midday, as we were leaving the village of Bucquoy where we crossed the Amiens road, we heard cannon on our left. So had the battle already begun?[6] We must get going at once if we were to take part in it. We were ordered to hurry. We crossed the Arras–Amiens railway line at Achiet-le-Grand station. We halted for a few moments. It seemed that the struggle hereabouts had been hot. The station was almost completely demolished. As we could make out the smoke of the battle in the distance, I climbed to the first floor for a better look. A shell had burst right in the middle of the station master's living-room and had left all the furniture in a pitiful state. The appearance of this little room was truly grotesque. You could no longer recognise the shape of any object, so greatly had the shell splinters and the flame from its charge disfigured, mangled, pulverised and consumed everything.

The march was resumed, but first of all we were deployed, and it was in combat order that we advanced into the open plain, in order to extend the right of our army. A few shells came in our direction, but without penetrating our ranks. In any case, night was falling and the fighting slackened and ceased altogether. We were halted, then directed to our respective billets. The regiment passed the night at Achiet-le-Petit on the other side of the railway. Given the immediate proximity of the enemy, I feared that we would have a disturbed night. But nothing happened. After having dined most comfortably thanks to the foresight of Michel who, having stayed in the rear to organise a dressing-station, had taken advantage of the circumstances to get some provisions, we rolled ourselves in our greatcoats and, stretched out and pressed close to one another on some heaps of straw, we fell fast asleep.

We were up early on the morning of the 3rd and, after an inspection of weapons and ammunition, we set out for the expected battle.[7]

We went back through Achiet-le-Grand and took the Bapaume road, going down to Bihucourt, which we kept on our left flank, and upward

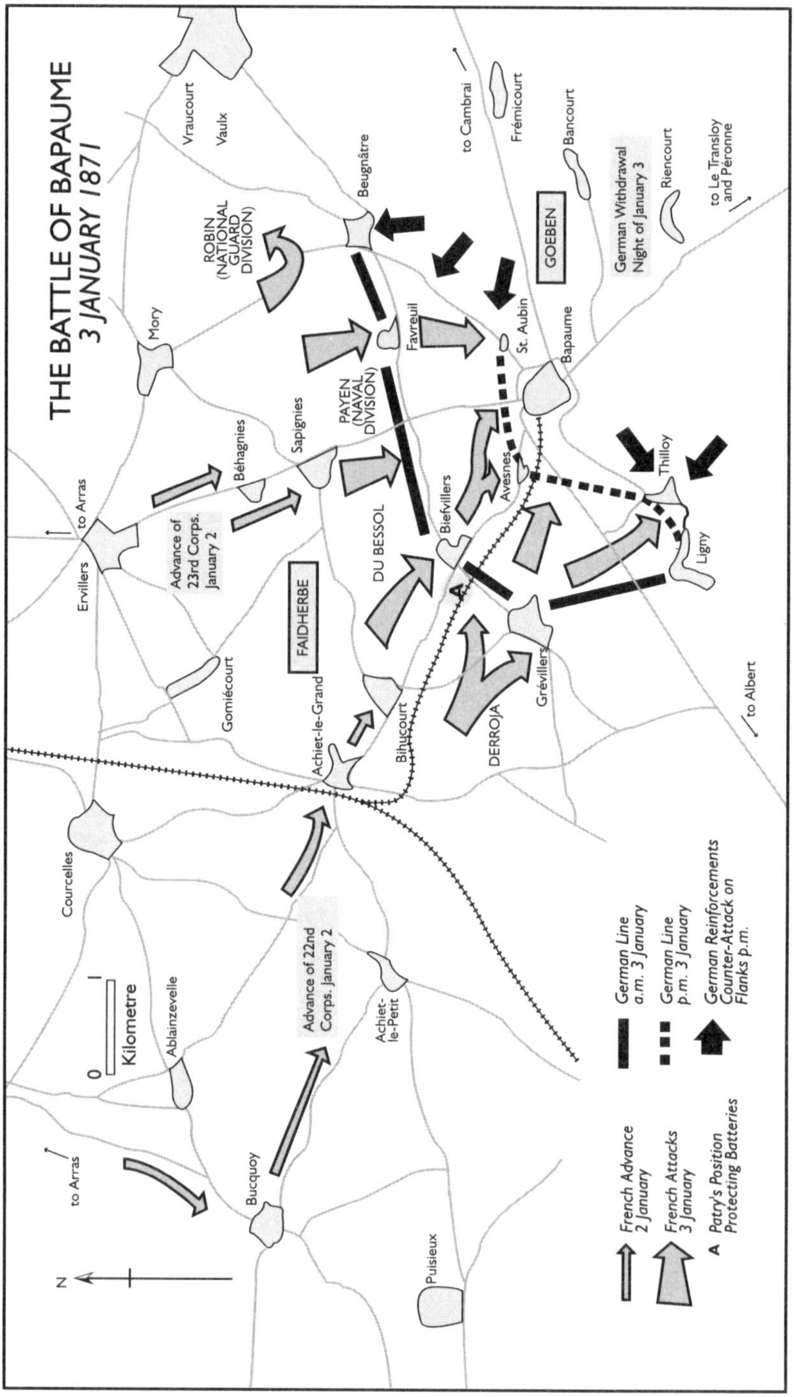
THE BATTLE OF BAPAUME
3 JANUARY 1871
Vraucourt
Vaulx
Beugnâtre
to Cambrai
Frémicourt
Bancourt
Riencourt
to Le Transloy and Péronne
German Withdrawal Night of January 3
GOEBEN
ROBIN (NATIONAL GUARD DIVISION)
Mory
Favreuil
St. Aubin
Bapaume
PAYEN (NAVAL DIVISION)
Sapignies
Béhagnies
Biefvillers
Avesnes
Thilloy
Ligny
to Arras
Ervillers
Advance of 23rd Corps. January 2
DU BESSOL
FAIDHERBE
A
Gomiécourt
Achiet-le-Grand
Bihucourt
DERROJA
Grévillers
to Albert
Courcelles
Advance of 22nd Corps. January 2
Achiet-le-Petit
Ablainzeville
0
1
Kilometre
to Arras
Bucquoy
Puisieux
N
French Advance 2 January
French Attacks 3 January
A Patry's Position Protecting Batteries
German Line a.m. 3 January
German Line p.m. 3 January
German Reinforcements Counter-Attack on Flanks p.m.

again onto the Biefvillers plateau. On reaching the crest we bore to the right, crossing the plateau at an angle. During this movement we received a lively fire from the defenders of the village, who were well posted behind walls and houses. We then turned to face the village and the attack commenced. The Germans put up a desperate resistance which soon weakened in the face of our great numerical superiority and which ceased after scarcely an hour; but not without having caused us serious losses since we were fighting without cover.

During this time our two divisional batteries of 4-pounder guns established themselves on the plateau which extends from Biefvillers towards Grévillers to the south, crossed by the line of the railway from Bapaume to Achiet-le-Grand, then under construction. My company was assigned to accompany these two batteries and to serve as their support. I did not relish this, because in that sort of position you generally catch all the enemy projectiles which have missed the batteries, and distance prevents you from using rifles. However, orders must be obeyed. I therefore separated with regret from the battalion, which entered Biefvillers, and I took the Grévillers road. I halted my company near the intersection of this road with the line under construction, which was in a deep cutting at this point and, climbing up to the plateau, I went to confer with the captain of the battery which was the closest to me.

The two batteries, separated by the railway track, had already opened fire at 1,800 metres against a line of enemy artillery established on the heights north of Bapaume. The enemy projectiles were raining down on the battery or, to be more precise, around the battery, which responded pluckily. It was an infernal hubbub. The enemy shells bursting very close to us, our guns firing very briskly, the distant noise of the enemy batteries: amidst the uproar made by all this I was astonished that our artillerists did not lose their senses.

I had never witnessed such a spectacle. So it was with great curiosity mixed with admiration that I gazed on these soldiers, so calm in the midst of this tempest of fire and iron, manoeuvring their guns with as much precision as if they were on the practice range; the NCOs directing the movements with perfect regularity, correcting the aim, supervising the bringing up of ammunition; the officers, telescope in hand, never taking their eyes off the enemy except to see if everything was going properly around them, and above all that their instructions concerning distances and allowance for wind were being observed. And all the while the enemy shells were raging. I wondered if there would be a single man left standing after an hour's fighting. And yet, after a struggle lasting three consecutive hours, I realised to my very great astonishment that the battery had suffered only relatively minimal losses after all. One thing that also surprised me very much – I who in the battles around Metz had always seen our artillery obliged to limber up and withdraw, or at least to change position, after a very short time – was that these two little batteries of 4-pounders held on for three hours without changing their position, and finally silenced the enemy artillery. At 1,800 metres our cannon were as effective as those of the Germans. They returned shot for shot, and their shots went right in the midst of the enemy: at Metz our artillery, opening its fire most of the time at such a range that it could not hit the enemy, took every shot without being able to return them, and for that very reason found itself constantly inferior. Would it not have been much better to lose people in getting closer to the enemy, to within the effective range of our guns, and to open the contest under conditions in which it could have been maintained rather more equally?[8]

Meanwhile I had to take the necessary measures for the protection of the two batteries. From our artillery position the terrain, quite bare of cover, inclined in a gentle slope towards Bapaume, which we could see fairly distinctly, forming a great mass of stonework. In front of the town were some scattered houses which I was told were part of a village called Avesnes-lès-Bapaume. To our right and on a hill was Grévillers, occupied by our men. I posted a hundred men on the slope about 300 metres in front of the batteries, between the road from Biefvillers to Bapaume and the railway under construction, deployed in skirmish formation under the orders of a lieutenant. With the rest of the company as reserve, I positioned myself between the two batteries in the shelter of the sunken road perpendicular to the railway. A few shells bursting in the air or on the crest of the sunken road wounded several of my men, whom I was able to have picked up by the personnel of a field-ambulance which was in the vicinity.

While we were awaiting, as well under cover as possible, the outcome of the action of our artillery, the two batteries fired without slackening their rate for a single instant. Suddenly the captain of the right-hand battery sent an NCO to ask me to come to talk to him. I hastened over and he told me with undisguised agitation that they were beginning to come under rifle fire. This was not credible, since if it had been so my skirmishers would have opened fire. But my whole line maintained the most profound silence. However, the captain was not mistaken, as I could see for myself. Artillerymen have a special intuition which seldom misleads them as to when there is danger of their being driven from the vicinity by enemy infantry approaching too closely. They suddenly become anxious and feel themselves distracted, which is quite rational, since they find themselves confronted by a threat that they cannot possibly ward off, being defenceless against it. I tried to figure out where this infantry fire could be coming from, but in vain. I saw nothing. Finally, in the large ditch formed by the deep railway cutting three or four hundred metres away, I spied a dark cluster of men who, hidden behind some trucks for moving earth which were placed across the track, were firing at their ease on our artillerists.

I immediately took twenty men with me and we hurled ourselves into the cutting at a run. I halted them after having passed about a hundred metres beyond the line of batteries and had them fire three or four volleys which, in spite of the trucks, put the overly bold enemy infantrymen to flight, not without bringing down several of them on the embankment. My skirmishers, who with their noses in clods of earth had noticed nothing, then opened fire upon them and sent their bullets after them until they had disappeared behind the little undulation in the ground in front of Avesnes-lès-Bapaume.

Two of my men had been wounded in this little escapade, one slightly in the head, the other mortally by a bullet through the neck. We brought this poor fellow back to our starting-point with great difficulty. He was choking and seemed about to yield his last breath at any moment. We leaned him against the embankment and were trying to stop the bleeding with handkerchiefs when there appeared from nowhere a man in religious orders, dressed in white, who seemed to be no more perturbed by the hubbub which was deafening us than if he had been saying Mass in a quiet chapel.

He came over to the dying man straight away and immediately spoke to him about his salvation, about eternal life, etc. The unfortunate man, who appeared to be still fully conscious but whose wound prevented him from uttering a word, sought to make it understood by feeble shaking of his head that he wished to be left in peace. The monk insisted and mingled his exhortations with prayers in Latin. Judging from the wincing features of the wounded man that this scene had lasted long enough, I drew the priest a little further off, telling him: 'Leave this man to die as he wishes. You can see well enough that he doesn't want to accept your spiritual help. He may be a Protestant or Jew, or perhaps nothing at all.' 'The latter, if anything,' he replied. 'It's incredible how these men from the North, though still very young, have retained little religious feeling. I have found the same lack of faith among nearly all the men I have wanted to help in their last moments.' 'Fortunately that does not prevent them from being dutiful men and, on the whole, sufficiently good soldiers.'

Although rebuffed in the exercise of his ministry, he nevertheless stayed in our midst, full of attentions towards the soldiers to whom he offered chocolate and a few cigars which he carried in a large satchel of dressings slung at his side. It gave me great pleasure to chat to him, for he was a highly intelligent man, very well informed and possessed of very large ideas, even in matters of religion.

The artillery contest still continued on our Biefvillers plateau. Towards midday, judging that the enemy was sufficiently shaken, General Derroja led his division forward against Avesnes-lès-Bapaume, bearing a little to the right towards the road from Bapaume to Albert.[9] The Germans greeted this attack by redoubling their fire. I had sent the order to my skirmishers to move forward, preparing to follow them with my reserve along the railway; but I saw no one move. Lying flat on the ground, demoralised and stupefied by this infernal cannonade which had been shaking their brains for three hours, they could no longer summon the necessary energy to get up and advance on the enemy. I rejoined them and walked up and down the line exhorting them, swearing at them, threatening them, without much result. Some of them lifted their heads, raised themselves on their elbows a little, then, as soon as I had passed by, dropped down to the ground again. It was necessary for the lieutenant, the NCOs and me virtually to apply ourselves to each individual in turn and, partly by reasoning and partly by more or less rough handling, we got them on their feet and started them forward. Once the line was shaken out and in motion, the advance on Avesnes was very soundly executed and the village fell into our hands in a very short time. Upon my word I had never been so hot in my life. Yet there were 15 degrees of frost that day, but despite that I was soaked in sweat.

Nothing is so hard as to lead forward under enemy fire men whose nerves are on edge after being stationary for a long time and who have thereby unlearned the exercise of their will. This problem is unknown in other arms of the service. In a cavalry charge, once the squadron has set off, how can a rider not go forward? Even if he wanted that, the horse would carry him along despite himself. In a battery fighting in a confined position (about 100 metres wide) all the men are well under their leader's hand; moreover they are naturally grouped around their respective artillery pieces. How could they escape their duty? Besides, in abandoning their gun would they not leave themselves defenceless against the enemy? That is not the case in the infantry where the men, once in skirmish order and well ensconced behind some shelter, in the end do not go forward unless they really want to. The leaders are obliged to supervise the advance and cannot occupy themselves with each man individually, and perforce neglect those who wilfully stay in the rear. Hence it is very difficult for company officers to carry along all their troops, and extraordinary and incessant efforts are required to push them forward and lead them right up to the objective. Those who have not fought in a war as infantry subalterns can have no idea of the forcefulness required in these modest jobs to get the men in hand once they have been dispersed and to make them advance against the enemy.

Our artillery had advanced too. Established on a little hill near Avesnes, it had opened fire on another objective to our right. On our side at least the action was flagging and seemed as if it would cease altogether. We wondered why we were not thrown against Bapaume which lay scarcely a few hundred metres in front of us, and above all why our artillery did not open the action in that direction to facilitate our entry into the suburbs.[10] Night was beginning to fall. In front of us the firing had ceased completely, but quite far off on our right there still echoed a fusillade which occasionally became rather lively. The situation seemed strange to us; but our astonishment became extreme when, instead of being led either against Bapaume or towards the spot where fighting was still going on, we were given the order to retire on Biefvillers. So we passed back over that undulating ground which had witnessed our day's struggle and was strewn with corpses; as many of ours as the enemy's. The cold was so intense that most of them were already stiff and hard. Most, not to say all, were barefoot. Well indeed, it is at such moments that shoes are at a premium! After having passed through Biefvillers, the regiment was halted at Achiet-le-Grand where it received the order to go into billets.

Our losses had been quite significant.[11] However, no member of our field-mess had been hit, and it was with great delight that all six of us met up again around an excellent meal that our far-sighted comrade Michel, who had been warned before us of our withdrawal, had succeeded in procuring everything while establishing his field-hospital. Naturally the conversation turned on the battle. Tramond did not stop fuming. Was it not possible, since we had conquered the ground that had been fought over, to go forward to complete the rout of the enemy, whose retreat could have been cut off by our right wing advancing through Thilloy? The fact is that the enigma was difficult to solve.

After dinner, in going to see my company settled in, I met the monk I had encountered that day. After our departure from the Biefvillers position, he had returned to the dying soldier's side to catechise him *in extremis*; but he had found only a corpse. 'Then that poor devil has departed for eternity without a ticket,' I said. And as the priest expressed great fears for the safety of his soul, I reassured him by telling him that, in dying in defence of the soil of his country, that man could certainly have gone nowhere else but to paradise.

On reflecting on this incident I have tried to recall whether, on a single occasion during the critical events of that war which was very murderous for us, I witnessed any manifestation, however feeble, of religious feeling in the soldiers around me, and I have been unable to recall from memory anything of that kind. Yet I have seen a fair number of people die around me; I have seen a great many severely stricken, and never at these supreme moments have I seen the minds of these poor men turn towards religion. Moreover, during the long course of this campaign I never heard the desire expressed by a soldier, not merely to perform any religious rite whatever, but even to have contact with a minister of religion. Naturally I am talking only about what happened in the camps, and not in the hospitals or field-hospitals where I very rarely set foot. Yet it is commonly accepted that without religious beliefs you cannot have good soldiers. That is just a saying. I am far from claiming that a strong and sincere faith in a man might in any way weaken the sense of duty; I believe indeed that it could only exalt it. But it is indisputable that this sense of duty is very real in the majority, independently of any link with any religious belief whatever. Reason and experience, moreover, are there to prove it.

We were greatly astonished on the evening of the 3rd, when we found ourselves in the enemy's positions which we had conquered after a day of struggle, to receive the order to return to the rear, right back to our point of departure. Imagine our stupefaction next day, the 4th, to find ourselves returning once more towards the strongholds of the north. After Amiens, after Pont-Noyelles, such a move was readily understood, since we had been worsted in those two encounters. But after Bapaume, where we had incontestably been the victors, this seemed to us an unparalleled blunder.[12]

On the 4th and 5th the regiment was billeted at Blairville, a little village on the Arras road. It was there that our supply convoy finally rejoined us, not without having suffered numerous mishaps, for it had been attacked by several squadrons of German cuirassiers which the escort had had great difficulty in driving off.

From the 6th to the 9th we were assigned to the small market-town of Croisilles. We were only a dozen kilometres from Arras. We heard no more of the enemy. My company mounted picket guard on the night of the 6th and the morning of the 7th, and saw absolutely nothing. During the three quiet days which we passed at Croisilles, recommendations for promotion were drawn up in order to fill up the gaps made in our ranks by the preceding fighting. Fernandez,[13] who had been promoted lieutenant after Pont-Noyelles in place of a lieutenant of the battalion who had been killed in that battle, was nominated for captain and confirmed a few days afterwards, still in our battalion and replacing the captain of the 4th Company killed at Bapaume. His career was progressing well. Having been made a sergeant-major at Metz in July 1870, a second lieutenant on 12 September, lieutenant on 30 December and captain on 10 January 1871, he could not believe his eyes when he saw himself with three gold braids on his sleeves. In fact this rank was fairly won and equally well maintained, for in this particular case at least luck had hit upon an officer of real worth. For the captains it was a slower process, since there were five competing for one vacancy for command of a battalion. However, I was recommended for this rank and, as I found myself the most senior captain in our regiment, I was able to conceive some hope of being appointed major before the end of the campaign.

During our stay in this place we received a rather large batch of items of every kind as a result of national donations: flannel shirts, vests, stockings and socks, woollen underpants, belts, etc. The men were able to clothe themselves warmly beneath their uniforms which the wear and tear of life on campaign had worn pretty thin. As there was more than could be distributed, the officers were authorised to provide themselves with what they might have need of. I laid claim to a superb pair of violet woollen stockings which gave me real bishop's legs when I took off my long boots.

Thanks to this generosity, the men did not have to suffer too much from the cold. Otherwise, the considerable wealth of these regions of the north saved them from all sorts of privations, except those imposed by the impossibility or irregularity of supply during critical moments when battle was near. In nearly all our billets we had found livestock to buy or to requisition, and it can be affirmed that not a man had to suffer from lack of food. Also the state of sanitation had always been excellent. I do not believe that I had ten men sick in my company during the whole of the campaign.

On the 10th we left Croisilles and, after a march of scarcely ten kilometres, we reached Ervillers on the road from Arras to Bapaume. In the evening, after dinner, the major kept us back and informed us that there was no point in going to bed, for the night was to be put to good use to carry out a surprise raid. Towards two o'clock we got our men up and set off down the road. We passed through Béhagnies, then, on coming out of the village, we left the road and entered the fields to surround completely the village of Sapignies, which was occupied by a fairly substantial party of cavalry. We positioned ourselves facing the exits from the village and awaited dawn. As soon as we could just about see clearly, we swiftly penetrated the village by every street at the same time and went from house to house picking up men and horses; the former half asleep, the latter tethered in barns and stables. We captured seventy riders and horses. Not a shot was fired, so discreetly and quickly had the affair been managed. It was an outpost of cuirassiers placed on picket guard in front of Bapaume, which had been reoccupied by the Germans a few days after the battle. The success of this raid certainly surprised us as much as the enemy. Could we have imagined indeed that a picket guard would guard itself so badly?[14]

Once the prisoners had been gathered up, each company had been reassembled at the exit of the village corresponding to the sector of action which had been assigned to it. Mine was on the road from Bapaume. I had formed the men in two ranks and roll-call had begun when nearly all of us together saw a German cuirassier who, having passed beyond the last house in the village, was trying to reach the Bapaume road by way of a rather steep slope across fields. I immediately ordered weapons to be loaded and before he could disappear volleys from two squads each of about 150 rifles had dispatched three hundred bullets personally addressed to him. Yet on arriving at the crest he broke into a brisk gallop which indicated in the clearest fashion that both horse and rider were in a state of perfect health. We had fired at 200 metres at the very most and none of our bullets had hit him; yet he must have felt their wind and believed himself lost. There was a lucky devil! And with all my heart I hope that he escaped as luckily from the dangers that he had to face in the last days of the campaign. The colonel, drawn by this fusillade that nothing seemed to justify, took stock of the incident. He seized the opportunity to give me a dressing-down in front of my company, saying with reason that men endowed with so little steadiness and who were such bad shots could not be well commanded. As he was the best of men, he made me understand a little while afterwards that if in doing this he had seemed hard on me, it was so that I could use his reproach with my men in order to exact more calm and obedience from them in the future.

After this little surprise raid the battalion departed on a reconnaissance to Favreuil, where there was no sign of the enemy. A few hours later we entered Bapaume which the Germans had just evacuated. We remained there until the 14th. My company took picket guard on the evening of the 12th. On the 13th, in the morning, we saw only a few enemy riders who came to prowl out of range around our advance posts. There we learned from local people that during the night of 3/4 January the Germans, considering the battle lost and fearing that our right wing would cut off their line of retreat on Péronne, had evacuated the town. There was great astonishment when, on the morning of the 4th with the Germans gone, no French troops from among those believed to be still in the immediate vicinity of the town had appeared in the suburbs. If, instead of making us abandon the battlefield on the evening of the 3rd for no reason, Faidherbe had only left us in the conquered positions, the enemy's retreat would not have escaped us. We would have entered Bapaume, and perhaps the Germans, seeing in this act an intention to pursue, would have raised the siege of Péronne, which we could have revictualled.

It was during our stay at Bapaume that news reached us of the capitulation of Péronne.[15] Thus our famous offensive undertaken on 1 January with the object of raising the siege of that fortified town – the possession of which was of capital importance to us because it defended the last crossing-point of the Somme still remaining to us – this offensive, in the course of which we had met and conquered the enemy in front of Bapaume, had had no result at all thanks to the timidity of our commanding general who had not dared or known how to profit from his success! It was truly discouraging.

On the 14th we set off down the road and, after a march of nearly twenty kilometres, entered Albert which the Germans had just evacuated precipitately on our approach. On the 15th the battalion was sent on reconnaissance towards Bray. It was the road we had travelled on our first day of campaigning on 26 November 1870. Bray was empty of all enemy troops, but on the left bank of the Somme we noticed cavalry patrols which were observing our movements.

CHAPTER V

FINAL DEFEAT AT SAINT-QUENTIN

16–27 January 1871

'The spectacle inside the courtyard was heart-rending.'

March towards the Oise – Bouchavesnes – Vermand – Tiring day of 18 January – 19 January, Battle of Saint-Quentin – La Neuville-Saint-Amand Farm – An eventful retreat – Valenciennes – Last shots

On the 16th the great flank march that was to lead us to Saint-Quentin began. Although we were in the immediate presence of the enemy, who pressed at our heels continually during these three days of marching, Faidherbe undertook this manoeuvre with the aim of proceeding towards the Oise against the enemy's communications. This was all that we knew, thanks to our major who kept himself informed by mixing with the generals. We did not suspect the danger to which we would be exposed, knowing nothing of the strength and position of the enemy army.[1]

The cold, so severe since the beginning of December, had given way to a very marked thaw. The roads were covered with mud, the utterly sodden fields were impassable. The smallest streams overflowing their bridges made crossings long and difficult. Leaving Albert early in the morning, after a most trying march (24 kilometres) we arrived at Bouchavesnes on the road from Péronne to Arras via Bapaume. The enemy had followed our movement by means of numerous cavalry patrols. One of them, met with unexpectedly in a fold of the terrain, passed through our column at the gallop in the interval between two battalions and was able to escape without hindrance. My company had to mount guard on the Péronne road. I had the greatest difficulty in establishing a few posts and sentinels, for the night was dark and the terrain beyond the road almost impenetrable. I stayed on my feet all night, for my men, a little on edge as a result of brushes with enemy, fired almost continually. In the morning we had to repel an infantry reconnaissance approaching from Péronne, according to what a wounded German soldier left in our hands told us.

On the 17th we set off again and once more put in a march of 25 kilometres by terrible roads which led us to Vermand. All along our route the cannon had thundered to our right, but quite distant from us. This could not but make us anxious, and you could guess from the men's preoccupied air that grave worry was besetting their minds. I sought to raise their morale, but without great success; and then, it has to be said, they were beginning to have had enough of it. If to that you add intense fatigue and a diet which had become deficient and very irregular, you can understand how little faith we were entitled to place in their resistance or their spirit in case of an encounter, which appeared imminent.[2]

After having supervised the quartering of my men in one part of the village and having provided for them to be fed, I went to the lodging that had been assigned to me. It was a very small house, the ground floor of which was occupied by a grocery store. There I found some very kind people who fussed around me and overwhelmed me with attentions. I was so dead beat that, forgoing dinner at the field-mess, I wanted to go to bed immediately: the more so as the bed allocated to me at the rear of the shop looked very enticing. But, in the face of the very gracious insistence of the mistress of the house, I felt myself obliged to share their meal, which besides was exquisite. Among other dishes there was a cabbage soup, the smell of which still titillates my nostrils twenty-five years later. I marvelled at the good sense of my hosts, so unpretentious in their lower middle-class manners. Their way of judging events, of expressing their patriotic anxieties, was very restrained but very proper. They had had no cause to complain at the presence of very disciplined German troops. Everything that had been taken had been paid for or requisitioned in the proper way. Finally, at about 8 o'clock, I was able to bid them goodnight and to retire. Heavens! What a comfortable bed! I scarcely had time to enjoy it, for I had only just put my head on the pillow when I fell fast asleep.

On the 18th at daybreak we were on the road to Saint-Quentin. The weather was wretched, with cold rain, mud, a gloomy and penetrating mist and, to cap it all, in the distance to our rear from about ten o'clock onwards there was a muffled but well-sustained cannonade which made us cock an anxious ear.

At midday we arrived at Saint-Quentin. We had taken five hours to cover some twenty kilometres. Arms were stacked in a street in the suburbs and the men began to make cooking arrangements; but the cannon thundered more and more and even seemed to draw nearer. Our rearguard was seriously at grips with the German 15th Division, which seized Caulaincourt and Trefcon from it in succession. General Derroja then ordered us to take up our weapons again and the regiment, tipping up its cooking-pots, set off on the march back towards Vermand in the direction of the fighting. After an extremely slow and laborious march, seeing that the column took five hours to travel a dozen kilometres, we arrived in the evening at the scene of the contest. It no longer consisted of anything but a very lively fusillade engaged at a distance between our men who occupied Vermand and the enemy, who was making the semblance of an attack on the village. In the darkness the gunshots looked like a shower of sparks.

We deployed in the orchards and took position on the left of the line of battle. After an hour or two, everything having reverted to the most complete quiet, we returned to Saint-Quentin. The night was dark; on the road you could scarcely make out the figure of the man next to you. The men were jaded. How many remained exhausted on the heaps of stones or in the ditches beside the road, seeking a semblance of rest in the melted snow, their teeth chattering, starving hungry![3]

On the morning of the 19th, before daylight, the division was reunited once more at Saint-Quentin and the 67th established itself in the suburb of Ille,[4] on the road from La Fère to the south of the town. I was making arrangements to collect food and to ensure that the men got as much rest as possible, when the cannonade once more boomed out ahead of us, towards the south, and in a few minutes became so unbroken that there was no doubt in my mind as to its significance. It was a real battle starting.[5] Breakfast was put off until later. I rapidly inspected weapons and had the battalion caisson replenished with the proper quantity of cartridges, then we started down the road for the battlefield. My battalion got in motion at about half-past eight and headed towards the hillock at Tout-Vent from where our artillery was responding to the German guns which were supporting the attack at Grugies. My company was at the head of the battalion which was thus marching with its left flank to the front, as one says in military language. At first we followed the main road from La Fère before

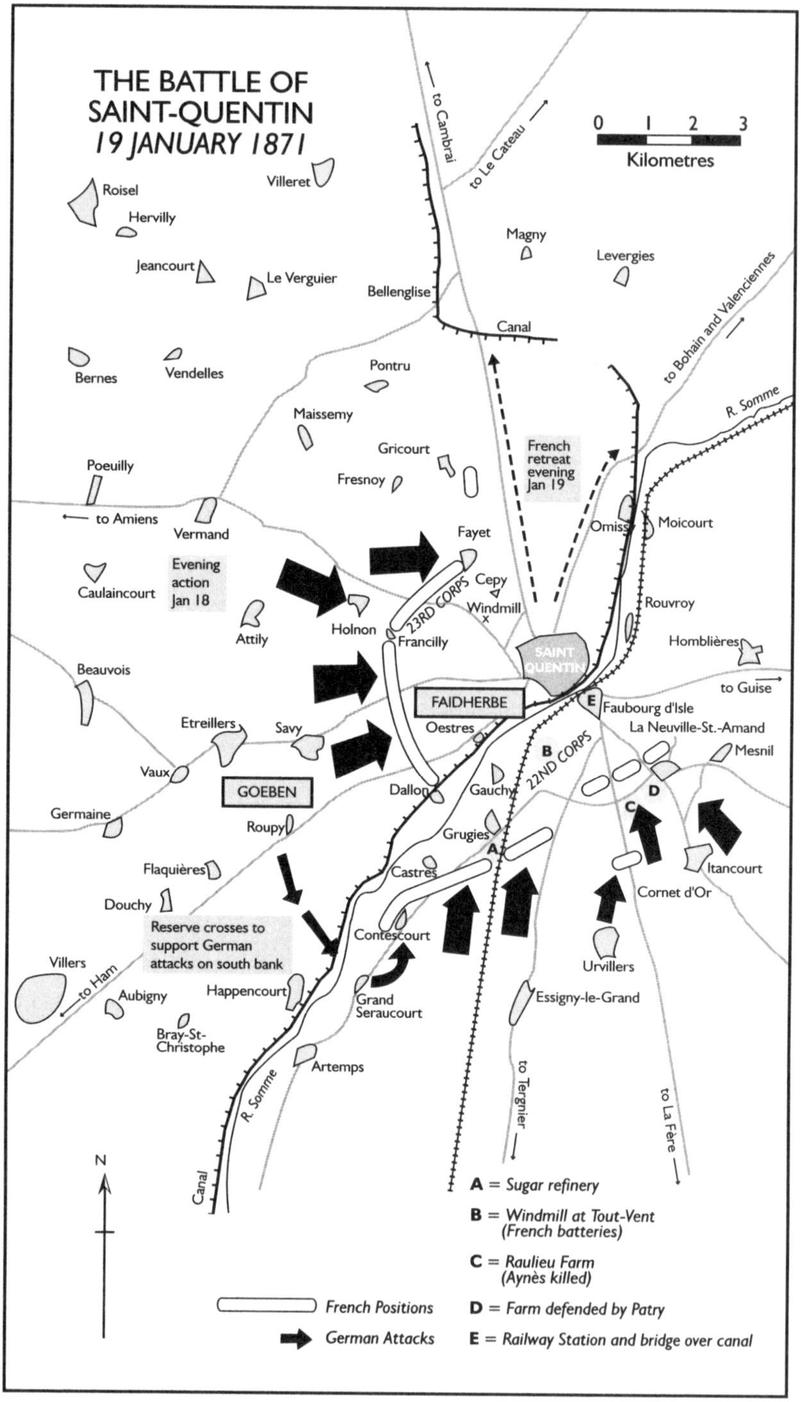

THE BATTLE OF SAINT-QUENTIN
19 JANUARY 1871
0 1 2 3
Kilometres
to Cambrai
to Le Cateau
to Bohain and Valenciennes
Roisel
Hervilly
Villeret
Jeancourt
Le Verguier
Bellenglise
Magny
Levergies
Canal
Bernes
Vendelles
Pontru
Maissemy
R. Somme
Gricourt
Fresnoy
French retreat evening Jan 19
Poeuilly
to Amiens
Vermand
Fayet
Omissy
Moicourt
Evening action Jan 18
Caulaincourt
23RD CORPS
Cepy
Windmill
Holnon
Attily
Francilly
Rouvroy
SAINT QUENTIN
Hombličres
Beauvois
to Guise
FAIDHERBE
Faubourg d'Isle
Etreillers
Savy
Oestres
La Neuville-St.-Amand
Mesnil
22ND CORPS
Vaux
GOEBEN
Dallon
Gauchy
Germaine
Roupy
Grugies
Flaquières
Castres
Itancourt
Cornet d'Or
Douchy
Reserve crosses to support German attacks on south bank
Contescourt
Urvillers
Villers
to Ham
Aubigny
Happencourt
Grand Seraucourt
Essigny-le-Grand
Bray-St-Christophe
Artemps
R. Somme
to Tergnier
to La Fère
N
Canal
A = Sugar refinery
B = Windmill at Tout-Vent (French batteries)
C = Raulieu Farm (Aynès killed)
French Positions
D = Farm defended by Patry
German Attacks
E = Railway Station and bridge over canal

turning right into a farm road which, sometimes deeply embanked and sometimes in the open, wound across the fields to reach the hill. The German shells which were missing our batteries came on to strike around us in the sodden clay and for the most part buried themselves in it without bursting, making a frightful whistling and sending up volcanoes of mud.

I was marching in front and to the left flank of my company, beside the sergeant who was serving as its guide, when I suddenly felt a strong pressure from him on my right arm. At first I yielded to it without paying much attention, but as this pressure continued more strongly, and as the company's direction was deviating far too perceptibly to the left of the road as a consequence, I said to the sergeant: 'Why are you pushing me like that? March straight ahead and keep to the right rather than to the middle of the road.' But he, with his face already very flushed by the prospect of combat, indicated to me by a most expressive glance a man all dressed in black coming down the road very rapidly in our direction. It was a priest who, doubtless drawn by curiosity, had wanted to see a battle from up there and, quickly edified, was returning with great strides to take refuge in the midst of his flock. 'Well!' I asked the sergeant. 'How can the presence of this priest affect the direction you should point the company in?' Still working hard at bearing to the left, he replied: 'Captain, he must not pass to our left, for that would bring us bad luck. From the way in which I have marched he will be forced to pass to the right and we shall have warded off evil fortune.'

I could not help laughing and I allowed him his whimsy. The priest hurried by, brushing the right flank of the company, and the sergeant breathed easily. Yet this subtle tactic did not bring good fortune to the poor fellow who had applied it so conscientiously; in fact he took a bullet in the arm one hour later. On the very road from La Fère where he had been wounded and in the midst of heavy firing, Michel applied a temporary dressing and then, giving him a friendly tap on the shoulder, said to him: 'It's only a scratch which will get you a medal; but all the same go and have a lie down in the hospital that has been set up in town.' He had scarcely spoken these words when a bullet hit the unfortunate sergeant in the head and knocked him dead into the arms of the doctor who, with his imperturbable phlegm, cried out: 'Oh! The brute! He has made me waste my time and my bandages! I haven't got that many either.'

After having passed the priest we arrived on the height of Tout-Vent. Major Tramond then halted the battalion and massed it a little in rear of the crest, the companies in line one behind the other, mine in front. We had the men sit on the ground in order to keep them out of the enemy's fire as much as possible. Then the officers went up to the batteries to see what turn the battle was taking.

Quite far off on rising ground to the south enemy batteries were venting their fury on ours. In the low ground two firing lines of infantry separated by about 500 or 600 metres were filling the hollow formed by the terrain with whitish, fleecy smoke which rippled like curtains of watered silk. On our right the crackling of unbroken volleys indicated desperate fighting.[6] On our left nothing yet: we found ourselves on the extreme left wing of the line of battle. We had been there for about half an hour without any very appreciable change in the situation when Major Tramond, who never lost his sense of priorities even in the most critical situations, proposed that we might as well take lunch where we were while awaiting events. Michel, equally resourceful as master of the field-mess or dedicated doctor, signalled to a man who quickly unbuckled his knapsack and took from it a most agreeable lunch. At the moment when he was unwrapping the paper containing a very fine-looking ham, the commander of the brigade, Colonel Aynès, arrived at the gallop and told Major Tramond to follow him immediately with his battalion.[7] Farewell ham! Farewell feast! I had had nothing in my stomach since the evening of the day before yesterday. The cabbage soup of the good grocer of Vermand had well and truly gone down after the many kilometres I had marched the day before. Everything was put back in the knapsack and each of us took his regulation place, with our stomachs empty but our hearts steadfast.

Led by the brigadier, the battalion moved in mass formation towards the La Fère road, which it crossed. There it was halted. Although we were in rear of the crest of the plateau the bullets were falling thick and fast. Colonel Aynès called on Major Tramond for two companies and he quite naturally gave him the two he had immediately to hand, that is to say mine, the 5th, and the following one, the 4th, commanded by Captain Fernandez. The colonel, thereupon addressing himself to me as the most senior, said: 'Captain, you will go with these two companies to that farm which you see over there; you will occupy it strongly and you will defend it to the last extremity. The position is very important. It anchors our extreme left and it covers our only line of retreat.'

I received this order without turning a hair; but my puzzled look and anxious features no doubt made an impression on the colonel, for, without taking his eyes off me, he added: 'You have understood properly, haven't you?' Then, encouraged by his benevolent manner, I said to him: 'But colonel, what do you mean by the last extremity?' 'You will not leave that farm except on a verbal or written order from me.'

I knew what to do. I immediately put the two companies in motion, then, halting them in a deep ditch by the road where they were sheltered from fire, I swiftly gained the plateau on which the farm in question stood, in order to make a brief reconnaissance.

The farm consisted of a square enclosure with fairly high walls. The entrance, formed by a great arched gate, was on the side facing the enemy. Once through the gate you saw to the left, in the corner, the dwelling-house consisting of one storey and a corn loft. On the side facing the enemy it was completely protected by a huge barn containing stores of forage, tools, etc. Here and there, spaced out along the other walls, were the bakehouse, some little low animal sheds, a pile of hop poles, etc. The courtyard was occupied by the remnant of a troop in strange dress which I did not recognise at all; *francs-tireurs*, no doubt.[8] These men seemed to be all at sea. They were very agitated and were preparing to depart. Their commander, a man of advanced age wearing much gold braid, seemed completely flustered. I could get no precise information from him about what had happened there before my arrival. I returned rapidly to seek out my troops. Fernandez and I made quick work of getting our men in and organising the enclosure for defence, to which indeed it lent itself very well. Outside, to guard the flanks, I posted to right and left two lines of skirmishers who, taking cover in furrows, immediately opened fire on Saxon troops coming down from Itancourt, a village built on the high ground opposite us.

Once these dispositions had been taken, I sought to come to a precise estimate of the situation. To my right and several hundred metres away was a large farm[9] surrounded by an orchard bounded by a thick thorn hedge. A very violent infantry fire was enveloping it as if in a halo of smoke. I supposed that it was occupied and defended by the other three companies of the battalion. To my left, also several hundred metres away, was the village of La Neuville-Saint-Amand. It was to this flank that my attention turned. Was this village occupied by our men? Undoubtedly not, if I recalled the words of Colonel Aynès. However, I could see men moving on its outskirts who seemed to be armed. I had every interest in determining this point, for my downfall in short order could come from that direction if the enemy were occupying that village. I therefore resolved to go and see for myself. As all was going well at the farm and around it, I broke into a run, for the terrain separating me from the village was completely without cover and was swept by enemy fire. On approaching the village I recognised red trousers. It was a company of the 1st Battalion placed there a short while ago. Its commander assured me that there were no more French troops to his left. I returned to my post immediately, very pleased to know that both my flanks were well secured.

In our part of the field the fighting dragged on very slowly. All the same we maintained a fairly steady fire for about two hours when suddenly, from the windows of the first floor of the house, I saw to my right enemy infantry rushing upon our line and, a few minutes later, our troops defending the farm situated on my right flank hastily retreating on Saint-Quentin, at the same time that the village of La Neuville was evacuated without a fight by the company occupying it.[10] I came down into the courtyard, expecting from one moment to the next to receive the order from Colonel Aynès to evacuate the farm. My men, being well concealed behind the walls of the yard, suspected nothing and kept up such unbroken firing that it was impossible to hear yourself speak. On our front the attack was broken; but what would happen if we remained isolated on the battlefield for long with no support on either our right or left? I was very perplexed, for I saw nobody coming. My comrade Fernandez shared my intense anxiety.

The Germans had quickly brought us under a troublesome fire. The Saxon battalion which had just taken the farm on our right bore down on our right flank while the Prussian battalion which had penetrated into La Neuville menaced our left. The men posted in the furrows halted this double envelopment while frontal firing was maintained from the farm. Seeing the difficulty his infantry would have in taking this redoubt of sorts, from which we were resisting under cover from his fire, the enemy halted his offensive movement. I was already rejoicing at this respite, which would have allowed us to receive either the order to retreat or reinforcements, when a shower of shot cut short my pleasure. A battery of artillery (perhaps only three guns) established about 150 metres away in front of Itancourt, was coming into action to prepare for the decisive infantry attack. What a dance we had then! Shells succeeded each other with incredible rapidity, some passing over the courtyard with such a shrill whistling that they made everything shake, others penetrating the roof of the barn, sending its timbers flying, or passing through the house, knocking down dividing walls, making holes in floors, smashing furniture to smithereens, or still more bursting right in the middle of the yard with an infernal uproar. I began to be unsure which way to turn amidst this tumult in which the screams of the wounded were painfully mingled.

Our losses, minimal until now, became more and more serious. My comrade Fernandez, who commanded the 4th Company, was hit in the shoulder by a shell splinter, his lieutenant was wounded in the face, my lieutenant had already withdrawn, severely bruised; directing the fight was becoming difficult. I devoted all my efforts to reassuring my men, who were becoming frightened under this hurricane of metal and fire unleashed around them. I begged them not to fire, to save their cartridges to resist the infantry attack which could not be long in coming. Wasted labour! They carried on firing without being able to see anything. To answer noise with noise brought them a satisfaction which kept them occupied and at all events held them at their posts.

My NCOs did not spare themselves, going from one man to another, and we were thus able to keep all our people in hand. I went to take a look at my skirmishers outside. In crossing the courtyard I saw a great stream of blood mixed with remnants of fabric and pieces of clothing flowing from the hole at the entrance to the oven. It was a man who, crazed by fear, had sought safety in the bake-oven, and had been reduced to mincemeat by a shell which penetrated the masonry. Outside everything was going well and my skirmishers were not suffering to speak of from the cannonade, which was passing over their heads. Just as I re-entered the courtyard a shell bursting in the barn set fire to the stored hay. In a few minutes, under the impulsion of a south-westerly wind, the barn was on fire and the conflagration had spread to the other buildings.

Then the men lost their heads. With nothing able to hold them, they abandoned their posts and rushed in disorder towards the gate which had remained wide open. I forestalled them in an attempt to stop them and keep them together as a unit, but I was quickly pushed aside and the mad disorderly race towards Saint-Quentin began.

With outstretched arms I held back a group of twenty men close to the gate. Seeing that they were about to escape me, and doubtless at the end of my powers of persuasion, despite myself – oh, very much despite myself! – I hurled at them as a last resort this piece of arch-pomposity: 'So is there no one who will have the courage to die here doing his duty?' I had not finished speaking before a smile came to my lips, as if I had heard a mouth other than my own utter these memorable words. The consequences were not long in following: all the men whom I had hoped to keep back by this bombastic address took flight towards the town like a covey of pigeons and I found myself almost alone, surrounded by six or seven enlisted volunteers, men already mature, full of courage and dedication, who in the course of the campaign had always formed the real backbone of my company. This outcome, which I have reflected on very often since, has inspired me with profound scepticism on the subject of the effect which the words spoken by a leader can have on thirty or forty thousand men in perilous circumstances.

What was to be done? The cannonade was still going on, but I was well aware that at the moment when the enemy noticed the evacuation of the farm, which could not be long delayed, the cannon would fall silent to leave the rifles to do their work, and then we should be surrounded and taken prisoner.

The spectacle inside the courtyard was heart-rending. The men wounded in the course of the action had sought refuge in the house and had taken off some of their clothing in order to tend themselves. Now as the flames reached them they tried to escape by dragging themselves along painfully, all bloody and dishevelled; but the flames overtook them and they were burned alive. A man still in the barn strove to beat a path of escape; he was seized by the flames, blinded by the smoke. He caught fire standing upright like a match and fell into the blazing mass, producing a shower of sparks. Being unable to do anything for these poor men and no longer having the means to defend my post which had ceased to exist since it had burned down, and having no more soldiers, I chose to make a run for it while there was still time. I assembled my bodyguard, who had crammed themselves with cartridges taken from the wounded, and we got out.

The enemy infantry was already approaching and was about to surround us.[11] My lads put up an infernal fire which enveloped us in smoke. We took advantage of it to pass through the enemy line, not without some knocks, but at all events without serious damage. Forgetting that I had a sword at my side, I had picked up a hefty cudgel in the courtyard of the farm which served me better for knocking away the rifles of the Germans and for thumping on their helmets than the mostly lead blade of my sabre. We reached the La Fère road and began a race at full speed. The rifle fire followed us for a few moments, but the rapid movement of its targets rendered it harmless. We hurried down in this fashion for two or three kilometres until we reached the first houses of the suburb of Ille. There I found the Major[12] who on seeing me grabbed me in his arms and hugged me most tenderly. To excuse their escapade, the men of my battalion had taken good care to tell him that I had been killed at the farm. At the news of my death my orderly, Guyonne, whom I had left that morning very badly stricken with bronchitis at a house in the suburb, had got up despite the urgings of the people with whom he was staying and, quite alone, had reached the part of the battlefield pointed out to him in order to find at least the body of his captain. I did not see him again until several days afterwards. Fortunately he had escaped the enemy.

I learned that Colonel Aynès had been killed at the farm situated to the right of mine.[13] He had therefore been unable, while there was still time, to give me in person or have sent to me the order to evacuate the farm and follow the general retreat of the brigade. Our resistance in that farm, prolonged quite involuntarily, had at least had the result of allowing our artillery positioned at Tout-Vent to make its withdrawal in safety along the main road.

At this moment, at about half-past three, the battle was finished, at least for those of us who had fought on the left bank of the Somme, but unfortunately it was irrevocably lost. The Twenty-second Corps was in full retreat on the Le Cateau road. For my part I busied myself with rallying the remnant of my company, without great success. As I was scouring the suburb of Ille for this purpose I met the commander of our division, General Derroja, who amidst a group of soldiers of all arms was attempting, by having barricades of a sort constructed out of carts, tables and sacks of wheat – for it was market day – to defend the suburb step by step and so to retard the advance of the enemy, who besides was pursuing us only very feebly. I attached myself to him. When night fell we withdrew.[14]

The Germans had already occupied the railway station and from there were firing salvoes which swept the tracks.[15] I quite believe that I jumped over the two tracks at a single bound. I then found myself, after having crossed the bridge over the canal, alone, or nearly so, in a square where a boulevard and several streets met. Which should I take to go northward? How could I get directions? All the houses were shut up tight. In vain I rained blows on several doors, thumped on venetian shutters or ground floor windows. Nothing. The German batteries were already beginning to bombard the town, and the bursting shells had so terrified the inhabitants that not one dared show himself. I gave way to melancholy reflections, believing that before long I would be taken prisoner, for I was so tired that I literally could no longer drag myself along, when my attention was drawn by two horsemen passing by. Fearing that these men were the enemy, I threw myself into the corner of a gateway and from there, to my great and joyful surprise, I saw outlined in the uncertain evening light the familiar silhouette of our dear Doctor Michel mounted on his big white horse. He was followed by his orderly who rode a horse which had been snatched from the enemy – he and I both – and was still wearing the harness of the Prussian hussars. This noble lad gave up his mount to me of his own accord and helped me to get myself in the saddle, for I was utterly incapable of lifting a leg.

Michel and I entered the first street we came to at a trot and followed it until it took us out of town. There we found a little tavern with its lights on and still open, where we learned with great delight that we were on the Valenciennes road! So off we went for Valenciennes! At six in the morning we were at Bohain, at eleven o'clock at Solesmes where we had a semblance of lunch – or I did at least. I had had absolutely nothing at all since the evening of the 17th, and yet I found it impossible to swallow what there was. At three o'clock we arrived at Valenciennes. We dismounted at the Hôtel du Commerce. Once the horses were settled in the stable and in good hands I asked for a room. At four o'clock I was in bed and fast asleep.

I did not wake until twenty-four hours later, but feeling very hungry! I was all stiff, not only from the exhaustion of these last few days but also from the twenty hours' ride I had just made; I who had not sat astride a horse for several months. But if my body was bruised, my mind was fresh and cheered by this long and comfortable sleep. I vividly went over in my mind the recent events which had led me there. During the almost hand-to-hand fight I had put up to get away from the La Neuville Farm I had suddenly felt a sharp pain in my lower right jaw. I had put my hand on it and, finding no trace of blood, I was very perplexed. I got an explanation of the mystery when I looked at myself in the mirror. The right tuft of my beard had been carried away by a bullet and numerous little points of blood had replaced the missing hair roots. In dressing myself I counted several holes in my clothing caused by German bullets; one on the inside of the knee of the left leg. The bullet had passed through my trousers leaving a very conspicuous circular hole. Several others had pierced my coat which had come unbuttoned in the excitement of combat and so had presented a large surface to projectiles. But my hide was intact, which was the main thing.

I also remembered that throughout the whole of the of the battle I had been haunted by a recollection of the waltz from *Le Petit Faust*[16] sung by Van Ghel in the role of Mephisto:

> I am Mephisto, faithful servant
> Of the fallen angel men call Satan:
> Like him I hate the mortal race.

From the time I entered the farm until the time I got away, this air had not left me and despite myself it was continually on my lips.

Michel and I, after having made a few purchases of underwear and toilet articles of which we were in very great need, and being refreshed by a wholesome bath, took ourselves to *Le Rocher de Cancale* which had been pointed out to us as the best restaurant in town, and there we took a dinner suited to our appetites. The next day, after a night's sleep nearly as long as the previous one, we went to the garrison offices and got the necessary directions to enable us to rejoin the regiment. We were told that its reassembly point was Beaurains, a little village three or four kilometres south of Arras on the road from Péronne. The entire day was spent completing the necessary formalities. On the 22nd at nine o'clock in the morning men and horses departed by railway. At midday we were at Arras and by the afternoon in Beaurains where we found some of our comrades from our battalion and field-mess.

I immediately enquired about my company. It consisted of a very small nucleus of scarcely fifty men, among whom was the second lieutenant, young de Linières, the son of our colonel, who had replaced Fernandez after Bapaume, and two NCOs and most of the volunteers.

The regiment lingered at Beaurains from 23 to 25 January. The men returned little by little and my company reached the total of 86 rifles, but no more. What a waste! To think that two months beforehand to the day, on leaving Lille, we had had 200 men present for duty! Certainly our losses had been great and I estimate that at Bapaume and at Saint-Quentin they must have amounted to 30 and 50 respectively. But to arrive at 114 there is still a margin to be accounted for. Undoubtedly the greater part of the 34 missing quite simply must have returned to their villages after the disaster of Saint-Quentin. In any event, I never heard another word about them.[17]

On the 26th the regiment left Beaurains for billets at Mercatel, four kilometres further along the same road. On that day my company mounted its last guard. On the morning of the 27th a reconnaissance party of German hussars advanced quite close to my line of sentinels, which they doubtless had not seen. They were received by a brisk fire which laid low only one of the four riders, and yet it was not possible to take him. His comrades picked him up and disappeared. Only the half-dead horse and the horseman's head-dress were left in our hands. These were the last shots of the campaign fired by my soldiers.

CHAPTER VI

ARMISTICE

28 January–17 March 1871

'Nobody wanted any more of the war. . .'

Armistice, 30 January 1871 – Mercatel – Voting in the elections for the National Assembly – From Arras to Dunkirk – Cherbourg – Peace – Coutances – En route for Paris – At the Trocadéro – Reunion with friends – At the Luxembourg

After the 27th the regiment did not move from Mercatel. On the 30th we were given the news of a twenty-one days' armistice.[1] We therefore more or less resumed garrison life. The proximity of Arras made life fairly pleasant for us. From time to time our field-mess was enlivened by the presence of the colonel's young children whom Madame de Linières brought along on her visits to her husband.

Recommendations for promotion had been drawn up a few days after the battle. I had featured in them for the rank of major, but I had no more success than after Bapaume. However, I had had a moment of real hope, for our battalion commander, Major Tramond, had been made a lieutenant-colonel and, given the truly phenomenal promotions which were meted out at this period, it was no very great pretension on my part to hope that I might replace him. Someone else was appointed. He was a captain of light infantry, Monsieur Pichat, who indeed had all the required qualities to fill this much coveted position worthily. I recognised with hearty goodwill that he was in every respect my superior and we were soon united in a solid and durable friendship.

To finish with these shabby questions of reward: one day when I had the chance to talk with General Derroja, who still commanded our division and who took great interest in me, I told him that I thought a recommendation for major was premature for me and that it would be best, if he was so minded, to nominate me for the Cross of the Legion of Honour which it would be easier for me to obtain. He approved my point of view and did the necessary. But, as power in the matter of nominations of every sort then devolved upon General Faidherbe, my recommendation, after a thousand tribulations, gained no result until the following 3 June.

The commanding general, wanting to take stock of the state of his army, reviewed us during the course of February. The troops made a good appearance to be sure, and the few who remained were certainly ready to resume the campaign – materially, it must be said, for in terms of morale it was a different matter. Nobody wanted any more of the war, myself included. We had struggled for two months knowing very well that it was absolutely impossible for us to change the course of events. If we had been better led, clearly the results obtained would have been more substantial; but then the enemy, sensing serious danger from our direction, would the sooner have accumulated large forces which would have crushed us. Saint-Quentin would have taken place several weeks sooner, that is all. This certainty of not being able to achieve anything useful, combined with a deep physical weariness, caused us to accept the end of the war with great satisfaction. Yet I cannot deny that this little campaign in the north, which we carried through in particularly interesting circumstances, had strangely appealed to me and it has remained one of my fondest memories, for after all it was really at that time that I learned my profession. I had done so with very young men who had not even fired a shot before finding themselves facing the enemy. And yet I must vouch that these men bore themselves very well on the battlefields, and from that point of view I had not discerned any real difference between their attitude and that of the soldiers I commanded at Metz who had from two to six years' service.[2] It is true that the officer corps was excellent, since it was almost entirely composed of NCOs who had escaped from Metz or Sedan.

During the course of February we had the elections for the National Assembly. Two lists had been distributed in our camps, for the army was invited to participate in the vote.[3] One was headed by the name of Monsieur Thiers, the other by that of Monsieur Gambetta.[4] On the day before voting several men of my company asked me to enlighten them on the merits of these lists and on their political significance. I therefore called my soldiers together and gave them this simple and short speech: 'Having never engaged in politics in my life, I cannot instruct you on the opinions of the men who are soliciting your votes. What I can say to you with complete certainty is that the Thiers list stands for the conclusion of peace and the Gambetta list for continuation of the war.' The next day when the votes were counted up I found that not a single Gambetta slip had been put into the ballot-box.[5]

On the 17th there was a great stir in Mercatel. The news had just arrived of our departure by stages for Dunkirk, whence we would be embarked for Normandy. If the war continued we would operate on the left wing of Chanzy's army.[6] Fortunately I had acquired, on payment of a hundred francs, one of the horses taken at Sapignies. It was a big Mecklenburger, still quite young, about five years old, spare and very ungainly, but at least it was an animal with four feet whereas I had only two in rather poor condition, still all swollen to the ankles through the excessive strains of recent days. So the prospect of putting in a few days' march held no fears for me.

On the 18th we set out and reached Lens, on the 19th Estaires, and on the 20th Cassel where we stayed on the 21st. On the 22nd we arrived at Dunkirk. During this pleasant journey I had one surprise after another. We were in fact received everywhere like conquerors. The crowd, pressing around us, acclaimed us with shouts of 'Long live Faidherbe!' 'Long live the Army of the North!' In the evening, while the soldiers were fêted by the inhabitants, the officers generally were invited for drinks, either by the municipality or by members of a private club.

It was at one of these receptions that I discovered the reason for this enthusiasm. Faidherbe was a native of the north and moreover he passed for a fierce republican, a qualification which in everybody's eyes endowed him with every military talent. One evening, finding myself among a group of notables of the town who appeared very intelligent and who heaped polite attentions on me, I had to listen to a rather fanciful account of our campaign, which according to them had been nothing but a series of victories. I tried to correct their completely erroneous understanding, but I promptly had to give up the attempt, for I saw that not only was I not convincing them, but that I was even offending them, which I would not have wished to do for anything in the world, for they were charming hosts. I therefore drank with them to the glory of Faidherbe, to the glory of the Army of the North, to Bapaume, to the Republic, to my great deeds, etc., and I thereupon went to bed, thinking myself a bit of a hero for all that! It's amazing what champagne can do!

On 23 February we embarked in the packet steamer *L'Atlantique*. After a completely calm passage of nineteen hours we disembarked at Cherbourg where we remained until 2 March. It was during our stay in that town that we learned of the conclusion of peace[7] with a widespread and general satisfaction, for we did not relish at all the prospect of resuming the campaign in the west. We had been told of the events which had taken place in every theatre of operations while we were fighting in the north, and we were perfectly aware that, in having to fight in addition the enemy armies set free by the fall of Paris, we would once again be marching from defeat to defeat until we were driven back against the sea.

On 2 March we left for Saint-Lô by railway, then from there we were directed to Coutances. There we began to settle ourselves as if we were going to stay for some time. The officer corps even made an official visit to the bishop. But our sojourn was not of long duration: on the 5th we returned to Saint-Lô, on the 6th we were put into trains and off we went for Paris! We got off at Mantes, where we camped on a large plateau entirely without cover and swept by a devil of a wind. The cold had returned and our situation was not at all pleasant. The men, who had been issued with shelter-tents at Cherbourg, lamented their billets in the north, and with good reason. Fortunately camp was broken the next day, and on the 8th we reached Poissy, where we made our camp near the river.

Next day we started out early, for we had to enter Paris the same day. We passed through Saint-Germain, still occupied by German troops who had been confined to the town's barracks for the occasion. The whole population was out, crowding the street we were marching down. We were the first French troops the inhabitants had seen for a very long time; for five long months they had bowed groaning under the burden of foreign occupation. Thus it was with a sigh of happiness that they gazed upon us; their hands sought ours, their eyes devoured us. You could read on the faces of all these poor people the anxiety of the past and the hope of a better future. To avoid adding to their troubles they dared not acclaim us as their hearts prompted them to do, but we had no need of any outward show on their part to feel all the sympathy we inspired in them, and to understand their inner joy. From time to time, from the crowd dominated by a forest of hats waved in the air, came an isolated shout of 'Long live the Army of the North!' followed by a redoubling of affectionate gestures. The women clapped their hands, some blew kisses. We were so pressed by the crowds of these very demonstrative people that our march was slowed up by it and delayed by all this touching, which was a delight to us. I was personally very moved, for I thought of the feelings that would have stirred my parents' hearts, if they had been in this crowd, on seeing their son pass, returned to them whole.

I do not know why, but Major Pichat was absent for several days and, as the most senior officer, I was in command of the battalion. Mounted on my big nag, I was following the drums and bugles section, which remained silent by order of higher authority. Full of pity, I was observing the expressions of sympathy from the crowd which surrounded me and which filled the gap separating the drums from the head of the column when, from a group of thoroughly fashionable-looking people, a very pretty young woman, dressed sombrely but with great elegance and exquisite taste, rushed towards me and, placing a bouquet of violets in my hand, said to me: 'You deserve these! Thank you!' Needless to say I did not know this lady at all and her gracious offering was in no way personal to me; but that made me prize it the more highly. I felt so moved by this unreasoning but very fine gesture that great tears came to my eyes and fell on the bouquet. Not having known, unfortunately, the sweet intoxication of triumphal returns, it is difficult for me to make a comparison. But I doubt that it could leave a more sweetly charming impression in the heart than that which I felt at the touch of these flowers, which constituted my only crown of laurels.

After leaving Saint-Germain we entered the war-ravaged zone. We passed through Bougival, which was half-destroyed. Gutted houses, roads obstructed by trenches, trees with all their branches cut off, devastated gardens: that was what we met with at every step.[8] We finally entered Paris by way of Courbevoie and halted on the hillock of the Trocadéro which at that time was covered with nothing but grass, and there we established our camp. We stayed at this site until the 17th. We were then allocated to the Luxembourg Garden where the brigade was fully reunited.

Since our disembarkation at Cherbourg we had changed commanders. The brigade which had formerly been composed of our regiment and a regiment of *Mobiles* found itself broken up, as the latter had stayed behind in the north. It was reconstituted by the addition of the 68th *de marche*, and placed under the command of a general whose name I have forgotten but who, like a real old style general, began at Mantes to upbraid and reprimand us severely. He was a big, red-faced man who always seemed to be furious and whose mouth was constantly full of invective. How we missed the ways – so courteous, so full of good comradeship – of our former commanders in the Army of the North, Generals Derroja and Aynès!

Having thus been disorganised from above, we had to suffer the same damage from below. Scarcely had we arrived in Paris when the volunteers who had enlisted for the duration of the war were sent back to their homes and, unfortunately for us, were replaced by men belonging to the Army of Paris who, having since the capitulation been idle and mixing with the most unwholesome elements of the populace, were animated by the most deplorable spirit of indiscipline. On 16 March my company received a large contingent of men of the 106th, with a few NCOs from whom I did not expect much good.

As we had a great deal of free time during the week which the regiment spent at the Trocadéro, I had taken advantage of it to see once more those of my acquaintances who had not left Paris. It was a very great pleasure to meet again after having passed through such hard trials. The Parisians, shut up in their city for such a long time, were very curious to know what had gone on outside. Thus it was with great insistence and an insatiable demand for detail that my old friends interrogated me about what I had done during the campaign. One thing astonished me a great deal: that was to find in Paris, where only a vague echo of events that had occurred in the provinces could have got through, the same admiration for Faidherbe and his army that I had noted in the north. I did not seek to undeceive them and allowed myself once more to pass as a hero. I think that in the end I began to believe it myself just a little.

But what filled me with glee at our evening meetings in one or other of the boulevard cafés was to hear them rambling on matter-of-factly about military matters. Most of them had merely served in the National Guard. The ramparts had been their only field of battle; and yet they told all sorts of tales about it! Ah! How at Champigny[9] the *mitrailleuses* had mown down entire battalions! How one fellow belonging to some company or other of *francs-tireurs* could not take his absinthe if he hadn't killed his Prussian; and he had had it every day. One, but never two, that was his principle. And spies! Paris was full of them. It was they who had always warned the Germans on the day before about the sorties which were due to take place. Up there on the sixth floor of that house, at that window at the corner of the street, a spy waved signal-lamps at night which alerted the Germans, who must have had wonderful eyes to be able to see from six or seven kilometres away a paraffin-lamp burning in an attic window in the centre of Paris. And treason! All the military leaders, Trochu, Ducrot,[10] etc., had betrayed us. Only Bellemare found favour with them; he was the hero of Le Bourget.[11] Ah! Le Bourget! If you had seen the marines rushing upon the Germans with the bayonet, their boarding-axes between their teeth, and making such a massacre of them that their corpses served us as barricades. The members of the government had also been traitors. But all the same we at last had a republic. The twenty years of imperial corruption were washed away. The nation, re-tempered in the school of misfortune, had regained control of itself and everybody was ready to work with determination to put the country back on its feet.

And these men, who for the most part belonged to the upper class of society, spouted all this foolish nonsense with all the seriousness in the world, their voices trembling with an emotion which seemed real. I could not believe my ears, and when I tried to revive our old scoffing banter of former times I felt that I was out of tune in this chorus of puritans. It is true that they did not sing this song for very long. Already the charming ladies of sin exiled for the duration of the siege were returning with their hands and lips full of consolations. The big restaurants were reopening their salons and riotous living was starting up again just as in the accursed times of corruption. But it was brusquely disturbed by the Commune, which burst out like a thunderclap and once more upset the joyful existence of these grave patriots.

PART THREE

THE COMMUNE

THE COMMUNE

18 March–24 June 1871

'My heart was filled with a profound distaste. . .'

18 March – Rue de Charonne and Place de la Bastille – Amid the popular flood – Without troops – Return to Versailles – Camp at Satory – Reconstitution of the field-mess – Reflections on the civil war – Diary (April and May) – Decorated once, and again

On 18 March at two o'clock in the morning our brigade, commanded by General Wolf[1] who had succeeded our very choleric big man with the red face, departed from the Luxembourg, where we left our pitched camp, and was led by way of the outer boulevards towards the Bastille. The march was extremely slow and interrupted by many halts. It was dawn when we entered the Place de la Bastille. On this part of the march we had met hardly anyone to speak of, but in the neighbourhood of the square the Parisians were appearing in ever greater numbers and became a crowd.

These people appeared for the most part to be very excited. 'What are you going to do?' they said to us. 'A *coup d'état*, for certain. The Republic is to be overthrown again.[2] But this won't be the last word.' These words gave me much to reflect upon. After all, what were we going to do? Why this stealthy movement carried out by night? A *coup d'état*? But against whom? The government whose orders we were executing could not be thinking of overthrowing itself. It is true that Thiers was the government. Now Thiers was nothing but an old Orleanist.[3] Had he perhaps conceived the plan of handing over power to his old masters? In that case it could in fact be a *coup d'état*; and the task began to seem somewhat repugnant to me. To start a civil war in the disastrous circumstances in which the country found itself, materially and morally ruined by this awful war, seemed to me not only culpable but even criminal, and if I had been able I would have slipped off then and there, for my heart was filled with a profound distaste at the thought that I might perhaps in a moment be obliged to fire on fellow countrymen. And what for? To bring the Orleanists back to the Tuileries.[4] In my judgement the return of a fallen regime, whatever it might be, could be no compensation for a probable massacre of the populace of Paris.

It was while ruminating on these more or less bitter thoughts that I found myself in the Place de la Bastille at the foot of the bronze column.[5] Just at that moment a fireman was engaged in replacing a red flag, which had been set in the hand of the figure surmounting the monument, by a tricolour. A very dense crowd which we had managed to push back into the avenues leading into the square was giving itself over to rather hostile demonstrations. I no longer understood a great deal about what was going on. Why this red flag? What did it represent in the eyes of the people more than the national flag? What interest did the Parisians have in sheltering behind this worst emblem of disorder, especially in the present circumstances? That would finally be seen well enough!

I received the order to go and occupy the Rue de Charonne, with express instructions to prevent any kind of assemblage, especially of National Guards;[6] but not to use either cartridges or bayonets for that purpose. I stationed myself at a cross-roads near a church and from there, after having placed double sentinels in all the adjacent streets, I had the area scoured by frequent patrols.

I was never more at a loss in my life. I had been ordered to disperse any assemblies and the street was nothing but one great assembly in which my company was positively drowned. I myself had the greatest difficulty in moving, being surrounded by a crowd of people, men and women, who pressed me with questions. None of these people were in any way hostile and they talked to me good naturedly. 'You wouldn't fire on the people, Citizen Captain. You're a brave officer; your soldiers have told us so. You're not a dirty capitulator,[7] keeping your powder for us after not daring to burn it against the Prussians. What have you come to do here? You see, we're not doing anything wrong. We're only keeping watch because those scoundrels want to quietly do away with the Republic to land some other Badinguet[8] on us. But we don't want any of it and we'd rather get ourselves killed than submit to such infamy.' I reassured them as best I could, advising them to go home, telling them that the street had to be left clear, that we had no intention of staging a *coup d'état*, but that order and calm had to be assured. Little by little I was all but carried along by the flood into a wine merchant's shop, and those around me begged me to down a glass. I consented on condition of a strict promise that they would not try to make my men drink. I managed to extricate myself. My company was still in ranks in the street, surrounded, but their order unbroken by the people of the quarter who were chatting with the soldiers. But meanwhile the street remained full of people.

Suddenly I heard a bugle sound the assembly, and a hundred paces away I saw a National Guardsman blowing his instrument with all his might. I ran, or at least I tried to run, to join him and demand an explanation, but he disappeared before I could reach him. Some while afterwards in almost the same place I saw a cluster of rifle barrels appear above the crowd. This time I was luckier, and found myself facing forty armed National Guards who were assembling. A lieutenant was ordering them into ranks. I addressed myself to him, begging him to send his men home, seeing that I had orders to disperse all armed assemblies by force! He replied that he didn't care a damn and that if the sight of his troop displeased me, I had only to go elsewhere. That did it. I felt my anger rising, but I restrained myself, for I saw straight away the gravity of a conflict in this street surrounded by a crowd which was inoffensive and in no way ill disposed.

'Look comrade,' I said to him. 'You have your orders and I have mine. Let's arrange things so that we can both keep to them. If you absolutely must assemble your men, choose somewhere else out of my sight and that of my sentinels, and everything will work out for the best.' He reflected for a few seconds then, making his choice, albeit unwillingly, he said to me: 'You're a decent sort, all the same.' He gave the order to march by the right and disappeared, lifting a great weight from my conscience.

At last, at about eleven o'clock, the order reached me to rejoin the regiment in the Place de la Bastille. I carried it out with enthusiasm. But already a new press of people, coming from I don't know where, had altered the feelings of the crowd towards us. We were called capitulators, assassins, hirelings of Bismarck.[9] Not wishing to let my troops be broken up, I ordered them to form ranks and to fix bayonets. Finally I emerged on the Place where I found the rest of the battalion.

Expecting that we would occupy the square for some time, the colonel had arms stacked and the men were permitted, under the supervision of

NCOs, to get something to eat in the shops of the neighbourhood. The officers could go and take lunch, but only half at a time, in the eating-places adjoining the square. Fernandez and I entered a restaurant displaying the name 'The Four Sergeants of La Rochelle'.[10] We stayed there about an hour, and imagine our shock when we came out to see the Place de la Bastille completely empty of troops but crowded with people, and violently excited people at that. Some fanatic was in the process of replacing a red flag in the hand of the figure on top of the column. We decided that the best thing would be to separate and get out of our predicament singly.

So I entered the crowd to make for the Rue Saint-Antoine, and from there the Luxembourg. I made headway only with great difficulty, noticed only by the people immediately next to me, who allowed me to make my way in peace. But in the Rue Saint-Antoine, right from the start, some rather sinister-looking fellows, having spotted me, abused me without respite, hurling at me the customary insults of that epoch: 'Capitulator, scoundrel, assassin of the people, coward in the face of the enemy, etc.' I was not unduly ruffled by this. However, by attracting attention to me they stirred up those around me who jostled me and drove me into a shop doorway.

'What do you want?' I asked them. 'I don't understand your insults at all. I have never had any quarrel with the people of Paris, so I can't have assassinated anybody.'

'Then where do you come from?'

'From the Army of the North.'

'You fought the war with Faidherbe?'

'Yes.'

A complete change came about immediately. These same men whom I had seen disposed to disembowel me wanted to carry me in triumph.

'You've got to respect that one,' they said to the others. 'He's a brave man. He's one of Faidherbe's soldiers. He wouldn't have fired on the people, etc., . . .'

Once extricated, I moved off quickly, keeping close to the houses and promising myself that if some new difficulty should befall me I would play the soldier of Faidherbe, which at that moment was a magic name. And in fact I was able to escape the clutches of these madmen twice more by invoking this talisman. This gallant Faidherbe! If he never did anything for me either during the war or afterwards he had at least rendered me the service, without disturbing himself, of having saved my skin, to which at that time I attached a certain value.

Once at the Hôtel de Ville[11] I was saved! I hastened to take advantage of the space which allowed me more elbow-room to cross to the left bank where the most profound quiet reigned. I learned there that many columns of infantry coming from the right bank had headed towards the Invalides and the Champ-de-Mars. I took the same direction and at about five o'clock I found my regiment on the esplanade. Fernandez had also managed to escape the claws of the popular lion without injury.

On the esplanade of the Invalides on the evening of 18 March two complete infantry divisions were massed in good order, well under the control of their commanders, forming a corps of about 20,000 men. We awaited orders. It was there that the events at Montmartre became known to us; the murder of the generals, the defection of the 88th, etc.[12] From the Rue Saint-Dominique[13] we saw emerge a brougham drawn by a single horse. All I could see of the gentleman inside was his grey overcoat. The brougham stopped in the middle of the square; the two generals of division approached and held a confabulation through the door of the carriage with the man in question. After a halt of a few minutes, the brougham set off again towards the west at a fast trot. It was the Minister of War who was making his retreat to Versailles in good order.[14] At nightfall the regiment returned to its camp at the Luxembourg. I went to find a bed in town in the area nearby, permission to do so having been accorded to officers.

This episode at Montmartre upset me. Who would believe that, in order to carry off a few cannon improperly kept by the National Guard, it was necessary to occupy the whole of Paris militarily as if for a day of rioting? But if the government had really wanted to take some cannon out of the hands of the National Guard, there was no lack of them in the Luxembourg Garden. There was a whole artillery park of them, guarded by a post of only a few men of the National Guard, and for two days we had been camping next to these cannon which were not difficult to take in this case, and the seizure of which would not have caused any popular uprising. No: these events of 18 March were certainly not contrived by the government for the purpose of snatching from the hands of the National Guard some cannon which were no bother to anybody where they were and which besides could not have been used for mischief. Somebody had certainly had an idea at the back of his mind, the realisation of which failed in the face of the determined attitude of the people of Paris and the wavering attitude of a fraction of the army. What was this idea? No one will ever know, for it could only be avowed in the event of success. Such was my opinion at the time and nothing that has happened since has changed it.[15]

On the morning of the 19th, between eight and nine o'clock, I reported to camp for duty as usual. The regiment was no longer there. At the entrance to the Rue de Fleurus the regular army sentinels had been replaced by some National Guardsmen. I then learned that the regiment, having received the order during the night to report to Versailles, had left early in the morning; that at the moment when the head of the column was passing through the gates the colonel had been arrested by a group of National Guards, unhorsed, and dragged before the Central Committee[16] for interrogation; that the greatest confusion had then reigned among the troops, that disorder was at its height, and finally that only half the regiment had been able to extricate itself and get away while the other half, overwhelmed by a throng of National Guardsmen, had disbanded, dispersed and scattered in the various districts around the Luxembourg. And indeed, staring through the iron gate, I could not see a single red kepi; only the little tents of our camp standing unoccupied on the muddy ground of the garden.

I came away extremely worried. What should I do? Evidently I must leave straight away for Versailles. But was that really where the regiment had gone? Besides, I was very anxious about my horse and my orderly. In the end, as matters were not pressing,[17] I returned to the hospitable house where I had found refuge and friendship since my arrival in Paris. It no longer exists now: that dear old house that witnessed my marriage and the birth of my children has lately given way to a big apartment building. It didn't look much from the outside, but the interior was so comfortable, so well laid out, and furnished with such good taste. During the war a temporary hospital providing care for more than twenty wounded was established in the billiard room, opening onto a garden which was small, admittedly, but very prettily laid out. Because of its isolated position jutting out at the corner of the Rue Vaugirard and the boulevard of the same name, it had to some extent been more exposed than others to German shells and it had suffered some chips out of its walls.[18] Its residents, old friends of my family, had been obliged to take refuge in its cellars for several weeks. It was in this charming nest, in this warm and affectionate atmosphere, that I had the good fortune to live during the few days in March that my regiment spent in Paris. It was there and during this same time that the biggest event of my life was decided, for a long-standing closeness with a dear childhood friend suddenly turned into mutual love which was crowned a year later by our marriage.

Everybody was greatly astonished when they saw me return so soon and with such news. Scarcely a few minutes after my arrival we heard the sound of horse's hooves on the pavement. It was Guyonne, my orderly, who, ever canny and seeing that things were going wrong at the Luxembourg, had mounted the horse and, after having made a wide detour, had just arrived. The stable was empty, the horses of the household having been eaten during the siege, so the Prussian horse was installed there and Guyonne was lodged in the house.

I deemed it prudent to get out of my uniform, for I wanted to wander around Paris to witness the strange events which were not slow in developing. With trousers that were a little too short and, by way of contrast, a frock-coat that was a little too big, I was well disguised in an outfit in which nobody would recognise me. I walked the streets of Paris for three days without seeing anything much, but hearing some very rum things indeed. However, this excitement did not seem to me to presage in any way the formidable insurrection that was shortly to break out.[19]

Finally, on the 23rd, having received a visit the day before from Fernandez and Michel who had come from Versailles in civilian dress to tell me that my absence was having a bad effect on the regiment, I decided to depart. So leaving Guyonne, the horse and my sword in the safekeeping of my friends, I did up my military outfit in a parcel and took the train at Montparnasse station. At Clamart a post of National Guards stopped the train; a few guardsmen made only a token inspection of the carriages, and I reached Versailles. That same day I rejoined the regiment which was encamped on the Satory plateau. Of my entire company there remained only a sergeant and the three officers.

In the first days of April the regiment received the number of men and officers necessary to reconstitute its thoroughly depleted ranks from the depot of the 67th Line Regiment stationed at Alaise: and on Easter Sunday, 9 April, after having heard Mass in camp, it was directed towards the theatre of operations.

Our colonel from the Army of the North, Monsieur de Linières, had been released by the Central Committee. He had been retained in the regiment as lieutenant-colonel, and a colonel from the Army of Paris, Monsieur Landrut, had come to take command of the regiment.[20] He quite naturally came to eat at the same field-mess as his lieutenant-colonel, and I found myself once again with all my commanders as messmates. Colonel Landrut was in fact a most likeable man, very straightforward, tolerant, and more like a comrade than a commander to his officers, by whom he was esteemed and liked. Our table was further augmented by the adjutant of the battalion, Captain de Brouard, a former colonel of *Mobiles* in the north, with whom I had nothing but excellent relations. There were thus eight of us, making a hard task for Michel, who took duty to the point of devoting nearly all of his time to managing the field-mess.

After having passed the day of the 10th in camp at Vaucresson, on the 11th we reached the outpost line at Courbevoie and once again heard shells and bullets whistling past our ears.

To say that this campaign was not much to my liking would be quite contrary to the truth. It was not at all to my liking, any more than to those around me either. I had tried to get out of it and for that purpose had gone to see the officer in charge of personnel, General or Colonel Hartung,[21] armed with a recommendation from my brother-in-law, an old companion in arms of his. I had asked him as the greatest favour to be sent to Algeria, where affairs seemed to be heading for serious trouble.[22] He had firmly promised to do so and, armed with this promise, I had asked my colonel (this was right at the beginning of April) for permission to take leave for a couple of days to go and visit my sister who lived at Laval, while awaiting my appointment. He had freely granted me this and I had gone down all dressed up to Chantiers station, where I had bought my ticket.

But while waiting for the train I was seized by scruples. If during my short absence my company were to go into action, what remorse should I feel – I who would have left it without real necessity; I who as its leader should set an example in all circumstances and without debate? The train was in the station; I was about to get aboard when a force superior to my will, or if you like my will overcoming my desires, drew me away from the beckoning train and, with my ticket in my pocket, I returned to Satory. I said that I had missed the train and there was no further question of going. Poor human nature, what great efforts it takes to prevent you from miring yourself in the swamp of the most cowardly compromises of principle! I did well, besides, all other considerations apart, for my appointment to an African regiment never came through.

At bottom this great desire of mine to see myself assigned to an African unit derived from several causes. The principal one, which perhaps was only secondary in my rather troubled mind, was to avoid waging civil war, which was cruelly repugnant to me. The one which I admitted as secondary, but which was perhaps the principal reason, was to take advantage, under cover of these changing events, of the few days of administrative delay that must ensue to go to see my dear parents at Grenoble and my sister at Laval. I loved them so much – these souls so full of affection for me – and I knew that they had suffered so much during this campaign in which rare, very rare, news of me had reached them from time to time. Besides, I was impatient to tell them, especially my sister, godmother to my fiancée, about the state of my feelings, so novel for them and for me, who until then had seen love as only a remote deity. In the end I overcame all this, and I could only congratulate myself on having done so, for after all self-respect, whatever it may cost, is still the greatest personal satisfaction one can obtain, when one is sure of acting impartially.

No, I disliked this campaign, and although until then I had never thought of my carcass, I now contemplated with very marked displeasure the prospect of seeing it injured through some mischance. But once we got going this cloud of apprehension disappeared, for I have never been a fatalist, considering such a belief utterly degrading to our individuality, which can find honour only through use of its free will.

At first this war, as it developed, promised nothing of interest from the technical point of view. After the great operations of the Army of the North in the open air, to pass one's days and nights in cellars or behind walls was hardly alluring, and that is what befell us. Moreover, from the political point of view it was a blundering and even dishonest war, for it would have been possible to come to an understanding with our adversary at any time. With a few minor concessions it would have been easy to reduce this insurrection to nothing. At bottom, its leaders did not rightly know what they wanted. And should we not have put proposals to them, as we were incontestably the stronger party? And that would have been all the

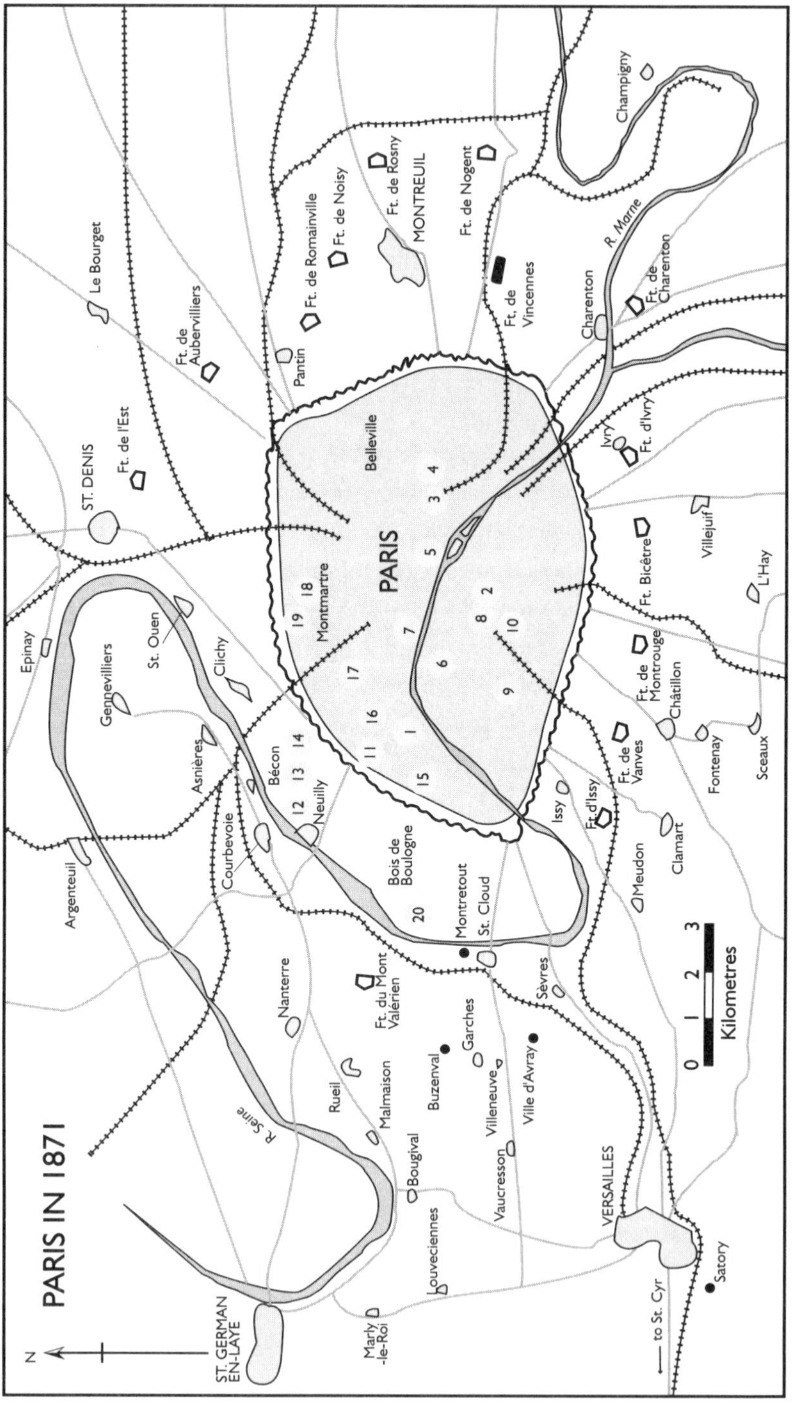
PARIS IN 1871
N
PARIS
Montmartre
Belleville
ST. DENIS
Ft. de l'Est
Le Bourget
Ft. de Aubervilliers
Pantin
Ft. de Romainville
Ft. de Noisy
Ft. de Rosny
MONTREUIL
Ft. de Nogent
Ft. de Vincennes
Charenton
Ft. de Charenton
R. Marne
Champigny
Ivry
Ft. d'Ivry
Villejuif
Ft. Bicêtre
L'Hay
Ft. de Montrouge
Châtillon
Fontenay
Sceaux
Ft. de Vanves
Ft. d'Issy
Issy
Clamart
Meudon
Epinay
Gennevilliers
St. Ouen
Clichy
Asnières
Bécon
Neuilly
Courbevoie
Argenteuil
Bois de Boulogne
Montretout
St. Cloud
Sèvres
Nanterre
Ft. du Mont Valérien
Garches
Buzenval
Ville d'Avray
Villeneuve
Vaucresson
Rueil
Malmaison
Bougival
Louveciennes
Marly -le-Roi
R. Seine
ST. GERMAN EN-LAYE
VERSAILLES
Satory
to St. Cyr
0 1 2 3
Kilometres

easier, as communications between Paris and Versailles were always open, almost right up to the last day.

In any case, if the Paris insurgents had been found to be uncompromising, would it not have been easy, with the forces at our disposal, to reduce them in a short time without dragging things out interminably in front of the ramparts, the effectiveness of which Monsieur Thiers no doubt wished to demonstrate since it was he who had had them raised?[23] Even after all the truly unpardonable mistakes at the outset, such as the evacuation of Paris by a completely unimpaired army, and of the forts, which is not even explicable and still less excusable, could we not, since we were faced with undertaking a siege, have conducted operations by the regular method for such cases? This would have entailed establishing batteries, digging trenches and working our way straight towards the ramparts by regular stages. On two separate occasions (I am speaking only of my regiment) we were led by night right up to the edge of the counterscarp,[24] waiting for dawn to show us a gate being opened. I shall never believe that, of the one and a half million inhabitants shut up in Paris at that time, given the constant communication that existed between the place and us, one hundred willing men could not have been found to open a gate for us. Or perhaps all Parisians supported the insurrection – which is not to be credited.[25]

Then why did it take two months to retake Paris, which could have been accomplished in a fortnight? Was it that Monsieur Thiers, after having juggled with the armies of the Republic and Napoleon,[26] and having finally realised his lifetime dream of being commander-in-chief of an army, wanted to prolong his pleasure? If it were not a case of a man whose patriotism was above all suspicion, one would be tempted to believe so. He was so happy when he came to rub shoulders with us. I saw him in our midst on two different occasions. Once he promised in the most solemn fashion that ranks acquired during the war would be confirmed to all those who had

Key to map opposite (some places mentioned by Patry)
1. Trocadéro. 2. Luxembourg Gardens. 3. Place de la Bastille. 4. Rue de Charonne. 5. Hôtel de Ville. 6. Les Invalides. 7. Tuileries. 8. Rue de Fleurus. 9. Rue de Vaugirard. 10. Montparnasse. 11. Porte Maillot. 12. Ave. de la Saussaye. 13. Bvd. du Château. 14. Bvd. Bineau. 15. Porte de Passy. 16. Place de l'Étoile. 17. Bvd. de Courcelles. 18. Rue Marcadet. 19. Porte Saint-Ouen. 20. Longchamp.

been in the Army of Versailles. The Commission for the Revision of Ranks held this assurance cheap. On the second occasion he made a speech in which he told us that at the moment everything was rotten in France, and that only the army remained upright and honourable. Why of course! What would have become of it without us?

Some alleged, in order to excuse the incomprehensible delays in taking vigorous action, that the troops were unreliable and could not be counted upon. What did they know about it? From the moment when they were properly established in the advanced positions they could just as well have held siege trenches and, instead of dawdling in front of Asnières and Neuilly, they could have advanced straight against the walls of the city, which could have been taken in a fortnight.

None of this escaped us, and it was for all these reasons that this campaign deeply repelled me. Thus the memories which I have retained of it are hardly pleasant to recall. Besides, they are of such little interest that the best thing is to pass over them in silence, for there is no practical lesson to draw from them from any point of view. So I shall content myself with copying out just as they are the notes I wrote up daily in my little field notebook:

11-12-13-14-15 April. Courbevoie, advance-posts, frequent cannonading during the day; intermittent rifle volleys.

16. Rest positions at Malmaison.

17-18-19 *idem*, in the camp huts at Saint-Cloud.[27]

20-21-22 *idem*, Rueil.

23-24-25. At the advance-posts at Asnières and Bécon; cannon and rifle fire on both sides of the Seine, chiefly around the railway bridge.

27-28-29-30. Rest in camp at Villeneuve-l'Étang.

1–2 May. Rueil, with picket guards on the plain.

During the night of the 2/3rd, march up to the rampart of the Porte Maillot and return without success.

4. Rueil.

5-6-7-8. At the advance-posts at Neuilly, Avenue de la Saussaye, Boulevards du Château, Bineau, Rue Eugène Sue. Rifle fire every night.

9-10. Rest at Rueil.

11-12. Bois de Boulogne. Second attempt to enter Paris meets no success.

13-14-15-16. Rest at Nanterre.

17-18-19-20. At advance-posts at Neuilly. Lively rifle fire nearly all the time.

21. Rest at Malmaison.

22. Set out at half-past midnight. Entry to Paris through the Porte de Passy without firing a shot. March into Paris. Avenue d'Eylau, Place de L'Étoile, Boulevard de Courcelles, Porte Bineau.
23. Capture of Montmartre by way of its northern slope, starting out from the perimeter railway. Rue Marcadet.[28]
24-27. On guard at the Porte Bineau, the only access point on the Saint-Ouen–Porte Maillot sector, to prevent all unauthorised entrance and exit.

Our losses during this accursed civil war were in all five officers killed, six wounded and one hundred and forty casualties in the ranks. Although this was not enormous, it was still far too many brave men struck down for an escapade of this sort which a government worthy of the name could so easily have avoided. In my company of seventy-five men I had two dead and five wounded.[29]

During this dismal affair, in which so many faults were committed on both sides,[30] only the Germans knew how to maintain a fully correct attitude. Yet it would have been good strategy for them, in order to add to our ruin and delay our revival, to provide covert encouragement to the Commune. Quite the contrary, as they had recognised the government of Monsieur Thiers, they scrupulously avoided putting the slightest obstacle in his way. They consented to a significant increase in our army, and to bringing forward the return of prisoners from Germany, who formed reliable bodies of troops whose contribution quickly made itself felt in the course of operations. Thus in this case, as in many others besides, they were fair-dealing and generous enemies.[31]

During the two months which the campaign lasted nominations for promotion and decoration were made on several occasions. I was the subject of several recommendations, both for the rank of major and for the Cross of the Legion of Honour, but none came to anything. Happily on 3 June the long-standing recommendations submitted from the Army of the North finally emerged from the ministerial files and I was made a Chevalier of the Legion of Honour. This reward certainly gave me the greatest pleasure, but much less than if it had been bestowed at the right time, that is to say during the armistice; for I really suffered during my stay in Paris in March at having reaped so little advantage from my two campaigns, particularly in comparison to the phenomenal promotions which had taken place in the Army of Paris and in the provincial armies. Be that as it may, it was with real satisfaction that I fixed the little red ribbon to my tunic and, immensely proud of my new adornment, called on my friends in the Rue Vaugirard, who had already been tipped off by Guyonne, who had left me at the Porte Bineau, that I had come through this period unscathed. How happy I was to see my dearly beloved fiancée. I had been very anxious about her during these two long months. The situation had not been without danger for the whole family in the midst of these madmen who respected nothing. Fortunately a Communard hospital had replaced that of the siege period, and the convention flag[32] made the house inviolable. My Cross was celebrated by these dear friends with all their hearts, and it was there that I truly appreciated its full value and experienced the pleasure that it gave me through the joy which they exhibited.

I again took possession of Guyonne and of my horse, which was even thinner than before. For want of forage this poor animal had lived on bread and leftovers from the table. He had grown accustomed to eating anything, the remnants of stew, of vegetables, and so on. But this regime had not fattened him up. I also recovered my sword from the Army of the North. For lack of this ineffective implement I had gone through the Commune with a simple wooden baton, a weapon which after all was quite sufficient, given the quality of the opponents we had to fight. For the entry into Paris we had been issued with large model Lefaucheux revolvers[33] for which we had to pay 30 francs. I have always believed that someone wanted to do a favour for some industrialist or merchant who possessed a considerable stock of these weapons and did not know how to get rid of them. Mine was much too heavy for my liking and was relegated to the bottom of my little trunk, from which it was removed only for the purpose of being fixed to a wall trophy once circumstances permitted me to be housed like ordinary mortals.

On 24 June Monsieur Thiers crowned his leadership as commander-in-chief with a review of his army passing over the turf at Longchamp.[34] On the same day appeared an order, as voluminous as a brochure, awarding an abundance of promotions and decorations to those who had helped to put down the insurrection and had assured him of the peaceful possession of the throne of his august predecessors. The numerous recommendations for the Cross made in my favour during the Commune bore fruit that day and I was named a Chevalier of the Legion of Honour for the second time.

No thank you! I declined to accept it! It is true that when you put on ribbon you should know when to stop, says the wisdom of the world.

In the face of this second award my friends and relatives, convinced that there had been a simple error, and considering besides that it was a Commander's Cross rather than an Officer's which should have been awarded me, strongly urged me to address a protest to the minister in order to have myself awarded an Officer's Cross which, according to them, the government had certainly intended to award me. For a moment I believed this was feasible, for after all it would be very acceptable. There was no lack of officers who had obtained two ranks in the Legion of Honour in the course of the campaign and who had certainly not done as much as me. But, after reflection, I renounced the idea. I considered myself very sufficiently provided for as I was, after a campaign in which none of us any more than the others had performed brilliantly. At hardly thirty years of age I found myself a captain and decorated; that was ample for me. On the other hand, if I acknowledged having in some slight way merited a reward, it was not so much for the services I had rendered during the war, since they could only be characterised as quite modest, my efforts having achieved no good for the country; it was not so much for those services as because, in escaping from Metz and in proceeding to take up arms again in the north, I had done a little more than was strictly my duty.

But as for the Commune, for that fratricidal war which every good citizen could wage only reluctantly, I felt that no reward was proper. In any case, I was very proud of having obtained my Cross by virtue of service in the Army of the North, and I should have been but little flattered to have obtained one by right of service in the Army of Versailles. And that is why I have been a Chevalier of the Legion of Honour for twenty-six years, delighted to be so, and without any desire to be anything else, since the only reason for promotion to a new rank would be that I had held the one below for such a long time. That is really not enough.

THE END

APPENDIX

THREE GENERAL ORDERS

(i) Bazaine announces the news of Sedan

TO THE ARMY OF THE RHINE

According to two French newspapers, of 7 and 10 September, brought to General Headquarters by a French prisoner who has been able to cross enemy lines, His Majesty the Emperor Napoleon has been interned in Germany following the Battle of Sedan and, the Empress and the Prince Imperial both having left Paris on 4 September, an executive power under the title of 'Government of National Defence' has been formed in Paris.

The members of it are:

Emmanuel Arago	Glais-Bizoin
Crémieux	Pelletan
Jules Favre	Picard
Jules Ferry	Rochefort
Gambetta	Jules Simon
Garnier-Pagès	General Trochu

Generals, officers and soldiers of the Army of the Rhine!

Our military obligations towards the country remain the same.

Let us therefore continue to serve it with devotion and with the same energy, defending its territory against the foreigner, and social order against evil passions.

I am convinced that your morale, of which you have already given so many proofs, will remain high in all circumstances, and that you will add new claims to the gratitude and admiration of France!

Ban-Saint-Martin, 16 September 1870

[Source: *Épisodes de la Guerre de 1870 et le Blocus de Metz, par l'Ex-Maréchal Bazaine* (Madrid, 1883), p. 178. Names of members of the Government, omitted by Bazaine, have been supplied from an official proclamation].

(ii) Faidherbe takes command

OFFICERS, NCOs, AND SOLDIERS

Called to the command of the Twenty-second Army Corps, my first duty is to thank the administrators and generals who have managed, in a few weeks, to improvise an army which has acquitted itself so honourably on 24, 26 and 27 November in front of Amiens.

Above all, let me express my gratitude to General Farre, who commanded you, and who, by a skilful retreat in the face of forces double his own, has saved you for the service of the country.

You will be resuming operations immediately with considerable reinforcements which are being organised every day, and your duty will be to force the enemy in his turn to yield ground to you.

Minister Gambetta has proclaimed that, in order to save France, he asks three things of you: discipline, moral austerity and contempt for death.

I shall exact discipline pitilessly.

If not everyone can attain moral austerity, I shall at least demand dignity and especially temperance. Those who today are armed for the deliverance of the country are invested with a mission too holy to allow themselves the least licence in public.

As for contempt of death, I ask it of you in the name of your own safety. If you will not risk dying gloriously on the battlefield, you and your families will die of destitution under the pitiless yoke of the foreigner. I do not need to add that courts-martial will do justice on cowards, for there will be none amongst you.

5 December 1870
General of Division
Commanding Twenty-second Army Corps
L. FAIDHERBE

[Source: Louis Faidherbe, *Campagne du Nord* (Paris, 1871), p. 85].

(iii) Conquer or die

Arras, 31 December [1870]

We are about to manoeuvre in the presence of the enemy. We must march and guard ourselves in a military fashion; not a single man must leave the ranks. Unit commanders will take care to ensure this; during our advances and our battles, cavalry will be placed in the rear to prevent stragglers from abandoning their posts. Unit commanders will take care to evacuate their sick, and those unable to march, to Arras.

At Pont-Noyelles we were unable to complete our victory because the enemy was close to a fortified city. Today, that advantage is in our favour.

I am therefore counting on you, when the order is given, to charge the enemy vigorously, in the French way, until he is put to flight.

The eyes of France are upon you; let each of you swear to conquer or die, and victory is certain.

By Order
Major General Farre

[Source: *Guerre de 1870–71, publié par la Revue d'Histoire, rédigé à la Section historique de l'Etat-Major de l'Armée* (Paris, 1901–13): *Armée du Nord II, Docs. annexes*, p. 132.]

BIOGRAPHIES

This section gives biographical information about some of the people who are mentioned in Patry's narrative and whose careers illuminate different aspects of the conflict.

BAZAINE FRANÇOIS-ACHILLE (1811–88) Bazaine was born at Versailles, though his father's family came from the village of Scy outside Metz which features in Patry's tales of outpost duty during the blockade. Bazaine's father was an army engineer who entered the Russian service and in effect abandoned the family he had left in France. Achille failed to get the necessary examination grades to enter the Ecole Polytechnique, so in 1831 he enlisted in a line regiment. He soon won promotions for his performance in combat and decorations for bravery. He served as a sergeant-major in the Foreign Legion in Algeria, then went with it to fight in the Carlist War in Spain. Back in Africa, he was in charge of an Arab bureau at Tlemcen in the province of Oran and took part in the expedition which captured the rebel leader Abd-el-Kader in 1847. In 1850 he was colonel of the 1st Regiment of the Foreign Legion. In the Crimea he succeeded to command of a brigade in the Legion following the death of its commander from cholera, and was made governor of Sebastopol after its surrender. In a successful Anglo–French amphibious operation he captured Kinburn at the mouth of the Dnieper in October 1855. In Italy in 1859 he won praise for the handling of his division at Melegnano and Solferino. Going to Mexico at the head of a division in 1862, he succeeded General Forey in command of the 38,000-strong expedition in July 1863. He was created a Marshal of France in 1864 and was virtually viceroy of Mexico. His territorial conquests were impressive, but it was impossible to hold on to them in the face of guerrilla resistance to the foreign occupation; which in turn led Bazaine to advise the new Emperor Maximilian to issue a draconian order for the summary execution of armed rebels. His relations with Maximilian deteriorated, and Bazaine had plenty of enemies to write letters to Paris accusing him of corruption and of intriguing to increase his own personal power. With the threat of intervention by the USA, Napoleon III withdrew his forces in 1867, leaving Maximilian to his fate. On his return to France, Bazaine commanded the Third Corps, then the Imperial Guard. It was the Third Corps which he led at the outset of the 1870 campaign, until Napoleon III appointed him to command the Army of the Rhine on 12 August.

Bazaine was popular in the country and all placed their hopes in him, but it would have taken an exceptional general with an excellent staff to extricate the French army at that point. Bazaine was not that man, and was tried beyond his capacity. In the battles around Metz he never gained the strategic initiative and allowed himself to be surrounded, failing to break out while at least a reasonable chance existed. His negotiations with the enemy, with a view to a Bonapartist restoration, were anathema to Republicans and were ascribed to a personal ambition to be regent and to control the country with his intact army. The capitulation of his army at the end of October was one of the worst humiliations in French history. Gambetta immediately issued a proclamation accusing him of treason, and a bitter attack in print by one of his own staff officers soon followed. After his return from captivity in Germany, Bazaine asked for a court of inquiry to answer the accusations against him. Although the Thiers government was not unsympathetic, a new ministry brought Bazaine to trial in late 1873. One of the Orléans princes presided. Bazaine was not found guilty of treason, but of having surrendered Metz without doing everything possible to save his army. He was stripped of his rank and honours and sentenced to death – a verdict immediately commuted to life imprisonment. After less than a year of imprisonment on the Ile Sainte-Marguerite, he escaped in August 1874 and settled in Spain. He lived out a miserable exile in Madrid, eventually deserted by the young wife he had married in Mexico. The enduring hatred in France against him was shown in the year before his death by press sympathy for the attacker when Bazaine was stabbed in the face by a demented ex-Communard. Bazaine was the French national scapegoat for defeat, and debate has continued as to whether the execration heaped on him by contemporaries was justified. It has been pointed out that the difficulties he faced were immense, that some of the calumnies against him were ill-informed or absurd, that as he had sworn his oath of allegiance to the Emperor and not to the unelected Government of National Defence he was acting properly and loyally in his dealings with the Empress, and that in October 1870 it would have been culpable to sacrifice his men needlessly. Yet ultimately his strategy was pusillanimous, his failure abject and ignoble. He might have lost no more men in breaking out than died in captivity in Germany, and, as his German opponents demonstrated, campaigns are not won by taking no risks. An enigmatic and inarticulate man, widely mistrusted, Bazaine was sufficiently out of touch with popular feeling to introduce in his defence a glowing testimonial from the German high command that he had acted very sensibly at Metz: in itself damning evidence in French eyes that the Marshal had failed to do his full duty in defence of his country.

BELLEMARE ADRIEN-ALEXANDRE-ADOLPHE CARREY DE (1824–1905) Graduating from Saint-Cyr in 1843, de Bellemare campaigned in Africa for five years, taking a bullet in his left side in 1845 and another in his right side during barricade fighting in Paris in the June Days of 1848. He served on the staff of General Lamoricière and taught at Saint-Cyr before further campaigns in the Baltic in 1854, the Crimea in 1856, Italy in 1859 and Mexico in 1862–3 where he was cited in orders after fighting outside Puebla. In 1870 he was colonel of the 78th Regiment stationed at Colmar. He distinguished himself in the frontier battles of Wissembourg and Froeschwiller and was promoted to brigadier-general on 25 August. After the disaster of Sedan he was among the thousands of French prisoners herded into the squalid, unhealthy Iges peninsula in a loop of the Meuse, but he slipped past the guards disguised as a peasant and escaped to Paris within a week. It was while commanding a sector of the defences during the siege that he mounted the spectacular attack on Le Bourget on 27 October that made him a popular hero. After the Battle of Champigny on 30 November he was promoted to command a division and led the centre column in the abortive Buzenval sortie on 19 January – the last effort to break out of the doomed capital. After the war the Commission for the Revision of Officers' Ranks reverted him to brigadier, but de Bellemare, always a stormy petrel, reacted fiercely and addressed a vain protest to the National Assembly. He also incurred displeasure by having an account of Le Bourget published in a Belgian newspaper. In 1873, while commanding in the Dordogne, he announced that if the monarchy were restored he would refuse to serve the regime. For this he was relieved of command by the Minister of War – not so much for being a strong republican but for breaking army rules against serving officers publishing expressions of political opinion. He was restored to service in 1874, but did not regain divisional command until 1879 when a Republican government came to power. He was promoted to command of the Thirteenth Army Corps in 1883, the Fifth in 1885 and the Ninth at Tours in 1886. (It was in this capacity that he dealt with the matter of Lieutenant-Colonel Patry's debts, which ended with Patry's dismissal from the army in 1887). Retiring to Nice in 1889 as a Grand Officer of the Legion of Honour, he presided over a gaming club: an occupation which compromised his repeated requests to be made a Grand Cross and Commandant at Les Invalides.

BESSOL JOSEPH-ARTHUR DUFAURE DU (1828–1908) After attending Saint-Cyr, du Bessol entered the Foreign Legion and was assigned to an Arab bureau. He distinguished himself at the siege of Sebastopol in 1854 and was promoted to captain, and returned to Algeria at the end of the war. He took part in the Kabyle expedition in 1857 and was decorated, then entered the Imperial Guard and fought with distinction at Magenta. He was twice cited for his service in counter-guerrilla operations in Mexico in 1863–4. Severely wounded at Rezonville in August 1870, he was promoted to lieutenant-colonel during the blockade of Metz, destroyed his Colour at the capitulation, then escaped via Belgium to Lille. In the Army of the North he moved rapidly from command of a regiment to that of a brigade and then to that of the 2nd Division of the Twenty-second Corps, and led his men in the hardest of the fighting at Pont-Noyelles, Bapaume and Saint-Quentin. While leading a brigade he was again badly wounded and had his horse shot under him; then at Saint-Quentin he was hit three times, so seriously that he was reported killed. After the war he was confirmed in the rank of colonel, but received brigade command in September 1871. As commander of the Toulouse district from 1875, he performed important services when the Garonne flooded. The doughty general ended his career in corps command in Algeria, and retired in 1893.

BISMARCK OTTO EDUARD LEOPOLD VON (1815–98) Bismarck was born at Schönhausen in Brandenburg, Prussia, his father being a landowner of the Junker class and his mother from a family of academics and civil servants. He studied law at Göttingen and Berlin, though he preferred drinking, socialising and duelling with fellow aristocrats to study. Impatient of the subordination required by the routines of the Prussian civil service, he resigned in 1839 and lived restlessly as a country squire until 1847, when he entered the Prussian Diet. His attacks on liberalism, Jewish emancipation and, later, on the revolutionaries of 1848 marked him as a vigorous rural reactionary. In 1851 his loyalty to the monarchy was rewarded by his appointment as Prussian representative at the Federal German Diet in Frankfurt, where he pointedly behaved as the equal of the representative of Austria, in defiance of the traditional deference shown to the dominant power among the German states. In 1859 he became Prussian ambassador to Russia, and in May 1862 in France, but was recalled from Paris in September and appointed Minister-President and Foreign Minister by the king. Bismarck's task was to break the two-year deadlock with the Liberals in parliament over army reforms. Failing to achieve a compromise, he arranged for taxes to be paid anyway to pay for the army reforms. In 1864 Prussia and Austria waged war on Denmark in a dispute over the duchies of Schleswig and Holstein. Two years later, Bismarck challenged Austria's dominance in Germany, which he had long resented, and in the ensuing Seven Weeks War Austria was decisively defeated at Königgrätz on 3 July 1866. Two of her smaller allies, Hanover and Hesse–Cassel, had their monarchies removed and, together with Frankfurt and Nassau, were annexed by Prussia. Bismarck's use of 'blood and iron' presented the liberals with a German political union north of the River Main, in partial fulfilment of their nationalist aspirations. When he made the concession of asking the Prussian parliament to sanction the military expenditure of the last three years retrospectively, it did so by 230 votes to 75. The creation of the North German Confederation was ratified in 1867, with representative constitutional forms, but with control of foreign affairs and war in the hands of Bismarck as Chancellor and Foreign Minister. During the next three years he tried various initiatives to bring the four South German states into the Confederation, and to have King William of Prussia made German Emperor. By early 1870 these efforts had stalled in the face of southern German opposition. Bismarck occasionally spoke of leaving unification to time, but sometimes of war with France as being inevitable if it were to be achieved. Whatever his precise intentions, in 1870 he secretly encouraged acceptance of the Spanish throne by Leopold of Hohenzollern–Sigmaringen, in full awareness of the likely reaction in France, which had a right to be consulted on such a matter. He spoke privately of wanting 'complications' with France. When the candidature became known in Paris in July, his reaction to French demands was at first intransigent and then deliberately provocative. In later years he was to boast of his opportunist editing of the 'Ems telegram' which precipitated war: he had in any case proposed to force a confrontation by demanding 'explanations' for Gramont's bellicose speech of 6 July, and recalling the Reichstag. He no more shrank from the use of force than he had in 1864 and 1866, and on 15 July took the mobilisation orders for the king to sign. A war in which France was seen to be the aggressor brought the South German states into willing alliance. Always adept at feeding the press, Bismarck fuelled the war fever by inciting a long campaign of national hatred against France. Accompanying the armies on campaign, he upheld military and popular demands for the annexation of Alsace–Lorraine, insisted on the bombardment of Paris over the resistance of the army high command, and managed the hard bargaining with the southern States which led to the creation of the German Empire in January 1871. Hailed as the hero of German national unity, he was made Imperial Chancellor and, on 21 March 1871, a prince. For the next two decades he was the dominating European statesman, and his prodigious diplomatic energies were devoted to trying to assure the security of the new Germany, principally by keeping France isolated. Internally, his aggressive political techniques for rallying support by targeting 'enemies of the Reich' were turned against Catholics (who were concentrated largely in Alsace–Lorraine, southern Germany and Poland), and then the Social Democrats. He tried to undermine socialism by restrictive laws in 1878 and by the introduction of state social security measures in the 1880s. Yet for all his political virtuosity in keeping his opponents at bay, he eventually lost control of the Reichstag and, after quarrelling with the new Kaiser, William II, resigned in 1890. Embittered, he retired to his estate, and spent his remaining years criticising his successors and writing memoirs which nourished nationalist legends of his omniscience and infallibility.

BOURBAKI CHARLES-DENIS-SAUTER (1816–97) The ship that carried General Bonaparte to Egypt in 1798 was piloted by a Greek, Constantin Bourbaki, whose intelligence and energy so impressed Napoleon that he later entrusted him with several important missions and made him a colonel. The family was naturalised in France in 1800. Constantin was killed in an Athens riot in 1825. His son Charles entered Saint-Cyr in 1834, later establishing a brilliant combat record as a Zouave officer in Algeria: particularly in defending a fortified camp near Sétif in 1840 with one battalion against thousands of Arabs. By the end of 1851 he was a colonel, promoted for his 'glorious conduct' of an expedition against the Kabyles. In the Crimea in 1854 he led a brigade in a spectacular charge which captured Telegraph Hill at the Alma, winning confirmation as a brigadier. At Inkerman his troops (including the 6th Line Regiment) fought off a strong Russian column, for which he was congratulated by Lord Raglan. Recovering from typhus, Bourbaki was wounded in the chest in the assault on the Malakoff on 8 September 1855. After convalescence in France he returned to Algeria, serving under MacMahon against the Kabyles. At Magenta and Solferino he commanded a division in Canrobert's corps. After a mission to Prussia in 1864, he advocated the introduction of breech-loading rifles, and in 1869 became an aide to the Emperor. On the outbreak of war in July 1870 he was given command of the Imperial Guard, which he led to re-establish the French positions around Rezonville on 16 August. His role on 18 August was controversial. According to Bourbaki he received no orders, but used his artillery to hold back the Germans at Amanvillers and covered the retreat of the other corps. But others described him as acting temperamentally, flying into a rage and turning his column around rather than involve it in the rout of the French right, which it might have saved: upon which his men joined the general retreat anyway. During September a reluctant Bourbaki was ordered on a fruitless diplomatic mission from Metz to the Empress in England. Before leaving, he insisted that the Guard should not be engaged in his absence. Refused permission to re-enter Metz by the Germans, he offered his services to the Republic. His unconcealed pessimism in organising the Army of the North in October caused concern, and he was recalled to command an army on the Loire, but proved unable to achieve a great deal. Such was his reputation, however, that in December he was put in command of the Army of the East, with the mission of relieving besieged Belfort and disrupting German communications. Fighting at Villersexel on 9 January 1871 and continuing his advance, Bourbaki was blocked by a smaller German force along the line of the Lisaine in three days of battle in Siberian conditions. The French retreat then became a nightmare of cold, hunger, and exhaustion, with two German armies closing in. Believing his army lost, on 24 January Bourbaki received a dispatch from Freycinet at the War Ministry, ordering movements which were now impracticable and implying slowness. Stung by criticism and confessing his despair at the situation, Bourbaki wired back: 'You have no idea of the suffering the army has endured . . . Believe me, to exercise command at this time is martyrdom.' On 26 January, with orders to relieve him on their way, he gave instructions for the retreat, then went to his room in Besançon and shot himself in the right temple. The bullet flattened as it penetrated his skull and was extracted by Dr Mathais. The Army of the East, hemmed in against the Jura mountains by the Germans, staggered over the Swiss border to be disarmed and interned on neutral territory rather than captured. Bourbaki recovered slowly, and after the war was appointed to corps command at Lyon by Thiers. With the advent of a republican government headed by Freycinet in 1879, he and a number of other generals associated with MacMahon were removed. He was placed unwillingly in the reserve in 1881. Having twice failed to enter the Senate, Bourbaki lived in seclusion until his death.

BOYER NAPOLÉON (1820–88) General Boyer, Bazaine's emissary to the Germans during the blockade of Metz, had entered Saint-Cyr in 1839. After service in Algeria in 1847–8 he became aide-de-camp to General Le Flô, took part in the siege of Rome in 1849 and was appointed aide-de-camp to Saint-Arnaud in 1851. After the Marshal's death in the Crimea he served on the general staff of the Imperial Guard. He campaigned in Italy in 1859, Syria in 1860, and in the Mexican expedition was on the staff of General Forey, its commander. When Bazaine succeeded Forey, the industrious but aloof Boyer became his aide-de-camp and confidant, and was suspected by other generals of encouraging Bazaine in intrigues. After their return to France in 1867 he remained Bazaine's intimate, and in October 1870 he was the Marshal's choice to conduct talks with Bismarck, then the Empress, with a view to a peace which would allow the army to march out of Metz and establish a regency. When Boyer first returned from captivity in Germany in April 1871 he was confirmed as a brigadier-general. But when the dealings with the enemy in which he had been involved came under scrutiny at Bazaine's trial in 1873, Boyer's reputation was tarnished by association with his master. He was given no further employment and was formally retired in 1879.

BRAYER MICHEL-SYLVESTRE-PHILIPPE-AMILCAR-ALDEBERT, COUNT (1813–70) The aloof and handsome brigadier, whose death in battle on 16 August 1870 caused Patry to ponder the nature of historical evidence, was born in Paris, the son of one of Napoleon's generals. A graduate of Saint-Cyr, Brayer served in Algeria, was wounded and taken prisoner in the Crimea, fought in Italy and was promoted brigadier in 1860. He was created a count by decree in 1869, and on the outbreak of war was appointed to command the 1st Brigade in the 1st Division of the Fourth Corps of the Army of the Rhine.

CANROBERT FRANÇOIS-ANTOINE CERTAIN (1809–95) The son of a royalist officer, Canrobert graduated from Saint-Cyr in 1828 and served brilliantly in Algeria, rising to brigadier in 1850. He became aide-de-camp to Louis-Napoleon and took part in the coup of 1851. In the Crimea he was wounded at the Alma. Shortly afterwards cholera, which devastated his division, carried off Marshal Saint-Arnaud, and command of the expedition passed to Canrobert. He marched on Sebastopol and commenced the siege, being wounded again at Inkerman. With his flowing locks and earthy, genial manner, he cut a dashing and popular figure with his men and enjoyed good personal relations with Lord Raglan, commanding the British forces. However, he became increasingly frustrated and overwhelmed by the problems of high command. In May 1855, after the Anglo–French expedition to Kertch was recalled at the last minute by orders telegraphed from Paris by Napoleon, he relinquished command to Pélissier. He took corps command for two months before returning to France, being elevated to Marshal in 1856. Leading the Third Corps in Italy, he won fresh renown for his part in the victories of Magenta and Solferino, and in the 1860s enjoyed the reputation and rewards of being considered the country's most illustrious soldier. When war came in 1870 he steadfastly refused supreme command. He mustered the Sixth Corps at Châlons, but discovered that even he could not bring discipline to the Paris *Garde Mobile*. He declined command of the capital and agreed to serve under Bazaine, his junior. In the defence of his position at Saint-Privat on 18 August he was at his best as a front-line leader, as usual setting an example of personal bravery, though ultimately his position was outflanked and overwhelmed. In Metz he spoke at one point of a breakout at any costs, and refused to go as Bazaine's emissary to the Empress, but eventually accepted that captivity was inevitable. After the war, he served the Thiers government and rejected opportunities to stand as Bonapartist candidate, though he did attend Napoleon III's funeral. Elected Senator for his native Lot, he voted with conservatives in the Chamber, but spoke only on army issues.

CHANZY ANTOINE-ALFRED-EUGÈNE (1823–83) One of the few French generals to emerge from 1870–1 with an enhanced reputation, Chanzy had started his career at 16 as a ship's boy in a troop transport. He then enlisted in the artillery and while serving managed to pursue a course at the Lycée de Metz and qualify for Saint-Cyr. Graduating near the top of his class, he spent sixteen years in Algeria, fought in Italy at Magenta and Solferino, then in 1860 went to Syria where he was valued for his knowledge of the Arabs. After a spell in the French garrison in Rome, he returned to Algeria and was recommended for brigadier by MacMahon in 1868. In 1870 he asked to return to France and was put in command of the Sixteenth Army Corps, where he soon showed his mettle as a leader. After taking part in the victories of Coulmiers (9 November) and Villepion (1 December), he was given command of the Second Army of the Loire. Chanzy showed an all too rare aggression and determination, making repeated attacks in extreme cold on the Germans north of the Loire. The arrival of more German troops made his task all but hopeless, but Chanzy never admitted this, even after the rout of his army at Le Mans on 11–12 January 1871. He was re-organising his troops at Laval when the armistice came, and was strongly in favour of resuming hostilities. Chanzy had been proclaimed a hero by Gambetta, but remained his own man politically. He refused to accept the appointment to his staff of Lissagaray, a future member of the Commune and its historian. When one of his choices, an Orléans prince, was escorted from the country by the government, Chanzy took another of the princes on to his staff under an assumed name. In February he was elected Deputy for the Ardennes without even standing as a candidate, also receiving 60,000 votes in Paris. On his way from Tours to Versailles via the capital, Chanzy arrived at the Gare d'Orléans on 18 March in full uniform, and was almost lynched by a mob which apparently mistook him for another general. Arrested by the National Guard, he was released by the Central Committee a few days later after taking an oath – which he kept – not to fight against the Commune. His view was that the insurrection was 'a senseless and wicked revolt by a few wretches whom France disowns'. In the National Assembly he sat on the centre left, opposed the peace terms and argued for continuation of the struggle against Germany. After the fall of the

Commune he also introduced the law to dissolve the National Guard. Elected President of the Assembly in May 1872, he accepted corps command later that year and in 1873 became Governor-General of Algeria. He was appointed a Life Senator in 1875, and in 1879 was named ambassador to Russia. Passing through Berlin to take up his post, he was treated with marked courtesy by the Kaiser and Bismarck, and was received with great honour in Russia by the Tsar. Chanzy's tact and courtesy made his three-year mission a success, but he resigned when Gambetta came to power and took command of the Sixth Corps. He died suddenly at his headquarters at Châlons. His reputation and popularity for his spirited resistance during the war endured after his death. A monument was raised by national subscription at Le Mans in 1885, and the room in Les Invalides which holds the Army Museum's collection pertaining to the war of 1870–1 is named in his honour.

CISSEY ERNEST-LOUIS-OCTAVE COURTOT DE (1810–82) Born into a noble Burgundian family, de Cissey entered Saint-Cyr in 1830 and from 1837 served in Algeria, where he was on the staff of General Bugeaud. In 1850 he was appointed aide-de-camp to the governor-general, General Pélissier, and was promoted to colonel in 1852. He continued on Pélissier's staff in the Crimea, and after the battles of the Alma and Inkerman was cited in orders for the fourteenth time. He achieved brigade command in March 1855 and after the fall of Sebastopol returned to Algeria. In 1858 he was recalled to France and appointed Director of Military and Maritime Affairs at the Ministry for Algeria and the Colonies. He gained divisional rank in 1863 and was made a Grand Officer of the Legion of Honour in 1867. In 1870 he won plaudits for his handling of the 1st Division of the Fourth Corps at Borny and Rezonville, although it was among those driven from the field on 18 August. De Cissey was named by Bazaine as one of the officers on the French side charged with negotiating capitulation, though there was little he could do to obtain favourable terms. Returning to France after internment at Hamburg (during which his wife died), he commanded the Second Corps in the Army of Versailles. Although he was credited with saving the left bank of Paris from destruction by the speed with which he retook it, he was certainly less sparing of people. It was during the repression of the Commune that the sinister side of the clever and able but ambitious, overbearing and ruthless general showed to the full. Under his direct orders summary executions of Communards who had stopped fighting were carried out during 'Bloody Week'. He applied the brutal methods of the French army in Algeria to the Paris insurgents, whom he regarded as scum. While eating lunch in a restaurant he ordered the cold-blooded shooting of the Republican deputy Millière. Although he was supposedly reprimanded for this act by MacMahon, he was confirmed as a Grand Cross of the Legion of Honour and was appointed Minister of War by Thiers on 5 June 1871 in the wake of the fighting. His tenure of office was marked by efforts to put into practice some of the lessons of the war, including the introduction of breech-loading cannon, reform of the conscription system with obligatory service and a territorial reserve, together with improvements in military hygiene and small arms. He instituted the Commission for the Revision of Officers' Ranks and a series of inquiries into the surrender of fortified places during the war. He also promoted the introduction of specialised military journals. Resigning in 1873 and taking command of the Seventh Corps, he served again as Minister in 1874–6. In his second term he focused on reform of the medical and supply services and the staff. He had been elected to the Assembly in July 1871 and became a Senator in 1876, voting always with the right and supporting MacMahon. In 1878 he took corps command at Nantes, but in 1880 a civil trial created a scandal by linking de Cissey during his period of ministerial office with a young woman suspected of being a German spy. He was relieved of command by the War Minister, General Farre, and although exonerated by a court of inquiry he remained in the reserve until his death.

COFFINIÈRES DE NORDECK GRÉGOIRE-GASPARD-FÉLIX (1811–87) The military governor of Metz in 1870 came from a family which had been ennobled in the 16th century. Nevertheless, while a student at the École Polytechnique he led a section of artillery to Versailles during the revolution of 1830. An outstanding pupil, he entered the École d'Application at Metz the following year and on graduation joined the engineers. In Algeria he won the Legion of Honour for saving a comrade from capture in battle while wounded himself. On returning to France in 1837 he prepared a report for the Minister of War on the methods of conquest in Algeria. In the Moroccan expedition of 1844 he was charged with coastal reconnaissance, then commanded a column in the assault on the town of Mogador. Within a few years he was Director of Engineering and a War Ministry spokesman in the Chamber of Deputies. After a further study mission in Morocco he was seconded to Argentina and conducted the first survey of the basin of the River Plate – for which he was decorated by both the Argentinian and French governments. Back in France in 1850, he was in Mâcon when a riot broke out and was presented with pistols by the city authorities for his part in suppressing it. In the Crimea as chief of staff of the engineers, he took part in the final operations against Sebastopol and was promoted to brigadier. In 1860, after the Italian campaign, he became commandant of the École Polytechnique and created a chair in history, first held by Victor Duruy. From 1865, as a divisional commander, he was involved in planning the fortifications of Metz, although the Chamber did not vote sufficient credits to complete the work. His role in 1870 was to be controversial. As chief engineer of the Army of the Rhine, he was responsible for the bridges over the Moselle, and was later much criticised for failing to destroy those which were of use to the Germans while making insufficient arrangements for the passage of the French army. Taking on the additional role of military governor of the garrison on 7 August, he seemed at times to see the strategic situation solely in terms of defending the city. His arguments to Bazaine against abandoning the protection of the fortress appear to have had a baleful influence on the Marshal's resolution, and helped to create a situation where escape became impossible. Nevertheless there was tension between the two men as the blockade tightened. Coffinières had to organise rationing and cope with serious unrest in the city, and was more prepared than Bazaine to recognise the Government of National Defence. After imprisonment in Hamburg he returned to France. He retired in 1881 and wrote a defence of his conduct at Metz.

DERROJA JEAN-BARTHÉLEMY-XAVIER (1822–1909) Born in the eastern Pyrenees, Derroja entered Saint-Cyr in 1841. He saw combat in Algeria, at the siege of Rome and in the Crimea, fought at Robechetto, Magenta and Solferino as a major, and in 1870 was garrisoned at Arras. As lieutenant-colonel of the 33rd Infantry, he fought in all the August battles around Metz, being twice cited in orders and promoted to colonel of the 15th Infantry in September. At the capitulation he walked through the lines wearing his colonel's uniform and made his way through Belgium to Lille. Initially made commandant at Cambrai, his energy and capacity for higher command became evident when he led a brigade in a bayonet charge at Villers-Bretonneux on 27 November. At the re-organisation of the Army of the North in December he was given the 1st Division of the Twenty-second Corps and led it with skill and distinction throughout the campaign. During the Commune he commanded a brigade in General Faron's division which was in action on the left bank and around the Place de la Bastille in the May fighting. His proven ability as a strategist and tactician ensured that his wartime promotion to brigadier was confirmed in 1871. He achieved divisional rank in 1879 and returned to Amiens to command the Second Corps in 1881. In the 1880s he was also active on the general staff committee and the commission for public works. Well respected as a brave, educated and modest soldier, Derroja became a Grand Officer of the Legion of Honour in 1882 and retired five years later.

DUCROT AUGUSTE-ALEXANDRE (1817–82) Born in Nevers, the son of a lieutenant-colonel, Ducrot graduated from Saint-Cyr in 1837 and took part in many campaigns in Algeria. As head of an Arab Bureau in 1846 he showed that he had negotiating as well as military skills. He reached the rank of colonel in 1853, having already been cited in orders nine times, wounded twice, and awarded the Legion of Honour. In 1854 he took part in the Baltic campaign, being present at the bombardment of Bomarsund. After a spell in the Imperial Guard he was promoted brigadier in 1858 and took part in the Italian and Syrian campaigns before returning to Algeria. Made a divisional commander in 1865, he wrote little-heeded letters to his superiors from his headquarters at Strasbourg warning of Prussian military preparations. When war came, he commanded the 1st Division of MacMahon's corps at Froeschwiller on 6 August. After the defeat and retreat he took command of the First Corps of the Army of Châlons. When MacMahon was wounded at Sedan on 1 September he designated Ducrot to succeed him. Ducrot had graphically summed-up the French strategic position: 'We are in a chamber-pot, and we are about to be **** upon.' Nevertheless, he claimed that he could have saved at least part of the army by timely withdrawal, but at that point General de Wimpffen arrived with orders from Paris putting himself in command and insisting that the army stay and fight. Encirclement and surrender followed. After the capitulation Ducrot escaped disguised as a worker, though the Prussians were to accuse him of having broken his word to surrender himself as a prisoner at Pont-à-Mousson. Arriving in Paris, he was given command of two corps, but his attempts to break the Prussian ring with raw troops failed on the Châtillon plateau on 19 September and again on 21 October. At the end of November he led the Second Army in the most formidable French attempt to break the German lines, but was repulsed in three days of fighting on the Marne at Champigny. Having foolishly declared that he would return only dead or victorious, he re-entered the capital on 4 December alive and beaten. He was by now very unpopular with Parisians and at odds with his colleagues. Despite his bravery during the Buzenval sortie on 19 January 1871, the late arrival of his corps was blamed for the failure. Elected as a monarchist Deputy for Nièvre with a large majority, Ducrot sat on the right of the Assembly and gave vent to his extreme anti-republicanism and aversion for democracy. He engaged in polemics, called for inquiries into the wartime activities of republican leaders and insulted Garibaldi, who had come to fight for France. In 1872 even the monarchist Assembly was growing tired of this behaviour and showed its contempt by silently voting down one of his calls for an inquiry. Resigning, Ducrot took corps command at Bourges and began suspending republican newspapers and demanding that the gendarmerie furnish him with lists of 'dangerous' individuals. He had a statue of 'La Résistance' in Dijon taken down because it wore a revolutionary Phrygian bonnet. In 1877 he was accused of being the author of a series of articles in *Le Figaro* attacking republican institutions. Finally, in 1878, following republican electoral victory, he was removed after breaching regulations by passing on the blessing of the Pope at a review of his troops, and placed in the reserve. He wrote several volumes of military history dealing with Sedan and the siege of Paris.

EUGÉNIE (1826–1920), EUGÉNIA MARIA DE MONTIJO DE GUZMAN, COUNTESS OF TEBA, was born at Granada, daughter of a Spanish nobleman. She became Empress of the French on her marriage to Napoleon III in 1853, and bore him one son, Louis, the Prince Imperial, in 1856. A renowned beauty, Eugénie was the centre of fashion at the Imperial court and set the tone and style of Second Empire society. She was a devout Catholic and conservative by instinct, and sought to influence her husband's policies in that direction; though not always with success, particularly before 1860. She advocated the ill-fated Mexican expedition and a continued French presence in Rome, and in 1866 favoured French mobilisation for a show of strength on the Rhine to check Prussia. In 1870 she was strongly in favour of war, which she saw as being in the best interests of the country and the dynasty. Although she denied having boasted

'This is my war' and there is no evidence that her influence on Napoleon was decisive, it was undoubtedly significant: and she was the recognised patroness of the war party and of advocates of the authoritarian Empire. Acting as Regent for the Emperor after his departure for the front, she presided over a government headed by General Palikao, which was more congenial to her than the liberal Ollivier ministry which fell on 9 August. When the news of Sedan reached Paris it precipitated revolution, and the by now deeply unpopular Empress escaped from the Tuileries in a carriage on 4 September and made her way to England with the help of her American dentist. Moving from a hotel in Hastings to Chislehurst, she appealed to the King of Prussia to allow Bazaine's army in Metz to be resupplied while negotiations took place, but the Germans would not agree and Eugénie was reluctant to commit the dynasty without knowing the extent of their demands. She lived for half a century after the war, maintaining her links with European royalty. The Prince Imperial, centre of her hopes for an eventual restoration, was killed by Zulus in 1879 at the age of 23 while serving as an officer in the British army. During the First World War she was quick to tell young men, particularly her own servants, of their duty to enlist to fight Germans, and had the satisfaction of seeing 1870 avenged in 1918. She died in Madrid, and was brought back for burial in Farnborough Abbey, which she had had built in the 1880s as a mausoleum for Napoleon III and their son.

FAIDHERBE LOUIS-LÉON-CÉSAR (1818–89) Faidherbe's reputation in France rests on his years spent as a colonial administrator, quite apart from his role in the winter campaign of 1870–1. Born in Lille, the son of a hosiery merchant and former sergeant-major, he attended the École Polytechnique and École d'Application before joining the engineers and going to Algeria. In 1848 he was posted to Guadeloupe to work on Fort Joséphine, 'the Gibraltar of the Antilles', showing characteristic energy and efficiency combined with a reserved but irascible temperament. He returned to Africa in 1850, creating the post of Bou-Saada in the desert and taking part in several military expeditions; including the disastrous one led by Bosquet in the winter of 1851, in which he owed his survival to his rescue by a soldier when he had collapsed from exhaustion in a mountain blizzard. Recovering from severe frostbite, he was sent to Senegal as Deputy Director of Engineers. There followed years of arduous (and often unauthorised) punitive expeditions against native tribes, followed by colonisation and the extension of French power into inhospitable regions of Africa. He became Governor of Senegal in 1854, presiding over the construction of the Port of Dakar and of settlements, barracks, hospitals, schools, a museum, and the establishment of a printing-press and posts and telegraphs. Debilitated by tropical diseases, in 1860 he asked for leave to convalesce. After two years of commanding a subdivision in Algeria, he returned as Governor of Senegal, being promoted to brigadier in 1863. Ill health again forced him to give up his functions, and in 1865 he moved to command a division at Bône, Algeria. In July 1870 he was convalescing at Lille and asked to join the Army of the Rhine: but

Faidherbe was a strong republican and was sent back to Algeria by the imperial authorities. The Government of National Defence was more receptive to his requests, and on 3 December, promoted general of division, he arrived to take command of the improvised Army of the North. He claimed to have relieved Le Havre by his advance in December 1870, but his battles at Pont-Noyelles and Bapaume bore no fruit, and he failed to relieve the siege of Péronne. The account of the campaign which he published just after the war, dedicated to Gambetta, was couched in the terms of an official report but is also a careful, politically conscious apologia – for the general was always very protective of his reputation. Nevertheless, Faidherbe showed courage, energy and determination, which were badly needed in 1870–1, and his offensive spirit made the Germans respect him and fear for their communications. His army was decisively defeated at Saint-Quentin on 19 January. Confirmed as a general of division after the war, he was elected deputy for the Département of the North, his immense popularity being attested by 400,000 votes. However, he soon resigned from the monarchist dominated Assembly and set off on a scientific mission to Egypt, Jerusalem, Italy, Sicily and Malta. After failing in 1876, he was elected to the Senate in 1879 and voted for the expulsion of the Orleans princes. In 1880, after 44 years of service and 27 campaigns, he received the Grand Cross of the Legion of Honour and shortly afterwards was appointed Grand Chancellor of the order by the republican government. Suffering from rheumatism and progressive paralysis of the limbs, from 1875 he moved about in a mechanical wheelchair. In addition to his achievements as a soldier and colonial administrator, Faidherbe wrote several works on geographical, archaeological and anthropological subjects. In his last years he was a hero to the advocates of French colonial expansion.

FARRE JEAN-JOSEPH-FRÉDÉRIC-ALBERT (1816–87) Educated at the Lycée de Grenoble, Farre went on to graduate first in his class at the École Polytechnique and chose a career in military engineering. He was employed on a succession of projects in the 30 years before 1870: the construction of Fort Nogent in the Paris fortifications and works around Lyon and Algiers, as well as a study of the defences of Oran. He took part in the 1857 Kabyle expedition and commanded the engineer troops in Rome in 1859. He was then chief of engineers at Le Havre, Toulon, Rome again, and was director of engineering at Arras and Lille with the rank of colonel when the war broke out. As Bourbaki's chief of staff, he played a key part in organising the Army of the North in October and November 1870. When Bourbaki was transferred, Farre, now a brigadier, was left in temporary command and led his raw army of 25,000 forward in an attempt to block Manteuffel's advance, only to lose the Battle of Amiens on 27 November. Faidherbe arrived a few days later, and Farre stayed on as his chief of staff throughout the campaign. An outspoken republican and protégé of Gambetta, Farre's promotion to general of division was not ratified by the monarchist Assembly after the war. He was not given further employment until recalled as director of engineering at Algiers in 1872, where he tackled the repairs needed after the destruction of the Kabyle revolt. He was promoted to divisional command in 1875, became president of the fortifications committee and Governor of Lyon, then Minister of War in the Freycinet government in 1879 with the support of republicans but opposed by MacMahon. His suppression of the promotion board system, and of military chaplains and drums, combined with staff reforms and changes in personnel, made him unpopular with many soldiers and civilians. He also had to grapple with serious problems in Algeria and Tunisia. Although allowed to stay on beyond retirement age, he resigned as Minister in 1881 but continued as a Life Senator, voting with the left.

FERNANDEZ EUGÈNE-ANTOINE-MANUEL-JOSEPH (1847–1916) Born in Bordeaux, Fernandez joined the 6th Line Regiment in 1865 and was made a sergeant-major on the outbreak of war in 1870. He was wounded in the head by a shell splinter on 16 August, was promoted to second lieutenant in September and escaped with Patry. Following his rapid promotions in the Army of the North (lieutenant, December 1870; captain, January 1871, in the 67th *de marche*) he was wounded in the left arm by a shell-burst at Saint-Quentin on 19 January in the action described by his friend. After the war he remained in the 67th, but was reverted to lieutenant by the Commission for the Revision of Officers' Ranks in 1872. However, he continued to command a company while his captain was on detached duty at Saint-Cyr, and regained the rank of captain in 1875. He was a major, garrisoned at Toul with the 118th Infantry, when on 1 August 1893 he received a knife wound in the groin while tackling a criminal being pursued by the police. He took command of a battalion in the 29th Infantry at Le Havre later that year, and was colonel of the 160th by the time of his retirement in 1907. Recalled on 2 August 1914, he commanded until January 1916 the subdivisions of Evreux and Rouen, a city then bustling with British troops passing to and from the Western Front.

GAMBETTA LÉON-MICHEL (1838–82) Gambetta's father was a Genoese grocer whose family had settled in Cahors a generation earlier, though legally Léon acquired French citizenship only on coming of age in 1859. He came to Paris in 1857 to study law and was admitted to the bar in 1861. Entering vigorously into opposition politics, he frequented left-bank cafés such as the Procope, once associated with the revolutionary Danton with whom he was later to be compared. He was a powerful orator and charismatic figure: stout, bearded and lacking his right eye, which had been damaged in a childhood accident and removed in 1867. Coming to prominence as a defence lawyer, in 1868 he turned the case of Delescluze (who had organised a collection for a memorial to Baudin, a Deputy killed in the *coup* of 1851) into a public indictment of the imperial regime. In the election campaign of 1869 his Belleville manifesto encapsulated the radical republican programme. He was elected in Belleville – a working-class suburb of Paris – but chose to sit as a Deputy for Marseilles, where he was also elected. Convinced that a republic could be achieved through electoral means, he denounced all compromise with the 'Liberal Empire' and was dismayed by the results of the plebiscite in May 1870 which heavily endorsed it. Whilst critical of the government in July, he voted for war credits and in August called for the arming of the National Guard. He played a leading role in the revolution of 4 September, declaring to the crowd that had invaded the Chamber (possibly with his connivance) that the Empire was overthrown. Elected to the Government of National Defence, he secured the Ministry of the Interior by entering the building first and signing himself as Minister in a telegram to the provinces announcing the change of regime. After the siege began he left Paris by balloon from Montmartre on 7 October, receiving a grazed hand from a Prussian bullet during the flight. Arriving at Tours, he made himself the dominant figure in the Delegation that was in effect responsible for governing France outside the capital. He also assumed the role of Minister of War, though he appointed an able deputy, Charles de Freycinet, to oversee military operations. The energetic enthusiasm with which Gambetta sought to mobilise and direct new armies boosted the spirit of resistance, but also gave rise to accusations of dictatorship. In later years Frenchmen were to take pride in his achievement and give him due credit for having saved the national honour in an otherwise ignominious defeat. Yet for all that he could do, by the winter of 1870–1 his patriotic exhortations to fight on to the bitter end were outstripping military and political reality. The elections of February 1871 showed that his die-hard Republican zeal did not represent the mood of the country as a whole. His decision to step down rather than force the issue with the Paris government of continuation of the war was not the least of his services to France. After a protest against the peace terms in the Assembly at Bordeaux he resigned and retired to Spain, not re-entering politics until after the Commune. Re-elected in July 1871, over the next decade he was the most prestigious and effective spokesman for the republican cause and an adept parliamentary leader. Regarded by conservatives as, in Thiers' phrase, 'a raging madman', he caused controversy in a speech at Grenoble in 1872 by hailing the political advent of 'new social strata' – small proprietors, traders and industrialists – and in 1877 by memorably denouncing clericalism as the enemy of the Republic. In 1877 he received a suspended three months' prison sentence for supposedly making a disrespectful remark about President MacMahon. Yet Gambetta was no rash extremist: indeed, many of his colleagues mistrusted his growing opportunist tendency to compromise for political advantage. The decisive republican triumph in the 1877 elections, in which he co-operated with Thiers, was in large measure his achievement. His ascendancy and great popularity seemed to entitle him to lead the government, but the hostility of Presidents MacMahon and Grévy meant that he was not called upon to form a ministry until 1881, and even then he was defeated within three months on an electoral reform issue. Disheartened, he went into seclusion. Whatever the future may have held, Gambetta's career was cut short at the age of 44 when he died from complications following an accident with a revolver.

GISLAIN CHARLES-PAUL (1825–1905) A native of Chablis, Gislain joined the army in 1845 and attended Saint-Cyr. On 8 November 1870 he became lieutenant-colonel of the 67th *de marche* in the Army of the North. His leadership of one of the assault columns that captured Ham in December won him a colonelcy that was confirmed after the war. He then commanded a brigade in du Bessol's division of the Twenty-second Corps and fought in all the battles of Faidherbe's army. He held post-war command in the South of France, and as commander of the subdivision of Constantine (Algeria), took part in an expedition to Tunisia in 1881. Returning from Africa in 1886, he held brigade command at Saint-Quentin before being promoted to divisional command at Lyon (1887) and Clermont-Ferrand (1889). He retired in 1890.

GRAMONT ANTOINE-ALFRED-AGÉNOR DE (1819–80) Gramont, scion of a noble family, studied at the École Polytechnique and then at the École d'Application at Metz. Graduating in 1839, he became a second lieutenant in the artillery but resigned in 1841. As an officer in the Paris National Guard in 1848 he helped suppress the June Days insurrection. Handsome and charming, he entered public life in 1851 and, as an aristocrat reconciled to the Bonapartist regime, pursued a diplomatic career. He became minister plenipotentiary at Cassel, then Stuttgart (1852) and Turin (1853), where he later negotiated for Piedmontese entry into the war against Russia. Known as the Duc de Guiche, he succeeded to his father's title as Duc de Gramont in 1855. As ambassador to Rome in 1857 he fulfilled his role with skill but his sympathy for reform made him suspect at the pontifical court and to many conservative Catholics of his own class at home. From 1861 he represented France at Vienna, taking a leading part in the cession of Venetia to France, then Italy, in 1866. In May 1870 he succeeded Count Daru as Foreign Minister in the Ollivier ministry. When news of the Hohenzollern candidature reached Paris in July, he determined that France must react firmly to Prussian machinations in Spain and made a speech in the Chamber on 6 July (reviewed and approved beforehand by both Napoleon and Ollivier) declaring that a Prussian prince on the Spanish throne would upset the balance of power in Europe and jeopardise the interests and honour of France. If the German people did not have the wisdom to prevent this, 'strong in your support and in that of the nation, we shall know how to discharge our duty without faltering or weakness'. At first his strategy succeeded, and the candidacy was withdrawn on 12 July. But then Gramont, urged on by popular excitement and pressure from the political right, which was all too eager to goad the liberal Ollivier government with accusations of weakness, pressed his advantage too far. In conference with Napoleon that night, and apparently without consulting the rest of the cabinet, he drew up instructions for the French ambassador to seek a promise from the King of Prussia not to authorise any prince of his house to renew the candidacy. Gramont was pushing for a public acknowledgement of the part the Prussian government had played behind the scenes in promoting the candidacy, but King William politely but firmly made it clear that he regarded the matter as closed. In publishing an edited version of the 'Ems telegram', portraying a curt rebuff, Bismarck delivered what Gramont excitedly called 'a slap in the face' to which France must respond by declaring war. Believing the army to be ready, Gramont gave the Chamber the over-optimistic impression that Austria and Italy would join France. Had France won, Gramont would no doubt be remembered as a great statesman, but the first defeats toppled the Government on 9 August. When disaster followed, Gramont was reviled. He and his Scottish wife took temporary refuge in London, then returned quietly to France. Ostracised, his career and reputation ruined, in his remaining years he wrote justifications of his conduct in 1870 under a pseudonym.

HARTUNG EDMOND-HENRI-DAVID (1819–96) The officer whom Patry approached to secure a posting in 1871 was a veteran of Algeria, the Crimea and Italy, but since 1860 had been engaged in personnel work at the Ministry of War. Between 7 and 11 July 1870 Colonel Hartung worked to draw up the final order of battle for the army, only to be told that the Emperor had changed his mind and wanted the army to operate as one large unit instead of in three wings as had been originally envisaged. All the plans had to be redrawn on the very eve of war. Promoted brigadier on 14 July, Hartung served as Director of Personnel and after the war became General de Cissey's chief of staff when he became Minister of War. He subsequently held several senior commands, interrupted briefly after his handling of a strike situation in the North in 1881.

LADMIRAULT LOUIS-RÉNÉ-PAUL (1808–98) Ladmirault belonged to a noble family which had been prominent since the 18th century, and included an ancestor who had fought at Fontenoy in 1745. In the 1790s his family had fought in Condé's royalist army against the Revolution. Graduating from Saint-Cyr in 1829, Ladmirault served in Algeria for 22 years. Intelligent, capable, courtly and brave, as a Zouave officer he soon made a reputation. He led a column in a murderous assault on Constantine and in 1842 commanded an expedition against the Beni-Manasser. Succeeding Cavaignac as colonel of Zouaves in 1844, he won further laurels fighting the Kabyles and rose to brigadier before returning to France to command a division at Boulogne in the 1850s. He took two severe wounds at Solferino in the Italian campaign, and afterwards found riding painful. From 1865 he was Deputy Governor of Algeria and chief of staff to MacMahon, transferring to command of the Second Corps at Lille in 1867. On the outbreak of war in 1870 he commanded the Fourth Corps. In the August battles the sight of his burly, imperturbable figure on horseback, wearing a white havelock, was said to have been reassuring to his men. But while there was no question of his bravery, his generalship on 16 August when he commanded the French right was later to be the subject of controversy when Bazaine implied that failures were the fault of his subordinates. These criticisms were vigorously challenged by Ladmirault's admirers. The General himself, a monarchist, strongly Catholic, conservative aristocrat, evidently felt some disdain for Bazaine. On returning from imprisonment at Aachen, Ladmirault commanded the First Corps of the Army of Versailles, which in May 1871 turned Communard defences from the north and occupied the hill of Montmartre. Said to have opposed the worst excesses of the repression, some of his subordinates had no such compunctions. He was rewarded for his services by being made Governor of Paris in June, retaining the post until 1878. After an initial failure in the 1876 elections he entered the Senate, representing his native Vienne. He was Vice-President of the Senate in 1876–7 and was re-elected in 1879 and 1882.

LAVEAUCOUPET SYLVAIN-FRANÇOIS-JULES MERLE DE LABRUGIÈRE DE (1806–92) Laveaucoupet, one of the most able French divisional commanders in 1870, entered Saint-Cyr in 1824 and progressed in 1827 to the École d'Application d'État-Major to study staff duties. As a second lieutenant in a line regiment from 1830, he took part in the conquest of Algeria and rose steadily in rank in the following years, moving to staff work in 1836. In 1849 he became *chef de cabinet* to the Minister of War, and subsequently chief of staff of the 3rd Military Division with the rank of colonel. In Italy in 1859 he was wounded in the left shoulder at Magenta on 4 June, received a bayonet thrust in his face five days later, and had two horses shot from under him on the 24th. On 30 June he was promoted to brigadier, commanding the 1st Brigade of the 1st Division of the Second Corps. He was promoted to general of division in 1868 and in July 1870 was given command of the 3rd Division of Frossard's corps of the Army of the Rhine. In the frontier battle at Spicheren on 6 August his division held the French right with great steadiness. Defending well-chosen high ground, his men delivered withering chassepot fire on the assaulting Germans, cleared the Gifertswald at the point of the bayonet, and withdrew in good order only at dusk, undefeated on their sector of the front. However, so severe had been the division's casualties that it was used to garrison Metz during the heavy fighting later in the month. In the last stages of the blockade, Bazaine considered appointing Laveaucoupet to command of the garrison, as the Marshal was dissatisfied with Coffinières' handling of growing civil disorder. Laveaucoupet, however, declined the assignment. At the capitulation he was following orders to collect the Colours to deposit at the Arsenal when he learned that they were not being destroyed as supposed. He thereupon gave verbal orders to his colonels to return them to their regiments and to burn them, in defiance of Bazaine's instructions. In April 1871 Laveaucoupet commanded the 2nd Division of the First Corps of the Army of Versailles, in which Patry was serving, but the general reached retirement age and went into the reserve at the end of that month.

LEBOEUF EDMOND (1809–98) Leboeuf's grandfather had been a member of the general council of the Paris Commune during the Revolution and his father had been director of the grand chancellery of the Legion of Honour and Master of Requests at Napoleon I's court. Edmond entered the École Polytechnique in 1828, took an active part while a student in the revolution of 1830, and graduated from the École d'Application at Metz in 1832. Thereafter he rose steadily as an artillerist, including service in Algeria, becoming chief of the artillery general staff at the outbreak of the Crimean War, taking command of the Second Corps' artillery in 1855 and that of the Imperial Guard in 1856. In 1859 he commanded the artillery of the Army of Italy, playing a key role at Solferino. Afterwards he was named aide-de-camp to the Emperor and an Inspector-General of artillery – one who was not unduly impressed by the new breech-loaders. In August 1869 he moved from corps command at Toulouse to the Ministry of War, being made a Marshal of France in March 1870 – the last to be created until 1916. In the July crisis he was anxious that German military preparations would put France at a fatal disadvantage and strongly urged the calling up of the reserves. When, on 14 July in the wake of the 'Ems telegram', the Council of Ministers was considering whether to call a European Congress, he insisted with vehemence that he would resign if war were not declared. He argued in the Chamber that the army was well prepared and armed and had the best opportunity it was likely to get to win a war which he believed was inevitable. He claimed that 'If the war lasts a year, we will have no need to purchase a single gaiter button', which was to be much quoted as a boast that the army was ready 'to the last gaiter button'. On mobilisation, he assumed the role of chief of general staff of the Army of the Rhine, but after the initial defeats he was execrated in Paris and stepped down. For the rest of the campaign he commanded the Third Corps. Described as a 'superb-looking man with wonderful moustaches', he fought well in all the battles around Metz. After imprisonment in Germany he settled in the Hague until August 1871, then returned to France. He attended the funeral of Napoleon III, but otherwise lived in seclusion at his château on the Orne which he had acquired in 1860. He began, but never finished, his memoirs. A generation after his death, in 1944, his château was destroyed in the Battle of Normandy.

LECOINTE ALPHONSE-THÉODORE (1817–90) Graduating from Saint-Cyr in 1839, Lecointe fought in Algeria, the Crimea, Italy (where he was wounded in the arm at Magenta) and Mexico. By 1870 he was colonel of the 2nd Grenadier Guards. Losing heavily at Borny on 14 August, his regiment lost a third of its effectives on 16 August and he was wounded in the leg. Escaping to Lille at the capitulation of Metz, he was named brigadier on 14 November, was energetic in helping to form the Army of the North, and fought at Villers-Bretonneux. He obtained permission from Faidherbe for the raid on Ham, and his direction, careful planning and briefings to his officers were largely responsible for its success on 9–10 December. He was appointed to command of the Twenty-second Corps, the best troops in the Army of the North, with Derroja and du Bessol as his divisional commanders. His sang-froid and firmness under fire and the benevolent air of the white-bearded general inspired confidence in his men at Pont-Noyelles and Bapaume. Although Faidherbe, in an article in *Le Temps* in 1884, hinted that Lecointe's men had given way too quickly at Saint-Quentin,

Lecointe's orders from Faidherbe had been few and late, and in the circumstances his men did well to hold up the Germans for as long as they did and to avoid a rout. After the war Lecointe commanded a division at Lille, then a corps at Toulouse, and from 1884 was Inspector-General of infantry schools. Having served as military governor of Lyon and Paris, he sat in the Senate for his native Eure.

LE FLÔ ADOLPHE-CHARLES-EMMANUEL (1804–87). Le Flô was the Minister of War whom Patry saw hurrying away in his carriage on 18 March 1871. A native of Finistère, Le Flô entered Saint-Cyr in 1823 and distinguished himself in North Africa. In 1848 he became a general and was elected Deputy for Finistère, sitting on the right of the Constituent Assembly. He was also sent on a diplomatic mission to Saint Petersburg. Re-elected in 1849, he became suspicious of Louis-Napoleon and changed from a supporter to a strong opponent. Foreseeing the *coup d'état* of 1851, he supported an unsuccessful motion to give the president of the chamber the power to summon the army to its defence. On 2 December, the night of the *coup*, he was arrested and incarcerated at Vincennes and then Ham, being expelled from France by decree in January 1852. Living in Belgium, then England, he was authorised to return in 1857, living in seclusion at his château. His offer of his services in 1870 was refused by the imperial authorities, but with the revolution of 4 September he was made Minister of War: though in sympathy he was an Orleanist rather than a republican. Once the siege began his authority extended only to the capital, where he carried out Trochu's directions with regard to the fortifications, manpower reserves and food stocks. Re-elected in 1871 and retained in his post by Thiers, he directed the concentration of troops around Paris in February–March 1871, though in such a way that many of the troops arriving were those who were due for imminent discharge. Le Flô was doubtful about the attempt to recover National Guard cannon on 18 March. Whether or not he was unduly influenced by his escape from a mob that day, it was his judgement that the only way to preserve the cohesion of the army was to evacuate the capital. Thiers had already fled for Versailles when Le Flô gave the controversial evacuation order, over the opposition of civilian ministers, so abandoning arms, munitions and forts to the insurgents. With Thiers exercising personal control, he seems to have had little influence over the operations against the Commune. Nevertheless, police executing foreigners and army deserters among the Communards claimed to be acting under orders from the Ministry of War. After the fighting was over, on 5 June, Thiers replaced Le Flô by General de Cissey, partly to reassure conservatives in the Assembly. Le Flô showed more aptitude for diplomacy, returning to Russia as ambassador. He refused a seat in the Senate in 1875.

LORENCEZ CHARLES-FERDINAND LATRILLE DE, COUNT (1814–92) The commander of the 3rd Division of the Fourth Corps in 1870, he was the son of a general and grandson of Marshal Oudinot of First Empire fame. He had graduated from Saint-Cyr in 1832 and served as an officer of *chasseurs à pied* in Algeria before returning to command of a line regiment in France in 1852. Promoted to brigadier in the Crimean War, he was wounded in the assault on the Malakoff redoubt on 18 June 1855. In 1862 he led a reinforcement of 4,500 men to Mexico. He entered Orizaba and advanced on Puebla, but was unable to dislodge a larger Mexican defending force. Withdrawing to Orizaba in May, he beat off pursuit but could do no more without reinforcements. In September fresh troops arrived, but he was superseded by General Forey and recalled to France the following month. From 1864 to 1870 he performed duty as an Inspector-General of Infantry. On 16 August 1870 his division arrived too late to join in the fighting on the French right, but it was one of the last to withdraw after the battle on the 18th. He did not return from captivity in Germany until August 1871, and retired in 1879.

MacMahon Marie-Edmé-Patrice Maurice de, Count (1808–93) MacMahon's family was of Irish extraction, having settled in France after 1688. His father, a friend of King Charles X, became a peer of France. After initially training for the priesthood, MacMahon opted for the military life and entered Saint-Cyr in 1827. Such was his record in Algeria that by 1853 he was a general of division and Grand Officer of the Legion of Honour. It was on 8 September 1855 that he won enduring fame with his successful assault on the Malakoff redoubt, the key to Sebastopol, which he defended against all Russian counter-attacks, announcing 'Here I am and here I stay.' This feat caused the city to fall to the allies, and MacMahon received the Grand Cross and was later made a Senator. After his prominent role in putting down the Kabyle revolt in 1857 he assumed command of forces in Algeria. In Italy in 1859 he led the Second Corps and was created a Marshal of France and Duc de Magenta in recognition of his crucial role in the victory of Magenta on 4 June. Solferino added to his reputation. He represented Napoleon III at the coronation of William I of Prussia in 1861, and in 1864 was appointed Governor-General of Algeria. In implementing the Emperor's policy the Marshal was less than politically adept, and by 1870 was offering to resign in the face of opposition from both the colonists and the Church. In July 1870 he was recalled to command French forces in Alsace, but with insufficient troops available was defeated at Froeschwiller on 6 August. His wing of the army then began a chaotic retreat to Châlons, where he reorganised it with reinforcements and under orders from Paris set out to rescue Bazaine in Metz. Hampered by supply problems and bad weather, he was soon pushed north-eastwards by relentlessly pursuing German armies. MacMahon underestimated the immediate danger on 31 August, for he ordered his exhausted troops to rest around Sedan the following day. On 1 September his army was surrounded and bombarded into surrender, though MacMahon, being badly wounded early in the day and having tried to take the offensive, was not blamed for defeat in the same way as Bazaine at Metz. Returning from captivity in March 1871, he was placed in command of the Army of Versailles in April. Moving with care, he supervised the operations which had overcome all Communard resistance by the end of May. In 1873 MacMahon succeeded Thiers, being voted President for a seven-year term by the Assembly, many of whom looked on him as a safe caretaker until the monarchy could be restored. MacMahon was a monarchist – he became splenetic if the *Marseillaise* was played in his presence – and his period in office, with Broglie as his first prime minister, was strongly aristocratic and conservative in tone. However, while he resisted republican influences and insisted that there should be an upper chamber in the new constitutional system, he tried to do his duty scrupulously and would not countenance schemes for a restoration by improper means. Reluctantly accepting a republican ministry under Jules Simon in 1876, he forced its resignation on 16 May 1877. When a majority of deputies rejected a new Broglie government, he dissolved the Chamber. Although MacMahon was acting legally, he was challenging the principle of rule by a parliamentary majority, and in the ensuing elections, despite the strenuous and ruthless efforts of the government to ensure victory, republicans triumphed. After this clear rebuff MacMahon stayed in office for a year, then resigned in January 1879 over republican demands for the dismissal of conservative generals. Presidential powers had been decisively checked, and for the remaining decades of the Third Republic no president attempted to dissolve the Chamber of Deputies, which was henceforth the focus of political power.

NAPOLEON III (CHARLES-LOUIS-NAPOLÉON BONAPARTE) (1808–73) Prince Louis Napoleon was the nephew of the Emperor Napoleon. His (probable) father was the Emperor's brother Louis, King of Holland, and his mother Hortense Beauharnais, daughter of the Empress Josephine by her first marriage. After Waterloo Louis-Napoleon lived with his mother in exile, mostly in Switzerland, and gained his first military experience with the revolutionary cause in Italy in 1831. The death of his elder brother, followed by that of his cousin in 1832, left him the heir of the Bonaparte dynasty, which he saw himself destined to restore to power in France. However, an attempted *coup* at Strasbourg in 1836 led to his expulsion, and another fiasco at Boulogne in 1840 ended in his imprisonment in the fortress of Ham. In 1846 he escaped to London, where he served as a special constable in the Chartist demonstrations of 1848. In February that year revolution in France overthrew the July monarchy and the country remained in turmoil for months. Judging his opportunity carefully, he returned to take his seat in the Assembly of the Second Republic after being elected in five departments in September. Taken for a fool by sophisticated politicians, he exploited the power of his name in the countryside to such effect that he was elected President of the Republic in December with 5½ million votes – nearly four times as many as his nearest opponent. Positioning himself as the man of order in the face of continuing turbulence, in 1851 he attempted to have his presidency extended by legal means: a move narrowly blocked by Thiers and other monarchists in the Assembly. With the support of a group of generals, Louis-

Napoleon planned and carried through a *coup d'état* in December. There was some bloodshed in Paris and resistance elsewhere in France. Mass arrests and deportations followed, but a plebiscite endorsed his seizure of power by 7½ million votes to just over 2 million noes or abstentions. In November 1852 the Prince President called another plebiscite, and with the approval of nearly 8 million voters became Emperor. The Second Empire gave France eighteen years of relative stability and growth, though at a cost in political liberty. Growing political opposition was registered in the elections of 1863, and particularly those of 1869, when the regime seemed to be in severe difficulties. Yet in May 1870 a plebiscite endorsing moves towards a 'Liberal Empire' again produced a 'yes' vote of more than 7 million, much to the dismay of the Empire's opponents. Napoleon's downfall was to come not directly from within, but through war – an instrument he had previously used to advance his policies and prestige. In 1852 he had declared that 'the Empire means peace', but he made war in the Crimea, Italy, China, Cochin-China, Syria and Mexico. In 1866 he was aware that the country was not eager for a war against Prussia in support of Austria, but his policy over the next four years of seeking 'compensation' on France's eastern frontier for Prussia's growth increased diplomatic tension, while his attempts at army reform were emasculated by a mistrustful Chamber. After the disaster of 1870 which cost him his throne, Napoleon and his ministers portrayed themselves as pressured into war by overwhelming popular excitement, and the image of a helpless man tortured by gall-stones, browbeaten by the Empress and swept along by events has been enduring. Yet, while Prussia provided the provocation and a strong French reaction to the Hohenzollern candidature was inevitable, it was Napoleon who, after some vacillation, backed Gramont in the demand for guarantees which risked a war he might have had the courage to prevent. Gambling on victory to strengthen his regime and re-establish France as the arbiter of Europe, he set in motion a military machine that required energetic and professionally skilled central direction. Napoleon proved unfit to provide such leadership. After failing to find death on 1 September on the field of Sedan, where he ordered a surrender to stop the slaughter of his troops, Napoleon was sent in captivity to Wilhelmshöhe in Germany. Going into exile in England in 1871, he died after an operation for gall-stones at Chislehurst, Kent, in January 1873.

OSMONT AUGUSTE-ADOLPHE (1818–90) Patry's benefactor on 17 August, the chief of staff of the Fourth Corps, was a soldier of ripe experience. A native of Montpellier, he graduated from Saint-Cyr in 1838 and then attended the École d'Application. His intelligence and military talent gained him several important missions. He was present at the siege of Rome in 1849 and in the Crimean campaign was charged with reconnoitring the roads from Gallipoli to Adrianople and onward to Varna. Commanding at Eupatoria from September 1854 to February 1855, with two French companies plus 200 British and 400 Turks, he repelled repeated attacks by the blockading Russians, meanwhile having to feed the populace and coping with the cholera raging in the town: a feat which won him the Legion of Honour and promotion to lieutenant-colonel. He fought at Magenta and Solferino, then commanded in Nice before postings to Alexandria and Beirut in preparation for the Syrian campaign. Going to Mexico as a divisional chief of staff, he was soon fulfilling that function for the whole expedition. In 1866 the Emperor Maximilian appointed him Minister of War with the task of reorganising loyal Mexican forces. However, Bazaine, Osmont's commander, saw this as part of a move to retain French support and strongly disapproved. The subsequent coolness between the two men was evident when in 1870 Bazaine refused to have Osmont as chief of staff of the Third Corps. He was little more welcome to General Ladmirault in the Fourth Corps, who habitually bypassed him. In the battle of 31 August outside Metz Osmont was wounded by a shell splinter in the right shoulder. Interned at Cologne after the capitulation, he refused to accept the conditions imposed on officers and was sent to stricter imprisonment in a fortress at the mouth of the Vistula. In the Army of Versailles he commanded a brigade, and was confirmed at divisional rank in June 1871. Thereafter he commanded the province of Oran, being active in colonisation work, and was sent on a diplomatic mission to Morocco by President MacMahon. He transferred to Algiers in 1878, and then held command of three corps in succession before retiring in 1883. In 47 years of service, Osmont had spent 32 abroad, had taken part in 40 campaigns, had been wounded twice and cited in orders nine times.

PELLETAN PIERRE-CLÉMENT-EUGÈNE (1813–84) A journalist and left-wing politician, Pelletan, who came from a family of Protestant pastors in Charente, was a vocal and effective spokesman for republicanism and anti-militarism. In his early career he began by studying law but broadened his interests to philosophy and political economy, studying at the Sorbonne and the Collège de France and travelling widely. He became an adherent of the ideas of Saint-Simon, and came to notice for his articles in many journals, particularly Girardin's La Presse. A friend of Lamartine's, he was active in the 1848 Revolution but failed to win election to the Constituent Assembly. In 1855 his outspoken views on restrictions on political liberty earned him a three-months' prison sentence and a fine. He wrote several books, including in 1863 *The New Babylon*, criticising Haussmann's remodelling of Paris, and in 1864 a pamphlet called 'Who loses wins', arguing that military defeat was actually beneficial to a country because it reduced the influence of the military caste in civil society. Elected as a Deputy for Paris in 1863 and 1869, in the Chamber he vigorously challenged the need for increased military expenditure. In 1868 he founded and edited *La Tribune* with Alexandre Glais-Bizoin. In the wake of the plebiscite in May 1870, against which he protested and which seemed to undermine all the republican electoral gains of the previous year, there was a division in the republican movement. Pelletan was clearly identified with the *gauche fermée*, which included Gambetta, who would not compromise with the Empire or with those who were prepared to work within it for gradual reform. On the outbreak of war he voted against war credits and his name was included with Gambetta's on a list of republicans whom Ollivier briefly thought of arresting. He was chosen as a member of the Government of National Defence on 4 September 1870 when the Empire was overthrown, but did not receive a ministerial post. He concerned himself with the administration of hospitals and the National Guard, and for a short while deputised at the Ministry of Education. Elected Deputy for the Bouches-du-Rhône in 1871, he remained a staunch republican, entering the Senate in 1876, becoming its Vice-President in 1879 and being made a Life Senator six months before his sudden death. His son Camille (1846–1915) was to be an even better-known radical.

ROSSEL LOUIS-NATHANIEL (1844–71) Born at Saint-Brieuc in northern Brittany, Rossel was the son of an army officer from Nîmes. His mother was British, and the closely knit family were strong Protestants. He was educated at the military school of La Flèche from 1855, passing on to the École Polytechnique in 1862 and the École d'Application at Metz in 1864. Graduating second in his class in 1866, Rossel entered the Corps of Engineers, being stationed at Metz, then Montpellier, and from 1869 in Bourges, where he supervised building projects and was promoted captain. He had shown early signs of a precocious intelligence, and his interests were wide-ranging. In 1868 he undertook the translation of John Stuart Mill's *On Liberty* and wrote a prize-winning essay on the repair of military bridges which was published in 1869. From the beginning of 1870, under the pseudonym of 'Randall', he began writing trenchant articles on military subjects for *Le Temps*. On the outbreak of war he thought of resigning to serve as a private but got permission to go to Metz as captain of a depot company of the 1st Engineers. He was scathingly critical of what he denounced as the cowardice and incapacity of the generals, and in October wrote a circular calling for a sortie and made efforts to persuade officers such as General Clinchant to lead one. After an unsuccessful attempt at escape he was summoned before Bazaine, but, unlike a colleague, was allowed to go free after an interview. His attempts to promote a break-out at the capitulation proving abortive, he escaped from Metz on 30 October and eventually reached Tours via Luxembourg, Belgium and England. During November he was sent to Lille and submitted reports to Gambetta on the resources for defence in the north. Returning in December, he was made a colonel in charge of a camp at Nevers. Frustrated and disgusted by the armistice, he was ardent for continuing a guerrilla war against the Germans. On hearing of the revolution of 18 March 1871 in Paris, he immediately wrote a barbed letter of resignation from the army, not hesitating to place himself 'on the side which did not sign the peace and does not count in its ranks generals guilty of capitulations'. In the capital he took charge of the revolutionary forces of the 17th arrondissement, though in trying to impose discipline in the wake of the abortive offensive of 1–2 April he was briefly imprisoned. The Commune then appointed him chief of staff to Cluseret, its War

Delegate. His prodigious efforts to organise the defences in a military manner created some opposition within the Commune, and the severe examples he tried to make as President of the Court-Martial were overturned by a commission of revision. Nevertheless, when Cluseret was arrested on 30 April the Commune appointed Rossel to succeed him. His energy created enthusiasm, as did his spirited reply to the 'insolent summons' to surrender sent by a former comrade now serving in the Versailles forces to the Communard defenders of the vital Fort d'Issy. But for all Rossel's attempts to galvanise the defence and impose discipline and centralised organisation in regular army style, the fort was lost on 9 May. Sickened by lack of support at the fighting front and by the undermining of his orders in the confusion of conflicting committees, Rossel resigned in disgust, publishing news of the defeat and a withering letter denouncing the Commune's incompetence and propensity to discuss rather than act. His letter provoked a bitter debate, and it was decided to court-martial him. However, he contrived to escape detention and stayed incognito at a hotel in the Boulevard Saint-Germain, observing the defeat of the Commune almost with detachment. Denounced by a police informer, he was arrested on 7 June, identified, and imprisoned at Versailles. After two trials, during which his intelligence, sincerity and courage aroused considerable sympathy, he was condemned to death. The Thiers government, and the army to which he had belonged and which he had fought against, were unforgiving. He was executed by firing squad at Satory on 28 November 1871.

ROUSSET LÉONCE (1850–1938) Born in Toulon, the son of a colonel of artillery from Metz, Rousset attended the prestigious Louis-le-Grand school in Paris before entering Saint-Cyr in 1868, emerging as a second lieutenant at the outbreak of war. After his wounding on 31 August, which his messmate Patry describes, he went into captivity but returned to fight against the Commune. He served in Algeria for several years, gaining successive promotions, before becoming an eminent teacher of tactics and military history at Saint-Cyr. His historical *tour de force*, the six-volume *La Seconde Campagne de France: Histoire Générale de la Guerre Franco-Allemande 1870–1871* (1895–9) won an academy prize and was followed by a study of the Fourth Corps in the Metz campaign and a critical essay on Frederick the Great, Napoleon and Moltke. However, Rousset's pronounced nationalist opinions, expressed in newspaper articles in *Le Gaulois*, *La Liberté* and other journals, brought him into official disfavour and in 1898 he was posted in disgrace to an infantry regiment in Épinal. He left the army in 1900, publishing his letter of protest. In 1902 he was elected Deputy for Verdun on the *Patrie française* ticket, defeating the republican candidate. He stirred up controversy by an attack on primary school teachers, but was also active on several commissions and in defending the economic interests of his constituents, and was noted for his interventions in the Chamber on military matters. Having acted independently of any party, Rousset was defeated and lost his seat in 1906. He subsequently wrote more books and articles, both about aspects of 1870–1 and, in the 1920s, about the campaigns of the First World War. He received the Legion of Honour and several foreign decorations, and lived almost until the eve of the Second World War.

THIERS MARIE-JOSEPH-LOUIS-ADOLPHE (1797–1877) Born in Marseille, an illegitimate child brought up by his mother and grandmother in modest circumstances, Thiers studied law in Aix and came to Paris in 1821. He began a successful career as a prolific and talented journalist and historian. His prominent role in the 1830 revolution as editorialist of *Le National*, mouthpiece of the liberal opposition, helped his election to the legislature and entry into government. As Minister of the Interior in 1834 he dealt ruthlessly with disturbances in Lyon and Paris, exhorting the prefect of Lyon to act 'as though there were a war'. He first led a government in 1836, resigning over the king's wish to disband forces that he had gathered to intervene in Spain. Back in power in 1840, he brought France to the brink of war with Great Britain and the other powers over his support for Mehemet Ali in Syria. This became too much for an alarmed King Louis-Philippe, and in the wake of the war scare (as a result of which Paris was fortified) he was not recalled. A move to recall him in the final hours of the 1848 revolution came too late to save the monarchy. Under the Second Republic he was the recognised parliamentary leader of the 'Party of Order', the champion of property rights and of restricting the franchise to protect liberty from what he denounced in an angry debate as the 'vile multitude'. At first courted by the new President, Prince Louis-Napoleon, Thiers eventually came into open opposition and was among those suspected of an 'Orleanist plot' and arrested in the *coup d'état* of 1851. He was in exile for eight months and devoted himself to his writings on historical, scientific and artistic subjects until his return to parliament in 1863. He proved a trenchant critic of Napoleon III's foreign policy, warning of the dangers of German nationalism and declaring after the failure to support Austria in her war against Prussia in 1866 that 'there is not a single blunder left to commit'. But in July 1870 he was one of the few cool heads, protesting that the occasion of the war was badly chosen and accusing the government of blundering into it in a fit of pique. 'Do you want all Europe to say', he asked in the Chamber on 15 July, 'that although the substance of the quarrel was settled, you have decided to pour out torrents of blood over a mere matter of form?' He would not join the Government of National Defence, but at its request undertook a mission to the neutral courts of Great Britain, Russia, Austria and Italy in September and October of 1870 in a vain attempt to persuade them to use their influence to secure a peace favourable to France. Judging the continuation of the war senseless, he opposed the extreme republican view that it should be fought to the bitter end. Elected head of the government with overwhelming support in February 1871, following the armistice, he negotiated the peace preliminaries with Bismarck. He sought to impose order on the dissident National Guard in Paris by sending troops into the city in the early hours of 18 March. The result was insurrection. Thiers fled to Versailles and from there energetically oversaw the military suppression of the Paris Commune – during which the Communards destroyed his house in the city.

The extent of Thiers' personal responsibility for the shooting by the army of large numbers of Communards who had stopped fighting has been disputed. He declared that expiation would be complete, but eventually (some said belatedly) acted to halt some of the worst excesses. He had in any case few compunctions in doing what he saw as necessary to restore internal order and France's position abroad. He was confirmed as President and, as the only French statesman with the prestige to see through the peace negotiations and deal with Bismarck, he concluded the treaty with Germany and then successfully raised loans to pay the indemnity, enabling German occupation to end ahead of schedule. He brought the Assembly to heel several times by threatening to resign, knowing that he was indispensable. However, his didactic, opinionated manner and dogmatism on the many issues on which he considered himself an expert (including military reform) made him enemies. An incessant talker, short and stout with a peak of silver hair and small spectacles, 'Adolphe I' was a gift to cartoonists. Once he had settled matters with Germany, he was vulnerable. In May 1873, disillusioned by his firm maintenance of the Republic, the monarchists were able to defeat him in a parliamentary vote, and he resigned the presidency. In 1877 there seemed a good possibility that he would be elected President a second time with republican support, but he died during the campaign. Shortly before his death he had received an ovation in the Assembly as the liberator of French territory, and his funeral in Paris became a demonstration of republican solidarity, attended by large and respectful crowds, including former enemies.

TROCHU LOUIS-JULES (1815–96) Attending Saint-Cyr in 1835–7, then the École d'Application d'État Major, Trochu served in Algeria in 1841–7, being an aide-de-camp from 1844. After personnel work at the Ministry of War in the early 1850s, he went to the Crimea as aide-de-camp to the expedition commander, Marshal de Saint-Arnaud and, on his death, to Canrobert. Promoted to brigadier in November 1854, he served as army chief of staff until taking brigade command in July 1855. In the assault on Sebastopol on 8 September he was wounded and cited in orders. More staff duties followed until he took command of a division in Italy, winning distinction at Solferino by his attack on the Austrian left. From 1860 he was Inspector-General of Infantry, coming to notice for his book *L'Armée française en 1867*, a radical critique of French military preparedness. This work cost him imperial favour, but confirmed his reputation for brilliance and made him the toast of the opposition. On the outbreak of war he was snubbed by being posted to command an observation force in the Pyrenees: but with the defeats of early August all his predictions seemed to be vindicated. When sounded, he said that he would consent to become Minister of War only if he were allowed to denounce in the Legislature all the mistakes of the government since 1866. Although this condition was not accepted, he was put in command of the Twelfth Corps at Châlons on 12 August and a week later was made Military Governor of Paris, in command of the defences of the capital. Mistrusting his popularity, the Empress and Palikao treated him with hostility, and during the revolution on 4 September he made little attempt to defend the regime. A Breton Catholic and Orleanist, he accepted the presidency of the new republican government with some reservations, feeling it his duty to prevent further social upheaval, and did so only on condition that 'family, property and religion' would be respected. Hailed in the press and in popular song as the man with '*Le Plan*' that would save the capital, Trochu was a capable organiser of the defences with a penchant for bombastic proclamations. However, he had a professional's contempt for amateur offensive plans, was more than doubtful about the quality of the National Guard, and pessimistic about the prospects for raising the siege. When, after three months, the 'Great Sortie' (largely planned by Ducrot) was finally attempted, it failed. Meanwhile, Trochu saw maintaining order as his priority. He and other members of the government were temporarily held hostage in the Hôtel de Ville by revolutionary National Guards on 31 October, but he remained calm, escaped, and organised loyal battalions to rescue his colleagues. Government authority was restored without loss of life, for Trochu restrained the impetuous Ducrot from conducting a bloody repression. The revolutionary leaders were arrested and a referendum on 3 November bolstered the government. But military inaction and failure caused all the hopes that had been placed in Trochu as a saviour to turn to disillusion, and his civilian colleagues became exasperated. In December he proclaimed that 'the Governor of Paris will not capitulate', but with food stocks running low, the capital could not hold out much longer. He directed the Buzenval Sortie on 19 January and, if its utter failure exploded the myth that the 'people in arms' could defeat a hardened professional army, it also proved the end for Trochu. His resignation was demanded the next day by the mayors and the Paris clubs. As he felt it would be dishonourable to resign, the government removed him by suppressing his post of Governor of Paris. Trochu, after trying to find death in the front line on 21 January, stayed on as President of the Council. After the Armistice he proposed the arrest of Gambetta if he failed to accept the government's decision. In the February elections he was elected as a Deputy and, after formally surrendering his powers to the President of the New Assembly, took his seat as an Orleanist, remaining until July 1872. Trochu later refused any further honours and withdrew from public life.

WILLIAM I (WILHELM FRIEDRICH LUDWIG OF HOHENZOLLERN) (1797–1888) The second son of Frederick William III of Prussia (reigned 1786–1840), William was old enough to remember the defeat of his country by France in 1806. He was commissioned in the Prussian army the following year at the age of 10, was a captain in the German War of Liberation in 1813, and took part in the campaign in France against Napoleon I in 1814. For his bravery at Bar-sur-Aube, his father awarded him the Iron Cross – an order which had been instituted the year before. Conservative and a conventionally devout Protestant, he remained first and foremost a professional soldier, for whom the needs of the monarchy and the army took priority. On the succession of his childless brother, Frederick William IV, in 1840, he became heir presumptive and vice-governor of Pomerania. Nicknamed 'Prince of Grapeshot' for his bloody dispersal of demonstrators in Berlin in March 1848, he went briefly to London to escape unpopularity. Becoming Military Governor of Westphalia, he crushed insurrection in Baden in 1849 – the virtual end of a year of revolution in Germany. He became Regent in 1858 following his brother's stroke. His rule was at first welcomed as a 'New Era' in which moderate Liberals were taken into the ministry and the government seemed disposed to conciliatory policies. William became king on his brother's death in 1861. Prussia's poor military preparedness had been demonstrated on mobilisation during the war between France and Austria in 1859, and army reform was needed. But the terms on which William insisted – three years' service with the Colours, a significant increase in the number of regiments, and subordination to regular army requirements of the *Landwehr* (a territorial reserve of citizen militia) – brought confrontation with the Liberals in the Prussian parliament. William was ready to abdicate rather than make any concession that would dilute the reforms or undermine his authority over the army. He was persuaded to appoint Bismarck as his Minister-President in 1862 to overcome parliamentary resistance. So began an often tempestuous twenty-six years' working partnership between the king and his principal servant, which within a decade achieved the unification of Germany under Prussian leadership. William got his army reforms, which in 1866 enabled Prussia to defeat her rival Austria and her allies. After victory at Königgrätz (Sadowa), Bismarck with difficulty persuaded William to make a moderate peace. In 1870, however, it was William who was more moderate, not having known or approved of the extent of Bismarck's intrigue concerning the Spanish throne. He influenced his Sigmaringen cousin to decline the throne, the acceptance of which he knew would be a provocation to France. At an interview in the Kurgarten at Bad Ems on 13 July, the King was perfectly polite to the French ambassador, Benedetti, and willingly reiterated his approval, as head of the House of Hohenzollern, to the withdrawal of the candidature. But he would not accede, as King of Prussia, to a humiliating public and formal guarantee that it would never be renewed. It was the account of this interview which Bismarck edited and published which provoked France into declaring war on 15 July. William, having returned to Berlin amid cheering crowds, signed the mobilisation order the same day and accompanied his armies into France, being present at Gravelotte and Sedan. Making his headquarters at Versailles during the siege of Paris, he had often to arbitrate quarrels between Moltke and Bismarck, his military and political advisers. After much hard political negotiation with other German princes and arguments over the exact form of title, William was proclaimed German Emperor in the Hall of Mirrors at Versailles on 18 January 1871, the 170th anniversary of the Kingdom of Prussia. After the war, he presided over the new Reich with dignity for another seventeen years, surviving two assassination attempts in 1878. Although he always remained mindful of the risks Germany had run in 1870, he bequeathed an authoritarian, militarist state which, in the less stable hands of his grandson, Kaiser William II, was to overreach itself in 1914–18.

WOLFF CHARLES-JOSEPH-FRANÇOIS (1823–1901) Patry's brigade commander during the Commune had spent most of his career after graduating from Saint-Cyr in 1843 in Africa, where he was in command of an Arab bureau, and was wounded in an expedition against the Kabyles in 1856. Returning to France in 1862, he was part of a commission which considered recommendations on infantry tactics and produced a report in 1867 identifying the problems posed by increased firepower. He was promoted to brigadier in 1869. In 1870 he commanded the 1st Brigade of the 1st Division of the First Corps of the Army of the Rhine and fought at Froeschwiller and Sedan, where he was wounded twice. Returning from captivity, he was twice cited in orders for his service against the Commune. From 1874 he held a command in Algiers, where he founded a military academy. He achieved Corps command in 1878 and was a member of the Defence Committee and the War Committee (*Comité supérieur de la guerre*). He received the Grand Cross of the Legion of Honour in 1883.

NOTES

Patry's few original footnotes are indicated as such where they occur and appear in quotation marks. All other notes have been supplied by the translator to provide relevant additional information or to explain references which would have been familiar to Patry's contemporaries and compatriots but which would seem to require some explanation as a courtesy to modern readers. The Biographies on pages 283–314 provide brief information about some of the people mentioned in the text. Some notes indicate (without attempting to be exhaustive) where further information on particular topics may be found. Readers who wish to learn more about the Franco-Prussian War and the Commune are also referred to the suggestions for Further Reading at the end of this book.

Abbreviations used in the Notes

To save lengthy repetition, the following abbreviations are used for frequently cited works:

Bazaine, *Épisodes*. *Épisodes de la Guerre de 1870 et le blocus de Metz, par l'ex-Maréchal Bazaine* (Madrid, 1883).

Dossier Patry. *Dossier Patry, M. G. L.*; Série 5Yf56338, Service Historique de l'Armée de Terre, Fort de Vincennes (Patry's unpublished service record in the French Army historical archives).

Faidherbe. Louis Faidherbe, *Campagne de l'Armée du Nord* (Paris, 1871).

GGS. *The Franco-German War, 1870–1871*, translated from the German Official Account by Captain F. C. H. Clarke, R.A (London, 1874–84). (The official history by the German Army General Staff.)

Guerre. Guerre de 1870–71, publié par *la Revue d'Histoire*, rédigé à la Section historique de l'État-Major de l'Armée (Paris, 1901–13). (The official history by the French Army General Staff.)

Historique. Jules Léon Méjécaze, *Historique du 6e Régiment d'Infanterie* (Paris, 1889).

Howard. Michael Howard, *The Franco-Prussian War: The German Invasion of France, 1870–1871* (London, 1961).

Lehautcourt. Pierre Lehautcourt (pseudonym of General Barthélemy Edmond Palat), *Histoire de la Guerre de 1870–1871* (7 vols., Paris, 1901–8).

Rousset, *4e Corps*. Lt-Col Léonce Rousset, *Le 4e Corps de l'Armée de Metz, 19 juillet–27 octobre 1870* (Paris, 1899).

Rousset, H. G. Lt-Col. Léonce Rousset, *Histoire Générale de la Guerre Franco-Allemande* (1870–71) (2 vols., Paris 1912).

Translator's Foreword

1 For losses in 1870–1 see François Roth, *La Guerre de 70* (Paris, 1990), pp. 507–10, and on prisoners *ibid.*, p. 418.

2 Martin van Creveld, *Supplying War: Logistics from Wallenstein to Patton* (Cambridge, 1977), p. 102, following H. von Molnar, 'Über Ammunitions–Ausrüstung der Feld Artillerie', in *Organ der Militär-Wissenschaftlichen Vereine*, 1879, pp. 591–3.

3 Martin Middlebrook, *The Kaiser's Battle* (London, 1978), p. 52. For further comparisons of material and consumption in 1870 and 1914 see van Creveld *op. cit.*, pp. 110–11.

4 Lyn Macdonald, *To the Last Man: Spring 1918* (London, 1998), p. 292 fn.

5 The text of the Treaty of Frankfurt is reprinted in Roth, *op. cit.*, pp. 731–6. See also *ibid.*, pp. 495–506, 527–51. An English translation can be found in Robert I. Giesberg, *The Treaty of Frankfort: A Study in Diplomatic History, September 1870–September 1873* (Philadelphia, 1966), pp. 283–93.

6 On commemoration of the war see Roth, *op. cit.*, pp. 680–726, and Annette Becker, 'War Memorials: A Legacy of Total War?' in Stig Förster and Jörg Nagler eds., *On the Road to Total War: The American Civil War and the German Wars of Unification, 1861–71* (Cambridge, 1997), pp. 657–80.

7 See Roth, *op. cit.*, pp. 607–79; Stéphane Audoin-Rouzeau, *1870: La France dans la Guerre* (Paris, 1989), pp. 315–22, and his essay 'French Public Opinion in 1870–71 and the Emergence of Total War' in Förster and Nagler, *op. cit.*, pp. 393–411; also Allan Mitchell, *The German Influence in France After 1870: The Formation of the French Republic* (Chapel Hill, 1979).

8 The essential bibliographical source for 19th-century writing on the war is Barthélemy Edmond Palat, *Bibliographie générale de la Guerre de 1870–1871* (Paris, 1896).

9 Not always the right lessons – see Witold Zaniewicki, 'L'impact de 1870 sur la pensée militaire française', in *Revue de Défense Nationale*, Aug.–Sept. 1970, pp. 1331–41.

10 David Clarke ed., *Roger de Mauni: The Franco-Prussian War* (London, 1970).

11 Jean-Frédéric Bazille, killed at the Battle of Beaune-la-Rolande, 28 November 1870, one week short of his 29th birthday. Monet, Sisley and Pissarro (whose studio was ransacked by German troops) came to London to work. Renoir was called up and served uneventfully in the 10th Cavalry in south-western France.

12 See Roth, *op. cit.*, pp. 685–8; Jean Humbert, *Édouard Detaille: l'héroïsme d'un siècle* (Paris, 1979); Philippe Chabert, *Alphonse de Neuville: l'épopée de la défaite* (Paris, 1979); François Robichon, *La peinture militaire française de 1871 à 1914* (Paris, 1998), pp. 124–40, and his article 'Emotion et sentiment dans les panoramas militaires après 1870' in *Zeitschrift für Schweizerische Archäologie und Kunstgeschichte* (Zürich), vol. 42, 1985, pp. 281–87. For a contrasting depiction

of French defeat by Swiss cyclorama artists see André Meyer and Heinz Horat, *Les Bourbakis en Suisse et le grand panorama de Lucerne* (Lausanne, 1983). Perhaps the most singular and haunting image of the war is Gustave Doré's *The Enigma* (1871), which hangs in the Musée d'Orsay. The Musée d'Orsay has produced a *carnet parcours* on the art of the conflict: Pierre Sesmat, 1870–71: 'L'Année Terrible' (Paris, 1989).

13 On French officer training and education see Richard Holmes, *The Road to Sedan: The French Army 1866–1870* (London, 1984), pp. 180-9; also Thomas J. Adriance, *The Last Gaiter Button: A Study of the Mobilisation and Concentration of the French Army in the War of 1870* (Westport, Conn., 1987), pp. 25–9; David B. Ralston, *The Army of the Republic: The Place of the Military in the Political Evolution of France, 1871–1914* (Cambridge, Mass., 1967), pp. 19–20; Douglas Porch, *The March to the Marne: The French Army 1871–1914* (Cambridge, 1981), pp. 38–40; Michael Howard, *The Franco-Prussian War, 1870–1871* (London, 1961), p. 16; Pierre Chalmin, *L'Officier Français de 1815 à 1870* (Paris, 1957), pp. 149–93, 350–7; William Serman and Jean-Paul Bertaud, *Nouvelle Histoire Militaire de la France* (Paris, 1998), pp. 321–4.

14 Léonce Rousset, *Le 4e Corps de l'Armée de Metz, 19 juillet–27 octobre 1870* (Paris, 1899), pp. 299 ff, 374. Rousset's major work was his *La Seconde Campagne de France: Histoire Générale de la Guerre Franco-Allemande, 1870–71* (6 vols., Paris, 1895–9), reissued in a profusely illustrated 2-volume edition (Paris, 1912).

15 For example the novels of Abel Hermant, *Le Cavalier Miserey (21e Chasseurs): moeurs militaires modernes* (1887); Lucien Descaves, *Sous-offs* (1889); and Georges Darien, *Biribi* (1890). See Serman and Bertaud, *op. cit.*, pp. 605–8; Ralston, *op. cit.*, p. 258. Darien was later to produce, in *L'épaulette* (1905), a cynical debunking of the 'last cartridge' image of the war beloved by nationalists.

16 Émile Zola, *The Debacle*, translated with an introduction by Leonard W. Tancock (Harmondsworth, 1972). See also Roth, *op. cit.*, pp. 690–1; Ralston, *op. cit.*, pp. 207–8.

17 *Extrait du Registre des Actes de Naissance*, 1841, in *Dossier Patry, M.G.L.* (Série 5Yf56338, Service Historique de l'Armée de Terre, Fort de Vincennes).

18 Charles Fierville, *Archives des Lycées: Proviseurs et Censeurs, 1er mai 1802–1er juillet 1893* (Paris, 1894), p. 442, summarises Edouard Patry's career.

19 Or Guillemenot.

20 Édouard Patry to Minister of War, 26 April 1860; *Extrait du régistre des délibérations du conseil municipal de la ville de Tarbes, séance du 12 mai 1860*; Prefect of Hautes-Pyrénées to Minister of War, 8 August 1860; *Acte d'Engagement, Marie de Cahors*, 5 November 1860, all in Dossier Patry.

21 *Notes Particulières et Successives* 1870–80, *ibid.*

22 *Certificat de Mariage*, 10 June 1872, Mairie de Vaugirard, 15e arrondissement de Paris, and associated notary's adjudication, *ibid.*

23 *Rapport Particulier: Détail des Services*, 1884, *ibid.* The study for which Patry was congratulated was entitled *Campagne de France. Étude d'ensemble de la guerre franco-allemande de 1870–1871*. It was cited in the *Journal Militaire* of 21 April 1877.

Patry was in consequence made an Officer of the Academy on 21 August 1877.

24 General de Bellemare to Minister of War, 6 February 1887; *Note pour Monsieur le Ministre*, approved 18 February 1887, *ibid.*

25 General de Bellemare to Minister of War, 10 June 1887, *ibid.* On the problem of debt among French officers and the penalties for incurring it see William Serman, *Les Officiers Français dans la Nation (1848–1914)* (Paris, 1982), pp. 224–8.

26 *Rapport fait au Ministre*, 18 June 1887; *Rapport Particulier*, 25 July 1887, Dossier Patry.

27 *Notes Particulières et Successives*, 1896–1913, *ibid.*

28 *Rapport fait au Ministre*, 23 March 1914, *ibid.*

29 Patry to Minister of War, 13 August, 21 September 1914, *ibid.*

30 *Service de Santé, Certificat de Visite*, 29 January 1916; General Auger to Minister of War, 3 February 1916; *Rapport fait au Ministre*, 28 February 1916, *ibid.*

31 Annotated request from Chef du 2e Bureau (Pensions Veuves et Orphelins) to Archives, date-stamped 15 October 1917, *ibid.*

THE REALITY OF WAR

Introduction

1 The Crimean War of 1854–6 was fought by Turkey, France, Britain and later Sardinia against Russia. The principal campaign centred on the siege of Sebastopol in the Crimea. Although none of the armies involved showed to great advantage, French forces were initially the least badly organised and carried away the honours in the final attack on the city in September 1855. A total of 63,000 French died in the war, the great majority from disease and exposure (compared to 24,000 British, reflecting the relative size of their contingents). By the Treaty of Paris which concluded the war in 1856 the Black Sea was neutralised. Russia took advantage of France's predicament in 1870 to renounce her agreement to this condition.

2 The Italian War of 1859 was fought by France in alliance with Sardinia against Austria with the aim of driving that power out of the Italian peninsula. French mobilisation by rail and sea and her military performance compared well with her opponent and two bloody allied victories at Magenta and Solferino led to peace preliminaries at Villafranca. Of a field force of about 120,000 French troops, 17,000 died. Austria's cession of Lombardy was confirmed by the Treaty of Zurich. In not pressing further, Napoleon III was influenced partly by Prussian mobilisation on the Rhine in support of Austria: an operation which revealed Prussia's military deficiencies to her own leaders, stimulating army reforms from 1861.

3 For Cissey, Faidherbe, Derroja and Laveaucoupet see Biographies.

4 On the Legion of Honour see Glossary.

PART ONE: METZ

Chapter I: The Outbreak of War

1 The 6th Infantry Regiment claimed descent from the Normandy Regiment formed in 1597, through the Armagnac Regiment formed in 1776. After service in the War of American Independence the unit was formally constituted as the 6th in 1791. During the Revolutionary and Napoleonic Wars it served in Belgium, the Vendée, Italy, the Levant and Corfu, gaining distinction in the Leipzig campaign of 1813. It took part in the invasion of Algeria in 1830. In the Crimea it lost 1,600 men. At the Battle of Solferino on 24 June 1859 it captured enemy cannon and 400 men at a loss of 19 officers and 1,290 men. The regimental historian noted proudly that at inspections at Châlons in 1860 and 1868 it had been cited in orders for its discipline, appearance, instruction and good attitude. See *Historique*, pp. 98–109.

2 The French and Sardinian campaign against Austria in Italy in 1859 lasted only two months. The campaign of 1866 was the Seven Weeks War, principally between Prussia and Austria for mastery in Germany. It ended after Prussia's startling defeat of the main Austrian army at Königgrätz (Sadowa) on 3 July 1866.

3 See Glossary.

4 The Luxembourg crisis in spring 1867 arose from France's desire for 'compensation' on her eastern frontier for Prussian aggrandisement in Germany as a result of her victory against Austria in 1866. The Grand Duchy of Luxembourg was owned by King William III of the Netherlands but had a German federal garrison of Prussian troops. French hopes of Prussian acquiescence in a transfer to France, with compensation for the Dutch king, were publicly opposed by Bismarck, the Prussian Minister-President and North German Chancellor. National feeling in both Germany and France was aroused and war seemed imminent. However, an international conference in London in May resolved the situation by a compromise which blocked French plans. The Powers collectively guaranteed the neutrality of Luxembourg, the federal fortress was demolished and Prussian troops withdrawn. On the outbreak of war in 1870 Bismarck published evidence from 1866 of similar French designs on Belgium, so influencing opinion in Great Britain and other neutral countries against France.

5 The Crimea commemorative medal, instituted by Queen Victoria in 1856 and awarded to all allied troops who had served in the campaign prior to the capture of Sebastopol in September 1855. The ribbon was pale-blue with a pale-yellow border. An example in the Musée de l'Armée in Paris is illustrated in Paul Willing, *L'Armée de Napoléon III (2): L'Expédition du Mexique (1861–1867) et la Guerre Franco-Allemande (1870–1871)* (Les Collections du Musée de l'Armée, Arcueil, 1984), p. 60.

6 Second Lieutenant Rotté was killed by a bullet through the heart while carry-

ing the Colour at the Battle of Inkerman on 5 November 1854. The 6th lost 530 men killed and wounded in the battle. See *Historique*, pp. 99–103.

7 See William I in Biographies. The reference to King William I of Prussia as 'Emperor' is an anachronism, as he did not become German Emperor until January 1871.

8 News of the offer of the Spanish throne to Leopold of Hohenzollern-Sigmaringen, a member of the Prussian royal house and a serving Prussian officer, first reached Paris on 2 July and was confirmed the next day. The indignant French diplomatic and popular response in the following days persuaded the Hohenzollern-Sigmaringen family to renounce the candidacy on 12 July.

9 Respectively the Foreign and War Ministers and the leading cabinet 'hawks'. See Biographies.

10 Not content with withdrawal of the Hohenzollern candidacy, which many foreign observers considered a diplomatic victory for France, Gramont and Napoleon III agreed that the King of Prussia should be asked to give a guarantee that the candidacy would not be renewed. It was the rejection of this demand on 13 July, aggravated by Bismarck's deliberately provocative editing of the 'Ems telegram' announcing the news publicly, that led to the French decision for war on 15 July. See Further Reading for items on the causes of the war.

11 Under the French system, each regional Department had a central prison.

12 Military preparations had begun in the last days of the diplomatic crisis before mobilisation was ordered on 14 July and war credits were voted by the French Chamber on the 15th by 246 votes to 10. Prussia ordered mobilisation that same day. The South German states soon mobilised in fulfilment of their military agreements with Prussia, so converting the Franco-Prussian conflict into a Franco-German war.

13 See Glossary.

14 Colonel H. Labarthe commanded the 6th Regiment from 1865 to 1874. See *Historique*, p. 127.

15 See Glossary.

16 From 1857 to 1867 French troops had been armed with muzzle-loading rifled muskets fired by means of the hammer striking the percussion cap to ignite the powder. The army was suspicious of breech-loaders because it feared that troops would waste ammunition. Following proof of the effectiveness of the Prussian needle-gun in 1866, the new breech-loading chassepots were introduced. Meanwhile, the old percussion weapons were converted to breech-loaders '*à tabatière*', so called because the breech mechanism resembled a snuffbox. See Paul Willing, *L'Armée de Napoléon III (2): L'Expédition du Mexique (1861–1867) et la Guerre Franco-Allemande (1870–1871)*, (Les Collections du Musée de l'Armée, Arcueil, 1984), pp. 65, 69.

17 Sebastopol, the chief port of the Crimea, was evacuated by the Russians after a successful French assault on the Malakoff redoubt on 8 September

1855. MacMahon, who commanded the assault, was also the victor at Magenta in the Italian war, where on 4 June 1859 54,000 French defeated 58,000 Austrians, inflicting 5,700 casualties and suffering 4,500.

18 Édouard Patry died in Paris on 10 November 1880, aged 66, having retired four years previously. See Charles Fierville, *Archives des Lycées: Proviseurs et Censeurs, 1er mai 1802–1er juillet 1893* (Paris, 1894), p. 442.

19 Patry's father had been appointed inspector at the Grenoble Academy on 27 August 1866. See Fierville, *op. cit.*, p. 442.

20 *Lift up your hearts* (exhortation from the Latin Mass).

21 Before 1870 conscription was by lot, but those with money could always buy themselves out of service. Reform in 1872 allowed shorter service for those studying to be teachers or priests, which in practice still favoured the wealthier classes. Patry's comments echo the political debate on conscription in the 1880s, during which anti-clerical republicans protested at exemptions and hospital duties for priests. Equality of service was not introduced until 1905. See Ralston, *op. cit.*, pp. 40–1, 48, 101–15, 305–6.

22 The shrine of Notre-Dame de la Salette is in the southern French Alps fifteen km north of the town of Corps (south-east of Grenoble). On 19 September 1846 two children, Mélanie Calvat (14) and Maximin Giraud (11) claimed to have spoken with the Virgin Mary, who then disappeared in a halo of light. After investigation, official church recognition was given in 1851 and a shrine was built in the spectacular isolated mountain-top location. The post-war years in France saw a strong Catholic revival, with increasing numbers of pilgrims visiting Lourdes, la Salette and other shrines, and the founding of the Church of the Sacred Heart at Montmartre in 1873.

Chapter II: On the Frontier

1 The First Division of the Fourth Corps of the French Army of the Rhine consisted of two infantry brigades: the 1st Brigade (Count Brayer) was formed of the 20th Battalion of Chasseurs (De Labarrière), the 1st Infantry Regiment (Frémont) and the 6th Infantry Regiment (Labarthe) in which Patry served; the 2nd Brigade (De Golberg) was formed of the 57th Regiment (Giraud) and the 73rd Regiment (Supervielle). The division also included two batteries of 4-pounders and one of *mitrailleuses*, plus a company of engineers. Present for duty with the division on 1 August 1870 were 287 officers and 7,583 men. Order of battle on 1 August in Rousset, *HG I, pièce justicative* No. 2, and conveniently in Paul Willing, *L'Armée de Napoléon III (2): L'Expédition du Mexique (1861–1867) et la Guerre Franco-Allemonde (1870–1871)* (Arcueil, 1984, pp.124–7. The best sources of figures for French mobilisation are Aristide Martinien, *La Guerre de 1870–1871. La Mobilisation de l'Armée: Mouvements des Dépots (Armée active) Du 15 Juillet au der Mars 1871* (Paris, 1911), and Lehautcourt Vol. 2, *Les Deux Adversaires* (Paris, 1902). Martinien's figures for strengths on 1 August are conveniently reprinted in Thomas J.

Adriance, *The Last Gaiter Button: A Study of the Mobilisation and Concentration of the French Army in the War of 1870* (Westport, Connecticut, 1987), pp. 148–9.

2 In contrast to the German practice, the larger units to which French regiments were assigned on mobilisation did not correspond to peacetime territorial commands. Moreover, the notably greater confusion and loss of time and motion on the French side were compounded when Napoleon III decided to change the command structure of the army after mobilisation had begun, and then failed to follow consistently a single plan of operations. See Richard Holmes, *The Road to Sedan*, pp. 172–9; Gary P. Cox, *The Halt in the Mud: French Strategic Planning from Waterloo to Sedan* (Boulder, 1994), pp. 183, 185–6; Howard, pp. 63–74, 77–82. See also items on 'Mobilisation' in Further Reading.

3 Patry's footnote 1897: 'Currently a major and teacher at the Military Academy'. See also Biographies.

4 On this occasion Patry's memory seems to have erred, for his service record indicates that he was not awarded the Order of the Nicham Iftikar of Tunis (3rd Class) until 10 October 1874, and did not become a Commander of the Order of Isabella the Catholic of Spain until 5 December 1879. See summary of '*Décorations et Médailles*' in the file constituted September 1915 in Dossier Patry.

5 It had been widely expected, and not only in France, that the war would begin with a French invasion of Germany. Unknown to Patry and his messmates, successful action had been launched on the frontier that day to the south-east at Saarbrücken, where the French Second Corps advanced in parade-ground formation under the eyes of the Emperor and the Prince Imperial and drove off a Prussian regiment. Much acclaimed by the Paris press, this minor victory was not exploited and was to be the last successful initiative by the French imperial army. The expedition in which Patry had taken part on the Fourth Corps front had been intended only as a reconnaissance. See Rousset, *4e Corps*, p. 40.

6 On Patry's brigade commander, General Count Brayer, and his corps commander, General Ladmirault, see Biographies.

7 The reference is to a post-war command, when the Second Corps had its headquarters at Amiens, and not to the operations around the city in November–December 1870 which form the background to Part Two, Chapter I, of Patry's narrative.

8 Possibly an allusion to the Prussian eagle symbol.

9 The Cadenbronn Line was part of a defensive plan devised by General Charles Frossard in 1867, but not formally adopted in 1870. The position, extending along high ground in Lorraine from Sarreguemines to Forbach, was selected to block the route from the frontier to Metz. Although the defensive positions occupied by the French forward corps in the battles of 6 August 1870 were close to those recommended by Frossard, in the event they were occupied in nothing like the strength he had envisaged as necessary to block the Prussians. See '*Mémoire Militaire*' by General Frossard dated May 1867 in

Guerre I: Annexe, pp. 79–115, and on Cadenbronn particularly *ibid.*, pp. 94–7; also Holmes, *The Road to Sedan*, pp. 169–70; Adriance, *op. cit.*, pp. 55, 128; Howard, pp. 45–6, 92, 98, 122–3; Cox, *op. cit.*, pp. 183–4.

10 *From one [offence] you may learn all.* From Virgil, *The Aeneid*, Book 2, line 65.

Chapter III: Retreat to Metz

1 On 4 August 1870 the isolated division of General Abel Douay (6,600 men), holding the frontier town of Wissembourg on the River Lauter, was surprised by 50,000 Germans – three corps of the Crown Prince's advancing Third Army. After a few hours of desperate defence, during which Douay was killed, his division was forced to retreat with the loss of nearly one-third of its men killed, wounded or captured. German casualties were 1,550. Douay was the first of eighteen French generals of the imperial army killed and 49 wounded in the first three months of fighting – see Aristide Martinien, *Guerre de 1870–1871: État Nominatif par affaires et par corps des officiers tués ou blessés dans la première partie de la campagne (du 25 juillet au 29 octobre)* (Paris, 1902).

2 Commander of the right wing of the French army, the First, Fifth and Seventh Corps in Alsace. See Biographies.

3 In fact it was the Germans who had inflicted double defeats of the advance corps of both the left and right wings of the French Army on Saturday 6 August. At Spicheren the French Second Corps under General Frossard was forced to retreat by the German First Army. At Froeschwiller the Crown Prince's Third Army overcame the French force of 48,000 under MacMahon. In both battles the numerically inferior and outgunned French inflicted punishing casualties on the Germans in ferocious fighting, but were ultimately outflanked and compelled to retreat. Losses for the day in the two battles totalled over 20,000 French (including prisoners) and 15,000 Germans. With MacMahon's defeat, Alsace was lost. News of the defeats precipitated the fall of the Ollivier ministry in Paris. The two halves of the French army fell back, out of contact with each other. In Lorraine the left wing began a withdrawal towards Metz. The Fourth Corps, including Patry's unit, was withdrawn from the frontier as part of this rearward movement.

4 Principally the victories of Austerlitz (2 December 1805) against Russia and Austria; Jena–Auerstadt (14 October 1806) against Prussia; Eylau (8 February 1807) and Friedland (14 June 1807) against Russia. It was these three countries which, with Britain, had invaded and defeated France in 1814; and for a generation after Napoleon I's final defeat at Waterloo in 1815 remained vigilant against any dangerous revival of French expansionism. Though taking care to declare his peaceful intentions at the beginning of his reign, within a decade Napoleon III had taken advantage of their isolation to defeat two of the former allies.

5 The name means literally 'The Ponds'. Les Étangs was on the left of the line which the French high command briefly contemplated holding along the French Nied, ten miles east of Metz, to hold back the German advance.

6 See chassepot in Glossary. The carbine was a shortened version of the standard infantry weapon, for use by mounted troops. Illustrated in Paul Willing, *L'Armée de Napoléon III (2): L'Expédition du Mexique (1861–1867) et la Guerre Franco-Allemande (1870–1871)* (Les Collections du Musée de l'Armée, Arcueil, 1984), p. 68.

7 i.e., in ironic contrast to receiving the enemy.

8 One league = 4 kilometres = 2½ miles.

9 The Standard Bearer Hotel. The name illustrates the fact that Metz had strong army connections even in peacetime. Besides being a fortified city with a large arsenal, it was the home of the École d'Application, the national academy for training all engineer and artillery officers.

10 Napoleon III had arrived in Metz from Saint-Cloud on 28 July. Ill, irresolute, pessimistic and discredited by the defeats of 6 August, he was clearly unequal to the military crisis and finally passed command of the Army of the Rhine to Bazaine on 12 August. With political power now effectively wielded in Paris by the Empress and General Palikao, the new Minister of War, Napoleon was little more than an unpopular figurehead. Leaving Metz on the 14th, staying the first night in the village of Longeville-lès-Metz and the second at Gravelotte (where the house he stayed in still stands), he finally departed from the army at dawn on the 16th, travelling to Verdun and then on to Châlons where MacMahon was assembling his forces. On the strong advice of the Empress that it would be seen as an admission of defeat fatal to the dynasty, Napoleon did not return to Paris.

11 Major G-E de Saint-Martin.

12 Patry's regiment had taken part in the closing phases of the battle later known to the French as Borny and to the Germans as Colombey-Nouilly. It had been precipitated in the afternoon of the 14th by a German brigade commander, von der Golz who, fearing that the French were making good their escape from Metz, attacked their rearguard east of the city. Units of the French Third Corps thereupon halted their withdrawal and soon had the Germans pinned down. More German divisions then hastened to support von der Golz and the battle escalated. On the French side two divisions of Ladmirault's Fourth Corps which had started westwards were recalled to support the 2nd Division of the Corps (Grenier) which was fighting around Mey Wood. Cissey brought his 1st Division to bolster Grenier's line at a crucial stage of the battle, and it was this action in which Patry's regiment was involved. The Germans lost 5,000 men in the battle, the French nearly 4,000. General Decaen, commander of the Third Corps, was mortally wounded. Marshal Bazaine was struck in the left shoulder by a shell fragment. Both sides claimed victory. Strategically, the battle failed to prevent the French withdrawal through Metz, but did impose an important delay. For French dispositions see Rousset, *4e Corps*, pp. 65–90, and Rousset *HG* I, p. 138. The German official account is in *GGS*, Pt. I, vol. I, pp. 303–38. General narrative and analysis in Howard, pp. 140–4.

13 Mey Wood had been held by Commandant Lefèvre with his 2nd Battalion of the 64th Infantry Regiment, part of the 2nd Brigade of Grenier's 2nd Division of the Fourth Corps. The 64th had the grim distinction of being one of the two worst hit regiments in the battle, losing from all causes eighteen officers and 249 men – see Rousset, *4e Corps*, pp. 76–7, 82, 366. In contrast, Patry's regiment lost only one officer and five men wounded at Borny, see *ibid.*, pp. 366–7; *Historique*, p. 112.

14 The Île Chambière which bisects the course of the Moselle at Metz and makes two crossings necessary to reach the western bank.

15 The much maligned *Intendance*, which functioned largely independently of field commanders. For its organisation and analysis of its failures during the campaign see Holmes, *The Road to Sedan*, pp. 73–86; Adriance, *op. cit.*, pp. 86–8; Rousset, *HG* I, pp. 26–8; Howard, pp. 65–71 and *passim*; Stephen Shann and Louis Delperier, *French Army 1870–71: Franco-Prussian War 1: Imperial Troops* (Osprey, 1991), pp. 33–4.

16 Boasting and exaggeration were popularly supposed to be characteristics of natives of Gascony (a reputation preserved in the English word 'gasconade').

17 German patrols reached Pont-à-Mousson, on the Moselle 20 miles south of Metz, on 12 August, and the river crossings were seized by Prince Frederick Charles' Second Army on the 13th. From this point (and crossings below it) large German forces were able to bypass the French positions around Metz and strike out for the crucial road to Verdun to intercept the ponderous westward passage of the French army.

Chapter IV: Days of Battle

1 The battle of 16 August 1870 was to become variously known by the names of the villages along the Metz–Verdun road which formed its seven-mile east–west axis: commonly Mars-la-Tour, Rezonville, or by the Germans Vionville. The battle began at about 9.00 a.m. with German cavalry, soon supported by infantry advancing from the south, striving to seize and hold the Verdun road. The Germans sent forward ever more troops during the day to sustain their determined attacks, eventually engaging some 64,000 infantry, 13,000 cavalry and 246 guns (*GGS* Pt. I, vol. 2, Appendix XXVI, p. 26). The French, despite having perhaps double these numbers within reach on the plateau west of Metz, mounted only piecemeal counter-attacks which failed to bring their numerical superiority to bear to good strategic purpose. For items on the battles around Metz see Further Reading.

2 The regimental history of the 6th puts the time at about 4 o'clock, see *Historique*, pp. 112–13. The official records also report that there were no stragglers in Cissey's division, despite the oppressive heat of the rapid approach march – see *Guerre: Metz II, Docs. annexes*, p. 285; Rousset, *4e Corps*, p. 146.

3 The 16th Westphalian Infantry Regiment was part of Wedell's 38th Brigade in the German X corps. Advancing to attack what they thought was the

French flank, they received frontal chassepot and *mitrailleuse* fire at short range, with appalling results. Wedell's brigade suffered a staggering 2,615 casualties – well over half its strength. Of these, the 16th lost 533 killed, 808 wounded and 424 missing (see *GGS*, Pt I, vol.1, pp. 406–7 and Appendix XX1, p. 135). Credit for capturing the 16th's Colour, which was later triumphantly displayed in Metz, was claimed by the 57th Regiment in Cissey's 2nd Brigade. It was one of only two Colours captured by the French during the war. See *Guerre: Metz II, Docs. annexes*, pp. 296–7; Rousset, *4e Corps*, p. 147; Rousset, *HG* I, pp. 158–9, *HG* II, p. 396; Lehautcourt V, pp. 278–88, 295.

4 Called *Le Fond de la Cuve* – literally 'The bottom of the tub'.

5 The charge was made at about 5.00 p.m. by 600 men of the Dragoons of the Prussian Guard under Colonel von Auerswald with the aim of disengaging Wedell's mutilated brigade and halting the French pursuit. The brunt of the attack fell upon the 13th Regiment of Grenier's 2nd Division and the 1st Regiment of Cissey's 1st Division. The Germans lost heavily in the attack, but claimed to have successfully accomplished their objective. Among the German wounded was Herbert Bismarck, son of the Prussian Minister-President and North German Chancellor. He was shot in the thigh and helped off the field by his brother Wilhelm, whose horse had been shot from under him. For French reports of the action see *Guerre: Metz II, Docs. annexes*, pp. 286–8, 297; also Rousset, *4e Corps*, pp. 151–4; Rousset, *HG* I, pp. 158–9; Lehautcourt V, pp. 289–98 and 292 fn. The German account is in *GGS*, Pt. I, vol. 2, pp. 407–8.

6 The failure of the commander of the Fourth Corps, General Ladmirault, to order an attack at this point was to become yet another disputed 'might have been' in the post-war years. At the time, the absence of Lorencez's 3rd Division was given as one reason for withdrawal – see the official reports of Ladmirault and Cissey in *Guerre: Metz II, Docs. annexes*, pp. 280–4, 287–90. Bazaine accepted these explanations and stated in his own report that 'General Ladmirault recognised that the Tronville position was too strongly held for him to be able to take with his two divisions, and he had to limit himself to containing the enemy and establishing himself on the ground he had won.' In later years, however, there were bitter recriminations about responsibility for the lost opportunity. Bazaine, (*Épisodes*, p. 87) and his defenders blamed Ladmirault's slowness and failure to communicate. Ladmirault's supporters, including Rousset, (*HG* I, p. 160) and Albert de Mun, pointed out that he had plenty of good reasons for acting prudently, and pushed the blame back on Bazaine. Later 'Pierre Lehautcourt' [General Palat], no defender of Bazaine, blamed Ladmirault's 'fatal inaction', and his hostile critique has been followed by Michael Howard and David Ascoli, who draw a telling contrast with the aggressive boldness of his opponent, General Voigts-Rhetz, commander of the outnumbered German X Corps (Lehautcourt V, pp. 297–8, 345; Howard, pp. 158–9 and David Ascoli, *A Day of Battle: Mars-la-Tour 16 August 1870* (London, 1987), pp. 189–93, 199). Ladmirault's biog-

rapher noted that with hindsight, on learning after the war that the Germans on his front had been much weaker than he had supposed, Ladmirault blamed himself and lamented 'If only I had known.' See J. de la Faye [pseudonym of Marie de Sardent], *Le Général Ladmirault (1808–1898) (Préface par le Comte Albert de Mun)* (Paris, 1901), pp. VII-IX, 208–25.

7 The number of squadrons engaged may have only been half that indicated by Patry, but this was nevertheless the last big cavalry battle in western Europe, involving more than 5,000 men. The Germans had marginally the better of it and held the ground at the end of a relatively short struggle. See *Guerre: Metz II*, pp. 516–48; *GGS*, Pt. I, vol. 1, pp. 409–12; Howard, p. 159; Ascoli, *op. cit.*, pp. 200–3.

8 See Biographies. Photograph in Rousset, *HG* I, p. 150. Brayer's aide, killed with him, was Captain de Saint-Preux.

9 An account based on available evidence is offered in Rousset, *4e Corps*, p. 144. Colonel Labarthe of the 6th took temporary command of the 1st Brigade.

10 The Battle of Arcola was fought on 15–17 November 1796, during Bonaparte's campaign in Italy. Patry was correct in suspecting that Bonaparte's role in the storming of the bridge had been improved by propaganda. See Jean Tulard, Napoleon: *The Myth of the Saviour* (London, 1984), pp. 56–62.

11 On Bazaine see Biographies. Bazaine did draw his sword during the battle but, characteristically, only as a defensive reaction when he found himself surrounded by charging German hussars. His critics were later to speculate how much better it might have been for his army had he been killed or captured at that point. See Bazaine, *Épisodes*, p. 82; Philip Guedalla, *The Two Marshals* (London, 1943), pp. 183–4; Ascoli, *op. cit.*, p. 153.

12 French casualties on 16 August totalled 13,761, of whom 1,196 had been killed outright. Unlike the 1st Regiment on its left, which suffered 195 casualties, Patry's regiment escaped lightly, having lost two men killed and seven officers and fifteen men wounded. Losses in the Fourth Corps as a whole had been 1,561 killed, wounded and missing. Total German losses on 16 August were 15,790. See *Guerre: Metz II*, pp. 608, 609, 614; *GGS*, Pt. I, vol. 1, Appendix XXI, p. 142.

13 Bazaine's apparently perverse decision to abandon the battlefield and withdraw eastwards towards Metz was much debated by contemporaries and subsequent critics. He was obsessed throughout the battle with the danger of being cut off from Metz, his base of supplies. He rejected the options of either exploiting his advantages for an offensive or attempting a breakout to the west, maintaining that this would have entailed certain defeat and that the disorganisation of his units and supplies gave him no choice but to act defensively. See Bazaine, *Épisodes*, pp. 91–5. Whatever the motives for his relentlessly passive strategy, his decision would lead to his army being blockaded in Metz and seal its fate. For critical accounts see Rousset, *HG* I, pp. 170–1; Lehautcourt V, pp. 347–55; Howard, pp. 161–4: and for a defence,

Edmond Ruby and Jean Regnault, *Bazaine: Coupable ou Victime?* (Paris, 1960), pp. 156–65.

14 The French army was taking a defensive line running almost at a right angle to the east–west Metz–Verdun road, stretching along high ground from Rozérieulles in the south to Roncourt in the north. The Fourth Corps formed the right centre of the six-mile line, roughly from Montigny-la-Grange to north of Amanvillers. For detail of movements on the 17th see Rousset, *4e Corps*, pp. 188–215; *Guerre: Metz III, Docs. annexes*, pp. 35–6; Lehautcourt V, pp. 356–99, and particularly pp. 362–3 on Ladmirault's 'incomprehensible' order for Cissey's division to face east.

15 See Biographies.

16 See Biographies.

17 The German Second Army had spent the morning of the 18th probing for the French right wing, and mistakenly thought it had been found at Amanvillers. Observing the 'heedless unconcern' of the French troops, General von Manstein, commanding the largely Hessian IX Corps of the German army, ordered his artillery under General von Puttkamer to open fire from positions around Vernéville. Firing was corrected when the first salvoes were seen to overshoot the French front line. See *GGS*, Pt. I, vol. 2, pp. 23–5.

18 There is a heavy joke in the original French, to which Patry draws attention. The sentence can also be read as 'The big drummer of our band took a shot which holed his idiotic hide' (literally = donkey's skin).

19 Patry's footnote 1897: 'The line from Metz to Verdun.'

20 See Glossary.

21 The Bois de la Cusse. The German troops involved in this attack, led by General von Wittich, were battalions of the 49th Hessian Brigade, which suffered more than 600 casualties during the day. See Rousset, *4e Corps*, p. 253; Rousset *HG* I, pp. 198–9; *GGS*, Pt. I, vol. 2, pp. 43–4 and Appendix XXVI, p. 15. See also Ascoli, *op. cit.*, p. 238. Ascoli's work contains photographs of the terrain. In latter years French Fourth Corps veterans were apt to refer to the battle of 18 August as 'The Defence of the Lines of Amanvillers'. German grave mounds are still to be found in the fields around Amanvillers.

22 On Canrobert see Biographies. The village of Saint-Privat-la-Montagne, which gave its name to the battle of 18 August, was the anchor of the French right wing. After beating off a massed infantry assault by the German Guards Corps during the late afternoon and inflicting 8,000 casualties, Canrobert's Sixth Corps was finally outflanked and overwhelmed, so exposing the flank of Ladmirault's Fourth Corps on their left to the same fate. The last moments of the 6th Corps' resistance were to be immortalised in Alphonse de Neuville's painting, 'Le Cimitière de Saint-Privat' (1881), which was widely reproduced before 1914 and now hangs in the Musée d'Orsay, Paris.

23 Recorded in Colonel Labarthe's report and the regimental history as Vaillaut,

see *Guerre: Metz III, Docs. annexes*, p. 252; *Historique*, p. 114. The official list of officers killed and wounded however gives Vaillant (R.) – see Martinien, *État Nominatif*, pp. 62–3.

24 Colonel Labarthe's spelling agrees with Patry's, but the regimental history records Ravet, see *ibid.* Martinien, *op. cit.*, p. 63, gives Ravel (G.-H.-C.).

25 The regimental history states economically that after enduring a hurricane of fire since midday and resisting every enemy assault, the regiment fought valiantly until withdrawing at 8 o'clock and then reforming – *Historique*, p. 114. Rousset's account makes it clear that elements of other units of Cissey's division, from the 1st and 73rd Regiments, took part in the forlorn last charge between the Bois de la Cusse and the Jerusalem plateau, but with exactly the same results. Their leaders killed or wounded, General de Cissey himself unhorsed and his staff dispersed, surrounded by the fearful debris of battle, disembowelled horses and smashed wagons, the survivors had no choice but to abandon the Amanvillers plateau, which had now become 'nothing but a field of carnage where death mowed without respite'. Twenty-three German batteries were now 'pouring a rain of fire' on Amanvillers, extinguishing French cannon fire and forcing the remnant of the division to retreat pell-mell – Rousset, *4e Corps*, pp. 261–2; and for a critique of the implacably defensive French tactics, *ibid.*, pp. 270–6. See also Rousset, *HG*, I, p. 202 and Lehautcourt V, pp. 623–5. The official reports by Ladmirault, Cissey and Labarthe can be found in *Guerre: Metz III, Docs. annexes*, pp. 23—52.

26 Second Lieutenant Pincherelle was cited for bravery and received the Chevalier's Cross of the Legion of Honour. Colonel Labarthe and Captain Laguire were also cited for bravery on 18 August. See *Historique*, p. 115.

27 If the French right wing had been defeated and forced to withdraw to Metz, at the southern end of the battlefield, around Gravelotte, the Germans had been brutally punished for a series of frontal assaults against entrenched French positions. So severe and demoralising had their losses been that German commanders were very slow to grasp that they had won a strategic victory. See Howard, p. 180. On the French side, Bazaine had not directed the largest battle of the war at all, and thought of little but resting and resupplying his troops in Metz, regardless of its outcome. See Rousset, *HG* I, pp. 196–8; Howard, pp. 172–3, 181.

Chapter V: Two Sorties Fail

1 Literally 'Before the Bridges'.

2 An ironic reference to the German triumphal entry into Paris at the end of the war, on 1–3 March 1871.

3 The regimental history gives the losses of the 6th Regiment (all companies) on 18 August as twelve officers killed, ten wounded, and 266 NCOs and men killed, wounded and missing: total 288 – *Historique*, p. 114. Rousset, *4e Corps*, pp. 366–7, gives a breakdown of thirteen officers and 41 men killed, twelve officers and 177 men wounded and 48 men missing: total 291. *Guerre:*

Metz III, p. 732, varies only slightly as to the number of officers. The strength of the regiment had been 67 officers and 1,735 men on 12 August. After the battles of 14, 16 and 18 August it was reduced to 38 officers and 1,453 men on 24 August. Overall, on 18 August a French force of 112,800 had fought a German army of 188,332. French losses were given officially as 13,218, German as 20,163 (*Guerre: Metz III*, pp. 738, 740; *GGS* Pt. I, vol. 2, Appendix XXIV, p. 23); see also Howard, pp. 167, 181, and discussion in François Roth, *La Guerre de 70* (Paris, 1990), pp. 88–94.

4 For citations in the 6th Regiment see *Historique*, p. 115.

5 The sortie from Metz on 26 August was intended as an attempt to break through the comparatively lightly defended German lines east of the city and to join with MacMahon's relieving army. But at a council of war that afternoon Bazaine vacillated under the urging of some of his generals that the army could not sustain itself in the field and should not abandon Metz. Finally, Bazaine cancelled the operation, the staff work for which had in any case been abysmal. The fiasco is narrated in Rousset, *4e Corps*, pp. 281–3; Rousset, *HG* I, 289–93; Lehautcourt VII, pp. 68–94; Howard, pp. 259–62.

6 Denis Auguste Marie Raffet (1804–60). A pupil of the Napoleonic painter Baron Gros, Raffet became famous as a graphic artist and lithographer for his dramatic representations of the troops of the Revolutionary and Napoleonic wars.

7 A reference to the imminent French loss of the greater part of Lorraine which, with Alsace, was formally ceded to Germany by the Treaty of Frankfurt in May 1871. In practice, German military occupation of the two provinces had begun even before the fall of Metz, with the King of Prussia appointing a governor-general of Alsace–Lorraine on 21 August 1870. See François Roth, *La Lorraine dans la Guerre de 1870* (Nancy, 1984), p. 61, and the same author's *La Guerre de 70*, pp. 376 ff. Strasbourg, the chief city of Alsace, was to fall on 28 September after six weeks' bombardment. The provinces remained German until 1918.

8 Following the failure of the attempted sortie on 26 August, plans were made for another, again towards the north-east, on the right bank of the Moselle. Urgency was added on the 30th when a message was received from MacMahon dated the 22nd, telling Bazaine that help was on its way from the direction of Montmédy. See Bazaine, *Épisodes*, p. 168; Howard, p. 262.

9 Partly for political reasons, in the decades after the defeat of 1870 French governments remained cautious about how far they should imitate the model of the German General staff which had played such a key role in achieving victory. On post-war reform of the French staff see Allan Mitchell, *Victors and Vanquished: The German Influence on Army and Church in France after 1870* (Chapel Hill, 1984), pp. 82–92; Ralston, *op. cit.*, pp. 89–92, 155–61; Porch, *op. cit.*, pp. 45–53.

10 French cannon were familiarly known as the 4, 8, 12 and 24. These were rifled muzzle-loaders made of bronze. Under the patronage of Napoleon

III, the 12 became the standard field-piece from 1853. (As the 'Napoleon', it was the most widely used gun on both sides in the American Civil War.) The 24 was a heavy gun for siege use. Although the conventional translation 'pounder' is used here for convenience, shell weights had been expressed in kilograms since 1858. On armament and organisation of the French artillery in 1870 see Rousset, *HG* I, pp. 24–6; Lehautcourt II, p. 115; Holmes, *The Road to Sedan*, pp. 227–31; Stephen Shann and Louis Delperier, *French Army 1870–71: Franco-Prussian War 1: Imperial Troops* (Osprey, 1991), pp. 20–1, 36–8; Paul Willing, *L'Armée de Napoléon III* (1852–1870) (1) (Arcueil, 1983), pp. 72–3. Prussian breech-loading steel artillery, introduced from 1861, was to demonstrate decisive superiority in 1870–1.

11 The dilatory French advance (partly caused by Fourth Corps troops having crossed the route of those of the Sixth Corps), with no attempt at surprise, was a godsend to the watching Germans, who hastened to take advantage of the opportunity to summon reinforcements to the threatened point of their lines of investment. The lull led them to speculate that the attack would not take place until the next day. See GGS, Pt. I, vol. 2, pp. 494–7. Bazaine, *Épisodes*, p. 169, blamed the slowness and indecision of his subordinates.

12 Yet Forstreuter's name is not listed in the German official history among those of the seven officers of this regiment who were killed. The East Prussian Grenadiers also lost 95 men killed, twelve officers and 186 men wounded, and 28 men missing. See *GGS*, Pt. I, vol. 2, Appendix LVIII, pp. 115, 118.

13 Rousset, *4e Corps*, pp. 366–7, gives the losses of the 6th Regiment on 31 August/1 September as two officers killed and seven wounded, sixteen men killed, 174 wounded and 51 missing; total 250. The regimental history differs only in stating the number of wounded officers as twelve – see *Historique*, pp. 116–17. Total French casualties in the sortie were 3,554. German losses, detailed in *GGS*, Pt. I, vol. 2, p. 530 and Appendix LVIII, pp. 115–20, were nearly 3,000.

14 The regimental history of the 6th similarly expressed disappointment that the 1st Battalion's gallant charge at Servigny went unexploited – *Historique*, pp. 116–17. In fact, some Third Corps battalions were sent to reinforce the gains at Servigny on the evening of the 31st, but too few to make a decisive difference. Bazaine, whose orders throughout were lax, had retired to sleep at Saint-Julien (Épisodes, p. 170). His direction of the sortie of 31 August hardly suggests that he seriously intended a successful breakout, and provided further grounds for charges at his subsequent trial that he was a traitor, rather than merely grossly incompetent. Rousset, in *4e Corps*, pp. 287–318 and *HG* I, pp. 293–309, and Lehautcourt VII, pp. 169–72, give scathing analyses of Bazaine's leadership. The German official account is in *GGS*, Pt. I, vol. 2, pp. 490–531; Cissey's attack is described *ibid.*, p. 507, and German counter-attacks pp. 508, 510–11. For narrative and discussion of the bungled operation see Lehautcourt VII, pp. 104–201; Howard, pp. 262–6.

Chapter VI: Shut up in Metz

1 At the start of the war the eight corps (including the Imperial Guard) of the French army on the frontier were collectively styled the Army of the Rhine, and that title continued in formal use for Bazaine's force. However, three corps under MacMahon had become separated from the others and had formed the nucleus of the Army of Châlons from 21 August. By the end of August it was clear that no French soldier was going to see the Rhine except as a prisoner, and the name Army of Metz became a widespread term of convenience for the forces trapped in the city.

2 Planning and construction of an outer ring of forts at Metz had been going on since 1867 to protect the city from the increased range of the latest artillery. Clockwise from the north the forts were St-Eloi, St-Julien, Queuleu, St-Privat, St-Quentin and Plappeville. At the outbreak of war, however, work was still unfinished on most of them. See Bazaine, *Épisodes*, pp. 309–11; Rousset, *HG* I, p. 285; Lehautcourt VII, pp. 205–6; Howard, p. 141; Holmes, *The Road to Sedan*, pp. 154–6, and the same author's *Fatal Avenue* (London, 1992), pp. 200–2; François Roth, *La Lorraine dans la Guerre de 1870* (Nancy, 1984), p. 14.

3 About 170,000 troops were trapped in Metz. Cases of diarrhoea, dysentery and typhoid increased as the weeks went by and smallpox and typhus appeared before the end. In total the medical services had to treat 43,000 sick and wounded and some 7,000 men died in the hospitals. See Roth, *op. cit.*, p. 45, and his *La Guerre de 70* (Paris 1990), pp. 250–6; also Howard, pp. 276–80.

4 Abraham Fabert (1599–1662), a native of Metz and an outstanding military engineer and administrator, was appointed Governor of Sedan in 1642. In 1650 he became the first commoner to be made a Marshal of France, and added to his reputation by his conduct of the siege of Stenay in 1654. His statue, erected in 1841, stands in the Place d'Armes in Metz, next to the cathedral. The words of his inscribed on the plinth seemed pointed in 1870: 'If, to prevent a place entrusted to me by the king from falling to the enemy, I had to throw my life, my family and all my goods into the breach, I should not hesitate to do so.' For a contemporary illustration of the statue see the *Illustrated London News*, vol. 57 (12 November 1870), p. 505.

5 See Biographies.

6 On civilian morale in Metz see Rousset, *HG* I, p. 328; *Cassell's History of the War between France and Germany 1870–1871* (London, 1899), vol. I, pp. 263 ff; Roth, *La Lorraine dans la Guerre de 70*, pp. 44–6. The civilian population of the city was about 70,000, including 20,000 country people made refugees by the fighting. Rations for adult civilians were reduced progressively during the blockade from 750g to 450g to 300g of bread per day. A report dated 8 October by Coffinières, reprinted in Bazaine, *Épisodes*, pp. 197–8, reckoned that the total civilian and military population of Metz at 230,000. With stocks in hand, he estimated that rations of 300 grammes per day would last until 20 October at the furthest. Civilian mortality in the city in 1870 was three

times greater than in 1869. On supplies and rationing see Lehautcourt VII, pp. 208–17, 309, 358–61.

7 Sardanapalus, the eponymous subject of a play by Lord Byron, was a king of ancient Nineveh with a reputation for luxury and feasting. Patry's disgust at the price may be gauged by the fact that a captain's annual salary in 1870 was 2,533 francs: thus, even at his new rank, the omelette cost about ten days' pay.

8 For example, in *Épisodes*, p. 92, Bazaine asserted that his soldiers were not the equals of those of the First Republic and of the First Empire: but compare his eulogy, *ibid.*, p. 251.

9 Lieutenant L.-F.-M. Jacques is listed as having died on 8 September from a wound received on 18 August – Rousset, *4e Corps*, p. 373; *Historique*, p. 114. There were an estimated 15,000 wounded in hospitals in Metz at this time, excluding 2,000 in private homes. See Lehautcourt VII, pp. 307–8; Roth, *La Lorraine dans la Guerre de 1870*, pp. 43–4.

10 MacMahon's Army of Châlons, ordered by the government in Paris to relieve Bazaine's army in Metz, instead found itself pursued north-eastwards by the German Third Army and the Army of the Meuse. Surrounded at Sedan near the Belgian border, it was forced after fierce fighting on 31 August and 1 September to surrender. The Emperor Napoleon III and 104,000 men became prisoners and were soon en route for captivity in Germany. After such a decisive victory, German hopes were high for an early end to the war. They sent news of the disaster to Bazaine in Metz on 3 September, and on the 6th exchanged 700 prisoners from MacMahon's army for Germans held in Metz, ensuring that the news spread in the city despite Bazaine's reluctance to publicise it. See Lehautcourt VII, pp. 218–23.

11 When the news of Sedan reached Paris it precipitated the fall of the imperial regime in a bloodless revolution. Amidst crowds of demonstrators, the Republic was proclaimed on Sunday 4 September. The republican Deputies for Paris formed a Government of National Defence. The Empress Eugénie fled to England. German troops started from Sedan for Paris on 7 September and had completely invested the capital by the 20th.

12 On the Guard see Glossary. The Guards regiments were the favoured élite and symbol of the imperial regime. In the plebiscite of May 1870 they had, as expected, strongly supported the regime while nearly a sixth of the army as a whole had voted against it – see Holmes, *The Road to Sedan*, pp. 136–43. The Guard was formally abolished by a decree of the republican government on 21 October 1870. On their return from captivity in 1871 the men were assigned to other regiments. See Paul Willing, *L'Armée de Napoléon III (1852–1870)* (1) (Arcueil, 1983), p. 34.

13 See Biographies, and also Paul Baquiast, *Les Pelletan: une dynastie de la bourgeoisie républicaine* (Paris, 1996).

14 Republican Deputies had been vocal in opposing army reform in the 1860s, fearing the power it would give an authoritarian regime. They favoured a

militia system instead. Léon Gambetta's 1869 Belleville electoral manifesto had demanded the suppression of standing armies as 'the cause of ruin for the nation's finances and businesses, source of hatred between peoples and distrust at home'. Another member of the new government, Jules Ferry, had privately exulted at the first French defeats in 1870 because 'the Emperor's armies have been beaten.' The opposing stances on army reform had been memorably expressed in December 1866 when Jules Favre asked Niel, the Minister of War, 'Do you want to turn France into a barracks?' 'Take care', came the reply, 'that you don't turn it into a cemetery.' See Howard, p. 33; J. P. T. Bury, *Gambetta and the National Defence: A Republican Dictatorship in France* (London, 1936), pp. 18, 285–7; Robert Tombs, *The War Against Paris, 1871* (Cambridge, 1981), p. 17.

15 Text in Bazaine, *Épisodes*, p. 178. For a translation see Appendix, item (i).

16 i.e. Bazaine.

17 See Biographies.

18 Officers on campaign were expected to pay their own way for equipment, clothing and living expenses, and the supplement was a modest recognition of the additional expenditure involved. On the wartime allowance see Pierre Chalmin, *L'Officier Français de 1815 à 1870* (Paris, 1957), pp. 213–18; William Serman, *Les Officiers Français dans la Nation (1848–1914)* (Paris, 1982), pp. 190–1; and on officers' income generally *ibid.*, pp. 185–201.

19 See above, Chapter IV, pp. 90–1.

20 For cuirassiers see Glossary. For illustrations of the uniform see Willing, *op. cit.*, p. 34.

21 See Glossary.

22 The head-dress of the lancers, the *czapska*, was similar to that worn by Prussian cavalry units. See Stephen Shann and Louis Delperier, *French Army 1870–71: Franco-Prussian War 1: Imperial Troops* (Osprey, 1991), p. 11 and plate B; Willing, *op. cit.*, pp. 40–1 and plate VI.

23 See above, Chapter IV, p. 91.

24 Patry's remarks, though in one sense progressive, illustrate the divisive snobbery and inter-arm rivalries which persisted in the French army for decades. In 1886 reformers complained that 'the army should have a uniform, not a series of costumes'. Retention of red trousers was also a politically sensitive issue. Nationalists attacked an attempt to introduce drab uniforms in 1911, seeing it as part of a drive by governments after 1900 to reduce the prestige and morale of the army. Long after most other European armies had adopted camouflage wear, the French went to war in 1914 in red *képis* and trousers, just as they had in 1870, and suffered the consequences. It took the proven impact of the machine-gun to cause the *pantalon rouge* to disappear from 1915. On the uniform question in army reform see Ralston, *op. cit.*, pp. 323–4, and Porch, *op. cit.*, pp. 42, 184–5.

25 A 20-franc coin.

26 See Glossary.

27 The balloon service for mail which operated from Metz in September was ceased by the military authorities in early October after several captures made it a security risk. Other means of communication included carrier pigeons, which often finished their mission in the pies of Prussian sentinels. See *Cassell's History*, vol. I, pp. 251–4; Gérard Lhéritier, *Les Ballons Montés* (Nice, 1989), p. 73.
28 Small-scale raids south-east of Metz were mounted on September 27–8 to secure provisions from nearby villages and had some limited success, though at a cost of nearly 400 men and without holding any ground. The Germans, who lost 345 men, responded by burning five villages near the lines of investment to discourage further attempts. The inhabitants were given two hours to leave. See Rousset, *HG* I, pp. 319–20; Lehautcourt VII, pp. 256–67.
29 See Glossary.
30 See Biographies.
31 Spelt Billaudel in Bazaine, *Épisodes*, p. 189, Lehautcourt VII, p. 317 and Rousset, *HG* I, p. 322.
32 Most probably a misprint for 9 September, date of the heavy bombardment described earlier in this chapter – see above, pp. 134–5, and also Rousset, *HG* I, pp. 312-13; Lehautcourt VII, p. 229.

Chapter VII: Capitulation

1 Literally 'at order arms'.
2 The main attack on 7 October was by Sixth Corps and the Guard north of Metz on the left (western) bank of the Moselle, with supporting attacks to right and left by parts of the Third and Fourth Corps respectively; 400 wagons were assembled to bring off captured supplies. Although French troops advanced with vigour and took their objectives, German artillery fire once more proved overwhelming and the ground won could not be held against counter-attacks. Nor could many provisions be brought away. French losses were nearly 1,300, German more than 1,700. See Rousset, *HG* I, pp. 323–4; Lehautcourt VII, pp. 329–46; Howard, pp. 267–8. An eye-witness account from the German side by the correspondent of the London *Daily News* is in Archibald Forbes, *My Experiences of the War Between France and Germany* (London, 1871), I, pp. 354–72.
3 Left-wing activists led a series of protests and demonstrations in Paris against peace negotiations and the conduct of the war by the Government of National Defence, particularly on 5 and 8 October. A much more serious demonstration was to come on 31 October after news of the fall of Metz. In Lyons a revolutionary attempt by the Russian anarchist Michael Bakunin on 28 September was scotched by the National Guard. In the south, a *Ligue du Midi* and similar associations gave expression to radical and decentralising political aspirations which led to some disturbances; particularly in Marseilles, Saint-Etienne and Toulouse at the end of October. However, reports of towns seeking German garrisons as protection against disorder seem to have

concerned principally Rouen and Le Havre in the north. See Rousset, *HG* I, p. 331; Bury, *op. cit.*, pp. 228 ff; Stewart Edwards, *The Paris Commune 1871* (London, 1971), pp. 70–88, 96; Audoin-Rouzeau, *op. cit.*, pp. 166–9; Howard, p. 236.

4 Eugénie. See Biographies. Having escaped from France to Hastings, the exiled Empress had by this time settled at Chislehurst in Kent.

5 General Boyer was sent to German headquarters to propose that Bazaine's army should be allowed out of Metz on this basis. Bismarck, finding the Government of National Defence intransigent, showed a passing interest in the idea of a peace negotiation with the imperial dynasty when he met Boyer at Versailles on 14 October. See Boyer's account of his mission in Bazaine, *Épisodes*, pp. 219–24; also Albert Sorel, *Histoire Diplomatique de la Guerre Franco-Allemande* (Paris, 1875), vol. 2, pp. 1–29; Lehautcourt VII, pp. 357–90; summary in Howard, pp. 278–9. Relevant documentation is reproduced in Edmond Ruby and Jean Regnault, *Bazaine: Coupable ou Victime?* (Paris, 1960), pp. 241–58, 359–73. On diplomatic negotiations during the blockade of Metz see also Maurice Baumont, *L'Échiquier de Metz: Empire ou République* (Paris, 1971).

6 On 12 and 13 October there were hostile demonstrations against any idea of capitulation by National Guards and civilians outside the Hôtel de Ville. On the 14th, Coffinières issued a conciliatory address which recognised the Government of National Defence (as Bazaine had not), but the military authorities remained apprehensive of further trouble right up to and during the capitulation. Bazaine, unpopular and mistrusted by the predominantly republican, anti-Bonapartist National Guard of the city, largely kept out of the way throughout the siege at a villa in the suburb of Ban-Saint-Martin. See Bazaine, *Épisodes*, p. 195; Rousset, *HG* I, pp. 327–9; Lehautcourt VII, pp. 391–4; *Cassell's History*, vol. I, pp. 285–92.

7 Later prominent in the Paris Commune, after which he was executed. See Biographies. Rossel's own account of his attempt to organise a breakout appeared in a short pamphlet published in 1871: *Les Derniers Jours de Metz*. See also Edith Thomas, *Rossel 1844–1871* (Paris, 1967), pp. 191–227.

8 Bazaine took steps to defuse the situation after learning of a meeting of officers on 10 October. He reprimanded Rossel and gave assurances to a delegation that he would not consider capitulation. Those involved in the breakout plan also had difficulty in finding a general willing to replace Bazaine or lead the movement against orders. On the day of the capitulation, a serious attempt did seem imminent, with particular unrest among the engineers and the Third Corps. However, General Clinchant, who had agreed to lead the sortie, was dissuaded at the last moment, by appeals to the honour of the army, not to break the protocol that had been signed with the Germans. While he was being harangued at Bazaine's headquarters, the dissident troops were quietly disarmed. General de Cissey took steps to ensure that his own troops obeyed orders. The threat of collective action passed, but many individual officers succeeded in escaping on their own initiative. See Lehautcourt

VII, pp. 394–401, 503-6; Bazaine, *Épisodes*, pp. 195, 214; Rousset, *HG* I, pp. 329–30; *Cassell's History*, vol. I, p. 304; Baumont, *op. cit.*, pp. 310–13; Tombs, *The War Against Paris 1871* (Cambridge, 1981), pp. 15–16.

9 After reporting back to Bazaine after his interview with Bismarck at Versailles, General Boyer passed through the lines once more for an audience with the Empress to discuss a regency supported by the Army of the Rhine. Eugénie, though anxious for a truce at Metz, was reluctant to commit herself to accept undefined German demands. For their part, the Germans doubted Bazaine's ability to bring an end to French resistance, and the military were opposed to any arrangement that did not involve the capitulation of Metz. Neither side being able to offer the guarantees sought by the other, Bismarck wrote to Bazaine formally breaking off negotiations. See Rousset *HG* I, pp. 330–3; Lehautcourt VII, pp. 431–40; Bazaine, *Épisodes*, p. 228; Howard, pp. 278–80.

10 Grandson and namesake of Louis-Philippe (1773–1850), last king of France, who had tried vainly to abdicate in the child's favour when his regime fell in 1848. The Count (1838–94) was thus representative of the House of Orléans (the liberal branch of the French monarchy) and pretender to the French throne. The Orleans princes had arrived in Paris in September to offer their services to the country, but were promptly invited to leave for Belgium by the republican Government.

11 On the negotiations for capitulation, signed on 27 October, see Lehautcourt VII, pp. 454–92; Rousset, *HG* I, pp. 333–8, and the terms of capitulation reprinted *ibid.*, *pièce justicative* No. 15, pp. xi–xii (also in Bazaine, *Épisodes*, pp. 245–6).

12 Having secured Metz and France's principal army, the Germans would be in a position to release the large forces which had been investing the city in time to take on the hastily raised and trained French provincial armies. The chance that the French could break the German ring around Paris would then become remote.

13 The 4th Battalion of the regiment had been captured at the Battle of Sedan, after which the Germans besieged Mézières, where the garrison included the depot battalion of the 6th. Mézières held out under bombardment from 5 September to 1 January 1871, when it too surrendered. The whole of the 6th Regiment was thus captive in Germany. '*Situation douloureuse et à jamais inoubliable!*' lamented the regimental history, even if the unit had done its duty honourably. The 6th Regiment was reformed at Périgueux in January 1871 with a few escapees. It was formally reconstituted on 16 August 1871, mainly from elements of other units, and went to garrison Rochefort. See *Historique*, pp. 120–2.

14 See for instance the paintings by Dujardin-Beaumetz and Lucien Mouillard reproduced in Rousset, *HG* I, pp. 337, 339.

15 According to Rousset, *HG* I, p. 337, 53 Colours were surrendered out of a possible 84, leaving 31 burned or otherwise destroyed or disposed of.

16 Patry's laboured protestation notwithstanding, many officers and men felt very differently about the issue and burned or cut up their Colours rather than surrender them: or handed them in at the arsenal in the belief that they were to be burned. Colours were specifically covered by Article 3 of the protocol of capitulation, and Bazaine became apprehensive (with reason) of German reaction if they were not handed over as stipulated. Nevertheless, many of his troops felt that his behaviour on this point was duplicitous and that he had been much too eager to please the conquerors: they never forgave him for inflicting this symbolic humiliation on them. This is the view expressed in the detailed accounts by Rousset, *HG* I, pp. 335–8 and Lehautcourt VII, pp. 493–9. Lehautcourt remarks, p. 499 fn., that Patry's view seems to be exceptional. Bazaine's own version is in *Épisodes*, pp. 239–44. See also Howard, pp. 281–2; Ruby and Regnault, *op. cit.*, pp. 269–94; and Baumont, *op. cit.*, pp. 321–6. In 1946, following the end of the Second World War, some of the Colours were brought back to France from Berlin.

17 As a result of the capitulation, the French surrendered Metz and 173,000 men, including three Marshals of France and more than 50 generals and 6,000 officers, plus more than 1,400 cannon with 3 million projectiles, 72 *mitrailleuses*, 200,000 rifles with 23 million cartridges, and 53 Colours. See Rousset, *HG* I, p. 335. An engraving of the surrender can be seen in the *Illustrated London News*, vol. 57 (12 November 1870), pp. 492–3. For descriptions of the capitulation and the scenes in Metz itself see Lehautcourt VII, pp. 500–17; *Cassell's History*, vol. I, pp. 298–309; Forbes, *op. cit.*, pp. 407–76.

18 Of the men of Bazaine's army captured at Metz, 11,000 were to die in captivity in Germany – Rousset, *HG* I, p. 339. On prisoners of war see François Roth, *La Guerre de 70* (Paris, 1990), pp. 418–33, and Manfred Botzenhart, 'French Prisoners of War in Germany, 1870–71' in Förster and Nagler *op. cit.*, pp. 587–93.

19 Commander of the Imperial Guard. See Biographies.

20 Bazaine took care to involve his corps commanders in councils of war, which ended in majority acceptance of his major decisions. Although there was some opposition to capitulation, most them concluded that it had become inevitable. See Bazaine, *Épisodes*, p. 239 and *passim*; Lehautcourt VII, pp. 346, 441–3; Rousset, *HG* I, pp. 333–4; Howard, p. 281.

21 Bazaine was reviled and insulted as he left Metz, keeping an armed escort for his personal protection: see Lehautcourt VII, p. 512; *Cassell's History*, vol. I, p. 309. His refusal of military honours at the capitulation was attributed to well-founded fears for his personal safety. He became the scapegoat for French defeat and was tried, found guilty and imprisoned in 1873. Rousset encapsulated the judgement of his generation when he wrote in 1899 that 'One man alone is inexcusable; he who sacrificed to who knows what guilty dreams the marvellous instrument of war which France had entrusted to him.' – *4e Corps*, p. 187. Later historians have generally discounted the charges of deliberate treason widely held by contemporaries: see for instance the judicious assess-

ments in Lehautcourt VII, pp. 518–23; Howard, pp. 282–3, and François Roth, *La Lorraine dans la Guerre de 1870* (Nancy, 1984), pp. 49–51. For items on Bazaine see Further Reading.

22 Literally 'take English leave'.

Chapter VIII: Escape

1 As after the capitulation at Sedan, German difficulties in coping with such enormous numbers of prisoners often provided opportunities for escape, particularly for officers. Several thousands succeeded in doing so, and joined the French provincial armies. The Army of the North, for instance, included some 5,000 escapees. See Howard, pp. 291, 391 and fn.; François Roth, *La Guerre de 70* (Paris, 1990), p. 419.

2 According to the aspersions of Livy, Capua was 'a city of great wealth and luxury' where 'no extravagance was spared, no sensual pleasure unindulged'. See Livy, *The War with Hannibal* (translated by Aubrey de Sélincourt, Harmondsworth, 1965), Book XXIII, pp. 168, 170–1.

3 Literally 'for how much less time', i.e., than in ancient Capua.

4 Patry's experience illustrates the division of opinion in the post-war French army over the morality of escaping and whether loyalty to the army code took precedence over patriotism. The notion of an officer's duty to escape and serve his country (axiomatic in the 20th century) was by no means accepted in conservative military circles. The Commission for Revision of Ranks (see Glossary) strongly disapproved of such behaviour. See Ralston, *op. cit.*, pp. 32, 164–5; Tombs, *The War Against Paris 1871* (Cambridge, 1981), p. 98. In his own service record Patry was careful to record that he had escaped without having signed any engagement or abused any safe-conduct. See '*Situation Militaire: Narration Faite Par L'Officier*' completed and signed by Patry on 19 September 1871, in Dossier Patry.

PART TWO: THE ARMY OF THE NORTH

Chapter I: To the Somme and Back

1 Although by November 1870 the Germans controlled a corridor of territory between the French frontier and Paris, the north-eastern corner of the country remained unoccupied. Having sufficient population, industry, fortresses and communication by sea, it had the potential to serve as a base for organised resistance. On the organisation of the Army of the North, see Faidherbe, pp. 8–14; Rousset, *HG* II, pp. 179 ff; Howard, pp. 291–2, 390–1. The operations of the 'Army of the North' were to extend beyond the boundaries of the administrative Département du Nord, of which Lille was the chief city, and into the neighbouring *départements* of Pas de Calais, Somme and Aisne.

2 General Bourbaki had avoided being taken prisoner at Metz in singular circumstances. He had been sent out of the city in September on a futile mis-

sion to the Empress Eugénie in England to discuss the possibility of a regency. On returning to France he was refused passage through the lines by the German military authorities. Frustrated at the delay, Bourbaki decided to offer his services to the Government of National Defence and was sent to command the gathering forces in the north on 18 October. However, his disagreements with the local republican authorities and pessimistic assessment of the situation caused him to be posted to another command on 18 November. See *Guerre: Armée du Nord I*, pp. 9–22, 32–3; Faidherbe, pp. 9, 12; Rousset, *HG* II, pp. 186–7; Howard, pp. 292–3.

3 The Lefaucheux was one of a number of native makes of revolver in use among French officers. After the outbreak of war, home-produced weapons were supplemented by government purchases of imported foreign makes. For illustrations of the 1858 'navy' Lefaucheux revolver and of the shorter and lighter 1870 model, see Paul Willing, *L'Armée de Napoléon III (2): L'Expédition du Mexique (1861–1867) et la Guerre Franco-Allemande (1870–1871)* (Les Collections du Musée de l'Armée, Arcueil, 1984), p. 70.

4 See Glossary.

5 On Faidherbe and Farre see Biographies. Faidherbe became a Grand Officer of the Legion of Honour on 15 June 1871. Farre became a Commander of the Order at about the same time, and a Grand Officer in 1880 when Faidherbe had become Grand Chancellor of the Order.

6 Following the capture of Metz, a German army of 40,000 men and 180 guns under General von Manteuffel was dispatched to deal with French troops gathering in the north, at that time numbering about 25,000 men. By 15 November the advancing force, comprising I and VIII Corps and the 3rd Cavalry Division of the First Army, had reached a line from Rheims to Rethel, while detachments besieged Mézières and La Fère. By 20 November the main body had reached the River Oise, and then followed the French in their withdrawal towards Amiens. See Helmuth von Moltke, *The Franco-German War of 1870–71* (reprint with an introduction by Michael Howard, London, 1992), pp. 177, 216–7; Faidherbe, p. 14; *Guerre: Armée du Nord I*, p. 38; *GGS* Pt 2, vol. 2, pp. 1–3; Pierre Lehautcourt, *Campagne du Nord en 1870–71: Histoire de la Défense Nationale dans le Nord de la France* (Paris, 1886), pp. 48–52; Rousset, *HG* II, pp. 187–93.

7 The Battle of Coulmiers, fought on 9 November 1870, was the first French victory of the war. The 70,000-strong Army of the Loire under General d'Aurelle de Paladines defeated 20,000 Bavarians under General von der Tann north-west of Orléans, then reoccupied that city. The news was a great boost to French morale, but only a temporary one. The Germans dispatched fresh forces, and after a further series of battles the Army of the Loire abandoned Orléans on 5 December and gave up its attempt to relieve Paris.

8 Patry's footnote 1897: 'He died a few years ago in Paris, where he commanded a division.' As a general, Tramond presided over the commission which in 1886 developed the Lebel repeating rifle that, with some mod-

ifications, became the standard French infantry weapon in the First World War.

9 Political and budgetary pressures to reduce the inflated number of officer posts in the decades following the war were resisted by the army with some success. Individual officers of course had a vested interest in opposing economies at their own expense, but the argument was influential that an adequate cadre of trained officers at captain's rank would be needed in case of another war; even if those posts were superfluous to regimental needs in peacetime. See Ralston, *op. cit.*, pp. 57–63, 136–7.

10 The 5th Battalion of the 91st Regiment of the *Garde Mobile*, from the Pas-de-Calais.

11 On the National Guard, see Glossary. Patry identifies these men as *gardes nationaux mobilisés*, that is, National Guardsmen subject to service away from their locality, as opposed to those of the *Garde Nationale Sédentaire* who were used only for local defence. The latter were generally older men with family responsibilities.

12 Patry's footnote 1897: 'Currently a doctor in Paris.'

13 The scene of heavy fighting on 27 November 1870, Villers-Bretonneux was to become so again nearly half a century later. On 24 April 1918 it was the nearest point to Amiens reached by the advancing Germans before they were halted by a crucial Australian counter-attack. On 8 August 1918 attacks in the sector by British, Canadian and Australian troops helped inflict what Ludendorff called 'the black day of the German army'. The town was rebuilt after the Great War. It is the site of the Australian National War Memorial and maintains strong cultural links with Australia. See Rose E. B. Coombs, M. B. E., *Before Endeavours Fade: A Guide to the Battlefields of the First World War* (London, 1976), p. 121.

14 The advancing German army of about 40,000 under General von Manteuffel was attacking extended French defensive positions along a line of villages east and south of the city of Amiens. The French force, consisting of about 25,000 men (one-third of them *Gardes Mobiles*) under General Farre, evacuated the city in disorder that night and retreated to the north and east towards Doullens and Arras. German casualties in the Battle of Amiens on 27 November 1870 were 1,300, French nearly 1,400 plus more than a thousand taken prisoner. The Germans occupied Amiens the next day and the citadel surrendered on the 30th. See Faidherbe, pp. 15–30; *Guerre: Armée du Nord I*, pp. 75 ff, 119; *GGS* Pt 2, vol. 2, pp. 5–16; Lehautcourt, *op. cit.*, pp. 60–74; Rousset, *HG* II, pp. 193–9.

15 See Glossary.

16 Faidherbe was officially appointed to succeed Bourbaki on 20 November, but, having to travel from Algeria, did not take up his command until the evening of 3 December. General Farre commanded in the interim, and then became Faidherbe's chief of staff. See *Guerre: Armée du Nord I*, pp. 32–3, 39, 138.

17 French forces in Paris had made a sally across the Marne in an attempt to break through the German lines south-east of the city. The offensive began on 29 November, but despite inflated early reports of success, piercing the reinforced German front proved a far tougher proposition than civilian enthusiasts of a '*sortie torrentielle*' had supposed. After five days of murderous fighting in bitterly cold weather, the French commander, General Ducrot, who had proclaimed that 'I shall only re-enter Paris dead or victorious', was forced to admit failure and return to the city. French casualties in what became known as the Battle of Champigny had been 12,000, German 6,200. As Ducrot withdrew, news arrived of the simultaneous failure of the Army of the Loire's rescue attempt from the south.

Chapter II: The Capture and Defence of Ham

1 Following his victory at Amiens on 27 November, General von Manteuffel moved to secure Normandy. Leaving part of his force under General von der Groeben to hold Amiens and its rail link with Laon, he set out with his main body on 1 December and occupied Rouen on the 5th. See Helmuth von Moltke, *The Franco-German War of 1870–71* (reprint with an introduction by Michael Howard, London, 1992), pp. 252–3; Rousset, *HG* II, pp. 204–6.

2 Vinciguerra, an adjutant in the 6th Line Regiment, had been cited in orders for bravery in the August battles around Metz. See *Historique*, p. 115.

3 See Biographies.

4 The German garrison at Ham, about 230 men in total, consisted of a party of the 3rd Field Railway Division sent to repair the railway between Laon and Amiens, together with an infantry guard from the 81st Regiment at La Fère.

5 The Corps commander, General Lecointe, obtained Faidherbe's permission for the raid on Ham and took great care to brief his commanders thoroughly and issue them with maps of the town. See *Guerre: Armée du Nord II*, pp. 36–8.

6 The medieval fortress of Ham, incapable of resisting heavy artillery, had latterly served as a political prison. Louis-Napoleon Bonaparte had been imprisoned there from 1840 to 1846 following the failure of his attempted coup at Boulogne. It was during his captivity that he studied social questions and wrote *The Extinction of Poverty*. In 1846 the future Emperor Napoleon III escaped disguised as a workman and made his way via Belgium to England.

7 Patry's figure agrees with a German account which gives three killed, three wounded and 221 captured. French losses were five killed and sixteen wounded. Official accounts are in *Guerre: Armée du Nord II*, pp. 36–8 and *Docs. annexes*, pp. 19–21. See also Rousset, *HG* II, p. 210 and Pierre Lehautcourt, *Campagne du Nord en 1870–71* (Paris, 1886), pp. 89–93. Patry had had an account of the Ham raid published in the year before his book appeared: 'La prise du fort de Ham, 9, 10, 11 et 12 décembre 1870', in *Revue Politique et Littéraire*, 1896.

8 The Germans had supposed that the French defeat at Amiens would make them incapable of an offensive for some time. Despite the pressing needs of reorganisation, Faidherbe had nevertheless determined to divert them. The successful small coup at Ham undoubtedly alarmed the Germans. It put the French astride their rail link between Amiens and Rheims; it was also, in Rousset's words, 'very mortifying' (*HG* II, p. 210) and demonstrated that the French still posed a danger. At first the Germans thought that the affair at Ham might have been a foray by the French garrison at Péronne. Over the next few days movements by larger French forces threatening La Fère and Amiens clearly showed, however, that an advance by the Army of the North had begun. The Germans temporarily evacuated Amiens and, instead of continuing their advance in Normandy, concentrated at Beauvais to counter the threat from Faidherbe. See von Moltke, *op. cit.*, pp. 252–4; Faidherbe, pp. 31–3; *GGS* Pt 2, vol. 2, pp. 26, 106–7; Lehautcourt, *op. cit.*, pp. 93–7; Howard, pp. 392–3.

9 Berlin's central park, taking its name from its origin as a royal hunting park.

10 The *feldmütze*, the German forage cap of the type still in use in 1914–18.

11 The French official account of the ambush, which took place near the hamlet of Vouël, mentions however that some of the 127 prisoners were wounded. See *Guerre: Armée du Nord II*, p. 45 and fn., and Tramond's report *ibid.*, *Docs. annexes*, pp. 26–7; Lehautcourt, *op. cit.*, p. 92.

12 The Army of the North included strong naval and marine contingents, commanded by naval officers. After the defeats of 6 August 1870 the French had abandoned plans for a seaborne expedition against the German coast. Retaining only sufficient men for naval defence, the Government redeployed sailors and marines to fight as artillerists or infantry. An estimated 57,000 served on land during the war. The marines distinguished themselves at Sedan, and naval battalions played an important role in stiffening the backbone of the largely untrained provincial armies. Naval battalions were conspicuous in the defence of Paris, as well as in the Army of the Loire and the Army of the North. See Rousset, *HG* II, pp. 445–50; also Stephen Shann and Louis Delperier, *French Army 1870–71: Franco-Prussian War 2: Republican Troops* (Osprey, 1991), pp. 18–20.

13 Patry's footnote 1897: 'The regular troops of the Army of the North included 279 officers who had escaped from Metz or Sedan.' This figure appears in Faidherbe, p. 87.

14 Patry's footnote 1897: '*Opérations de la première armée allemande sous Manteuffel d'après les documents officiels du quartier général de la première armée.*' The work Patry cites was a translation of Graf Herrmann Ludwig von Wartensleben, *Feldzug 1870–71. Die Operationen der I Armee unter General von Manteuffel* (Berlin, 1872). An English version was also published: *The Campaign of 1870–1871. Operations of the First Army under General von Manteuffel compiled from the Official War Documents of the Head-Quarters of the First Army* (translated by Col. C. H. von Wright, London, 1873). The passage quoted by Patry occurs on pp. 125–6

of the English edition. The French official account of the defence of Ham is in *Guerre: Armée du Nord II*, p. 45, and Tramond's report *ibid.*, *Docs. annexes*, p. 27; see also Lehautcourt, *op. cit.*, p. 93. The German official history gives a conveniently brief account of events at Ham. See *GGS* Pt 2, vol. 2, pp. 25–6.

15 General Edwin von Manteuffel, commanding the German First Army. Dissatisfied with von der Groeben's response to the French offensive, von Manteuffel would shortly supersede him and return to take charge of the Somme front himself.

16 Possibly a reference to 'the day of tiles' in Grenoble on 7 June 1788, in the early stages of the French Revolution, when royal troops were pelted with roof tiles by rioting citizens. As Patry's parents lived in Grenoble for five years from 1866, and as he was himself based there during his later services as an officer of the Reserve, the story of the episode may have come readily to mind.

17 Abbé Charles-François Lhomond (1727–94), born at Chaulnes, grammarian and author of such primers as *De viris illustribus urbis Romae a Romulo ad Augustum*, *Élements de la Grammaire Latine*, *Élements de la Grammaire Française*, *Doctrine Chrétien*, etc. His works continued to be a staple of schoolrooms in the century following his death, some also being translated into English, Russian and Italian.

18 Although Napoleon I had defended France in 1814 with a vigour and ingenuity which contrasted with the pusillanimity of his nephew in 1870, the outcome of that campaign and of Waterloo the following year brought the same result for eastern France: defeat and enemy occupation. The Prussian occupation was remembered as particularly oppressive. In their turn, the Prussians of that generation were paying France back for the occupation they had endured after the defeat of Jena in 1806 (much as Russian troops had scores to settle once they entered Germany in 1945). For treatments of occupation and resistance in France in 1870 see François Roth, *La Guerre de 70* (Paris, 1990), pp. 372–410, and Audoin-Rouzeau, *1870: La France dans la Guerre* (Paris, 1989), pp. 210–19, 261–91.

19 Irregular Muslim troops employed by Turkey, notorious for their depredations and indiscipline in the Danube region during the Crimean War of 1854–6.

20 *For hearth and home.*

21 See Biographies.

22 See Biographies. These generals were still with the army, but at different levels of command following reorganisation. General Derroja, as divisional commander, reported to General Lecointe, commander of Twenty-second Corps. Gislain, who had led the specially constituted column which attacked Ham, commanded a brigade in Lecointe's other division, du Bessol's.

Chapter III: Pont-Noyelles

1 Having probed towards Amiens, Faidherbe decided against trying to take it because the Germans still occupied the citadel there and threatened to bombard the city from it if the French attempted to enter. Learning of the ap-

proach of a large German relief force, Faidherbe then withdrew his army eight kilometres north-eastward to a strong defensive position astride the road to Albert on the heights east of the River Hallue, a tributary of the Somme. The French position, with commanding fields of fire and advance units in the valley guarding the approach roads, stretched for twelve kilometres from north to south, where it was anchored on the Somme. The village of Contay, situated on the right bank of the Hallue, was on the French right (northern) flank. See *Guerre: Armée du Nord II*, pp. 56–86, 87; Faidherbe, pp. 34–6; Pierre Lehautcourt, *Campagne du Nord en 1870–71* (Paris, 1886), pp. 101–3; Rousset, *HG* II, pp. 213–14; Howard, pp. 393–4.

2 See *Régiment de marche* in Glossary.

3 Fradin de Linières was to remain Patry's commanding officer for several years after the war. His annual reports on Patry's performance are preserved in the 'Notes Particulières et Successives, 1870–80' in Patry's service record (Dossier Patry).

4 Anatole Robin was a former captain of marines who had escaped from Sedan. He secured an appointment as a general, but was notorious for his incompetence, womanising and corruption. His division of National Guards was so unreliable that Faidherbe hesitated to put it in the front line. They were to perform badly at Bapaume on 2 and 3 January 1871. See Lehautcourt, *op. cit.*, pp. 105–6; Rousset, *HG* II, pp. 212–13, 220; Howard, pp. 392, 394, 396.

5 A German reconnoitring force advancing from Amiens on the Albert road on 20 December was attacked on all sides and forced to retreat by French forces commanded by General du Bessol. The Germans lost three officers and 69 men killed and wounded, the French seven killed and 20 wounded. See Herrmann von Wartensleben, *The Campaign of 1870–1871. Operations of the First Army under General von Manteuffel compiled from the Official War Documents of the Head-Quarters of the First Army* (translated by Col. C. H. von Wright, London, 1873), p. 143; *Guerre: Armée du Nord II*, pp. 69–71; Faidherbe, pp. 36–7; *GGS* Pt 2, vol. 2, p. 108 and fn.; Lehautcourt, *op. cit.*, pp. 108–9; Rousset, *HG* II, pp. 214–15. Querrieux was to be the centre of fighting again three days later during the Battle of Pont-Noyelles, some of it in the grounds of the château which was to serve as General Sir Henry Rawlinson's headquarters during the Battle of the Somme in 1916. See Toni and Valmai Holt, *Major and Mrs Holt's Battlefield Guide to the Somme* (London, 1996), pp. 39–40, 236; Martin and Mary Middlebrook, *The Somme Battlefields: A Comprehensive Guide from Crécy to the Two World Wars* (Harmondsworth, 1991), pp. 239–40.

6 Evidently Faidherbe carried out his reconnoitring in a carriage in order to accommodate Rear-Admiral Moulac, one of his divisional commanders, who was a poor horseman. The Army of the North was also very deficient in cavalry, which both limited its powers of reconnaissance and enabled the German cavalry to keep it under observation without much challenge. See Henri Daussy, *Comment le cheval de Faidherbe ne lui fut pas rendu par les Prussiens* (pamphlet, Amiens, 1886), p. 9; Rousset, *HG* II, p. 216 and fn.

7 Artaxerxes III, King of Persia 359–338 BC, who was detested by the priests of Egypt and contemptuously called by them 'The Ass'. When Artaxerxes conquered Egypt he took his revenge by slaughtering and eating Apis, their sacred bull. Thus his 'gift' was an ass in exchange for a bull. See *Plutarch's Moralia V* (translated by Frank Cole Babbitt, Loeb Classical Library, London, 1969), pp. 29, 77.

8 Also known as the Battle of the Hallue. After recalling some units from Normandy, the Germans reoccupied Amiens and by 22 December had succeeded in concentrating there a force of 22,600 men and 108 guns. General Manteuffel then advanced north-eastwards from Amiens in an attempt to drive the French away. Faidherbe's force numbered 41,000 with 82 guns, though many were untrained levies who could not match the discipline and experience of the Germans. Manteuffel's plan for 23 December was for the 15th Division of VIII Corps to attack the French left, while the 16th Division marched northward to try to turn their right. In the event, the Germans were drawn into a series of attacks on the villages along the Hallue, in front of the French left and centre. See *Guerre: Armée du Nord II*, pp. 78–9, 82; Faidherbe, pp. 37–9; Lehautcourt, *op. cit.*, pp. 110–21; Rousset, *HG* II, pp. 216–24; Helmuth von Moltke, *The Franco-German War of 1870-71* (reprint with an introduction by Michael Howard, London, 1992), pp. 254–7; *GGS* Pt 2, vol. 2, pp. 109–16, 118 fn.; Howard, pp. 394–5.

9 Pont-Noyelles itself, in the centre of the French line, had seen furious fighting on the 23rd, continued in the winter dusk by the light of burning houses. After attack and counter-attack it had finally been held by the Germans, who had similarly gained control of other disputed villages along the Hallue. The cannonade on the morning of the 24th was intended by both sides mainly to break up any offensive preparations the other might make, rather than as a prelude to an attack of their own. See Faidherbe, pp. 39–40; *GGS* Pt 2, vol. 2, pp. 116–17; Lehautcourt, *op. cit.*, p. 122; Rousset, *HG* II, p. 221.

10 The *Garde Mobile* did not wear red trousers like regular line infantry, but dark-blue trousers with a red stripe. Thus from a distance, and particularly in bad light, their predominantly dark-blue uniforms could cause them to be mistaken for Prussian troops. See Stephen Shann and Louis Delperier, *French Army 1870–71: Franco-Prussian War 2: Republican Troops* (Osprey, 1991), plates C and D.

11 Although Faidherbe's troops had fought the Germans hard in the villages along the Hallue on the 23rd, their evening counter-attack had failed and he felt that no more could be asked of them, particularly in such freezing weather and without food or shelter. Nevertheless, Patry's criticism of Faidherbe's failure to use his uncommitted troops for a concentrated attack on the German left on either the 23rd or the morning of the 24th had justification. Although the Germans were very wary of French numerical superiority and did not pursue, they had reclaimed the strategic advantage, for Amiens and their lines of communication were safe again for the moment as Faidherbe

retreated northward. German losses had been 950. The French had suffered 1,226 casualties and more than a thousand taken prisoner. For official reports see *Guerre: Armée du Nord II*, pp. 87–128; *GGS* Pt 2, vol. 2, pp. 117–8 and Appendix CXIV; also Faidherbe, pp. 39–42, Lehautcourt, *op. cit.*, pp. 123–4, and Rousset, *HG* II, pp. 222–4.

12 *Le réveillon* – a traditional supper after midnight Mass on Christmas Eve or New Year's Eve.

13 See Biographies.

Chapter IV: Bapaume

1 In fairness to Faidherbe, the grandiloquent phrases in question were Gambetta's, to which the general added a qualifying gloss in his order of the day of 5 December 1870. Text in Faidherbe, p. 85. (Also in *Guerre: Armée du Nord II, Docs. annexes*, p. 6, and *ibid.* p. 132 for the 31 December exhortation to 'conquer or die'). Translations of both orders are provided in the Appendix (items ii and iii).

2 The passage of this river in Epirus through dark gorges and underground caves in its course towards the Ionian Sea gave rise to the belief in ancient Greek legend that it was the entrance to the underworld. An oracle of the dead stood on its banks.

3 Nearly 40,000 French troops in all served in the Mexican expedition of 1861–7. Ostensibly intended to recover debts and protect the French community in Mexico, the expedition became an attempt by Napoleon III to establish a client monarchy in Central America. French conquests of territory under Bazaine could not be sustained in the face of determined guerrilla resistance, and troops were withdrawn after the end of the American Civil War when intervention by the United States seemed probable. Deprived of French support, Archduke Maximilian of Austria, who had accepted the Imperial crown of Mexico in 1864, was captured and shot by the Mexicans in 1867. The failure of the expedition was a severe blow to Napoleon's prestige at home and abroad and weakened France's position in Europe militarily and diplomatically. Some 2,000 French troops were killed and more than 7,000 died of disease in Mexico.

4 See Glossary.

5 Péronne was a key crossing-point of the Somme. Continued possession of it by a French garrison of 3,500 men under Commandant Garnier posed a threat to German communications, and it had been under observation by German cavalry since the end of November. On 27 December it was completely invested, and was heavily bombarded on successive days. When news of the town's predicament was brought to Faidherbe, he determined to advance to its relief from his positions south of Arras. See Faidherbe, p. 43; *Guerre: Armée du Nord II*, pp. 136–42; *GGS* Pt 2, vol. 2, pp. 119, 249–50; Pierre Lehautcourt, *Campagne du Nord en 1870–71* (Paris, 1886), pp. 137, 141–51; Rousset, *HG* II, pp. 231–7.

6 Uncertain of the exact position of the German force covering Péronne because of inadequate cavalry reconnaissance, Faidherbe had directed the Twenty-second Corps (including Patry's regiment) south-westwards towards Bucquoy on the Amiens road, while the Twenty-third Corps moved directly south towards Bapaume. The Germans proved to be concentrated on Twenty-third Corps' front along a line of villages north and west of Bapaume, where they were attacked by Payen's naval division. Finding no enemy around Bucquoy, Derroja's division on the French right was hurried eastwards in support of du Bessol's division which was fighting around Achiet-le-Grand, but was too far from the fighting to be able to join in that day. While Derroja's troops might have made a decisive difference on 2 January, on the French left Robin's National Guard Division, which was in a position to force the German right, allowed itself to be held up by a small German detachment. See Faidherbe, pp. 43–4; Helmuth von Moltke, *The Franco-German War of 1870-71* (reprint with an introduction by Michael Howard, London, 1992), pp. 304–5; *Guerre: Armée du Nord III*, pp. 15–31, 46–7; *GGS* Pt 2, vol. 2, pp. 233–5; Lehautcourt, *op. cit.*, pp. 152–9; Rousset, *HG* II, pp. 236–7; Howard, p. 396.

7 Having been unable to achieve a decisive outcome on the 2nd, Faidherbe's plan for the 3rd was to outflank and overwhelm the German positions north and west of Bapaume by a concentric attack. Derroja's division was on the French right, attacking towards Bapaume from the west. The German force defending Bapaume was VIII Corps under General von Goeben.

8 A related reason for the marked superiority of the German artillery in the first phase of the war of 1870 had been Napoleon III's misguided standardisation of French artillery time fuses. By puncturing the appropriate hole, French shells could be set before firing to explode at only two fixed ranges (four for shrapnel) between 1,350 and 2,850 metres. The inadequacy of this rigid system became evident when German batteries and infantry failed to oblige by staying at exactly those distances from the French guns. German shells, in contrast, could be fired at up to 3,500 metres and burst upon impact. In response, French production of percussion fuses was increased and the artillery of the provincial armies, for instance at Coulmiers and Bapaume, was able to demonstrate that German gunners could no longer dominate the battlefield as decisively as they had in August. See Lehautcourt II, pp. 116–17; Holmes, *The Road to Sedan*, pp. 227–9; Howard, p. 298.

9 The long straight highway (originally the Roman road) which connects Amiens and Cambrai had played a role in military operations in the region down the ages. The Battle of Pont-Noyelles (La Hallue) on 23 December 1870 had been fought astride it. In the Battle of the Somme in 1916 the road would form the central axis of the British offensive from Albert towards Bapaume.

10 Faidherbe felt scruples about bombarding a French town to dislodge the Germans defending it – a decision which Rousset judged 'honourable, no doubt, but perhaps excessive'. The outnumbered Germans had managed to

hold a contracted line around Bapaume only by hurrying up reinforcements from Péronne during the afternoon. This left the investing force around Péronne very thin, but as the French garrison there remained passive, the German move paid off. Faidherbe had 34,500 men and 86 guns at Bapaume. Although the Germans had a total strength in the region of 26,000 and 137 guns, the need to invest Péronne and other detachments reduced the numbers available to fight at Bapaume. The Germans claimed to have fought off the French with only 10,000 men. Faidherbe thought, however, that the force opposing him numbered twice that. See Faidherbe, pp. 45–6; *Guerre: Armée du Nord III*, pp. 7, 10, 34–69 and *Docs. annexes*, pp. 33–6; Carl Emil von Schell, *The Campaign of 1870–1871: The Operations of the First Army under General von Goeben compiled from the Official War Documents of the Head-Quarters of the First Army* (translated by Col. C. H. von Wright, London, 1873), pp. 24–36; *GGS* Pt 2, vol. 2, pp. 237–9, 252–3; von Moltke *op. cit.*, pp. 306–8, 311; Lehautcourt, *op. cit.*, pp. 165–9; Rousset, *HG* II, 239 and fn., 240–1, 245.

11 French losses at Bapaume had been over 1,300 killed and wounded and nearly 1,200 missing – *Guerre: Armée du Nord III*, p. 68; Rousset, *HG* II, pp. 241–2. German losses were 128 killed, 702 wounded and 236 missing, total 1,066. See H. von Wartensleben, *The Campaign of 1870–1871: Operations of the First Army under General von Manteuffel compiled from the Official War Documents of the Head-Quarters of the First Army* (translated by Col. C. H. von Wright, London, 1873), p. 198 fn.

12 Ironically, the Germans had been so hard pressed and were so low on ammunition that General von Goeben had determined to evacuate Bapaume that night and move to a defensive position south of the Somme. Thus both sides retreated after the battle. Faidherbe's caution and consideration for his troops had lost the chance to relieve Péronne and turned a hard-won French tactical advantage into a German strategic victory. See *Guerre: Armée du Nord III*, p. 67; Faidherbe, p. 47; Wartensleben, *op. cit.*, pp. 41–3; Schell, *op. cit.*, pp. 41–3; GGS Pt 2, vol. 2, p. 241; Lehautcourt, *op. cit.*, pp. 169–72; Rousset, *HG* II, p. 242; Howard, p. 397.

13 Patry's footnote 1897: 'Currently a battalion commander in the 129th Infantry.' On Fernandez's post-war career see also Biographies.

14 The German troops involved were two sections of the 6th Company of the 33rd Regiment and the 4th Squadron of the 5th Uhlans. French and German accounts of the number captured varied. General Derroja reported 39 men and twelve horses captured, and estimated about 30 killed and wounded. See *Guerre: Armée du Nord III*, pp. 94–5 and *Docs. annexes*, p. 89; Faidherbe p. 49. The Germans in contrast reported one man killed, one man and one horse wounded, eleven men and twelve horses captured and three horses destroyed. See *GGS* Pt 2, vol. 2, p. 255 and Appendix CXXVII, p. 125. Schell, *op. cit.*, p. 71.

15 Péronne surrendered on the 9th after a fortnight of bombardment. Although there were supplies of food and ammunition remaining, morale was low and

there were divisions with the civil authorities. Despite some opposition from his officers, in the absence of any sign of a relief column Commandant Garnier felt that he had no option but to capitulate. The Germans, who had been in constant anxiety in case there were a further French relief effort, occupied the town on the 10th. Faidherbe learned the news 'with stupefaction', but might have averted the capitulation by more effective and timely action. See Faidherbe, pp. 49–58, 89–91; Louis Cadot, *La Vérité sur le Siège de Péronne: Réponse au Général Faidherbe* (Pamphlet, Paris, 1872); *Guerre: Armée du Nord III*, pp. 89–90, 97–8; Schell, *op. cit.*, pp. 37–67; von Moltke, *op. cit.*, pp. 310–11; *GGS* Pt 2, vol. 2, p. 254; Lehautcourt, *op. cit.*, pp. 172–80, 188; Rousset, *HG* II, pp. 244–6.

Chapter V: Final Defeat at Saint-Quentin

1 By capturing Péronne, the Germans had secured their control of the line of the Somme, which they now held against any attempt by the Army of the North to interfere with their operations against Paris. Faidherbe was urged by the War Ministry at Bordeaux to make one more effort to divert the Germans while another sortie was attempted from Paris. He therefore feinted towards Amiens and Albert (hence the presence of Patry's unit there) but decided that, rather than attack the German line to the south-west where it was strongest, he would thrust south-eastwards towards Saint-Quentin and the Oise valley beyond, to try to pass the right of the German line and disrupt their rail communications, so drawing their forces away from Paris. Such a scheme might have succeeded with speed and surprise, but in the event Faidherbe was able to achieve neither. See Faidherbe, pp. 58–9; *Guerre: Armée du Nord IV*, pp. 1–35; Helmuth von Moltke, *The Franco-German War of 1870–71* (reprint with an introduction by Michael Howard, London, 1992), pp. 311–12; Schell, *op. cit.*, pp. 87–8; *GGS* Pt 2, vol. 2, p. 257; Pierre Lehautcourt, *Campagne du Nord en 1870–71* (Paris, 1886), pp. 195–9; Rousset *HG* II, pp. 351–3; Howard, pp. 403–4.

2 By the 17th General von Goeben, having succeeded Manteuffel as commander of the German First Army, had sufficient information from his cavalry to be sure that the French were moving towards Saint-Quentin. Having the advantage of good roads and interior lines, he immediately began shifting his forces eastward to catch the French in flank should they continue their advance – which they did. See *GGS* Pt 2, vol. 2, pp. 258–9; Schell, *op. cit.*, pp. 92–3; von Moltke, *op. cit.*, pp. 313–15; Lehautcourt, *op. cit.*, pp. 200–2; Rousset, *HG* II, pp. 353–5.

3 As Patry's account vividly illustrates, the French advance, made over bad roads and closely observed by German cavalry, was now in serious trouble. The hurried doubling back to Vermand of Aynès' brigade, to which Patry's regiment belonged, had been ordered by Faidherbe to disengage the rear of the French column, which had become entangled in a running battle with German forces intent on harassing and delaying it. With no hope now of

throwing off the Germans, let alone of achieving his original objective of cutting their communications, and with his supply arrangements in disorder, Faidherbe felt that his only option to keep his army together was to accept battle at Saint-Quentin. See Faidherbe, pp. 56–61; *Guerre: Armée du Nord IV*, pp. 48–76; Schell, *op. cit.*, pp. 110–26; *GGS* Pt 2, vol. 2, pp. 259–63; Lehautcourt, *op. cit.*, pp. 203–12; Rousset, *HG* II, pp. 255–8.

4 Patry uses this spelling throughout for the Faubourg d'Isle.

5 The German attack gave the French no time to complete their dispositions. Thus the two French corps would fight separate battles, with the city of Saint-Quentin (population 30,000), the River Somme and its bordering marshes, and the Crozat Canal between them. The Twenty-second Corps took position on hills south of the city and the river. The Twenty-third Corps defended the line north of the river and west of the city. Although the Germans also had to straddle the Somme and the canal, they managed to keep better contact between the two halves of their army. The German army numbered 33,000 men and 161 guns, the French possibly 43,000 men of varying quality and 102 guns. See Faidherbe, p. 62; *Guerre: Armée du Nord IV*, pp. 46–7, 75–82; Schell, *op. cit.*, pp. 127–8; *GGS* Pt 2, vol. 2, pp. 263–4; Lehautcourt, *op. cit.*, pp. 212–20.

6 The attacking forces in this sector were the German 16th Division and 3rd Reserve Division under General von Barnekow, captor of Péronne. Until after midday the Germans were unable to make headway in a series of frontal assaults around the village of Grugies and a sugar refinery. See *Guerre: Armée du Nord IV*, pp. 82–9; Faidherbe, p. 63; Lehautcourt, *op. cit.*, pp. 220–6; Rousset, *HG* II, pp. 260–1; von Moltke, *op. cit.*, pp. 316–17; Schell, *op. cit.*, pp. 130–7; *GGS* Pt 2, vol. 2, pp. 264–5.

7 The emergency which Aynès had to meet was the advance of the German 12th (Saxon) Cavalry Division under Count zur Lippe, which was advancing up the La Fère road, threatening to turn the French left. See *Guerre: Armée du Nord IV*, p. 90; Faidherbe, p. 63; Lehautcourt, *op. cit.*, p. 226; Rousset, *HG* II, pp. 261–2; Schell, *op. cit.*, pp. 136–7; *GGS* Pt 2, vol. 2, p. 266.

8 These were probably men of *La Compagnie Franche des Mobilisés de l'Aisne*, two companies of whom were present on this sector. See *Guerre: Armée du Nord IV*, p. 90 fn.; Lehautcourt, *op. cit.*, p. 234.

9 The Raulieu farm.

10 La Neuville was taken at about 1.00 p.m. by the 2nd Battalion of the 86th Regiment, which had arrived from Tergnier as a reinforcement from the German Army of the Meuse. The attack came at a time when Aynès had had to send four battalions away to the right to relieve pressure on the French line, leaving him only three thinly spread battalions to defend the extreme left of the French army. See *Guerre: Armée du Nord IV*, p. 92; GGS Pt 2, vol. 2, pp. 267, 271; Lehautcourt, *op. cit.*, pp. 234–5; Rousset *HG* II, p. 264.

11 The attacking Germans were a company of the 12th Rifle Battalion, fighting to the left of the 2nd Battalion of the 86th Regiment. These units suffered

about 80 casualties between them. For German accounts of the attack in this sector see *GGS* Pt 2. vol. 2, pp. 266–7 and Appendix CXXVII; Schell, *op. cit.*, p. 151. See also *Guerre: Armée du Nord IV*, pp. 91–2.

12 Tramond distinguished himself that afternoon by charging with the bayonet against the attacking Saxons, thereby rallying his men and helping to keep open the escape route of the Twenty-second Corps to Saint-Quentin. By also rushing up other troops and turning their artillery on the advancing Germans, the French managed to deter Count Lippe from immediately exploiting the disintegration of Aynès' left companies, so buying a little time before they were forced to withdraw by renewed German attacks all along the line in mid-afternoon. See *Guerre: Armée du Nord IV*, p. 94 and *Docs. annexes*, pp. 98–9; Faidherbe, p. 64; Rousset, *HG* II, p. 264 ; Lehautcourt *op. cit.*, p. 235; Schell, *op. cit.*, pp. 152–70; *GGS* Pt 2, vol. 2, p. 271.

13 Aynès was reported killed by a bullet through the forehead at the Raulieu farm at about 1 o'clock. The French official history paid tribute to his modesty and intelligence, his simplicity and heroism, and admitted that without his support his men's morale failed. See *Guerre: Armée du Nord IV*, p. 92, echoing Derroja's eulogy in his report, *ibid.*, *Docs. annexes*, p. 98.

14 West of Saint-Quentin, the Twenty-third Corps had also been defeated and forced to withdraw after fighting all day. Although the Germans proved unable to cut the French escape route to the north or to mount a rapid pursuit, they had achieved the decisive final victory in the Northern campaign. See Schell, *op. cit.*, pp. 170–2; Faidherbe, pp. 65–7; *Guerre: Armée du Nord IV*, pp. 113–50; Lehautcourt, *op. cit.*, pp. 240–5.

15 The most authoritative German account puts their occupation of the railway station at 5.15 p.m. They then entered the town and began taking prisoners. See Schell, *op. cit.*, pp. 169–70; Lehautcourt, *op. cit.*, pp. 239–40.

16 Operetta by the popular composer and impresario Florimond Hervé (1825–92), parodying the *Faust* of Charles Gounod (1859).

17 French casualties at Saint-Quentin had been 3,400, but another 11,000 men were missing – 9,000 of them taken prisoner by the Germans. In effect, Faidherbe had lost one-third of his army and the remainder were no longer capable of an offensive. German casualties had been 2,500. See *Guerre: Armée du Nord IV*, p. 148; *GGS* Pt 2, vol. 2, p. 276; Schell, *op. cit.*, p. 173; von Moltke, *op. cit.*, p. 323; Lehautcourt, *op. cit.*, p. 244; Rousset, *HG* II, pp. 269–70.

Chapter VI: Armistice

1 The armistice was signed at Versailles on 28 January, following negotiations between Bismarck and Jules Favre, acting for the Government of National Defence. Food stocks in the capital were at their limit, and the siege could no longer be sustained. The Army of the Loire had been defeated at Le Mans on 11–12 January, and the last effort at a sortie from Paris had been decisively repulsed at Buzenval on 19 January, the same day that Faidherbe was defeated at Saint-Quentin. The armistice was to last until 19 February, while

elections were held for a National Assembly that would meet at Bordeaux to decide on continuation of the war or acceptance of peace. See Howard, pp. 433 ff, and for text of the armistice *GGS* Pt 2, vol. 2, Appendix CLVI, pp. 227–30.

2 Patry's verdict echoes that of the regimental historian of the 67th *de marche*, who with pardonable hyperbole extolled 'our young men [who], without military instruction, badly armed, equipped and clothed, fought like veterans and astonished the battle-hardened troops of the enemy by their steadfastness and their courage'. See A. J. P. N. de Rocca-Serra, *Historique du 67e Régiment d'Infanterie* (Paris, 1889), p. 38.

3 Soldiers had been allowed to vote only since 1848, and then only by specific authorisation of the government for each election, not as an automatic right of suffrage. The army had been allowed to vote in the plebiscites of 1851, 1852, and most recently May 1870, but Napoleon III had not extended the right to other elections. See Holmes, *The Road to Sedan*, pp. 130–1; William Serman, *Les Officiers Français dans la Nation (1848-1914)* (Paris, 1982), p. 36.

4 On Thiers and Gambetta, see Biographies and Further Reading. Gambetta, who as Minister of the Interior had in effect governed France outside besieged Paris since October, visited Lille on 21 January to make his customary eloquent and impassioned appeals for continuation of the war at any cost. But his rhetoric was no longer enough. He had been told bluntly by Dr Testelin, the republican Defence Commissioner, that the mass of the nation would hold him responsible for their disasters and now wanted peace. See *Guerre: Armée du Nord IV*, pp. 3 and fn., 155; Howard, p. 403; J. P. T. Bury, *Gambetta and the National Defence: A Republican Dictatorship in France* (London, 1936).

5 Gambetta had resigned from the government on 6 February, so averting a confrontation over the issue of continuing the war, which might have precipitated civil disturbance. The results of the election, held on 8 February, gave conservative monarchists 400 seats in the National Assembly: a 2 to 1 majority over republican and other candidates. Bonapartists won only fifteen seats. The result was an overwhelming mandate for acceptance of peace. Thiers was elected in no less than 26 *départements*, making him leader of the new government virtually by acclamation. The Assembly met at Bordeaux on 13 February.

6 On Chanzy, commander of the Army of the Loire, see Biographies. General Faidherbe had concluded that an active offensive could no longer be sustained in the north. Following the armistice, it was therefore decided to transfer the best troops of the army – the Twenty-second Corps – to western France in case of a resumption of hostilities. Orders for embarkation were given on 15 February, and between the 17th and 25th 16,000 men and 60 guns were embarked at Dunkirk. The *Garde Mobile* and National Guard units which had fought with Faidherbe were demobilised and sent home. See Faidherbe's report in *Guerre: Armée du Nord IV*, pp. 160–2; also Faidherbe, pp. 69–70, 124–5; Rousset, *HG* II, pp. 271–2; Howard, p. 445.

7 The peace preliminaries were signed by Thiers and Bismarck on 26 February. France lost Alsace and much of Lorraine (including Metz) and undertook to pay an indemnity of 5 billion francs. German troops would stay in occupation of the north-eastern *départements* until the money was paid. France retained Belfort, which was still holding out at the armistice, but at the price of allowing a German victory parade through Paris. After eloquent protests at the loss of the two eastern provinces, on 1 March the French National Assembly voted to accept these terms by 546 votes to 107. The prompt ratification enabled the German victory parade which had commenced in Paris to be curtailed, much to the Kaiser's displeasure. That the parade had taken place at all, however, was felt as an affront by Parisians, increasing their contempt for the new government. See Howard, pp. 446–51. English text of the peace preliminaries can be found in Robert I. Giesberg, *The Treaty of Frankfurt: A Study in Diplomatic History, September 1870–September 1873* (Philadelphia, 1966), pp. 275–82.

8 Bougival, west of Paris, had been close behind the German front line during the siege and had seen fighting in October 1870 and again during the final sortie of 19 January 1871. Nevertheless, much destruction had been deliberately committed by the Germans while they were in occupation. See Howard, pp. 329, 334, 365.

9 See above footnote 16 to Part Two, Chapter I.

10 On Trochu and Ducrot see Biographies.

11 On Bellemare, who was responsible for Patry's dismissal from the army in 1887, see Biographies. On his own initiative, he had directed the surprise attack which captured Le Bourget, a hamlet north of Paris, from the Germans on the night of 27 October 1870. The feat won him much popular acclaim. It did little good for his commander, General Trochu, to point out that Le Bourget was an exposed point of little military value. When the Germans stormed back into Le Bourget on 30 October, taking 1,200 prisoners (though at the cost of 500 casualties) Trochu was savaged in the press. See Howard, pp. 334–6; Alistair Horne, *The Fall of Paris: The Siege and the Commune 1870–71* (London, 1965: Penguin edition, 1981), pp. 136–9.

PART THREE: THE COMMUNE

1 The correct spelling was Wolff – see Biographies – an infantry general not to be confused with General A. T. F. Wolf who had been *Intendant Général* in charge of the army commissariat administration at the start of the war. Wolff's command was the 1st Brigade of the 2nd (Laveaucoupet's) Division of the First Corps. At this point the Army was commanded by General Vinoy. Marshal de MacMahon would take over at Versailles on 6 April.

2 A reference to the *coup d'état* of 2 December 1851 when Louis-Napoleon, then President of the Second Republic, had dissolved the Assembly and had

himself first confirmed in office for ten years as Prince-President, then within a year proclaimed Emperor. Both moves were subsequently endorsed by a plebiscite, but the memory of the shooting of more than a hundred Parisians by nervous troops and the imprisonment and deportation of some 13,000 political opponents had been kept alive by the republican opposition in Paris in the late 1860s.

3 See Glossary for Orleanist and Biographies for Thiers. Thiers had been a leading politician and minister under the Orleanist 'July Monarchy' (1830–48). Although in the face of monarchist divisions he was to become the stalwart custodian of the Republic as the 'government that divides us least', on his first return to power in February–March 1871, backed by a monarchist Assembly, it seemed natural to suppose that he might act quickly to restore the monarchy. That prospect was anathema to Parisians, who had just voted for predominantly republican candidates.

4 The royal, and latterly imperial, palace in central Paris, originally taking its name from the tiles that were made in medieval times from the clay on the site. The Tuileries was to be deliberately burned by the retreating Communards on the night of 23 May 1871, during the climax of the fighting for central Paris. The building was gutted and subsequently demolished, and today the name is preserved only for the gardens laid out on its site.

5 The July Column, commemorating the Revolution of 1830 and the Parisians who died in it, 504 of whom are buried in the vaults beneath, together with some dead of the 1848 revolution. The gilded statue on top of the 52 metre-high column is a figure of Liberty.

6 The armistice had left the regular army with only 12,000 men in Paris, and hitherto the government had not dared to tackle the problem of disarming the National Guard. More than 200,000 men were still enrolled in the National Guard in March, and a significant proportion of them were extremely hostile to the government, which they felt had betrayed and insulted them, and whose first measures seemed calculated to alienate the capital and threaten their livelihoods. The very location of the government, which moved from Bordeaux to Versailles, safely outside the capital, emphasised the extent of mutual mistrust between rural conservatives and Paris radicals. In the previous three weeks the National Guard had seized additional weapons and ammunition, and a hard core was evidently intent on resisting government authority. Many National Guardsmen and their families in working-class districts were entirely dependent on their wartime pay, and had no intention of being disbanded.

7 *Capitulard* was a term of abuse applied to those who had favoured ending the war and accepting the harsh German conditions. Despite the evidence of the attempted sorties during the siege of Paris, it remained an article of faith among many Parisians that only treason in high places could have prevented the defeat of the besieging Germans, and that no mere professional soldiery could withstand the people in arms. Parisians felt that they had borne

the brunt of the war, and alienation between the capital and the provinces over acceptance of the armistice, and over the nature of the post-war order to be established, had now reached alarming proportions.

8 A derisive nickname for Napoleon III. It had originally been the nickname of Pinguet, a stonemason of Ham, whose identity Louis-Napoleon had assumed in order to make his escape from the fortress there in May 1846. See André Castelot, *Napoléon III: L'aube des temps modernes* (Paris, 1999), pp. 93–102.

9 The German Chancellor. See Biographies.

10 Named for Sergeants Bories, Goubin, Pommier and Raoulx of the 45th Line Regiment, who in 1822 had been implicated in an abortive carbonari plot against the reactionary royalist regime. The plot was infiltrated by government agents, and on their arrival at La Rochelle from Paris the men were arrested in March of that year. Brought back to the capital and tried, they were executed on 21 September 1822, so becoming martyrs in republican eyes.

11 The seat of the municipal government of Paris and the traditional venue for the proclamation of revolutionary regimes. Although the Commune was proclaimed there on 28 March, the Hôtel de Ville was burned to a shell by the retreating Communards on 24 May 1871. It was subsequently rebuilt and restored.

12 Troops sent to Montmartre in the early hours of 18 March to retrieve National Guard cannon parked there were soon surrounded by hostile crowds. Elements of the 88th *régiment de marche* fraternised with the crowd and were reluctant to obey orders. Other units failed to keep the crowds at a distance and found themselves overwhelmed. Unlike the situation encountered by Patry around the Place de la Bastille, the confrontation did not end in a stand-off and shooting broke out. Generals Lecomte and Clément Thomas (a former commander of the National Guard hated for his part in the repression of the uprising of June 1848) were captured by the crowd. During the afternoon both were murdered and their bodies defiled. See Tombs, *The War Against Paris 1871* (Cambridge, 1981), pp. 43–7 and Alistair Horne, *The Fall of Paris: The Siege and the Commune 1870–71* (London, 1965: Penguin edition, 1981), pp. 327–31.

13 The home of the French War Ministry, and sometimes used as a synonym for it.

14 This was General Le Flô (see Biographies), who himself had narrowly escaped the mob. Thiers had already fled to Versailles, seven miles to the southwest, convinced that the city was lost. Le Flô too was adamant that the army must evacuate the city to avoid being overwhelmed, and gave orders accordingly, though civilian ministers were less convinced that this was really necessary. For discussion of the government's decision to evacuate Paris see Stewart Edwards, *The Paris Commune 1871* (London, 1971), pp. 145–50 and Tombs, *The War Against Paris*, pp. 50–1.

15 The motives of the Thiers government in attempting to seize the National Guard cannon have been variously interpreted as conspiracy or miscalculation. That a symbolic seizure would have helped the situation is highly doubtful. Vain attempts had already been made by negotiation to recover the 417 cannon parked in working-class districts – principally at Montmartre and Belleville. The National Guard regarded the guns as theirs because they had been partly bought by popular subscription, but behind the issue of ownership of the guns was that of who ruled Paris. On the 17th the government had taken the decision to assert its authority by a pre-emptive military operation against the dissidents. By making such an attempt with insufficient troops, too widely dispersed, it had provoked insurrection rather than forestalled it. The less than enthusiastic attitude of the army on 18 March, illustrated by Patry's account, conditioned the government's cautious military strategy for putting down the insurrection. See Robert Tombs, 'The Thiers Government and the Outbreak of Civil War in France, February–April 1871' in *The Historical Journal*, vol. 23 (1980), pp. 813–31; and the same author's *The War Against Paris*, pp. 34–43.

16 The Central Committee of the National Guard. This recently formed body, outside the legal military hierarchy, represented a federation of the National Guard units in the city and was a focus for opposition to the government. An unachieved objective of the operation of 18 March had been to arrest the members of the Committee. With the evacuation of Paris by the government, the Central Committee found itself in charge of the capital and its formidable store of armaments by default. The mayors of the 20 arrondissements were the only other constituted authority until elections for a city council ('The Commune') could be organised a week later, on 26 March. See Edwards, *op. cit.*, pp. 153–86.

17 Later in the chapter Patry hints that his casual attitude towards rejoining his unit may have owed something to his disenchantment at what he considered to be a lack of recognition for his services on campaign.

18 The southern suburbs of the capital had suffered most severely during the German bombardment of Paris, which began on 5 January 1871 and lasted until the armistice: see Tombs, 'The Wars Against Paris' in Förster and Nagler, *op. cit.*, pp. 541–64, and the map *ibid.*, p. 547. For details of the incidence of damage caused by the bombardment in the locality Patry mentions (15th arrondissement), see H. De Sarrepont, *Le Bombardement de Paris par les Prussiens en janvier 1871* (Paris, 1872), pp. 177–8, 181–2, 275, 299–300, and map following p. 191.

19 Although Patry does not mention it, while he was in Paris there was a demonstration by the anti-revolutionary 'Friends of Order' on 22 March. The National Guard opened fire and killed a dozen of the demonstrators in the Rue de la Paix. Elections were held on the 26th and the Commune was proclaimed on the 28th. The first shots between government troops and Commune supporters occurred on 30 March, initiating civil war. See Horne, *op. cit.*, pp. 344–7.

20 Landrut, whose appointment dated from 3 April, remained in command until 1880, when he was succeeded by Colonel Fradin de Linières. The 67th *de marche* formally became the 67th Line Regiment in September 1871. See A. J. P. N. de Rocca-Serra, *Historique du 67e Regiment d'Infanterie* (Paris, 189), p. 40.

21 See Biographies.

22 Algeria had been invaded by French forces in 1830, and colonial occupation had been accompanied by years of brutal suppression of native revolts. Napoleon III had tried to follow a relatively liberal policy towards the Arab population, but in 1870 French colonists took political control in their own interests. This, together with the withdrawal of thousands of troops to defend metropolitan France, created the conditions for a major native uprising in 1871. Mutinies by some colonial troops who had been ordered to join the fighting in France began in January 1871. Revolt spread amongst the Kabyle tribes in February and on 16 March Mohammed el-Hadj el-Mokrani at the head of 6,000 men sacked and burned the town of Bordj-Bou-Arreridj. On 8 April Sheik El-Haddad declared a *jehad* (holy war) and soon 100,000 men were in arms against the French. The revolt was crushed by September and the Kabyles were severely repressed. More than 1,000 French troops and 2,000 Kabyles were killed in the fighting, besides civilians massacred. For summaries of this neglected aspect of 'L'Année Terrible' see Charles-Robert Ageron, *Modern Algeria: A History from 1830 to the Present* (translated by Michael Brett) (London 1991), pp. 47–53, and William Serman and Jean-Paul Bertaud, *Nouvelle Histoire Militaire de la France 1789–1919* (Paris, 1998), pp. 499–502.

23 Thiers had gained royal approval for plans to build new fortifications when he had been in power in 1840, and had championed the scheme in parliamentary debate the following year. Building work then proceeded on a 38-mile defensive wall with 94 bastions, a moat, and seventeen detached forts, at a cost of more than 140 million francs. Further hasty work had been done from August 1870 to put the forts in a condition to withstand a siege – see Howard, pp. 318–19. Thiers' pride in the fortifications did not incline him to underestimate the task of attacking them: but it should be remembered that the Germans had been too wary ever to attempt a frontal assault.

24 In fortifications, the wall of a defensive ditch on the side nearest the enemy, behind the glacis. For a diagram see Richard Holmes, *Fatal Avenue* (London, 1992), p. 362.

25 The government did in fact, albeit slowly, resort to regular siege methods, mainly to spare the army, given its doubts about the steadiness of many of the troops. Attempts on 2 and 13 May to enter Paris by arranging for gates to be opened were rejected as too risky – any breach of security might have exposed the troops to ambush and disaster. Only when siege operations had brought the Army of Versailles much closer to the city walls, on 21 May, was it able to enter Paris through an unmanned section of the defences at the south-western tip of the ramparts. See Tombs, *The War Against Paris*, pp. 125, 129, 145.

26 A reference to Thiers' reputation as a historian, his major works being *Histoire de la Révolution Française* (10 vols., 1823–7) and *Histoire du Consulat et de l'Empire* (20 vols., 1845–62). On his literary output see J. P. T. Bury and R. P. Tombs, *Thiers 1797–1877: A Political Life* (London, 1986), pp. 140–60, and on his conduct during the Commune *ibid.*, pp. 196–210. To his critics, Thiers appeared to have overweening confidence in himself as both a player and commentator on the stage of history. On many military issues he seemed to regard himself as having a monopoly of Napoleonic wisdom, and was not noted for intellectual modesty. His dogmatism on the need to complete the Montretout battery of heavy guns probably caused a week's unnecessary delay in the progress of the siege, and his propensity to interfere once provoked an outburst from even the normally deferential MacMahon. See Tombs, *The War Against Paris*, p. 129; J. S. de Sacy, *Le Maréchal de MacMahon, Duc de Magenta (1808–1893)* (Paris, 1960), p. 257.

27 Nearby had been Napoleon III's palace, eight kilometres west of the centre of Paris on a bluff above the Seine. Saint-Cloud had been the centre of magnificent receptions in the heyday of the Second Empire, and there the Emperor had signed the declaration of war against Prussia and set off for Metz in July 1870. It had made a convenient observation post for the besieging Germans until French gunners on Mont Valérien – probably with good republican zeal – shelled it on 13 October 1870. Many works of art were lost in the spectacular fire that resulted. Like the Tuileries, the palace was regarded as a symbol of the imperial past and not rebuilt. See *Cassell's History*, vol. I, pp. 380–2.

28 After entering the city the Army of Versailles advanced methodically, broadly from west to east on both sides of the Seine. On 23 May Ladmirault's First Corps acted as the northern wing of a two-corps pincer movement to take the hill of Montmartre which, as the centre of resistance on 18 March and a commanding artillery position, was expected to be strongly held by the insurgents. In fact, Montmartre was not heavily defended, and such barricades as there were faced mostly south and west rather than north. Resistance was therefore overcome with surprising speed. MacMahon's report speaks of Grenier's 1st Division of First Corps, rather than Laveaucoupet's 2nd Division, being the most seriously engaged that morning, though Wolff's Brigade took part in a final vigorous concentric attack which had cleared Montmartre by 1.00 p.m. For fighting in this sector on 23 May see *Cassell's History*, vol. II, pp. 473–4, and on the Communard defence Prosper-Olivier Lissagaray, *History of the Commune of 1871* (London, 1886), pp. 326–9; Edwards, *op. cit.*, p. 321. The last resistance in eastern Paris was crushed on 28 May. Patry's service record shows that during the campaign he was engaged in 'affairs' at Asnières, Neuilly and Montmartre.

29 Total casualties for the 117,000-strong Army of Versailles in the two months' campaign were officially given as 877 dead and 6,454 wounded. The number of Communards killed either in combat or shot after surrender has tradi-

tionally been put at between 17,000 and 20,000, but it has been suggested in recent years that the evidence supports a figure closer to 10,000. See Robert Tombs, *The Paris Commune 1871* (Harlow, 1999), pp. 179–80.

30 On the events of 'Bloody Week' and the atrocities committed by both sides see Edwards, *op. cit.*, pp. 313–50; Horne, *op. cit.*, pp. 433–97; and for an examination of the role of the army see particularly Tombs, *The War Against Paris*, pp. 163–93.

31 Patry is implicitly making the point that lurid stories current in nationalist circles that the Germans were secretly funding the Commune to promote anarchy in France were unfounded. German neutrality was on balance advantageous to the Versailles government: not only was the return of French prisoners of war from Germany to join the Versailles forces expedited; advancing Versailles troops were permitted to pass through the German lines, and Communards trying to escape through German lines to the east of the city were turned back. However, Bismarck acted more from diplomatic calculation than chivalrous disinterest, and used these concessions as a means of putting further pressure on the French in the hard bargaining over the terms of the treaty to end the war, which was signed at Frankfurt on 10 May 1871. See Howard, pp. 451–3; Tombs, *The War Against Paris*, pp. 134–7; Allan Mitchell, *The German Influence in France after 1870* (Chapel Hill, 1979), pp. 5–20.

32 The Red Cross flag. The Geneva Convention ('Convention for the Amelioration of the Condition of the Wounded in Armies in the Field') had been signed in 1864. The Franco-Prussian War marked an important stage in the history of the International Red Cross, being the first major war between European member states. See Caroline Moorehead, *Dunant's Dream: War, Switzerland and the History of the Red Cross* (London, 1998), pp. 60–86; and for a sceptical view John F. Hutchinson, *Champions of Charity: War and the Rise of the Red Cross* (Boulder, 1996), pp. 109–28. See also Bertrand Taithe, *Defeated Flesh: Welfare, Warfare, and the Making of Modern France* (Manchester U.P., 1999), pp. 155–79; and on Paris as a 'giant hospital', *ibid.*, pp. 83–98.

33 See note 3 to Part Two, Chapter I, on p. 340 above.

34 This seems to be a slip on Patry's part, as the review at Longchamp took place on 29 June. For a description see *Cassell's History*, vol. II, p. 520.

FURTHER READING

This highly selective list attempts no more than to point interested readers towards a fraction of the vast number of books and articles which deal with some aspect of the war of 1870–1. It is limited mainly to titles relevant to the themes of Patry's narrative. The emphasis is on books in English, though with some indication of the major works in French.

For convenience, works are arranged under headings, as follows:

1. Bibliographies

The standard bibliography, Barthélemy Edmond Palat, *Bibliographie générale de la Guerre de 1870–1871* (Paris, 1896) lists works published up to that date. For work which appeared over the following seven decades it can be supplemented by the 'Essai de bibliographie sur la guerre de 1870–1871' which appeared in the *Revue Historique de l'Armée*, 1971, No. 1, pp. 203–8 –a special issue of the journal entirely devoted to articles about the war. Six of the most significant modern French works about the war and the Commune are reviewed in Robert Tombs, 'L'Année Terrible, 1870–1871', *The Historical Journal*, 35 (3) (1992), pp. 713–24. The majority of the books listed below contain bibliographies, and the best approach is to explore them for titles of interest – particularly those in the histories by Howard, Roth and Audoin-Rouzeau (see section 5 below). For the period generally, Robert Tombs, *France 1814–1914* (Harlow, 1996), besides being the best recent survey of French history in the 19th century, includes a useful bibliographical guide.

2. Official Records

The German General Staff produced its official histories within a few years of the conflict, and these were soon translated as *The Franco-German War, 1870–1871*, translated from the German Official Account . . . by Captain F. C. H. Clarke, R.A. (5 vols., London, 1874–84; reprinted in facsimile edition by the Battery Press, Nashville, 1995–6). The records of the losing side were much slower to appear, and were never translated. They were published as *Guerre de 1870–71, publié par la Revue d'Histoire, rédigé à la Section historique de l'État-Major de l'Armée* (Paris, 1901–13). Each volume of the French records includes a formal narrative supported by the original documents on which it is based (*Documents annexes*). A useful supplemental volume detailing officer losses is Aristide Martinien, *État Nominatif par affaires et par corps des Officiers Tués ou Blessés dans la Première Partie de la Campagne (du 25 Juillet au 29 Octobre 1870)* (Paris, 1902).

3. The Second Empire

For short introductions to Napoleon III and his regime, see James F. McMillan, *Napoleon III* (Harlow, 1985); W. H. C. Smith, *Second Empire and Commune: France 1848–1871* (Harlow, 1985); the same author's *Napoleon III: The Pursuit of Prestige* (London, 1991); and Alain Plessis, *The Rise and Fall of the Second Empire, 1852–1871* (Cambridge, 1985). A wealth of information can be found in William E. Echard ed., *Historical Dictionary of the French Second Empire, 1852–1870* (Westport, 1985), and its sequel, Patrick H. Hutton ed., *Historical Dictionary of the Third French Republic, 1870–1940* (2 vols., Westport, 1986).

In French, the classic multi-volume work is Pierre de la Gorce, *Histoire du Second Empire* (7 vols., Paris, 1894–1905) – Volume 6 of the narrative runs from the beginning of 1870 to the defeats of 6 August, Volume 7 takes the story to the revolution of 4 September. More recent single-volume treatments include Louis Girard, *Napoléon III* (Paris, 1986), Pierre Miquel, *Le Second Empire* (Paris, 1998) and André Castelot, *Napoléon III: L'Aube des Temps modernes* (Paris, 1999). Information about many of the events and people of the period will be found in Jean Tulard ed., *Dictionnaire du Second Empire* (Paris, 1995).

4. Origins of the War of 1870

The most accessible account in English is William Carr, *The Origins of the Wars of German Unification* (London, 1991), and the most thorough analysis of the diplomatic crisis of July 1870 is Lawrence D. Steefel, *Bismarck, the Hohenzollern Candidacy, and the Origins of the Franco-German War of 1870* (Cambridge, Mass., 1962). The older account by Robert H. Lord, *The Origins of the War of 1870* (Cambridge,

Mass., 1924) is still valuable. M. R. D. Foot contributed a masterly chapter entitled 'The Origins of the Franco-Prussian War and the Remaking of Germany' to *The New Cambridge Modern History*, vol. X (Cambridge, 1960). French public reaction to the crisis is treated in Lynn M. Case, *French Opinion on War and Diplomacy During the Second Empire* (Philadelphia, 1954). On the German side, the documents captured in 1945 were fortunately translated into English as Georges Bonnin ed., *Bismarck and the Hohenzollern Candidature for the Spanish Throne: The Documents in the German Diplomatic Archives* (London, 1957). Bismarck's role is best followed in Otto Pflanze, *Bismarck and the Development of Germany: The Period of Unification 1815–1871* (Princeton, 1963, revised 1990); and for a caveat against taking Bismarck's own later account at face value see William L. Langer, 'Bismarck as a Dramatist' in A. O. Sarkissian ed., *Studies in Diplomatic History and Historiography* (London, 1961), pp. 199–216. Balanced observations on responsibility for the war are provided by S. William Halperin, 'The Origins of the Franco-Prussian War Revisited: Bismarck and the Hohenzollern Candidature for the Spanish Throne' in *Journal of Modern History*, vol. 45 (1973), pp. 83–91. The general histories in section 5 below also contain notable treatments of the origins of the war.

In French, major older studies of the crisis include Albert Sorel, *Histoire diplomatique de la Guerre Franco-allemande* (2 vols., Paris, 1875) and Pierre Lehautcourt, *Les Origines de la Guerre de 1870; la candidature Hohenzollern* (Paris, 1912). The prime minister in 1870, Émile Ollivier, left a long apologia for his government's actions in *1870: L'Empire Libéral* (16 vols., Paris, 1895–1912). For an overview of the foreign policy of the Second Empire see Pierre Renouvin, *Histoire des Relations Internationales: vol. 5, Part 1: Le XIXe Siècle. De 1815 à 1871* (Paris, 1954); and for the crisis in the context of Franco-German relations, Raymond Poidevin and Jacques Bariéty, *Les Relations Franco-Allemandes 1815–1975* (Paris, 1977) and Jacques Binoche, *Histoire des relations franco-allemandes de 1789 à nos jours* (Paris, 1996).

5. General Histories of the War

In English there is one great and unsurpassed work: Michael Howard, *The Franco-Prussian War: The German Invasion of France 1870–1871* (London, 1961). Now forty years old, this classic history has remained virtually continuously in print. Some fine essays by leading modern scholars from Great Britain, France, Germany and the USA are collected in Stig Förster and Jörg Nagler eds., *On the Road to Total War: The American Civil War and the German Wars of Unification, 1861–1871* (Cambridge, 1997). At the time of writing, two new histories are announced which are likely to offer significant new interpretations: one on the German wars of unification by Dennis Showalter, and another on the Franco-Prussian War by Robert Tombs and Stig Förster.

In French, the multi-volume histories by Léonce Rousset, *La Seconde Campagne de France: Histoire Générale de la Guerre Franco-Allemande, 1870–71* (6 vols., Paris, 1895–99), and Pierre Lehautcourt, *Histoire de la Guerre de 1870–1871* (7 vols., Paris, 1900–1908), are of enduring value. Both later produced two-volume editions, Rousset in the form of an illustrated version of his earlier work, *Histoire Générale de la Guerre Franco-Allemande, 1870–71* (Paris, 1912), and Lehautcourt in what was in effect an abridgement: *La Guerre de 1870–1871: Aperçu et Commentaires* (Paris, 1910). In recent decades more readily digestible works of note have included Michel Lhospice, *La Guerre de 1870 et la Commune en 1000 Images* (Paris, 1965), which provides a narrative connecting contemporary illustrations; and Michel Chanal, *La Guerre de 70* (Bordas-Connaissance No. 35, Paris, 1972), a concentrated and stimulating introduction. Two longer and admirable single-volume treatments appeared within a year of each other: Stéphane Audoin-Rouzeau, *1870: La France dans la Guerre* (Paris, 1989), and François Roth, *La Guerre de 70* (Paris, 1990). Both are particularly strong on the wider impact of the war on French society. Roth, a historian of Lorraine, illuminates both the short- and long-term effects of occupation on the region.

6. The French Army

The essential monograph is Richard Holmes, *The Road to Sedan: The French Army 1866–70* (London, 1984), while the problems of frontier defence are examined in Gary P. Cox, *The Halt in the Mud: French Strategic Planning from Waterloo to Sedan* (Boulder, 1994). Three works which deal with the army in the decades after 1870 nevertheless include insights into the defeat in their opening chapters. They are David B. Ralston, *The Army of the Republic: The Place of the Military in the Political Evolution of France, 1871–1914* (Cambridge, Mass., 1967); Douglas Porch, *The March to the Marne: The French Army 1871–1914* (Cambridge, 1981); and Allan Mitchell, *Victors and Vanquished: The German Influence on Army and Church in France after 1870* (Chapel Hill, 1984). Readily available handbooks, not to be overlooked, for either their text or plates, are Stephen Shann and Louis Delperier, *French Army 1870–71: Franco-Prussian War 1: Imperial Troops* and *2: Republican Troops*, in the Osprey Men-at-Arms series (Nos. 233 and 237, London, 1991).

In French, General Charles Antoine Thoumas, *Les Transformations de l'Armée Française: Essais d'Histoire et de Critique sur l'État Militaire de la France* (2 vols., Paris, 1887) is a mine of information, thematically arranged. It has a worthy (and more helpfully organised) successor in William Serman and Jean-Paul Bertaud, *Nouvelle Histoire Militaire de la France 1789–1919* (Paris, 1998). This major work, which also addresses the political and social role of the army, includes accounts of every military campaign of the period, including a 70-page treatment of the events of 1870–1. It encapsulates much of Professor Serman's earlier work.

On French officers see Pierre Chalmin, *L'Officier Français de 1815 à 1870* (Paris, 1957); William Serman, *Les Officiers Français dans la Nation (1848–1914)* (Paris, 1982); the same author's 'Les Généraux Français de 1870', in *Revue de Défense Nationale*, 1970, pp. 1319–30; and Jean Regnault, 'Le Haut Commandement et Les Généraux Français en 1870', in *Revue Historique de l'Armée*, 1971, No. 1, pp. 7–22. H. Roger de Beauvoir, *Nos Généraux 1871–1884* (Paris, 1885), includes useful synopses of the careers of several senior officers who fought in 1870. The collections of the Musée de l'Armée at Les Invalides are illustrated with informative supporting text in two attractive volumes by Paul Willing: *L'Armée de Napoléon III (1852–1870)* (Arcueil, 1983), and *L'Armée de Napoléon III (2): L'Expédition du Mexique (1861–1867) et la Guerre Franco-Allemande (1870–1871)* (Arcueil, 1984). In the same series, Jean Humbert et al., *Photographies Anciennes 1848–1918: Regard Sur Le Soldat et la Société* (Paris, 1985) is a fascinating collection of contemporary photographs. The depiction of the army in the paintings of the period is considered in the beautifully illustrated work by François Robichon, *L'Armée française vue par les peintres 1870–1914* (Paris, 1998).

7. Mobilisation

Treatments in the general histories cited above may be supplemented by Thomas J. Adriance, *The Last Gaiter Button: A Study of the Mobilisation and Concentration of the French Army in the War of 1870* (Westport, 1987); an essay by William Serman 'French Mobilisation in 1870' in the volume by Förster and Nagler cited in section 5; and chapter 3 of Martin Van Creveld, *Supplying War: Logistics from Wallenstein to Patton* (Cambridge, 1977).

In French, the best study is in Volume 2 of Lehautcourt's *Histoire de la Guerre* cited above. The most reliable compilation of statistics is Aristide Martinien, *La Guerre de 1870–1871: La Mobilisation de l'Armée: Mouvements des Dépots (Armée active). Du 15 Juillet 1870 au 1er Mars 1871* (Paris, 1911). See also Colonel E. R. Rocolle, 'Anatomie d'une Mobilisation', in *Revue Historique de l'Armée*, 1979, pp. 34–69.

8. The Campaign around Metz

The fullest account of the August battles in English is David Ascoli, *A Day of Battle: Mars-La-Tour 16 August 1870* (London, 1987), who argues strongly that 16 August was the decisive day of the war. Readers of Richard Holmes, *Fatal Av-*

enue: A Traveller's History of Northern France and Flanders (1346–1945) (London, 1992) should turn to the section on Lorraine for an expert overview of the campaign. An older account, George Hooper, *The Campaign of Sedan: The Downfall of the Second Empire* (London, 1887) has been conveniently reprinted (Worley Publications, 1998). An easily available and amply illustrated short account is Philipp Elliot-Wright, *Gravelotte-St.Privat 1870: End of the Second Empire*, No. 21 in the Osprey Campaign series (London 1993).

In French, the whole of Volume 5 of Lehautcourt's *Histoire de la Guerre*, cited in section 5, is devoted to the battles of 16–18 August. Of particular relevance to the operations in which Patry was engaged are Léonce Rousset, *Le 4e Corps de l'Armée de Metz, 19 juillet–27 octobre 1870* (Paris, 1899) and J. de la Faye, *Le Général Ladmirault (1808–1898)* (Paris, 1901). Among more recent work, François Roth, *La Lorraine dans la Guerre de 1870* (Nancy, 1984) is a fine short treatment that goes beyond the narrowly military sphere.

9. Bazaine

Although nearly sixty years old, Philip Guedalla, *The Two Marshals: Bazaine and Pétain* (London, 1943), is an engrossing read. In French, Bazaine's own apologia was published as *Épisodes de la Guerre de 1870 et le Blocus de Metz par l'Ex-Maréchal Bazaine* (Madrid, 1883). The best reasoned case for his defence was presented by two generals: Edmond Ruby and Jean Regnault, *Bazaine: Coupable ou Victime? A la lumière de documents nouveaux* (Paris, 1960), though the authors concede that he cannot be entirely exonerated of 'inadequacies, weaknesses and errors'. A sympathetic biography which disposes of many myths is Maurice Baumont, *Bazaine: les secrets d'un maréchal* (1811–1888) (Paris, 1978). The same author has also contributed a study of the political situation during the blockade of Metz: *L'Échiquier de Metz: Empire ou République, 1870* (Paris, 1971).

10. The National Defence

The relevant chapters in Howard on the war after Sedan may be supplemented by J. P. T. Bury, *Gambetta and the National Defence: A Republican Dictatorship in France* (London, 1936). Military events on the Loire can be followed in the older work by Colonel Lonsdale Hale, *The 'People's War' in France 1870–1871* (London, 1904), and through the eyes of a French officer in the *Garde Mobile* in David Clarke ed., *Roger de Mauni: The Franco-Prussian War* (London, 1970). Gerd Krumeich, 'The Myth of Gambetta and the "People's War" in Germany and France, 1871–1914', in the volume by Förster and Nagler cited in section 5, points to the proven ineffectiveness of untrained armies, while Sanford Kanter, 'Exposing the Myth of the Franco-Prussian War', in *War & Society*, vol. 4 (1986), pp. 13–30, challenges the French view of the period as one of heroic resistance.

For accounts of life in the capital see Robert Baldick, *The Siege of Paris* (London, 1964); Rupert Christiansen, *Tales of the New Babylon: Paris 1869–1875* (London, 1994); and also those works on the Commune in section 14 below which cover the siege of Paris.

In French, the indefatigable Pierre Lehautcourt matched his seven-volume history of the war up to the fall of Metz with eight volumes on *La Défense Nationale* (Paris, 1893–8). A recent study of conditions in the capital is Victor Debuchy, *La Vie à Paris Pendant Le Siège 1870–1871* (Paris, 1999). On guerrilla activity see Pierre Bertin, 'La Guérilla sur les Communications Allemandes dans l'Est de la France', in *Revue Historique de l'Armée*, 1971, No 1, pp. 187–202; and in the same issue Henry Lachouque, 'Résistants de 1870–71', pp. 62–7.

11. The Army of the North

After reading Howard, the reader has to go to the French sources, the most important of which, after the four volumes of the official records entitled *Armée du Nord*, is Faidherbe's account published immediately after the war and dedicated to Gambetta: L. Faidherbe, *Campagne de l'Armée du Nord en 1870–1871* (Paris, 1871). The pioneering historical study was Henri Daussy, *La Ligne de la Somme pendant La Campagne de 1870–1871* (Paris, 1875). Daussy also contributed over the years several illuminating pamphlets and articles about the northern campaign, such as *Comment Le Cheval de Faidherbe ne lui fut pas rendu par les Prussiens* (Amiens, 1886). Pierre Lehautcourt built on Daussy's work to produce *Campagne du Nord en 1870–1871: Histoire de la Défense Nationale dans le Nord de la France* (Paris, 1886) – which was later re-issued as a volume in his *La Défense Nationale*. A more popular account with attractive pen-and-ink illustrations is Edmond Deschaumes, *L'Armée du Nord (1870–1871): Campagne du Général Faidherbe* (Paris, 1895). Biographies of Faidherbe with chapters on the northern campaign are I.-M. Brunel, *Le Général Faidherbe* (Paris, 1892); André Demaison, *Faidherbe* (Paris, 1932); and, more recently Alain Coursier, *Faidherbe: du Sénégal à l'Armée du Nord* (Paris, 1989).

12. The German View

The architect of German victory left a lucid but clinically detached account of operations which modestly omits the role which his own judgement and force of intellect played in achieving an outcome that was by no means inevitable: Field Marshal Helmuth von Moltke, *The Franco-German War of 1870–71* (Introduction by Michael Howard) (London, 1992). Inside accounts from German Headquarters include the Crown Prince's own observations, published as A. R. Allinson ed., *The War Diary of the Emperor Frederick III 1870–1871* (London, 1927); and a vivid and informed account by a staff officer, Julius von Verdy du Vernois, *With the Royal Headquarters in 1870–71* (London, 1897). Bismarck's activities can be followed in the memoirs of his secretary, Dr Moritz Busch, *Bismarck in the Franco-German War 1870–71* (2 vols., London, 1879). A magnificent illustrated one-volume history of the war, *Krieg und Sieg 1870–1*, edited by Dr Julius von Pflugk-Harttung (Berlin, 1895-6), was translated as Major-General J. F. Maurice ed., *The Franco-German War, 1870–71. By Generals and other officers who took part in the campaign* (London, 1900).

Indispensable for following the operations of Faidherbe's opponents in the North are Count Herrmann von Wartensleben, *Campaign of 1870–1871. The Operations of the First Army under General von Manteuffel compiled from the Official War Documents of Head-Quarters of the First Army*, translated by Col. C. H. von Wright (London, 1873); and its sequel, Carl E. F. G. A. von Schell, *Campaign of 1870–1871. The Operations of the First Army under General von Goeben compiled from the Official War Documents of Head-Quarters of the First Army*, translated by Col. C. H. von Wright (London, 1873).

13. Contemporary British Accounts

The war was scarcely over before leading British newspapers rushed to publish compilations of their war reports or narratives, notably *The Daily News Correspondence of The War Between Germany and France 1870–1* (London, 1871) and *The Campaign of 1870–1 Re-published from "The Times" by Permission* (London, 1871). Accounts by the leading correspondents also appeared, for example Archibald Forbes, *My Experiences of the War Between France and Germany* (London, 1871) and William Howard Russell, *My Diary During the Last Great War* (London, 1874). Forbes, particularly, was markedly pro-German, but this owed something to the fact that the Germans were far more aware than the French of the advantages of welcoming foreign newspaper correspondents. Among other British memoirs of note are Charles Ryan, *With an Ambulance during the Franco-German War: Personal Experiences and Adventures with Both Armies 1870–1871* (London, 1896), and Ernest Alfred Vizetelly, *My Days of Adventure: The Fall of France, 1870–1871* (London, 1914).

Cassell's History of the War Between France and Germany 1870–1871 (2 vols., London, 1899) utilised many newspaper and eye-witness accounts to produce a 'popular' history of the war which in its unassuming way is a powerful anti-war book. The files of the *Illustrated London News* for the period contain a wealth of engravings as well as reports. Like most British journals, the *ILN* lamented a needless conflict, and optimists may pause at reading its editorial for 23 July 1870, which expressed the hope that 'Science will aid religion in making war impossible . . . Human nature will be unable much longer to face death on a battle-field, where individuality is lost, where personal bravery avails nothing . . . The war just commenced so recklessly will, perhaps, make a large contribution towards permanent peace by showing that, in these latter days, it can only be prosecuted under conditions too horrible, both in their certainty and their severity, for men to accept. This is the only solace we can discover in it – namely, a possibility that war may die by its own hand.'

14. The Peace and the Commune

Negotiations for peace can be followed in Robert I. Giesberg, *The Treaty of Frankfort: A Study in Diplomatic History, September 1870–September 1873* (Philadelphia, 1966). The impact of defeat on France in the following decade is treated in Allan Mitchell, *The German Influence in France after 1870: The Formation of the French Republic* (Chapel Hill, 1979).

On the Commune, the most influential history by a participant was Prosper-Olivier Lissagaray, *History of the Commune of 1871* (translated by Eleanor Marx Aveling, London, 1886). Most modern English-speaking readers discover the Commune through Alistair Horne's inspired narrative: *The Fall of Paris: The Siege and the Commune 1870–71* (London, 1965, and frequently reprinted in paperback since), which was followed by his illustrated account *The Terrible Year: The Paris Commune, 1871* (London, 1971). Of the works that appeared around the centenary, two significant scholarly contributions were Roger L. Williams, *The French Revolution of 1870–1871* (London, 1969), and a sympathetic treatment of the Communards by Stewart Edwards, *The Paris Commune 1871* (London, 1971). A decade later, a ground-breaking work based on careful research in the French archives brought the military opponents of the Commune out of caricature and into historical focus for the first time: Robert Tombs, *The War Against Paris 1871* (Cambridge, 1981) is invaluable for the role of the army in Paris in 1871, and incidentally makes skilful use of Patry's testimony. The same author's 'The Thiers Government and the Outbreak of Civil War in France, February–April 1871', in *The Historical Journal*, vol. 23 (1980), pp. 813–31, illuminates the Government's controversial decision of 18 March. Thiers' role can be followed in J. P. T. Bury and R. P. Tombs, *Thiers 1797–1877: A Political Life* (London, 1986). In addition to a number of articles on aspects of the Commune, Professor Tombs has also recently published *The Paris Commune 1871* (Harlow, 1999), which is the best available introduction to modern scholarship on the subject. The art of the period is superbly treated in John Milner, *Art, War and Revolution in France 1870–1871: Myth, Reportage and Reality* (New Haven and London, 2000).

From the mass of literature on the Commune in French, readers seeking short introductions can do no better than Jacques Rougerie, *La Commune* (*Que sais-je* series No. 581, Paris, 1988) and his richly illustrated *Paris Insurgé: La Commune de 1871* (Paris, 1995), while the most substantial modern single-volume treatment is William Serman, *La Commune de Paris (1871)* (Paris, 1986). Jacques Rougerie, *Paris Libre 1871* (Paris, 1971), explores and analyses the Commune through contemporary documents. For large illustrated volumes see Jean Bruhat, Jean Dautry and Émile Tersen, *La Commune de 1871* (Paris, 1970) and the sumptuous reissue of a 1939 work: Georges Bourgin, *La Guerre de 1870–1871 et La Commune (iconographie de l'époque réunie sous la direction de Max Terrier)* (Paris, 1971). On Thiers see Pierre Guiral, *Adolphe Thiers* (Paris, 1986). Contrasting biographies of commanders on opposing sides can be found in Jacques Silvestre de Sacy, *Le Maréchal de MacMahon, Duc de Magenta (1808–1893)* (Paris, 1960), and Edith Thomas, *Rossel, 1844–1871* (Paris, 1967).

INDEX

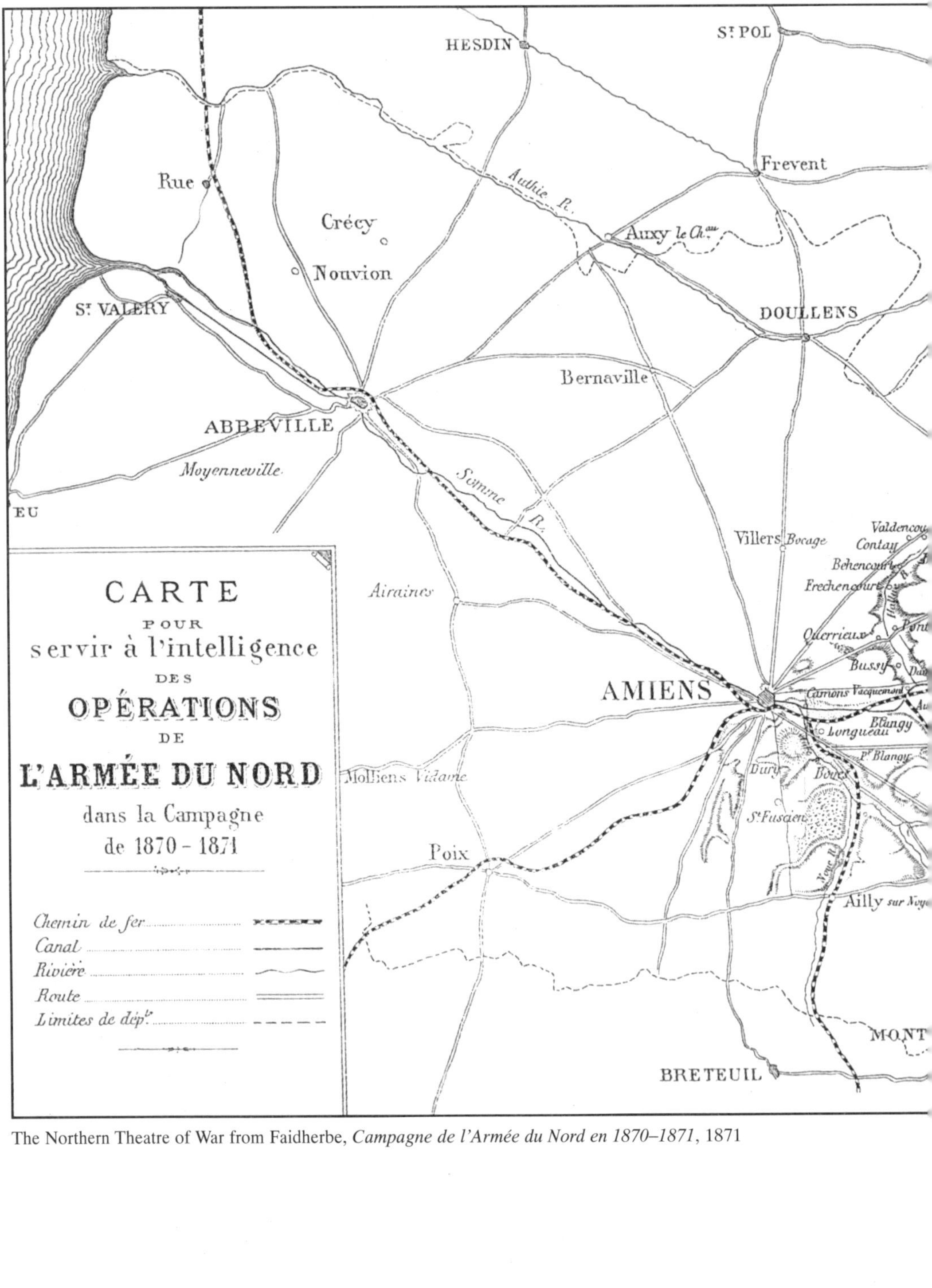

The Northern Theatre of War from Faidherbe, *Campagne de l'Armée du Nord en 1870–1871*, 1871